Noble and Joyous Histories: English Romances, 1375–1650

NOBLE AND JOYOUS HISTORIES

ENGLISH ROMANCES, 1375–1650

EDITED BY
Eiléan Ní Cuilleanáin & J.D. Pheifer

IRISH ACADEMIC PRESS

This book was typeset by
Seton Music Graphics, Bantry for
IRISH ACADEMIC PRESS
Kill Lane, Blackrock, Co. Dublin.

A catalogue record for this book
is available for the British Library

ISBN 0-7165-2379-5

ACKNOWLEDGMENT

The publication of this book has been assisted
by a subvention from the School of English,
Trinity College, Dublin.

Printed in Ireland
by Betaprint, Dublin.

In memory of

PROFESSOR W.F. PYLE, SFTCD

1907–1989

ego dormio, sed cor meum vigilat

Contents

Preface

The late Mr. Francis La Touche Godfrey, Lecturer in the History of Philosophy in the University of Dublin and one of Trinity's last life fellows, at a joint faculty meeting in the early 1970's convened to discuss proposals for an inter-disciplinary Moderatorship in English Studies, roused himself from a Churchillian torpor to puzzle more literal-minded colleagues by observing that 'there are no English philosophers'. The same might be said of English romances, but the essays in this book (which were not commissioned to support any preconceived thesis) make a strong case for the opposite view. The editors wish to thank their contributors for the patience they showed during its long gestation, and Michael Adams and his staff for the speed and efficiency with which they brought it to birth when it reached its term.

Introduction

European Tradition and English Romances

I

Like much else in medieval and renaissance literature, romance was originated by the ancient Greeks, but it emerged only gradually as an autonomous literary form. Though qualities later distinguished as 'romantic' were prominent in the *Odyssey* and in Euripides' tragi-comedies and the New Comedy that succeeded them, the earliest known example of a poetic narrative with a romantic plot in which love triumphed with supernatural help in a remote and exotic setting is the tale of Acontius and Cydippe, from the *Aetia* of the early-third-century Alexandrian poet Callimachus.[1] It tells how Apollo's oracle finally joined two virginal lovers in an exstatic union which more than compensated the sufferings love had inflicted on them:

οὔ σε δοκέω τημοῦτος, Ἀκόντιε, νυκτὸς ἐκείνης
  ἀντί κε, τῇ μίτρης ἥψαο παρθενίης,
οὐ σφυρὸν Ἰφίκλειον ἐπιτρέχον ἀσταχύεσσιν
  οὐδ' ἃ Κελαινίτης ἐκτεάτιστο Μίδης
δέξασθαι, ψήφου δ' ἂ ἐμῆς ἐπιμάρτυρες εἶεν
  οἵτινες οὐ χαλεποῦ νήιδές εἰσι θεοῦ.

I think not then that thou, Acontius, in that night's
  Place when thou the maiden's girdle touched
Would Iphicles' ankle skimming o'er the corn
  Or what Celaenean Midas e'er had gained
Have ta'en, and to my view would witness be
  Those who not unknowing are of that grim god.[2]

Romances of this type may already have been an established genre by the time Callimachus wrote. The allusive character of his work suggests that he was writing within a recognised convention, and another love-story, Jason and Medea's, was central to the third and fourth books of the *Argonautica*, an epic poem by his contemporary Apollonius of Rhodes. The fact that

1 *Callimachus*, ed. Rudolphus Pfeiffer, 2 vols. (Oxford, 1948, 1953), I, 70–84; *A Hellenistic Anthology*, ed. Neil Hopkinson (Cambridge, 1988), pp. 18–19.

2 Callinachius, Fragment 75, lines 44–9; Hopkinson, *Hellenistic Anthology*, lines 98–103. See further G. O. Hutchinson, *Hellenistic Poetry* (Oxford, 1988), pp. 28–32.

Jason and Medea 'did not live happily ever after'[3] gave their story an ironic twist which was typical of Hellenistic poetry.

Apollonius and Callimachus both influenced medieval romance indirectly. Apollonius' Medea was the model for Virgil's Dido, and his *Argonautica* was transmitted through a Latin version by Valerius Flaccus. The design of Callimachus' *Aetia*, ostensibly a poetic treatise on the origins of local customs, inspired the *Metamorphoses* and *Fasti* of Ovid,[4] whose tale of Pyramus and Thisbe became one of the earliest French romances and was translated by Chaucer in his *Legend of Thisbe*.[5] In its French version Pyramus and Thisbe became child-lovers like Flores and Blancheflor,[6] although in their case the thwarting of innocent passion ended tragically, and the widely popular *Floire et Blancheflor* was itself a product of the Ovidian tradition that nurtured Chrétien de Troyes,[7] to whom it supplied the name of Perceval's *amie*.[8]

Chrétien was a pivotal figure in the history of medieval romance. He, more than any other individual, was responsible for the literary form of the Matter of Britain, the mass of Celtic myth and legend whose 'natural magic' was a survival of 'the ancient religion of the world',[9] which became its dominant tradition. But the foundations he built on were laid in earlier romances like *Floire et Blancheflor*, in which the sensuality, delightful as it is, was subordinated to a moral theme. It was not the golden cup decorated with the legend of Paris and Helen that saved the lovers from death, but the magic ring which each pressed on the other, thereby moving even the Emir's stony heart. Chrétien's art was more subtle and elusive, and he used the marvels of Celtic folklore with powerful effect in episodes such as the *Joie de la Cort*, the shameful custom that Erec, the archetypal knight-errant, destroyed before returning to Arthur's court. He, the husband of Enide, was matched against her cousin's paramour Mabonagrains, his equal in strength and courage but his moral inferior, who impaled the

3 Hopkinson, *Hellenistic Anthology*, p. 195.

4 For Ovid's debt to Callimachus see Hutchinson, *Hellenistic Poetry*, pp. 291–5, 329–52. Acontius and Cydippe are the 'writers' of his last two *Heroic Epistles* (*Heroides* XX–XXI).

5 *Metamorphoses* IV 55–166; *Legend of Good Women*, 706–923. Cf. Jean Leclercq, *Monks and Love in Twelfth-Century France* (Oxford, 1979), pp. 69–72.

6 *Piramus et Thisbé*, ed. C. de Boer (Paris, 1921), 13–76. Cf. *Floire et Blancheflor*, ed. Jean-Luc Leclanche (Paris, 1980), 191–272; *Floris and Blauncheflur*, ed. Franciscus Catharina de Vries (Utrecht, 1966), E1-34.

7 Cf. Claude Luttrell, *The Creation of the First Arthurian Romance* (London, 1974), pp. 14–19, 56–7; Leclercq, *Monks and Love*, pp. 129–32. Chrétien compared Lancelot's ardour to that of Piramus in *Le Chevalier de la Charrete*, ed. Mario Roques (Paris, 1974), 3082–4.

8 See below, p. 165 and note 30.

9 W.B. Yeats, 'The Celtic Element in Literature', *Essays and Introductions*, (London, 1961), pp. 173–88 , at 176.

heads of his defeated opponents on stakes.[10] So much is straightforward, but the significance of the episode is not just a moral commonplace, as Luttrell pointed out:

> The episode is different in kind from the other adventures, because the combat takes place in a location which is unreal. The marvels impart symbolic power to the garden, and its attributes suggest a mental condition or state of life. Here, enclosed by insubstantial air, though as firmly as by iron, there is a terrestrial paradise of perpetual delights, from which no-one can issue without abandoning its fruits, only to be enjoyed inside it. The sight that meets Erec's eyes, a damsel of ravishing beauty sitting on a splendid couch, is like an emblem of a certain kind of life. We are not far from Alain's world of imagery, with its symbolic pictures and locations.[11]

'Alain's world' is the abstract world of his *Anticlaudianus* and *De Planctu Naturae*, familiar to us from Chaucer's *Parlement of Foules*, but the *Joie de la Cort*, being concrete, is more truly polysemous, and its inhabitants behave less predictably: Mabonagrains told Erec he was kept in the garden against his will and asked to be released, showing the equivocal nature of this *Joie*.

Episodes like the *Joie de la Cort* and Yvain's conquest of the *Chastel de Pesme Aventure*[12] look forward to the fully allegorized romance of the *Queste del Saint Graal* and the *Faerie Queene*, and there is little indeed in the later romances that was not foreshadowed in Chrétien; but this does not mean that the romance tradition was a closed one. The history of ancient romance did not end with the Hellenistic poets and their Roman disciples. Two prose romances of late antiquity entered the vernacular tradition at different points: the hero of *Apollonius of Tyre*, the Latin version of a lost Greek original, which was translated into Old and Middle English[13] and became the climactic tale of Gower's *Confessio Amantis*,[14] was the prototype of the young Tristan,[15] while Heliodorus' *Aithiopica*, a fourth-century Greek romance translated into Latin and English in the

10 *Erec et Enide*, ed. Mario Roques (Paris, 1973), 5319–6358.
11 Luttrell, *The Creation of the First Arthurian Romance*, p. 63.
12 Chrétien de Troyes, *Yvain*, ed. T.B.W. Reid (Manchester, 1942), 5107–809. See below, p. 179.
13 Josef Raith, *Die alt- und mittelenglischen Apollonius-Bruchstücke*, Munich, 1956 (Studien und Texte zur englischen Philologie 3). This edition includes the Latin text (pp. 92–119).
14 *Confessio Amantis* VIII. 271–2008 (*The Complete Works of John Gower*, ed. G.C. Macaulay, 4 vols. (Oxford, 1899–1902), III, 393–440).
15 For Apollonius' influence on the Tristan story see Helaine Newstead, 'The Origin and Growth of the Tristan Legend', *Arthurian Literature in the Middle Ages*, ed. Roger Sherman Loomis (Oxford, 1959), pp. 122–33, at 132.

sixteenth, became one of the models for Sidney's *Arcadia.*[16] Both, however, followed the basic pattern of *Acontius and Cydippe*, as did the Italian romances that supplemented the French tradition in the fourteenth, fifteenth and sixteenth centuries. The continuous development that can be traced from Chrétien and his imitators through the Prose *Lancelot* and the Prose *Tristan* to Boiardo and Ariosto remained unbroken.

Historically, therefore, the English romances discussed in the following pages belong to an international tradition established and carried on in foreign works, from which many were directly translated. How or why they are seen as differing from their models is a difficult question. Part of its answer may lie in the time-lag between them: the creative period of the French tradition was in the late twelfth and early thirteenth century, which coincided with the Dark Age of medieval English literature when Anglo-Norman flourished and English was hardly used. Romance in English thus began on a modest scale a century late and fully realized its potential a century later still in the works of Chaucer and the *Gawain* Poet, who were distanced from the classic French romance-writers by a gap as wide as that which separated Virgil and Ovid from Apollonius and Callimachus. Part of the answer may also lie in the nature of language itself; English sounds different from French or Italian as Latin sounds different from Greek. However that may be, English romancers viewed their material with fresh eyes from the beginning and expressed themselves more openly and emphatically: when Floris and Blauncheflour made love, 'Non oþer heuene hi ne bede | Bute eure swich lif to lede';[17] Ywain, Alundyne, Lunet, and the lion all lived happily 'Until þat ded haves dreven þam down'.[18] Such explicitness may be thought naïve, but it can also be sublime, as in passages like Balin's reply to the lady who told him he must fight with the knight that kept the *Isle des Merveilles*:

> 'That is an unhappy customme,' said Balyn, 'that a knyght may not passe this wey but yf he juste.'
>
> 'Ye shalle not have adoo but with one knyghte,' sayd the lady.
>
> 'Wel,' sayd Balyn, 'syn I shalle, therto I am redy; but traveillynge

16 *Heliodori Æthiophicæ Historiæ Libri decem*, tr. S. Warschewiczki, Basel, 1552; *An Æthiopian Historie*, tr. T. Underdowne, London, 1567(?). Cf. C.S. Lewis, *English Literature in the Sixteenth Century Excluding Drama* (Oxford, 1954), pp. 333–5.

17 *Floris and Blauncheflur* C553–4. Cf. *Floire et Blancheflor* 2491–3 *Se cele vie lor durast | ja mais cangier ne le rovast | Flores li biaus et Blanceflor*. Lady Holy-Church expressed the same idea in similar words: 'Of ooþer heuene þan her holde þei no tale' (William Langland, *Piers Plowman: the B Version*, edd. George Kane and E. Talbot Donaldson, London, 1975), I. 9).

18 *Ywain and Gawain,* edd. Albert B. Friedman and Norman T. Harrington, London, 1964 (Early English Text Society 254), 4026.

men are oft wery and their horses to, but though my hors be wery my hert is not wery. I wold be fayne ther my deth shold be.'[19]

In the hands of the masters this transformation was complete: the *Gawain* Poet turned Bertholais and the False Guinevere into Sir Bertilak and his Lady,[20] Chaucer turned *Il Filostrato* and *Teseida* into *Troilus and Criseyde* and *The Knight's Tale*.

II

If the medieval romances were founded in the continuous European tradition, later authors of romance, equally aware of that tradition, could not be as securely part of it. Writers and readers in the sixteenth century in England were in various fashions subjected to a traumatic sense of separation from the past, and from the Catholic mediterranean world. For them the process of adapting the native tradition or assimilating foreign material could not be simple. Many humanists disapproved not just of the obsession with fighting and sexuality but also of the sheer narrative delight of romance. Protestants looked at Ariosto as well as Malory across a gulf of space and time. And literature in English, to a critic like Sidney sympathetic to romance, as well as to the hostile Roger Ascham, appeared as an enterprise to be begun all over again with fresh standards, in spite of the universal acceptance of Chaucer's status as a national treasure.

The demands of the reader, and the demands *on* the reader, had changed. The figure of the woman as reader came into a new, sharper focus, and was to remain highlighted as the essential audience for romantic literature long after the romance of chivalry was dead. Since Dante's Francesca Da Rimini fell into sin by reading, with her brother-in-law and lover Paolo, of the amours of Lancelot and Guinevere it had been known that reading romances is dangerous: *Galeotto fu il libro e chi lo serisse*.[21]

19 Malory, *Le Morte Darthur* II. 17; *The Works of Sir Thomas Malory*, ed. Eugène Vinaver, 3 vols. (Oxford, 1947), p. 88.30–7, paraphrasing his reply to the senescal in *Merlin*, edd. Gaston Paris and Jacob Ulrich, 2 vols., Paris, 1886 (Société des anciens textes français), II, 46: '*Onques cortoise gent n'establirent ceste coustume, que elle est assés et mauvaise et vilainne; car quant uns chevaliers errans vient de lointainnes terres lassés et travilliés de grans jornées, quidiés vous qu'il soit si aasiés de combatre maintenant com sera li chevaliers de la tour qui ne fera fors que reposer?* (. . .) *Iceste chose ne die je mie, que sachiés vous, por moi; car je ne sui ne si lassés ne si travilliés, ains me plaist bien autant li combatres comme feroit li reposers.*'

20 Cf. Richard R. Griffith, 'Bertilak's Lady: The French Background of Sir Gawain and the Green Knight', *Annals of the New York Academy of Sciences* 314 (1978), 249–66, at 256–65.

21 *Inferno*, V. 137. Galeotto (Galehot) played the role of Pandarus in Lancelot's affair with Guinevere.

But in the sixteenth century women readers were shown fighting against the addiction. Erasmus had created in his colloquy *Abbatis et Eruditae* a piquant opposition between the representative of the new learning who was also a young married woman, Magdala (perhaps Margaret More), and the monk who protested at seeing Latin books rather than vernacular romances in her chamber. The sexual politics of women's reading, the prescriptive role of male authority-figures, are emphasised by his double assumption that romance reading is a waste of time, and that women's time is there to be wasted. The woman as the primary consumer of this kind of fiction is given a new profile by the monk's indulgence, and by Magdala's refusal to be moulded by his expectations which is in effect a resistance to seduction.[22]

Roger Ascham set his discussion of young gentlemen's education in the frame of a day spent reading Demosthenes with Queen Elizabeth in the intervals of her public business. He inserted another portrait of a lady reading, this time alone, as an example of the higher delights of learning:

> Before I went into Germany, I came to Broadgate in Leicestershire to take my leave of that noble Lady Jane Grey, to whom I was exceeding much beholding. Her parents, the duke and duchess, with all the household, gentlemen and gentlewomen, were hunting in the park. I found her in her chamber reading *Phaedon Platonis* in Greek, and that with as much delight as some gentleman would read a merry tale in Boccaccio.[23]

Lady Jane, because she had attained a 'deep knowledge of pleasure',[24] rose above both the indulgence of fiction and the aristocratic pastime of hunting which in romances often introduces magical and amorous adventures. Boccaccio was rejected as fashionable, corrupt, and foreign; he had in fact taken on his modern guise as the author of the Decameron's 'merry tales' rather than the scholarly humanist who inspired Chaucer's major works. By contrast, Malory was simply obliterated as an author in Ascham's account:

> In our forefather's time, when papistry as a standing pool covered and overflowed all England, few books were read in our tongue, saving certain books of chivalry, as they said, for pastime and pleasure, which, as some say, were made in monasteries by idle monks or wanton canons; as one for example, *Morte Darthur*, the whole pleasure of which book standeth in two special points—in open manslaughter

22 Erasmus, *Colloquies*, tr. Craig R. Thompson (Chicago, 1965), pp. 219–23.
23 Roger Ascham, *The Schoolmaster*, ed. Lawrence V. Ryan (Charlottesville, 1974), p. 36.
24 *Ibid.*

> and bold bawdry; in which book those be counted the noblest knights that do kill most men without any quarrel and commit foulest adulteries by subtlest shifts . . . This is good stuff for wise men to laugh at or honest men to take pleasure at. Yet I know when God's Bible was banished the court and *Morte Darthur* received into the prince's chamber. What toys the daily reading of such a book may work in the will of a young gentleman or a young maid that liveth wealthily and idly, wise men can judge and honest men do pity.[25]

In Ascham's view there was no possibility of a discriminating reader deriving any benefit from Malory. Chaucer was different: he came at the head of Ascham's list of English poets,[26] looming uniquely—all the others were from the sixteenth century—and unapproachable by imitators because he was too uncritically followed:

> Some that make Chaucer in English and Petrarch in Italian their gods in verses, and yet be not able to make true difference what is a fault and what is a just praise in those two worthy wits, will much mislike this my writing.[27]

Ascham's staid and penetrating ideal reader powerfully suggests her opposites: those who recklessly wallow in Malory, idolize Chaucer, Petrarch, and Ariosto, risk the contaminations of Boccaccio, readers whose sexual seduction will merely complete the effect of such intemperate reading. But the revival of romance as entertainment for serious people was at hand. In Sidney's *Arcadia* reading is indeed eroticised, but the women who read his romance may hope, like those within the book who read or listen to tales of adventure and love, to achieve a judicious and tempered delight. Philoclea gets Pyrocles to tell her his story to distract him from making sexual advances,[28] while Argalus and Parthenia's shared reading is an emblem of their ideal marriage:

> . . . he reading in a book the stories of Hercules, she by him as to hear him read; but while his eyes looked on the book she looked on his eyes, and sometimes staying him with some pretty question, not so much to be resolved of the doubt as to give him occasion to look upon her . . . .[29]

25 *Ibid.*, pp. 68–9.
26 *Ibid.*, p. 145.
27 *Ibid.*, p. 147.
28 Philip Sidney, *Arcadia*, ed. Maurice Evans (Harmodsworth, 1977), p. 331. On women as readers of romance see Caroline Lucas, *Writing for Women: the example of Woman as Reader in Elizabethan Romance,* Milton Keynes, 1989.
29 *Arcadia*, p. 501.

Mediaeval romances had addressed women as patrons, had made them judges of men's achievements in literature as in battle; Chaucer had identified them in the *Nun's Priest's Tales* as devoted readers.[30] Their narratives wound their way from the male world of fighting into erotic and magical complications (often dominated by women) and back again. Edmund Spenser's *Faerie Queene* and Philip Sidney's *Arcadia* emphasise other female presences, in particular that of Queen Elizabeth as the source of political power, and that of the Countess of Pembroke who was, as well as the critical patroness, the beloved sister and literary collaborator of the author. The peculiarly overpowering nature of these relationships is compounded by the fact that in the fictions there is no longer a feminine sphere as such: women are everywhere, presiding as queens, plotting as villains, founding dynasties, loving adventuring, teaching divine truth, or fleeing, or passively victimized; alternatively, taking on roles of rescuers which parody or contradict, the masculine, overloading the narrative with redundant female power.

Sidney and Spenser triumph over the difficulties posed by taking romance seriously in Protestant England. In the process they replace the inimitable classic Chaucer as the exemplary practitioners of the genre for the succeeding century. Sir William Alexander was to supply the lacuna in *Arcadia*, Ralph Knevett to produce *A Supplement to the Faery Queene* and Samuel Shephard (a prisoner, like Sir Thomas Malory) *The Fairy King*. But the work of those seventeenth-century Spenserians remained unpublished; chivalrous romance itself had come to look obsolete. Milton never wrote his planned Arthurian epic, and his tribute to the wondrous qualities of Chaucer and Spenser emphasises the fragmentary and the atmospheric:

> Or call up him that left half told
> The story of Cambuscan bold,
> Of Camball and of Algarsife,
> And who had Canace to wife,
> That owned the virtuous ring and glass,
> And of the wondrous horse of brass,
> On which the tartar king did ride;
> And if aught else, great bards beside,

30 Chaucer, *Nun's Priest's Tale* 391–3 (*Canterbury Tales*, VII. 3211–3): 'This storie is also trewe, I undertake, | As is the booke of Lancelot de Lake, | That wommen holde in ful greet reverence.' Chaucer quotations in this volume are taken from *The Riverside Chaucer*, 3rd ed., edd. Larry D. Benson and others, Oxford, 1988.

In sage and solemn tunes have sung,
Of tourneys and of trophies hung;
Of forests and enchantments drear,
Where more is meant than meets the ear . . .[31]

Meanwhile 'romance' became the name of a different kind of book, evolving into a sub-species of the novel. The situations, the pattern of ordeals and highminded devotion, sometimes even (as in Samuel Richardson's *Pamela*) the names, continued the archaic tradition. And the debate about the effects of romances on their readers remained a lively one up to the period of Jane Austen and Maria Edgeworth.

31 Milton, 'Il Penseroso', 109–20.

Time Structure in the Narrative Framework of *Sir Gawain and the Green Knight*

PIOTR SADOWSKI

Sir Gawain and the Green Knight (henceforth referred to as *GGK*) is by far the finest of all English medieval romances, and most certainly one of the most beautiful Arthurian stories ever composed. The strength of its position in European literature lies in the poem's superb poetic artistry, the consistency and balance of the plot, as well as in the precision of its internal structure. The unique manuscript dates from the end of the fourteenth century and was written in the dialect of north-west Midlands. Together with the three other poems contained in the manuscript,[1] *GGK* represents an outstanding artistic achievement of the late medieval English alliterative non-Chaucerian literary tradition.

The aim of the present article is to examine and interpret the temporal structure of the poem by analyzing the arrangement of the main elements of the plot with regard to different time-scales used in the framework of the narrative. Our main postulate is that there co-exist in the structure of *GGK* a number of simultaneous time-scales, mainly of cyclic character, which are parallel though interconnected, and carry in themselves certain specific meanings of paramount importance for the general import of the Gawain story. As has been amply illustrated by a number of *Gawain* scholars and critics,[2] the constituent elements of the poem: scenes,

1 British Library, Cotton Nero A.x. The other Middle English poems contained in the manuscript are *Pearl*, *Purity* (or *Cleanness*), and *Patience*, in all probability composed by the same author: cf. R.A. Cooper and D.A. Pearsall, 'The *Gawain* Poems: A Statistical Approach to the Question of Common Authorship', *Review of English Studies* 39 (1988), 365–85. The edition of *GGK* used in this article is *Sir Gawain and the Green Knight*, edd. by J.R.R. Tolkien and E.V. Gordon, 2nd ed. rev. Norman Davis, Oxford, 1967.

2 Selected aspects of the internal structure of *GGK* have been subject to scrutiny by such authors as A.K. Hieatt, 'Sir Gawain: Pentangle, *Luf-Lace*, Numerical Structure', *Papers on Language and Literature* 4 (1968), 339–59; D.R. Howard, 'Structure and Symmetry in *Sir Gawain and the Green Knight*', *Speculum* 39 (1964), 425–33; H. Kausmann, 'Numerical structure in Fitt III of *Sir Gawain and the Green Knight*', *Chaucer and Middle English Studies in honour of Rossell Hope Robbins*, ed. B. Rowland (London, 1974), pp. 131–9; L.N. Dendinger, 'The Dynamic Structural Balance of *Sir Gawain and the Green Knight*', *Essays in Honor*

episodes, certain descriptive passages, selected objects and symbols, are characterized by a very fine structural balance and symmetry, and very few medieval literary works can compare with *GGK* as far as consistency and harmony of the internal composition are concerned. In the present study, however, we shall be interested first of all in the general structural framework of the poem seen from the temporal perspective, and in the possible interpretative implications of the use of time in *GGK*.

I. THE QUEST-THEME

The story of *GGK* is too well-known to be even briefly summarized here, but it is useful to recall that the content of the poem reveals a pattern, typical for the chivalric romance and for its prototype, the heroic epic, which shapes the story's action according to a general regulating narrative principle that for want of a better term could be called the quest.[3] The quest is here understood as sequence of events and adventures involving the main protagonist leading towards some goal or solution. This implies a linear, goal-oriented and purposeful movement in time from one important happening and stage to another, usually framed within a fictitious life-span of some exemplary individual. As concerns the possible goal of the quest, let it suffice to say that in all pre-modern cultures the ultimate aim of human life had always been defined from a religious perspective as a kind of *post-mortem* spiritual 'reward', described as most valuable and precious, in the Christian context referred to as 'resurrection' or 'salvation', granted to those who adhere to the culture's religious rules and commandments. To a great extent all traditional narratives, to which category the romance on Sir Gawain undoubtedly belongs, are about individuals struggling to achieve such spiritual goals, usually through a series of difficult and dangerous adventures, and this is why the quest as a structural pattern is a universally dominant formal device arranging action in such narratives.

If we then accept the view that the story of *GGK* shows analogy with a quest-based epic narrative, there consequently follow certain implications of importance for the poem's interpretation. Firstly and most generally, Gawain's chivalric adventures can be viewed as a symbolic presentation of human life in search of higher, spiritual values through a series of tests and trials. Secondly, in the medieval context, dominated as it was by the teaching of the Church, Gawain's story can be interpreted as an allegory

of Esmond Linworth Marilla, edd. T.A. Kirby and W.J. Olive (Baton Rouge, 1970), pp. 367–78; D.J.B. Randall, 'A Note on the Structure of *Sir Gawain and the Green Knight*', *Modern Language Notes* 71 (1956), 319; L. Blenkner, 'Sin, Psychology, and the Structure of *Sir Gawain and the Green Knight*', *Studies in Philology* 74 (1977), 354–87.

3 Cf. E. Vinaver, *The Rise of Romance* (Oxford, 1971), p. 2.

of human life based on the doctrine of *imitatio Christi*, that is, a normative conviction that every Christian should follow and imitate in his life the example of Christ as presented in the Scriptures and the Christian tradition. The doctrine pertained particularly to chivalry, the clearly defined system of values and ideals of the aristocratic military elite of late medieval Europe.[4] Thirdly, the quest-theme in *GGK*, represented simultaneously as an allegory of human life in general, and of the life of a perfect Christian knight in particular, is embedded within the time scheme of the Church's liturgical calendar with its feast-days and customs, harmonized with the natural cycle of the seasons of the astronomical year. The main calendar time-scale of the poem is that of a solar year, from mid-winter celebrations at Camelot to the New Year feast in the same place a year later, and such a temporal perspective implies cyclicity, completeness and universality, since the full round of the year can easily be homologized with great historical or mythological cycles, as well as with a complete age of a society or of an individual life.

In short, the dynamic, quest-based structure of *GGK* brings in its train a possibility of discovering in the poetic texture of the poem simultaneously existing and interrelated time-scales referring to the mytho-historical, christological, seasonal, social, and individual layers of meaning.

II. PRINCIPLE OF CYCLICITY

It has not escaped the notice of scholars[5] that the poem is embraced by a significant reference to the mytho-history of Britain with its well-known story of the peopling of the country by Brutus and the descendants of the refugees from Troy.[6] The opening line of *GGK* reads:

> Siþen þe sege and þe asaut watz sesed at Troye

and it is followed by a brief account of the exploits of Aeneas, of his great-grandson Brutus, and finally of Arthur (3–26). All this is echoed almost at the very end of the poem[7] in an even briefer repetition of the chief legendary figures of Britain, though in a reversed order

4 Cf. D. Aers, '*In Arthurus Day*: Community, Virtue, and Individual Identity in *Sir Gawain and the Green Knight*', *Community, Gender and Individual Identity. English Writing 1360–1430* (London, 1988), ch. IV.

5 See e.g. Randall, 'Note on the Structure', Dendinger, 'Dynamic Structural Balance'.

6 The main source of the legend is *Historia Regum Britanniae* by Geoffrey of Monmouth, Book I.

7 A.K. Hieatt, 'Sir Gawain', pp. 346–7, regards 2525, the 'echoing line' ending the last stanza but before the bob and wheel, as the critical one in the poem, not the final line 2530. An additional point made by Hieatt is that number 2525 is a multiple of five, which is the number of Gawain's pentangle.

Þus in Arthurus day þis aunter bitidde,
Þe Brutus bokez þerof beres wyttenesse;
Syþen Brutus, þe bolde burne, boȝed hider fyrst,
After þe segge and þe asaute watz sesed at Troye (2522–5)

Such a device introduces a principle of cyclicity to the events described in the poem, because by returning to the point of departure the poet suggests that the beginning of an historical cycle is analogous to its end, and further, that every end is followed by a new beginning, since the fall of Troy that gave rise to the British race marked in itself the end of an older civilisation. Also, the references to Troy, Rome and later Arthur's Camelot were probably intended as a providential warning, since the glory of famous people and places always tends to fade away, superseded by decline and fall, most often due to some moral trespass or sin like pride, treachery or adultery for example.[8] The message inherent in cyclic history is therefore a double one, that of rise and fall, applied both to nations (Troy, Rome, Britain) and to individuals (Aeneas, Brutus, Arthur) and ultimately Gawain. The paradigm of ups and downs in the lives of great men is established vividly by a reference to Aeneas, the illustrious hero of the Trojan war. The figure is ambiguously referred to in *GGK* as

Þe tulk þat þe trammes of tresoun þer wroȝt
Watz tried for his tricherie, þe trewest on erthe:
Hit watz Ennias þe athel . . .[9] (3–5)

The legend of Aeneas' treachery, widely known in the Middle Ages,[10] constitutes in *GGK* a providential parallel for the chivalric exploits and deception of Sir Gawain, a figure often compared to Aeneas.[11] Both characters were exemplary heroes of their nations, both fell short of the heroic ideal for fear of their lives, and both used personal strength and will-power to rectify the wrongs they had done, and eventually purged themselves through trial and self-knowledge. In this way the pattern of rising and falling, of constant fluctuation between fame and shame, success and failure, set in a framework of cyclic time with its ever recurring beginnings and ends, constitutes the overall structural principle organizing the action in *GGK*.

8 Cf. L.S. Johnson, *The Voice of the* Gawain-*Poet* (Madison, 1984), pp. 38–45.
9 For a discussion of the ambiguity of these lines see note in Davis's edition, p. 70.
10 According to Guido de Columnis, *Historia Destructionis Troiae*, ed. N.E. Griffin (Cambridge, Mass., 1936), p. 218, Aeneas was sentenced to perpetual banishment by the Greeks he collaborated with at the downfall of Troy, for his deceit in concealing from them Polyxena, through whom Achilles had lost his life.
11 Cf. A. David, 'Gawain and Aeneas', *English Studies* 49 (1968), 402–9.

Also, as is easily seen in the poem, the larger mytho-historical cycles referring to Troy, Rome, and Britain are reflected on a smaller scale in Gawain's story, placed as it is in King Arthur's Camelot and the kingdom of Logres, and set within the calendar rotation of one year. Consequently, then, the annual cycle of a single story involving one individual life complements the universal cycle regulating the lives of whole nations.

III. THE YEARLY REVOLUTION AND HUMAN LIFE

As is well remembered, the crucial episodes of the poem, that is, the two parts of the Beheading Game, are placed on consecutive New Year's Days—the pivotal moments of the year that mark the end of one annual cycle and the beginning of a new one.[12] In an allegorical sense the New Year is a passage from one life or mode of existence to another, so that the beheading ceremony occurring on that day should be viewed as a kind of *rite de passage*, a symbolic death for the previous existence followed by a spiritual renewal to new life. On the other hand, the time intervening between the two critical moments marked by the New Year, filled with events and episodes coinciding with important liturgical feasts and seasons of the year, is an allegorical life-span of an individual man exemplified by Sir Gawain, conceived of as a penitential pilgrimage from cradle to tomb.

The symbolic homology between the seasons of the year and the ages of human life was so common in the Middle Ages that one can even venture a supposition that hardly any description of season or nature found in medieval literature ever functioned without at least some reference to human life or the state of the human soul in connection with a particular age of life. Nature viewed as a mirror of the human mind, and the sequence of the seasons as a progression of the stages of human life were very frequent themes in medieval poems and allegories, as in the fourteenth-century Stanzaic *Life of Christ*:

12 The problem of the 'beginning' of the year is a confused one and depends on usage and tradition. Astronomically speaking the solar year begins at midwinter solstice (22 December), when days start to grow longer (in the Northern Hemisphere). It is no accident that the Christian Feast of the Nativity coincides with midwinter since Christ had been identified with the *sol iustitiae* (Mal. 4: 2) conquering the forces of evil and darkness. The practice of reckoning the beginning of the year from 1 January came with the Julian calendar (46 BC), accepted by the Church and widely used in the Middle Ages.

March is likenet, is no3t to layn,
to childehede wel, as reden we.
Somer to 3outh likenet is,
that gro3yng time is cald expres,
harnest to monnes eld, i-wys,
is whiche is kyndle soburnes,
Winter to elde wihthouten wer
is likenet to wel and skilfully
wen mon is passit sixty 3er,
in four our life thus diuise I.[13]

GGK is no exception in this respect, as can be seen in the description of the passing of the seasons between the joyous Christmas and the sorrowful Feast of All Saints, the following year, the day of Gawain's departure from Camelot, at the beginning of Fitt II. The beautiful opening passage depicts a continuous flux of good and bad days, a constant oscillation between the life's ups and downs, rises and falls, according to the mutable nature of Fortune:

Forþi þis 3ol ouer3ede, and þe 3ere after,
and vche sesoun serlepes sued after oþer:
After Crystenmasse com þe crabbed lentoun,
Þat fraystez flesch wyth þe fysche and fode more symple;
Bot þenne þe weder of þe worlde wyth wynter hit þrepez,
Colde clengez adoun, cloudez vplyften,
Schyre schedez þe rayn in schowres ful warme,
Fallez vpon fayre flat, flowrez þere schewen,
Boþe groundez and þe greuez grene ar her wedez,
Bryddez busken to bylde, and bremlych syngen
For solace of þe softe somer þat sues þerafter (500–10)[14]

The condensed description of the passing of the yearly seasons from winter to winter contains a nostalgic realization of the brevity of life that leads inevitably towards decline of old age and death, 'as þe worlde askez' (530).

The analogy between the four seasons of the year and the habit of dividing human life into four ages is additionally underlined by the universally acknowledged internal division of the poem into four fitts marked by large, ornate capitals at lines 1, 491, 1126, and 1998 in the

13 *A Stanzaic Life of Christ*, ed. F.A. Foster, London, 1926 (Early English Text Society 166), 5075–84.

14 See also the following stanza until line 531. One cannot help comparing the lines on the renewal of life in spring in *GGK* (506–15) with the famous opening of Chaucer's *Prologue* to the *Canterbury Tales* (I. 1–12).

manuscript.[15] Now the tradition of dividing human life into four parts ('in four our lif thus diuise I') is well grounded in the Scripture where number four is almost always associated with life in 'this world' filled as it usually is with hardships, suffering, and penance. Four is, first of all, a number of the 'earthly' man created out of the four elements and inhabiting the four quarters of the globe. In the temporal sense the year in an easily observable way falls into four equal parts distinguished by the two solstices and the two equinoxes, a pattern readily homologized with the popular and natural division of the human life into childhood, youth, adulthood, and old age, as in Virgil's famous fourth *Eclogue*. In the Bible in turn numbers four, forty, and four hundred are frequent numerical symbols referring to life as a time of penance, suffering, privation and purification, followed—however—by a resurrection into a state of perfect heavenly bliss. For example, it took forty days for the Flood to purge the world of all sin and impurity (Gen. 7:17)[16]; for forty years did the Jews wander through the desert in search of the Promised Land (Deut. 2:7); similarly, Christ spent forty days in the Wilderness fasting and resisting Satan's temptations (Mark 1:13), the episode reflected in the liturgy in the forty days of Lent preceding Christ's Resurrection. In the like fashion Moses had spent forty days fasting and praying on Mount Sinai before the reception of the Law (Ex. 24:18). This is also why Jacobus de Voragine at the beginning of his *Legenda Aurea* divides the life on earth into four periods, describing the consecutive phases in terms of the earthly pilgrimage towards resurrection and unity with God.[17]

IV. THE FOUR FITTS

Very much in harmony with these popular medieval numerical conceptions is the earlier-mentioned textual division of *GGK* into four fitts, even though—it should be made clear—this division does not match precisely the four seasons or the ages of man, because the action is concentrated almost exclusively on the time around Christmas and the period between the All Saints' and the New Year. Given these modifications it still holds true, as D.R. Howard put it, that 'the specific events in Sir Gawain's life are presented in some measure as metaphors of the life of man, and specific spans of time as metaphors of the entire temporal

15 *Pearl, Cleanness, Patience and Sir Gawain Reproduced in Facsimile from the Unique MS Cotton Nero A x in the British Museum*, ed. I. Gollancz, London, 1923, rept. 1955.

16 On the number four in connection with man's purification (*ad hominem purificandum*) see Maximus Taurinensis, *Sermones* XV–XXVIII, *Patrologia Latina* ed. J.P. Migne, 221 vols. (Paris, 1844–64), 57, 561–90.

17 Jacobus de Voragine, *The Golden Legend*, tr. William Caxton, London, 1892.

world'.[18] The use of the allegorical fourfold pattern dividing the text of *GGK* into fitts, harmonized with the seasons of the year, the liturgical feasts referred to in the story, and the phases of human life, is presented in fig. 1. Accordingly, the successive parts of the romance contain the following simultaneous layers of reference:

Fig. 1. *Allegorical correspondences in the fourfold structures of GGK*

	Gawain's Adventures	Time of the Year	Liturgical Feasts	Ages of Human Life
Fitt I	Christmas celebrations ↓ First Part of the Beheading Game	Midwinter Solstice (25 Dec.) ↓ New Year's Day (1 Jan.)	The Nativity (25 Dec.) ↓ The Circumcision (1 Jan.)	Birth ↓ Infancy
Fitt II	Sojourn at Camelot ↓ Journey through North Wales	Winter ↓ Spring ↓ Summer ↓ Autumn	Lent ↓ Michaelmas (29 Sep.) ↓ All Saints' (1 Nov.) ↓ Christmas Eve (24 Dec.)	Childhood ↓ Youth ↓ Adulthood ↓ Old Age
Fitt III	Sojourn at Hautdesert ↓ Three Days of Temptation	Midwinter Solastice (25 Dec.) ↓ Last Day of the Year (31 Dec.)	The Nativity (25 Dec.) ↓ Christmas ↓ New Year's Eve (31 Dec.)	Old Age (cont.)
Fitt IV	Departure for the Green Chapel ↓ Second Part of the Beheading Game ↓ Return to Camelot	New Year's Day (1 Jan.)	The Circumcision (1 Jan.)	Death ↓ Resurrection

18 D.R. Howard, *The Three Temptations: Medieval Man in Search of the World* (Princeton, 1966), p. 251.

Fitt I

The Christmas festivity at Camelot coincides with the time around midwinter, that is, the astronomical beginning of the solar year. By the way of analogy it also denotes an 'absolute beginning' of life, suggested first by the initial reference to Troy and the implied beginning of a new mytho-historical cycle, and then by placing the crucial event of Fitt I, the first part of the Beheading Game, on 1 January, that is, on the first day of the calendar year. The resurrectional character of this period of the year is clearly emphasized in the Church's liturgy: the Feast of the Nativity (25 December) celebrates the spiritual 'rebirth' of mankind and a hope of redemption through the birth of the Saviour, and the Feast of the Circumcision (1 January), which closes Fitt I, refers to the day when Christ shed his blood for the first time and received the name of Jesus. Circumcision was conceived of by medieval theologians as the Old Testament prefiguration of the New Testament Baptism, and both are clearly associated with the 'death' to flesh and sin, and the 'rebirth' to new life (Deut. 10: 6, Col. 2: 11–15). It should be observed here that throughout the entire story the poet carefully alludes to the feast days on which significant events occur, and if these dates may appear merely ornamental to us today, both the poet and his audience would probably have recognised that Gawain's adventures recall the religious feasts and their moral and spiritual significance, reminding the reader of the 'the duties of the Christian warrior in the battle of life'.[19]

The Feast of the Nativity, as the very name indicates, also corresponds to man's biological birth or—as in the case of Sir Gawain—to his social and spiritual 'birth' in the sense of becoming aware of his role and responsibility as a Christian knight. Sir Gawain's acceptance of the challenge to the Beheading Game marks the emergence of his conscious Persona, the realization of his tasks and moral duties as a knight of the Round Table, and—in consequence—the recognition of the inevitability of death. From this perspective all the forthcoming events and adventures are to be looked upon as an expression of Gawain's growing spiritual maturity in his progression through life towards the final doom.

Fitt II

As already mentioned, the second part of the poem begins with a brief but memorable description of the passing of the seasons from early spring to the All Saints' Day, opening with a nostalgic remark that

> A ȝere ȝernes ful ȝerne, and ȝeldez neuer lyke,
> Þe forme to þe fynisment foldez ful selden. (498–9)

19 Johnson, *The Voice of the* Gawain-*Poet*, p. 56.

The whole passage is clearly a metaphor of the entire life-span with its successive phases from childhood to old age, stretched allegorically between two winters. The action in Fitt II is resumed at All Hallows (1 November), followed by the period of Advent (beginning 24 November) until Christmas Eve (24 December). Advent marks the beginning of the liturgical calendar and its moral significance is that of penance, purification, and spiritual preparation for the coming of Christ. Jacobus de Voragine refers to the period of Advent as a spiritual 'spring' and 'morning', because, as he says, it signifies the birth of the hope of redemption.[20] In the life of Christ this period corresponds to the last phases of the Saviour's gestation in Mary's womb, a preparation for his 'death' to Heaven and subsequent birth as mortal man. This is also why Advent and early winter coincide with old age in a man's life, marked with a growing awareness of the approaching death and filled (sometimes) with penitential thoughts. It is no accident, therefore, that in the poem the period between the All Saints' and Christmas Eve is a time of Sir Gawain's solitary journey through *þe Norþe Walez* and *þe wyldrenesse of Wyrale*, filled as it is with hardships and suffering. The wintry journey is a traditional occasion for penance in medieval literature, and the dangers, discomforts, and struggles with monsters (716–34) experienced by Sir Gawain in the wilderness are suggestive of the inner spiritual combat, the *psychomachia* of the Christian soul fighting the temptations of the flesh.[21]

Fitt III

In the third part of the poem the tempo of action slows down to encompass a period of only seven days between Christmas Eve and the New Year's Eve. Again the Feast of the Nativity, celebrated sumptuously in the castle of Hautdesert, establishes a religious context for the spiritual *renovatio* of mankind brought to the world by the birth of the Saviour. In terms of correspondences with human life the last days of the year refer to old age with its maturing realization of the irrevocability of death. In Gawain's story, in turn, it is a time of decisive trials and temptations whose outcome appears later to be of vital importance for his survival.

Fitt IV

New Year's Day is, as has been remarked earlier on, an allegorical passage between two cycles of life, a critical transition from one mode of existence to another illustrated by the elaborate ritual of Gawain's

20 Jacobus de Voragine, *ibid.*

21 Cf. H. Schnyder, *Sir Gawain and The Green Knight: An Essay in Interpretation* (Bern, 1961), pp. 46–51; J.A. Burrow, *A Reading of Sir Gawain and the Green Knight* (London, 1966), p 54; B.S. Levy, 'Gawain's Spiritual Journey: *Imitatio Christi* in *Sir Gawain and the Green Knight*', *Annuale Medievale* 11 (1965), 65–106, at 90.

'beheading' by the Green Knight. The ecclesiological, resurrectional significance of the Feast of the Circumcision provides a spiritual context for Gawains's symbolic 'death' during the beheading ceremony at the Green Chapel, followed by a confessions of his sins and a kind of 'last judgement' at the hands of the Green Knight, when Gawain obtains both a punishment for his faults and sins, and a reward for his virtues. The christological theme exemplified by Gawain's yearly round of adventures reaches its conclusion at the threshold of a new year, when the most perfect of knights has done the necessary penance, cleansed himself of his sins, and experienced a 'rebirth' almost in the Pauline sense:

> Þou art confessed so clene, beknowen of þy mysses,
> And hatz þe penaunce apert of þe poynt of myn egge,
> I halde þe polysed of þat ply3t, and pured as clene
> As þou hadez neuer forfeted syþen þou watz fyrst borne (2931–4)

The subsequent return and reintegration with the chivalric society at Camelot completes for Gawain the cycle of his adventures, from which he emerges as a 'new man', morally and spiritually superior to the fellow members of the Round Table.

V. THE SPIRAL OF LIFE

So far we have been analyzing the linear development of action in *GGK* within the mutually inclusive and interrelated larger cycles of Britain's mytho-history, the seasonal time, the liturgical year, and human life in general. But the story itself at closer scrutiny appears to consist of smaller recurrent periods, of a number of circles embedded within one another, following the paradigm of ups and downs established at the beginning of the poem by the meaningful allusions to Troy and Aeneas. Throughout the entire story both the revolution of the natural seasons with their continuous flux of good and bad days and a similar character of Gawain's peregrinations are suggestive of the concept of the Wheel of Fortune, very popular in the Middle Ages, expressing the mutability and inconstancy of fate, as in the Chaucerian *Romaunt of the Rose*:

> But froward Fortune and pervers,
> Whanne high estatis she doth revers,
> And maketh hem to tumble doun
> Of hir whel, with sodeyn tourn[22]

22 *Romanunt*, 5467–70.

The principle of oscillation between life's ups and downs illustrated by the consecutive episodes of the Gawain story implies a pair of opposites or extremes and an alternating, dynamic movement between them. Purely theoretically, let us call these opposing elements 'culture' and 'nature', tentatively defined in the following way:

Culture
In relation to *GGK,* Culture comprises a system of values and patterns of behaviour characteristic of the medieval courtly *milieu*; more specifically, the world of chivalry with its ethos and customs, represented in the poem by king Arthur's Camelot and Sir Bertilak's Castle of Hautdesert.

Nature
On the other hand, Nature refers to laws and forces that operate in the realm beyond culture and civilisation as opposed to it: for example, magic as opposed to established, institutionalized religion, wilderness as contrasted with human habitations, chaos as different from social and divine order, the realm of the unknown, the alien, the unpredictable as distinct from the familiar environment. This 'other' reality is represented in the poem by the wilderness of North Wales and the bleak surroundings of the Green Chapel.

Throughout the whole story the action constantly shifts between these two realms in a series of repeated descending and ascending movements as Sir Gawain's adventures and chivalric tests unfold, thus maintaining a state of dynamic balance between Culture and Nature. From this perspective Sir Gawain appears as a mediator between the two domains (as does the Green Knight from his side), periodically entering the world of Nature and the unknown and then reintegrating with civilisation. The periodical interplay between Culture and Nature placed within the dimension of linear time characterizing a simple flow of action in *GGK* can therefore be represented as follows:

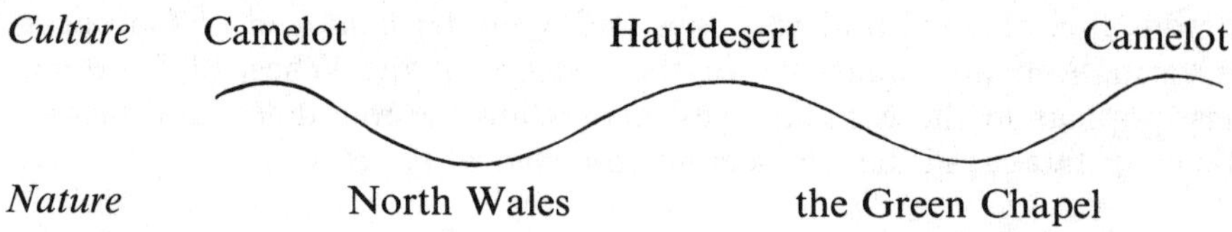

The sinuous diagram of Gawain's yearly sequence of adventures graphically reflects the oscillation between the realms of Culture and Nature—a principle responsible for the dynamic equilibrium of the story's internal structure. But the above scheme, clear and simple as it is, takes no account of the fact that Gawain's wanderings describe a regular circle, since both the beginning and end of the story occurs at Camelot on

New Year's Day. What is more, the periods of consecutive windings in the movements between Culture and Nature differ in length as the action develops, the principle being that of ever-decreasing time intervals between the successive episodes. Nor is the end of the story the same as its beginning, since the Camelot to which Sir Gawain happily returns from his perilous journey, is different for him than the one he had left the previous year. Due to his heightened moral sensitivity, Gawain now has a changed conception of chivalric duties, quite distinct from that of the other knights of the Round Table. Therefore the most lucid and effective way of presenting the internal dynamic temporal structure of *GGK*, one that takes into account the dimensions of both place and time, the differing length of the successive intervals, as well as the possible ultimate goal of Gawain's adventure, is a diagram that combines the linear and cyclic movements, namely the spiral. The dynamic structure of action in *GGK* thus understood is represented in fig 2.

Fig. 2 *The spiral time-flow of action in* GGK

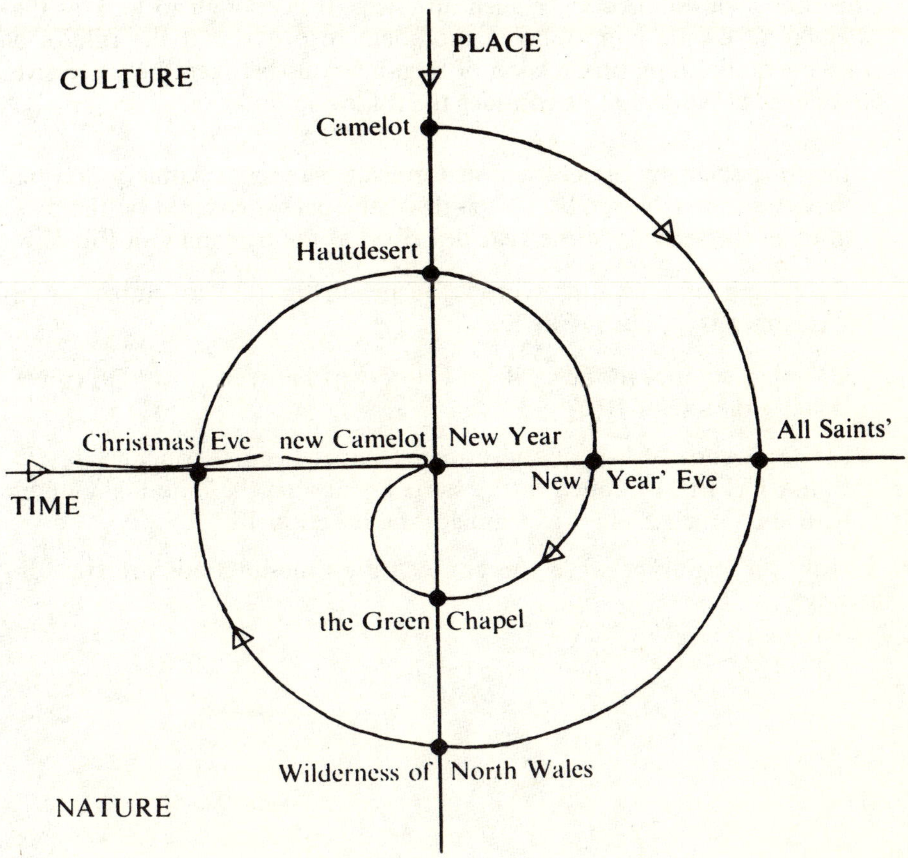

The diagram shows the winding flow of the story with the successive episodes alternating between Culture and Nature, as the curve of continuous time descends and ascends describing a spiral. The intersections of the curve with the horizontal axis of time mark the crucial moments in the year at which passages between the realms of Culture and Nature occur. On the other hand, the intersections of the spiral with the vertical axis of place shows locations where important events happen. Consequently, the upper part of the diagram contains places and episodes occurring in the sphere of Culture (Camelot, Hautdesert), while the lower part of the diagram describe *loci* belonging to Nature (Wilderness of North Wales, the Green Chapel). The constant interplay between the two realms is visualized in the repeated cyclic movements of the descent towards Nature (the right-hand side of the diagram) and of the following ascent toward Culture (the left-hand side of the diagram).

Also, as can be seen on the diagram, the curve of the spiral is divided into a number of ever-shortening arcs that correspond to the decreasing intervals between the succeeding episodes of the story. Neither a simple circle nor a sinusoid produce such an effect. It is enough to look at the calendar of events happening in the poem to prove that the rule of a constant diminishing progression of time-intervals between the successive episodes is at work. Let us consider the following data:

—the time spent by Sir Gawain at Camelot between 1 January and his departure on 1 November is 308 days, the period covered by the progress of the seasons of the year described at the beginning of Fitt II;

—the length of Gawain's wintry journey from 1st November to 24 December is 54 days (Fitt II);

—Gawain's sojourn at the castle of Hautdesert between 25–31 December lasted 7 days (Fitt III);

—the final show-down at the Green Chapel occured on one day, 1 January (Fitt IV), much in the same fashion as the initial encounter with the Green Knight at Camelot described in Fitt I.

Now the ratios between the consecutive time-intervals are the following:

$$\frac{308}{54} = 5{\cdot}7 \qquad \frac{54}{7} = 7{\cdot}7 \qquad \frac{7}{1} = 7$$

Of course, the quotients obtained are unequal, but they are comparable, circling around the average of 6.8. Equal figures in each case are by no means necessary, because what matters in the time structure of the poem is not mathematical precision but the reader's perception of time-flow organizing the action according to the principle of progressively diminishing intervals. This principle also reflects—when one comes to think of it—a subjective sense of the pace of life as one grows older: the more advanced the age the faster one's life-time seems to fly. Another observation that can be made from comparing the time-curve on the diagram with the text of *GGK* is that textual space and attention given to the described events are inversely proportional to their actual duration counted in calendar days. For example, the most critical scenes, that is, the two parts of the Beheading Game, each happen on one day, and yet at the same time each scene has almost an entire fitt devoted to it. On the other hand, the famous description of the round of the season occupying about four fifths of the whole year is economically packed in two stanzas only. If textural space, attention, and detail given to described events be indicative of their importance, as they undoubtedly are, then the poem should teach its readers that the first important event in life is one's birth (understandably enough), and then the moment of one's death and what directly precedes it. All the rest, no matter how long it may last, is but a tedious gestation of consciousness in preparation for the decisive, catastrophic experience of one's death, though not necessarily is it 'a tale told by an idiot' devoid of any sense.

Finally, the spiral diagram of action in *GGK* reveals yet another thing. As has been already remarked, from the perspective of Gawain's spiritual journey passing from ignorance and self-complacency through humility and penance to renewed spiritual integrity, the point of departure is not the same as the point of ultimate arrival. At first Gawain leaves Camelot, a symbol of the chivalric civilization with its values and ideals, a kind of medieval aristocratic paradise, then he undergoes his ordeal, gains self-knowledge, and finally returns a different man, perfected through his fall and humiliation, only now worthy of the name of a Christian knight which he so far merely nominally possessed. The old Camelot with its rash and immature king Arthur and self-complacent knights of the Round Table is therefore different and inferior to what might have been a new Camelot, filled with people like Gawain representing chivalry that is spiritually and morally renewed. A blithe and light-hearted reaction of both Arthur and the court to Gawain's story shows their complete misunderstanding of the spiritual import of the adventure, and in adopting the green girdle, the sign of Gawain's disgrace, as their badge of honour, the knights turn the meaning of the whole message topsy turvy and shut their eyes to any possibility of perfecting their moral and spiritual standards. In this way king Arthur's 'old Camelot' and Sir Gawain's would-be 'new

Camelot' fall apart, as our spiral diagram clearly shows. The postulated Camelot of renewed chivalry, a kind of New Jerusalem of knightly civilisation, is situated in the centre of the diagram, in the point zero which exists beyond space, time, and history, and which is as ideal and desirable as it is unattainable and unreal.

The remarks presented in this article have been intended to throw some light upon the overall structure of the Gawain narrative, and in particular to show to what extent an analysis of the poem's temporal framework can help to support arguments concerning the general symbolic meaning of the story. As has been pointed out at the beginning, an underlying structural pattern of *GGK* is that of a quest-theme typical of the traditional heroic epic and equally valid for its medieval variant, the chivalric romance. As a rule, a quest narrative describes a fictitional life and deeds of an exemplary character who expresses and personifies his culture's goals and ideals. Also, the quest-story is usually placed within a cyclic framework of mythical time, superimposed on a particular history and tradition with its customs and beliefs regulating people's lives according to the astronomical, seasonal, religious, social, and individual rhythms. In *GGK* the main protagonist appears as a paragon of chivalry and its specific values, being at the same time an archetypal human being, an Everyman figure, whose life was presented as an exemplification of the medieval doctrine of *imitatio Christi.* This is seen in the parallelism between Gawain's individual adventures and the episodes from the life of Christ reflected in the liturgical calendar. The synchronization of chivalric adventures with Christian feast-days gives profound spiritual significance to the story, and a simultaneous co-existence of manifold systems of religious, cultural, and psychological reference in a single plot, together with superb mastery of the internal structure and balance, produce a rare example of a poetic synthesis of the crucial concepts regarding man, society, and religion dominant in the Middle Ages.

Wonder and Boethian Justice in the *Knight's Tale*

HELEN COONEY

I

In the opening lines of *Piers Plowman*, Langland makes several references to the wonderful and the marvellous:

> In a somer seson, whan softe was the sonne,
> I shoop me into shroudes as I a sheep were,
> In habite as an heremite unholy of werkes,
> Went wide in this world wondres to here.
> Ac on a May morwenynge on Malverne hilles
> Me bifel a ferly, of Fairye me thoghte . . .
> Thanne gan I meten a merveillous swevene— (Prol.1–11)[1]

Most critics of the poem have not remarked on these references, presumably taking them to be simply part of what L.A. Hibbard has called 'the paraphernalia of wonder'[2] so characteristic of the romance genre, and indeed, instances of such references proliferate in the English and French romances of the period. A.V.C. Schmidt, proceeding, I think, from the same assumption, makes the following comment in his discussion of the progress of Will's quest in *Piers*:

> There is real progression. Will first seeks 'wondres' (Prol.4); he proceeds to seek Dowel (VIII.2); after his visions of Patience and Charity he grows 'wery of the world' (XVIII.4). Whilst at his final awakening it is not he but Conscience who sets out as a pilgrim (XX.381), it has become clear that Will has advanced from identification with the folk of the field (V.61) . . . to a real if implied identification with Conscience. . . . The quest 'wondres to here' has become one 'to seken Piers the Plowman' (XX. 383).[3]

1 William Langland, *The Vision of Piers Plowman*, ed. A.V.C. Schmidt, London, 1978.
2 *Medieval Romance in England* (Oxford, 1924), p. 228.
3 *Piers Plowman*., p. xx.

Implicit in Schmidt's words is the belief that the pursuit of 'wondres' is somehow a rather frivolous activity—something out of which Will, as he becomes more spiritually aware, is educated in the course of the poem. Yet I believe an awareness of classical and medieval ideas of wonder would suggest that the references to wonder in the opening lines of *Piers Plowman*, far from indicating a lack of wisdom and insight and a certain naïveté or even folly on the part of the dreamer, are the very means by which Langland announces the seriousness of his poetic purpose.

Both Plato and Aristotle speak of wonder as the point of origin of philosophy. In the *Theaetetus*, Socrates is recorded as saying: 'Wonder is the feeling of a philosopher and philosophy begins in wonder' (155D).[4] Similarly, Aristotle, when referring to earlier philosophers, declares that: 'It is owing to their wonder that men both now begin and at first began to philosophize' (*Metaphysics*, 982b.11–19).[5] St. Thomas Aquinas translates τὸ θαυμάζειν with the Latin *admirari*, a word that means 'to regard with wonder', and, commenting on the text of Aristotle just cited, says: 'But it is agreed that doubt and wonder proceed from ignorance. For when we observe any clear effects, whose cause is hidden from us, then we wonder about their cause.' Following Aristotle, he goes on to say that wonder is uniquely appropriate as a subject for poetry: 'And because of this, wonder is the cause which leads to philosophy, so it seems that the philosopher is on equal terms with the *philomythos*, that is to say, the lover of myth, something which is proper to poets. For this reason, the earliest thinkers, who explained the fundamental principles of things by means of myths of a certain sort, are called theologising poets.' He concludes: 'The reason why the philosopher is compared to a poet is this, that each is concerned with things that excite wonder' (*Commentary on Aristotle's Metaphysics* I.lect.3). The emotion of wonder, then, was seen to be uniquely bound up with philosophical enquiry, the search for

4 *The Dialogues of Plato*, tr. Benjamin Jowett, 4 vols. (Oxford, 1953), III, 251.

5 *The Works of Aristotle*, 17 vols., tr. D.A. Smith and W.D. Ross, Oxford, 1908.

6 '*Quia vero non actiua* [sc. *scientia vniuersalis*] *palam ex primis philosophantibus: nam propter admirari homines nunc et primum inceperunt philosophari* (. . .) *Qui vero dubitat et admiratur ignorari videtur; quare et Philomithes philosophus aliqualiter est. fabula nanque ex miris constituitur; quare si ad ignorantiam effugiendam philosophati sunt, palam quia propter scire studere persecuti sunt et non vsus alicuius causa*' (. . .) *Constat autem quod dubitatio et admiratio ex ignorantia prouenit. Cum enim aliquos manifestos effectus videmus quorum causa nos latet, eorum tunc causam admiramur et ex quo admiratio fuit causa inducens ad philosophiam. patet quod philosophus est aliqualiter phylomithes, idest amator fabule, quod proprium est poetarum. Unde primi qui per modum quendam fabularum de principiis rerum retractauerunt dicti sunt poete theologizantes* (. . .) *Causa autem quare philosophus conparatur poete est ista: quia vterque circa miranda versatur* (*Super metaphysica* (Venice, 1517), 5rab). See also the article on 'Wonder' in *The New Catholic Encyclopaedia*, 17 vols., Washington, 1981.

causes, and the search for truth. And since, as Piero Boitani points out, in poems such as *Piers Plowman* 'the narrative becomes philosophical and the search for truth is the object',[7] it seems to me that there could hardly be a more appropriate point of departure for Will's quest than the desire for marvels and wonders.

An appreciation of this more profound concept of wonder and its association with philosophy and truth may not, however, be unique to Langland. Such a concept may, for example, lie behind the *Pearl*-poet's statement that he was rapt from his body to 'gon in Godes grace | In aventure ther mervailes meven' (63–4).[8] And while wonder has always been recognised as an integral part of romance, it is interesting to find that references to wonder would appear to be characteristic of the fourteenth-century dream-vision poem too. Along with *Piers Plowman* and *Pearl*, one thinks of Chaucer's *Book of the Duchess*—

> Me mette so ynly swete a sweven,
> So wonderful that never yit
> Y trowe no man had the wyt
> To konne wel my sweven rede (276–9)[9]

—or his *House of Fame*

> No man elles me biforn,
> Mette, I trowe stedfastly,
> So wonderful a drem as I . . . (62–4)

Again, such references have generally been overlooked as being undeserving of comment, but it may be that these allusions to wonder signify not only, as in the world of romance, a movement beyond the ordinary and quotidian to a realm of the strange and marvellous, but also, and at the same time, entry into a more philosophical mode. Piero Boitani has pointed out that 'the genres of vision and dream generally invoke a penetration of the human spirit into a realm beyond the confines of ordinary experience, into a dimension where one discovers absolute truths and ontological realities, which appear only in veiled form in the sensible universe',[10] and according to A.C. Spearing, the dream-vision uncovers 'philosophical truths it would be impossible to know in waking life'.[11] There is a sense, then, in which the dream-vision is uniquely suited to

7 *English Medieval Narrative in the Thirteenth and Fourteenth Centuries* (Cambridge, 1982), p. 72.

8 *Pearl*, ed. E.V. Gordon, Oxford, 1988.

9 All Chaucer quotations are from *The Riverside Chaucer*, 3rd ed., ed. Larry D. Benson, Oxford, 1988.

10 *Ibid.*, p. 71.

11 *Medieval Dream-Poetry* (Cambridge, 1976), p. 18.

philosophical inquiry and revelation, and hence, I believe, a concomitant sense in which 'wondres' are singularly appropriate as its subject and point of departure. One might, of course, wish to follow Spearing in distinguishing between poems such as *Piers Plowman* and *Pearl,* behind which lies the ancient connection between spiritual or intellectual vision with doctrinal instruction, on the one hand, and the more secular tradition of the dream-poem represented by the *Book of the Duchess* or the *House of Fame*, on the other; yet an awareness of the concept of wonder or *admiratio* as it is found in classical and medieval thought ought to make us sensitive to those occasions in medieval poetry when allusions to the wonderful or marvellous might, as well as expressing a simple delight in the novel or fantastic, be pointing towards the link between wonder, philosophical enquiry, and the search for truth. Spearing points to the *Book of the Duchess* and the *House of Fame* as instances where 'nothing more is claimed for the dream than that it is "wonderful"',[12] yet this may in fact be a larger claim than he allows.

II

Although Boccaccio's *Teseida* was a 'classical' epic in twelve books, the plot which Chaucer borrowed from it for the *Knight's Tale* was full of the trappings of wonder characteristic of romance. As Ian Bishop puts it, 'it tolerates such contrivances as disguise, divine intervention and (most notoriously) co-incidence.'[13] Yet it is clear from his introduction to *The Canterbury Tales* that Larry D. Benson believes that Chaucer, far from being embarrassed by such 'absurdities' of plot, turns them to his advantage, and in so doing demonstrates an awareness of the link between the wonderful and the philosophical:

> Many medieval thinkers maintained that wonder, the emotion we feel when confronted with apparently inexplicable events, is an aid to philosophical and religious thought, since the mind is thus incited to seek out causes. In The Knight's Tale, Chaucer used the wonder arising from sudden reversals of fortune as occasions for philosophical meditation.[14]

The result is indeed 'a uniquely philosophical romance' which is concerned above all with discovering and laying bare the causes behind its erratic reversals of plot, and there are several instances in the narrative

12 *Ibid.*, p. 64.
13 *The Narrative Art of the Canterbury Tales* (London, 1987), p. 37.
14 *Riverside Chaucer*, p. 10.

which bear out the truth of Benson's remarks. Of the inherently improbable intervention by Duke Perotheus—a veritable *amicus ex machina*—on Arcite's behalf, Chaucer simply remarks:

> It happed on a day,
> To telle it yow as shortly as I may,
> A worthy duc that highte Perotheus . . .
> Was come to Atthenes his felawe to visite (1189–94)

Yet this sudden and unexpected—and, in that sense, wonderful—event (in 1022–32 Chaucer had deliberately created the expectation that Palamon and Arcite would languish in prison for ever) becomes the occasion for lengthy philosophical reflection, as each of the young knights poses a problem which casts its shadow across the ensuing narrative, Arcite questioning the nature of divine intervention in human affairs, and Palamon the apparently unjust suffering of the innocent. But perhaps the most striking example of the way in which a strange or wonderful incident prompts philosophical reflection on the causes of things comes in Part II of the tale, in the narrator's handling of the coincidence whereby the hunt just happens to lead Theseus and Emelye to the very grove where Palamon and Arcite are fighting. We have already heard, in the course of this second part, of a whole series of unlikely or coincidental events which have been ascribed to the mysterious force of 'aventure' (cf. 1465, 1516), but here Chaucer declares at once that the apparent coincidence has, in fact, been providentially ordained:

> The destinee, ministre general,
> That executeth in the world overal
> The purveiaunce that God hath seyn biforn,
> So strong it is that, though the world had sworn
> The contrarie of a thyng by ye or nay,
> Yet somtyme it shall fallen on a day
> That falleth nat eft within a thousand yeer . . .
> This mene I now by myghty Theseus . . . (1663–73)

Chaucer has kept Boccaccio's reference to the effect that this is something 'that might not happen in a thousand years' (*Teseida*, V. 77)[15] but the philosophical way in which he elaborates upon it means that our response goes beyond wonder at a remarkable coincidence to a sense of how marvellous are the workings of providence. It is as if Chaucer wished us to see in this event what Boethius calls 'this noble miracle of the ordre destynal' (*Boece*, IV.pr6.220–1). The third and final example of an apparently strange or mysterious event which

15 *Chaucer's Boccaccio*, ed. and tr. N.R. Havely (Cambridge, 1980), p. 120.

becomes an occasion for philosophical reflection is, of course, Theseus' great speech, insofar as it is a meditation on the cause and possible meaning of Arcite's sudden downfall and apparently senseless death in the scheme of things presided over by the 'Firste Moevere'.

But although Benson's comments are extremely valuable in alerting us to the link between the wonders of romance as they appear in the *Knight's Tale* and the philosophising so often attendant upon them therein, one may find, if one looks just a little more closely at Chaucer's handling of Arcite's fatal fall, that wonder is even more fundamental to the dynamics of the tale than his comments have suggested.

The climax of the action of the *Knight's Tale* comes at the moment when Saturn's 'furie' startles Arcite's horse and throws him to the ground, fatally wounding him (2684–93). As far as Theseus is aware, the contest had ended with Palamon's capture by Lygurge:

> And whan that Theseus hadde seyn this sighte,
> Unto the folk that foghten thus echon
> He cryde, 'Hoo! namoore, for it is doon!
> I wol be trewe juge and no partie.
> Arcite of Thebes shal have Emelie
> That by his fortune hath hire faire ywonne.' (2654–9)

But Chaucer, with a series of brief, dramatic questions, swiftly turns to the conflict this causes in the heavens:

> What kan now faire Venus doon above?
> What seith she now? What dooth this queene of love
> But wepeth so, for wantynge of hir wille,
> Til that hir teeres in the lystes fille?
> She seyde, 'I am ashamed, doutelees.'
> Saturnus seyde, 'Doghter, hoold thy pees!
> Mars hath his wille, his knyght hath al his boone,
> And, by myn heed, thow shalt been esed soone.' (2663–70)

The reader is privileged, as the protagonists are not, to see behind the scenes to the celestial quarrel, but Chaucer, with a nice sense of narrative tension, refuses to tell us in advance what Saturn's solution might be: we must wait to hear what happens. Yet the climactic moment, when it comes, is heralded, not (as one might expect) by a lengthy philosophical meditation, nor even by an expression of indignation or regret, but by a rather quiet, unemphatic and ostensibly candid statement by the narrator:

> But herkneth me and stynteth noyse a lite,
> Which a myracle ther bifel anon (2674–5)

And so, with only the briefest of pauses for reflection, the narrative continues in an entirely neutral and matter-of-fact way:

> This fierse Arcite . . .
> He priketh endelong the large place
> Lokynge upward upon this Emelye; . . .
>   Out of the ground a furie infernal sterte,
> From Pluto sent at requeste of Saturne . . . (2676 ff.)

Chaucer's reference to Arcite's fall at this climactic moment as a 'myracle' has generally—and perhaps not surprisingly, given its deliberate but, I believe, rather disingenuous unobtrusiveness—been overlooked by critics, but it is in fact an important indication of the extent to which wonder acts as a controlling idea in the tale. For a miracle is simply a wonder by another name. It means in general 'a wonderful thing', and is equivalent to the Latin *miraculum* which, of course, comes from *mirari*, 'to wonder'; and the Greek for miracles, τέρατα, literally means 'wonders', in reference to the feelings of wonder excited by their occurrence. Hence, the idea of wonder is to be found at the very heart of the *Knight's Tale*—a fact which must reflect its significance for Chaucer—though when we come to consider what precisely he meant by the term miracle here, we shall see that his invitation to the reader: 'herkneth me . . . Which a myracle ther bifel anon' is, for all its apparent simplicity, a profoundly ambiguous and challenging one.

But what then of Theseus' subsequent speech? If the reference to Saturn's fury as a miracle was indeed designed to provoke in the reader wonder as to its cause, surely that amazement is resolved by Theseus' great Boethian speech in which the Prime Mover is identified as the first and universal cause of all things? Many critics (notably Charles Muscatine[16] and P.M. Kean[17]) have assented to Theseus' words and have judged his speech to be a successful or even triumphant resolution of the issues raised by the tale; others have said that, as an attempt to justify Arcite's death and to answer the large philosophical questions raised by it, the speech fails. Elizabeth Salter, for instance, recognises that Chaucer had altered the Boccaccian narrative of the *Teseida* so as to attempt a philosophical justification of man's suffering. But this, she says, made heavy demands of him when he came finally to the point of resolution—demands which, according to her, he failed to meet.[18] Similarly, Derek Pearsall is of the opinion that 'his attempt to graft on to the consolatory platitudes of Teseo (*Teseida*, XII.7–18) an opening address in which he calls upon Boethius for his noble Platonic vision of a universe bound by

16 *Chaucer and the French Tradition* (Berkeley, Calif., 1957), pp. 183–6.
17 *Chaucer and the Making of English Poetry*, 2 vols. (London, 1972), II, 41–52.
18 *Fourteenth-Century English Poetry* (Oxford, 1983), pp. 143–81.

'the feyre cheyne of love' is unsuccessful, and he speaks of Chaucer's 'uneasiness', 'inconsistency' and 'evasion'.[19] Whether or not one agrees with such views concerning the failure of Theseus' speech, what is striking is that in almost every case the implication is that the failure is Chaucer's own. But while Theseus' speech has indeed every appearance of authority, it is after all spoken not by the narrator himself, but by a character within the tale—one, moreover, who lacks full knowledge of the cause of Arcite's death—and I shall attempt to show that it is questionable whether in fact Chaucer ever intended that the wonder excited by the 'myracle' of Saturn's fury and Arcite's fatal fall should be resolved either in Theseus' speech or anywhere else in the *Knight's Tale*, and whether he believed such a resolution to be possible.

The last words spoken by Troilus in *Troilus and Criseyde* occur at V. 1722: of Criseyde's betrayal and his subsequent fate he says simply and uncomprehendingly, 'I have it nat deserved.' The extent to which Troilus 'deserves' his sad fate and is himself responsible for his fall 'out of joie' becomes one of the central issues of the poem, as Chaucer continually explores the complex relationship between intention and reward in love, between Troilus' 'entente' and his 'fyn'. The use of the term 'tragedye' in the closing stanzas of the poem (V.1786) invites continued speculation about the true cause of the protagonists downfall. For however great our compassion for Troilus may be, there is, as Ian Bishop says, an uneasy sense that the element of human responsibility has been greater than Troilus himself is willing to allow, and greater than that allowed for in the standard medieval definition of tragedy.[20] Hence I believe one finds in *Troilus* a tension between the Boethian and characteristically medieval definition of tragedy as simply 'a lament that happy states are overthrown by the indiscriminate blows of fortune', or, as Chaucer has it, 'the dedes of Fortune that with an unwar strook overturneth the realmes of greet nobleye' (II.pr2.38–40) and that advanced, for example, by Nicholas Trevet in his commentary on the *Consolation*, where in place of the Boethian stress on the indiscriminate nature of fortune's blows and their unhappy consequences we find the rather more disturbing inference that sin invites tragedy: 'a tragedy was a song about great iniquities with the ancient deeds and criminal actions of kings as its subject-matter.'[21] Troilus' wretched 'I have it nat deserved', for all its undoubted pathos, nevertheless begs important moral questions about desert and culpability which are perhaps never finally resolved in the poem.

19 *The Canterbury Tales* (London, 1978), pp. 124–5.

20 *Chaucer's Troilus and Criseyde: A Critical Study* (Bristol, 1981), p. 76.

21 A.J. Minnis, *Chaucer and Pagan Antiquity* (Cambridge, 1982), p. 27. Minnis believes, however, that in *Troilus and Criseyde*, 'Chaucer is true to the letter and spirit of the auctor, not his interpreter', and says that 'There is no suggestion that the tragedy has been prompted by criminal or sinful actions.'

Troilus and Criseyde is often linked to the *Knight's Tale*, the shorter work being seen likewise to have love as its theme and to be profoundly Boethian in character. Yet however much Arcite's tragic fate may appear to invite comparison with Troilus' downfall, the situation in the *Knight's Tale* is in fact altogether different. Certainly Arcite's allusion in Part I part of the tale to 'the olde clerkes sawe | That, "who shal yeve a lovere any lawe?"' takes us back to Book III, *metrum* 12 of *Boece*—the *metrum* which tells the tragic tale of Orpheus and Eurydice and which in Boethius' hands becomes a warning against excessive concern with 'lowe thinges of the erthe' and neglect of 'the noble good celestial'. This story of a 'love that doublide . . . sorwe' has an obvious relevance for *Troilus and Criseyde* (practically all the classical lore found in this *metrum* is used by Chaucer in *Troilus*), and Arcite's allusion to the lawlessness of love reminds us that we are dealing here with essentially the same kind of earthbound love which distracts men from love of the true good, and which, in Boethian terms, duly and necessarily renders the lovers 'caytif' and subject to the arbitrary workings of fortune. Indeed, the allusion is but one of several instances, most notably in the early, Boethian speeches of Palamon and Arcite (1251–1333), which indicate either ironically or by omission that theirs, like Troilus', is love for a partial rather than the sovereign good and so renders them less than fully free. And just as Troilus' love had led to much suffering, so this is a love that causes in Arcite 'manye', an extreme form of 'the loveris maladye Of Hereos' (1373–4), and 'destreyneth' Palamon so 'That wood out of his wit he goth for wo' (1455–56), the disordered effects of which Theseus must attempt to regulate. Yet notwithstanding these same reservations and a similar ambivalence concerning the moral nature of the protagonists' love, it seems to me that the ethics and limitations of this kind of love are no longer the focus of Chaucer's interest in the *Knight's Tale*, as they had been in *Troilus*. The dying Arcite's bewildered 'What is this world? What asketh men to have?' has none of the ambivalence surrounding Troilus' 'I have it nat deserved.' There would appear to be no question that, for all that his love may—like Troilus'—fall short in Boethian terms, Arcite's death is manifestly undeserved. Indeed, it is almost as if the *Knight's Tale* were taking up where *Troilus and Criseyde* left off, insofar as it goes beyond an exploration of the merits and demerits of earthly love (the subject of Book III of *Boece*) to the more difficult and altogether more disturbing question of the unjust suffering of the innocent (the central theme of Books IV and V of *Boece*).

III

If justice really is the central issue of the *Knight's Tale*, then Chaucer's initial account of the conflict between Athens and Thebes serves at the outset to underline the fact that the attainment of justice is no easy matter. Creon's violation of the chivalric code, his villainous and tyrannous (961) treatment of the husbands of the weeping Athenian ladies is a manifest injustice which cries out for rectification. But though we are assured that in his defeat at the hands of Theseus,

> Creon was of Theseus yserved
> As he that hadde his deeth ful wel deserved (963–4)

the righting of this wrong leads to the perpetual imprisonment of the Theban cousins, Palamon and Arcite—a fate that is presumably, given that they are guilty of no outrage, undeserved, and, to that extent, unjust. Chaucer does not flinch from underlining the contrast between the triumphant state of the conqueror and the misery and subjugation of the conquered:

> And whan this worthy duc hath thus ydon,
> He took his hoost and hom he rit anon
> With laurer crowned as a conquerour;
> And there he lyveth in joye and in honour
> Terme of his lyf; What nedeth wordes mo?
> And in a tour, in angwissh and in wo
> This Palamon and his felawe Article
> For everemore . . . (1025–32)

The defeat of a tyrant has led to a situation in which the 'worthy' conqueror himself, though entirely free from blame, according to the laws governing medieval warfare, nevertheless appears to the conquered to behave tyrannously (1111).

However that may be, it soon becomes apparent that questions of justice and its obverse, tyranny, and of what men do and do not deserve, have shaped Chaucer's account in the early part of the *Knight's Tale* of Palamon and Arcite's situation both *vis-à-vis* the powerful conqueror Theseus, and in relation to the powerful and overwhelming love they feel for Emelye. Moreover, it would seem that Chaucer intended us to perceive certain parallels and similarities between the two kinds of suffering—that caused by imprisonment, on the one hand, and that born of love, on the other. Hence Arcite mistakes the cry which Palamon utters on being wounded by love of Emelye for an expression of the pain caused by imprisonment:

And therwithal [Palamon] bleynte and cryde, 'A!'
As thogh he stongen weere unto the herte.
And with that cry Arcite anoon up sterte
And seyde, 'Cosyn myn, what eyleth thee
That art so pale and deedly on to see?
Why cridestow? Who hath thee doon offence?
Fod Goddes love, tak al in pacience
Oure prison, for it may non oother be.
Fortune hath yeven us this adversitee . . . (1078 ff.)

And then Palamon, believing Emelye to be Venus herself, prays to her not for success in love, but—what is, I think, extraordinary—for release from prison:

'Venus, if it be thy wil
Yow in this gardyn thus to transfigure
Bifore me, sorweful, wrecched creature,
Out of this prison help that we may scapen . . .
Of oure lynage have som compassioun
That is so lowe ybroght by tirannye'. (1106–12)

The narrative immediately goes on:

And with that word Arcite gan espye
Wher as this lady romed to and fro. (1112–13)

Mention of the word 'tirannye' leads directly to an account of Arcite's falling in love, the implication being that here is another form of tyranny. Further, in describing Arcite's response to the intervention of Perotheus on his behalf and his consequent release by Theseus, Chaucer makes play of the fact that he is merely exchanging one form of prison for another:

'Allas that day that I was born!
Now is my prisoun worse than biforn.' (1223–4)

The association between the two kinds of suffering becomes quite explicit at 1295, as Palamon declares himself tormented on two sides:

'For I moot weep and wayle whil I lyve
With al the wo that prison may me yive,
And eek with peyne that love me yeveth also,
That doubleth al my torment and my wo.' (1295–8)

and, towards the end of Part I of the tale, Chaucer laments how winter doubles the 'peynes stronge'

Bothe of the lovere and the prisoner.
I note which hath the wofuller mester. (1339–40)

It is less, I think, that Chaucer wishes to differentiate between the lover Arcite and the prisoner Palamon, than that he wishes to suggest a kind of parallel, perhaps even an equivalence, between the two species of pain. And while Theseus' release of Arcite at Perotheus' request (an action which above all bespeaks a capacity for mercy) should alert us to important differences, Chaucer continues in Part II to evoke a suggestive resemblance between these two kinds of suffering. He asks concerning Palamon:

Who feeleth double soor and hevynesse
But Palamon that love destreyneth so
That wood out of his wit he goth for wo?
And eek therto he is a prisoner
Perpetuelly, noght oonly for a yer.
Who coude ryme in Engylyssh proprely
His martyrdom? (1454–60)

Vincent J. Dimarco points out thai 'the *Romaunt of the Rose* and the *Legend of Good Women* regularly refer to those who die for love in the language for martyrdom',[22] but there is here a pointed ambivalence as to whether Palamon's 'martyrdom' will be that of lover or prisoner. And again, while Arcite has been released from prison, one finds in his speech in the grove outside Athens the by now familiar expression of double sorrow: he laments first the suffering he continues to endure as a Theban and hence as an enemy of Theseus:

'Allas', quod he, 'that day that I was bore!
How longe, Juno, thurgh thy crueltee,
Woltow werreyen Thebes the citee?. . .
And now I am so caytyf and so thral,
That he that is my mortal enemy,
I serve him as his squier povrely . . .
Allas, thou felle Mars! Allas, Juno!
Thus hath youre ire oure lynage al fordo,
Save oonly me and wrecched Palamoun,
That Theseus martireth in prisoun.' (1542–62)

But then, with the mention of martyrdom, Arcite immediately turns his attention to the suffering he endures for love:

22 *Riverside Chaucer*, p. 832.

'And over al this, to sleen me outrely
Love hath his firy dart so brennyngly
Ystiked thurgh my trewe, careful herte
That shapen was my deeth erst than my sherte.' (1563–6)

While he believes Theseus to be martyring Palamon, Arcite clearly feels that love is in turn martyring him. Just as Theseus appears to the Theban knights to be a tyrant, so too does Cupid. It is precisely the tyrannous nature of Palamon and Arcite's love for Emelye that the narrator, uniting his point of view with theirs, and seeing how this love has broken the bonds of friendship and will not endure 'felaweshipe', apostrophises at 1623–7:

O Cupide, out of alle charitee!
O regne, that wolt no felawe have with thee!
Ful sooth is seyd that love ne lordshipe
Wol noght, his thankes, have no felaweshipe.
Wel fynden that Arcite and Palamoun.

And from consideration of the tyrannous lord who inflicts overwhelming passion on Palamon and Arcite and leaves them fighting 'up to the ancle . . . in hir blood' (1660) the narrative turns to tell of the lord who likewise inflicted suffering on them and is still their mortal foe. But here, in the account of how Theseus discovers the cousins fighting in a grove outside Athens, the illusion of tyranny in both its forms is finally broken down.

Palamon is conscious that justice demands their death: three times in his address to Theseus he alludes to the fact that this is what they 'deserve':

'Sire, what nedeth wordes mo?
We have the deeth disserved bothe two . . .
This is thy mortal foo, this is Arcite,
That fro thy land is banysshed on his heed,
For which he hath deserved to be deed . . .
For bothe han we deserved to be slayn.' (1715–41)

Theseus acknowledges that their own words damn them, and in his character as Martian and ireful 'conquerour' he is inclined to assent to Palamon's words. But the demands of strict justice are modified by 'pitee' and 'mercy', as Theseus demonstrates 'compassioun' for the cousins and 'foryeves al hoolly this trespaas' (1818). And, just as he reveals his own 'pitous' and 'gentil' nature, so now, looking up 'with eyen lighte' (1783), he apostrophizes Cupid, again, as the narrator earlier had done, in his character as tyrant, but in a tone which is transformed from one of solemnity and foreboding to one of tolerance and amusement:

> 'The god of love, a benedicite!
> How myghty and how greet a lord is he!
> Ageyns his myght ther gayneth none obstacles.
> He may be cleped a god for his myracles . . .
> Se how they blede! Be they noght wel arrayed?
> Thus hath hir lord, the god of love, ypayed
> Hir wages and hir fees for hir servyse!' (1785–1803)

Theseus duly recognises the power of love, but his words undermine the unwavering seriousness and intensity with which the young lovers have until now regarded Cupid: love is now seen as a phase through which Palamon and Arcite must go, something which is proper to their age, but which will pass with the natural processes of time. Cupid is still acknowledged to be a great and powerful god, but at the same time is regarded in a lighthearted, even flippant way which suggests that after all, love is something of a game. And in encouraging us to regard Cupid with humour, there is a sense in which Theseus unmasks and renders less threatening the tyrant who had so recently seemed to portend only disaster, leaving Palamon and Arcite bloody and desirous of death.

Hence, in this pivotal scene at the end of Part II of the the *Knight's Tale*, the illusion of tyranny in both its forms is at last dispelled and the tone of the narrative lightens accordingly. It is now the wise and mature and above all merciful and humane Duke Theseus, rather than the dark, anarchic forces of love, who is in control of events. By a chance coincidence which is clearly designed to beget faith in the benevolence of providence (1663 ff.), disaster has been averted, and it is with a sense of relief that we hear of Theseus' proposal for a tournament where each of the knights 'shal have his destinee as hym is shape' (1842–3)—a proposal which signifies the accommodation of a seemingly implacable and potentially destructive love into the order of the world of chivalry. It appears that we have now left behind disquieting notions of injustice, despotic rule, and martyrdom, of suffering which is at once inordinate and undeserved, and, above all, thoughts of dying for love. Under the aegis of Theseus love will be treated with all proper seriousness and decorum, but it seems no longer to be a matter of life and death. Reassurance that this is indeed the case comes with news of Theseus' modification, on the day of the tournament, of his first purpose: the knights may indeed fight for love, but no one must be allowed to die for it (2537–60). More and more, as the tale progresses, it is as if we are being encouraged in retrospect to read Palamon and Arcite's talk in the early part of the tale, of being slain by Emelye's eyes, for example, or of dying for love of her, not literally, but as figurative and conventional expressions of the courtly, chivalric code—a code by which it now appears their love has been safely accommodated.

But while Theseus does indeed wrest control of events from an apparently despotic and tyrannous love, thus showing this love to be amenable after all to the claims of moderation and good sense, and at the same time proving himself to be no tyrant but rather a benevolent and humane governor, it soon becomes apparent that his benign governance is to be challenged by forces which, insofar as they act capriciously, entirely in disregard of justice and take no account of men's merits or deserts, are truly tyrannous—forces which, moreover, truly do have (and will exercise ruthlessly) power of life and death over Palamon and Arcite.

Hence, though it may be with nascent feelings of optimism that we first hear, in Part III of the tale, of Theseus' construction of the lists (1881–1913), such feelings are quickly undermined by the actual account of the temples of Venus, Mars and Diana (1914–2088), since these gods—rather disquietingly, and for no reason that is yet apparent—are depicted solely in their malevolent aspects. Similarly, any sanguine expectations we may entertain on hearing of Theseus' elaborate preparations for the tournament (2190–207) are soon dispelled by the account of the celestial conversation in which the malevolent Saturn declares his intention to intervene in the 'divisioun' of Mars and Venus (2438–78). And, in due course, the splendid chivalric idyll over which Theseus presides on the day of the tournament, 'as he were a god in trone' (2529) is shattered by the advent of a 'myracle' (2675), Saturn's 'furie infernal' (2684), which startles Arcite's horse and casts him to the ground. At first it appears that the injury is not fatal: Theseus, we are told, comes home to Athens

> With alle blisse and greet solempnitee.
> Al be it that this aventure was falle,
> He nolde nought disconforten hem alle. (2702–4)

Many of the wounded knights are healed with 'salves' and 'charmes' and 'fermacies of herbes' (2712–3) and Theseus 'made revel al the longe nyght' (2717) and 'fully heeld a feeste dayes three' (2736). Such has been the sustained celebratory mood of the account of the tournament and its aftermath that the stark, explicit and scrupulously unemotional account of Arcite's death, when it comes (2742–61), is felt primarily as a violation of the orderly and decorous world over which a 'gentil' ruler presides and in which, crucially, love is a matter for ceremony and due gravity, but where the idea of death as a possible 'fee' for the 'servyse' of love seemed to have no place. The lapse here in the declamatory or panegyric or otherwise heightened style which has characterised Chaucer's writing of the chivalric milieu throughout the tale signifies the intrusion into that milieu of dark and primitive forces which, it appears, are way beyond its capacity to control. Theseus had expressly decreed that no man should die for love, but the reader may perhaps remember that in the temple of Mars there was depicted an 'ensample' of those 'who shal be slayn or elles deed for love' (2038), and such, indeed, is the tragic fate of Mars' knight. There has been, albeit unknown to the human protagonists, a conflict between the will of the gods themselves and the will of Theseus, godlike ruler of Athens—a conflict from which the gods emerge triumphant and in which Theseus, his intention frustrated, is indubitably the loser.

But the tale does not after all end with Arcite's death (though it might—and in the opinion of some critics, *should*—have ended with Arcite's last words to Palamon, since these mark the resolution of the conflict between love and friendship, an important theme of the *Knight's Tale*), as a still more important issue remains unresolved. The concluding part of the tale may, in one sense, be seen as a test of whether Theseus and the chivalric code by which he lives can accommodate the ultimate misfortune, death. And it seems that indeed it can: Theseus responds to Arcite's death in what is above all a decorous and appropriate manner, devising an elaborate funeral-rite worthy of the young knight, the orderliness and ceremony of which is intended to push back the encroachment of forces of disorder and chaos. In this way, the initial frenzy of grief which greeted Arcite's death becomes circumscribed by the rituals of the chivalric world. Moreover, the end of the mourning period is itself seen to be a matter of due process and decorum:

> By processe and by lengthe of certeyn yeres,
> Al stynted is the moornynge and the teres
> Of Grekes, by oon general assent. (2967–9)

and, again in due course, and in what appears to be a timely move, Theseus initiates a parliament with the object of healing the division between Athens and Thebes which has been outstanding since the beginning of the tale:

> Thanne semed me ther was a parlement
> At Atthenes, upon certein pointz and caas;
> Among the whiche pointz yspoken was,
> To have with certein contrees alliaunce,
> And have fully of Thebans obeisaunce. (2970–4)

Theseus is then allowed a lengthy speech which, it would seem, has the two-fold but effectually single purpose of consoling Arcite's friends for his death and hence opening the way for the marriage of Palamon and

Emelye. In this speech, Theseus evokes a transcendent order, a universe presided over by a Prime Mover and governed by love:

> 'The Firste Moevere of the cause above
> Whan he first made the faire cheyne of love,
> Greet was th'effect, and heigh was his entente.
> Wel wiste he why, and what thereof he mente' (2987–90)

By appealing to the principle of mutability, he conveys a sense that Arcite's death can in fact be accommodated within this order:

> 'That same Prince and that Moevere . . .
> Hath stabilissed in this wrecched world adoun
> Certeyne dayes and duracioun
> To al that is engendred in this place,
> Over the whiche day they may nat pace . . .' (2994–8)

He concludes, 'Thanne may I seyn that al this thyng moot dye' (3034), and draws the following—pragmatic—inference:

> 'Thanne is it wysdom, as it thynketh me,
> To maken vertu of necessitee,
> And take it weel that we may not eschue' (3041–3)

This inference justifies and legitimises the marriage of Palamon and Emelye, which Theseus duly proposes (3067–3089).

It is tempting to assent to Theseus' words here (as indeed the narrator himself appears to do in the closing lines of the tale), to conclude that his great speech represents the enunciation of a fundamental principle of cosmic harmony and the triumphant restoration of order to the social and civil spheres—an order which, moreover, insofar as it is reflected in the union of Palamon and Emelye, proves itself the earthly counterpart of the heavenly law of love. Arcite's death had threatened chaos and the dissolution of order, but it appears that we are entitled to conclude from Theseus' speech that seemingly intractable events have finally yielded to forces for good.

Such has been the view of a large number of the *Knight's Tale*'s critics, and such will be our reading of the tale if we unite our point of view with that of Theseus. But there is, I believe, one fact which effectively prevents us from doing so—the fact that he has not, any more than the other characters in the tale, been privileged to see beyond the surface of events to the true cause of Arcite's death. And his ignorance of the machinations of a malevolent Saturn, and hence of the true cause of the 'myracle' which kills Arcite, inevitably creates a gap between his point of view and that of the omniscient reader which prevents us from wholeheartedly assenting to his words. We are surely intended to recognise that Theseus, in deeming Arcite's fall 'but an aventure' (2722; cf. also 2703), falls some way short of the truth, and may well feel that his subsequent speech, for all its gravity, might have been a little less sanguine if he were fully aware that callous and indifferent forces had not only permitted but had actively caused Arcite's death. In fact, as several critics have pointed out, Theseus' adducement in this speech of a law of love is significantly—even violently—at odds with what we have witnessed in the events of the tale. To put it in the crudest terms, what we have seen is a manifestation, not of love, but of malevolence and cruelty. Theseus thanks the Prime Mover, Jupiter, for his 'grace' (3069), but we have seen no evidence of it; he concludes that 'gentil mercy oghte to passen right' (3089), yet the gods have demonstrated neither mercy nor even justice. Indeed, what we have witnessed is, above all, the perpetration of an injustice; it is, above all, the injustice of Arcite's death that cries out for comment. Yet any reference to, or any attempt to explain the workings of divine justice is conspicuously absent from Theseus' speech.

For many critics, the revelation of the injustice and malevolence of the gods and the consequent, apparently inevitable, negation of Theseus' Boethian certitudes—in particular, his assertion of a universal law of love—is at the heart of the *Knights Tale*.[23] But one ought to ask whether, if we do feel that Theseus' conclusion are very imperfectly reconciled with our experience of the tale, we are therefore, as Christian readers, entitled simply to marvel at the injustice and cruelty of these pagan gods and to conclude, as Alastair Minnis does, that 'the noble Athenians deserve better gods'?[24] The truth of the matter is, I believe, altogether more complex and more challenging. Chaucer does not allow his Christian audience any such serene historical relativism, for while Venus, Mars, Saturn and the rest may appear to be simply pagan gods, when we look more closely we can see that it is not as deities but as planets that they exert power: hence the care with which Chaucer identifies the propitious planetary hour at which the three petitioners attend with prayer their patron deities. Saturn's speech at 2453, 'My cours, that hath so wyde for to turne . . .', makes this plain, and it is because they are not independent pagan deities but planets that it is Saturn and not Jupiter who is seen to be in control of the heavens. Now, as has often been pointed out, the influence of the planets was well accepted in medieval lore as part of the agency of providence and of destiny, its 'ministre general'. According, to Boethius, for example, the planets, in the hierarchy of instrumentality, were related to God, the Prime Mover, as a secondary to a primary cause, having themselves—and this is

23 See, for example, Bishop, *Narrative Art*, pp. 26–59; Salter, *Fourteenth-Century Poetry*, pp. 143–81; Minnis, *Pagan Antiquity*, pp. 135–45.
24 *Ibid.*, p. 141.

what is crucial for the *Knights Tale*—no independence of causation (*Boece*, IV.pr6.41 ff.). Hence the apparently independent movers are themselves moved by other powers.[25] So vivid is Chaucer's account of the conversations and squabbles of the gods that we may become so engrossed in the fiction (Chaucer himself refers at the end of the celestial quarrel simply to 'goddes above' (2479)) as to forget that this quarrel is in fact, as Derek Pearsall says, 'a figurative account of planetary influences'.[26] Theseus' speech, his opening reference to an omnipotent 'Firste Moevere', may therefore come to the reader of the tale as something of a reminder—perhaps even a revelation—that there is a power beyond the planets by which they are moved. But if, instead of dismissing it as irrelevant or simply mistaken, we come to acknowledge that the (monotheistic) Boethian system outlined by Theseus is entirely compatible with what we have seen of the operations of the planetary gods, certain difficult and disturbing questions emerge.

Such an acknowledgement means, above all, that, since we are no longer able to attribute it to the caprice of a pagan deity, we are forced somehow to reconcile the injustice of Arcite's death with a belief in a God who governs all things by love. Hence, Theseus' speech, far from resolving the wonder aroused by the 'myracle' of Saturn's 'furie', serves only to heighten it. The familiar consolatory maxims found in the latter part of the speech might indeed, as they do in Teseo's speech in the *Teseida,* have increased our understanding of Arcite's death, or at least softened our feelings of outrage at it, had they not been so problematically prefaced by an emphatic assertion of a universal law of love which is radically at odds with what we have just witnessed. Alastair Minnis has said: 'There is no divine justice in *The Knight's Tale*; the pagan gods act arbitrarily and capriciously and they have their favourites.'[27] But in fact the situation with which Chaucer confronts us at the end of the tale is more distressing than that, in so far as it forces us to acknowledge that Arcite's manifestly unjust fate has been presided over and, more than that, has ultimately been caused by the one God who, it is said, holds the universe together by a 'feyre cheyne of love'. It is a dilemma which, far from being confined to the realm of pagan history, remote in space and time, has an obvious relevance to, and is only slightly less disturbing than, the Christian's besetting problem of how to reconcile unjust suffering with belief in a loving God. Hence the real significance of Chaucer's reference to Saturn's 'furie infernal' as a 'myracle'. The term was designed to excite wonder in the reader as to the cause of the fury, but this cause is not as obvious as it

25 See Jill Mann, 'Chance and Destiny in *Troilus and Criseyde* and the *Knight's Tale'*, *The Cambridge Chaucer Companion*, edd. Piero Boitani and Jill Mann (Cambridge, 1986), pp. 75–92.

26 *Canterbury Tales*, p. 128.

27 *Pagan Antiquity*, p. 136.

might first seem: if Saturn's sending of this thunderbolt is not simply the whim of a capricious god, but is indeed an anthropomorphic representation of a cosmological phenomenon, then Theseus' speech demands that it be attributed to the 'Firste Moevere', the God who controls all such secondary causes as agents of his providence. A miracle, in Christian theology, signified something extraordinary—a suspension by God of the normal workings of providence for a particular purpose, often (ironically enough) in answer to a prayer. Some such connotations may be present even in the pagan context of the *Knight's Tale*, and, if they are, they add to our feelings of outrage that the permissive will of God should extend to an action such as Saturn's.[28] Moreover, as evidenced, for example, by Chaucer's use of 'Cupid's miracles' as the antithesis to his 'crewel yre' in the *Parlement of Foules* (11), the term was invariably used of an intervention for good, but while the narrator's invitation, 'herkneth me . . . Which a myracle ther bifel anon', encourages the expectation that the impasse between Mars and Venus is to be resolved by a wonderful but, above all, benevolent act, what we subsequently witness is, of course, an intervention for ill. In retrospect, then, and in view of the appallingly cruel fate to which it refers, the apparently innocuous term 'myracle' will be seen to have been used by Chaucer with bitter irony. And in the light of Theseus' speech, the question arises: how can it possibly be seen as a manifestation of love?

Of course, one may say that the ill fortune of men does not necessarily negate belief in the benevolence of providence, and that there is, as Theseus says, a transcendent order of love, whose workings in this world are simply beyond man's limited comprehension. And, of course, orthodox medieval ideas of providence could and did reconcile God's goodness with the existence of evil by arguing that providence encompasses evil, as well as good, and finally turns everything to the good from which it comes—an idea which perhaps lies behind Theseus' assertion that Jupiter operates by 'Convertynge al unto his propre welle | From which it is dirryved' (3037–8). Aquinas, for example, said that God allows evil not in itself but for the good towards which it is directed, and held the belief that providence was indeed benevolent since in a great many cases there is a pattern whereby things turn out for the better.[29] It is possible that such an idea may be inferred from Theseus' closing words, in which he claims to turn evil to good, by

28 The retrospective projection of Christian values onto the pagan world of classical Greece which I am suggesting is implicit in the *Knight's Tale* is of course entirely in keeping with the synchronic view of history which prevailed throughout the Middle Ages and which Chaucer almost certainly shared.

29 *Videmus enim in rebus naturalibus provenire quod melius est aut semper aut in pluribus* (*ST* 1*a*, 103.1). References in this article are to St. Thomas Aquinas, *Summa Theologiae* (Latin text and English translation) London, 61 vols., 1964–81.

making 'O parfit joye' from 'sorwes two' (3071–2). But such a reading, insofar as it implies that the evil of Arcite's fate has somehow been transformed to a greater good, is, I believe, self-evidently facile and false to our experience of the tale: if such an orthodox notion is indeed suggested by Theseus' words, it must be in a near-parodic or, at best, ironic way. Chaucer does nothing to help the reader of the *Knight's Tale*, to soften the dichotomy between Arcite's cruel fate and the universal law of love. Indeed, proof of his desire to create a disturbing conflict between the First Mover's 'faire cheyne of love' and the injustice and caprice of the acts perpetrated by his agents is to be found in his (otherwise inexplicable) decision to present the gods, Venus, Mars, and Diana, solely in their malevolent aspects. Hence, the dominant emotion at the end of the tale is neither simple outrage at a pantheon of pagan gods nor joyful assent to Theseus' words—Chaucer having rendered both responses inadequate—but rather wonder at how a God who rules all things by love could have allowed such a 'myracle' to come to pass. It is a question which echoes down through centuries of metaphysical thought and is at the centre of all theodicies and their attempts to justify the ways of God to man. And if the challenge facing the reader at the end of the *Knight's Tale* really is that of how to reconcile apparent injustice with a belief in the benign control of a First Mover who turns all things to the good, then it is illuminating to discover that this situation is exactly replicated by the dilemma of Boethius himself in Book IV of the *De Consolatione Philosophiae* and I believe it is worth looking more closely at this part of *Boece* for any light it may cast of the *Knight's Tale*.

IV

Lady Philosophy has taught Boethius in Book III that 'God governth alle the thinges of the world by the governementis of bounte' (*Boece*, III.pr12.76–7). But his heart is still filled with 'wepynge and moornynge', and in Book IV, *prosa* 1, he declares that the greatest cause of his grief is that he cannot reconcile an awareness of the injustices of this world with belief in a good governor: 'that so as the governour of thinges is good, yif that eveles mowen ben by any weyes, or elles yif that evelis passen withouten punysschynge'; he begs Philosophy to consider 'how worthy it es to be wondred upon' (IV.pr1.18–23). Added to this, he says, there is another thing 'more to be wondrid uppon: for felonye is emperisse, and floureth ful of richesses, and vertu nis nat al oonly withouten meedes, but it is cast undir and fortroden undir the feet of felonous folk' (26–30). He goes on: 'Of alle whiche thinges there nys no wyght that may merveillen ynowghe ne compleyne that swich thinges ben don in the reigne of God, that alle thinges woot and alle thinges may and ne wole nat but only gode thinges' (31–6). Philosophy replies that 'that were a greet merveille and an abaysschinge withouten ende . . . yif it were as thou wenest'; 'But', she says, 'it nys nat so', and asserts that 'blissfulnesses cometh alwey to good folk and infortune to wykkede folk' (46, 54–6). She points again and again in the course of *prosae* 2, 3, and 4 to the suffering which is, inevitably, attendant upon vice since it removes man from the true good, and to the happiness which always accompanies virtue since it unites man with that good. Hence, Philosophy concludes, 'good folk been blisful and schrewes ben wrecches' (IV.pr4.97–8).

The narrator eventually assents to this view: 'Thus se I wel . . . eyther what blisfulnesse or elles what unselynesse is establishid in the dissertes of gode men and of schrewes' (IV.pr5.1–3). But while Lady Philosophy may have proved to his satisfaction that virtue is its own reward and vice its own punishment, Boethius continues to be troubled by the manifest injustices which he sees around him: 'But in this ilke fortune of peple I se somwhat of good and somwhat of yvel. . . . Thanne I merveile me gretly why the thinges ben so mysentrechaunged that tormentz of felonyes pressen and confounden good folk and schrewes ravysshen medes of vertu and ben in honoures and in grete estatz' (IV.pr5.4–25). He goes on (and here the relevance to our predicament at the end of the *Knight's Tale*, attempting to reconcile Theseus' speech with Arcite's death, becomes apparent):

> 'for I wolde wondre wel the lasse, yif I trowede that alle thise thinges weren medled by fortunows hap. But now hepith and encreseth myn astonyenge God, governour of thinges, that . . . yeveth ayeinward to good folk hardnesses and to schrewes he graunteth hem hir wil and what they desiren—what difference thanne may ther be betwixen that that God doth, and the hap of fortune, yif men ne knowe nat the cause why that it is.' (IV.pr5.27–39)

Philosophy declares that 'Ne it nis no merveile', and that Boethius should accept that 'alle thinges . . . ben don aryght' (40–8), and there follows a *metrum* in which Philosophy shows how, if the causes of natural phenomena like the movement of the stars are unknown to men, they will 'wondryn' (m5.8) at them, but that no man 'wondreth' (22) at the movement of the winds or the elements since he knows their 'causes'. Hence, she concludes, 'the moevable peple is astoned of alle thinges that comen seelde and sodeynly in our age; but yif the troubly errour of our ignorance departed fro us, so that we wisten the causes why that swiche thynges bytyden, certes thei scholde cesen to seme wondres' (m5.31–7). Yet Boethius remains unconvinced, troubled by the existence of injustice in a world where all things are directed to the good, and at the beginning of *prosa* 6 reminds Philosophy of her duty to 'unwrappen the hidde causes of thinges', and begs her to 'devyse and juge me of this matere, and that thou do me to undirstonden it. For', he says, 'this miracle or this wonder trowbleth me ryght gretly' (pr6.1–8).

Hence the question which is at the centre of the *Knight's Tale* is also fundamental to the *Consolation*, and the similarities between Boethius' dilemma here and that of the reader at the end of the *Knight's Tale* are obvious. Hardly less striking is the way in which—as I hope my emphases have shown—as the question of how to reconcile injustice with belief in a 'good governor' arises in Book IV of *Boece*, so expressions of wonder and astonishment occur with increasing and dramatic insistence, reaching a climax in the passage quoted from the beginning of *prosa* 6 in which Boethius declares that it is Lady Philosophy's duty to resolve 'this miracle or this wonder' (the Latin has simply *miraculum*). It is as if, for Boethius, this question above all was a subject for wonder, and I believe it is hardly claiming too much to say that it was Boethius' persistent expressions of wonder specifically in relation to this problem that inspired Chaucer's basic handling in the *Knight's Tale* of the story of unjust suffering he had borrowed from Boccaccio, leading him, as we have already seen, to set wonder at the heart of the tale.

The pervasive Boethian character of the *Knight's Tale* is unmistakable and has long been recognised and discussed by critics, yet it is strange that there has been no enquiry into whether Chaucer was at all influenced by what the *Consolation* has to say on the subject of apparent injustice and its relation to a good governor. It would be extraordinary, in view of the strong Boethian colouring of the tale, and especially if it is indeed the case that his treatment of his narrative material in the *Knight's Tale* was influenced by Boethius' presentation of this problem, if Chaucer were then to ignore entirely the *Consolation*'s resolution of it. I believe, therefore, that it is worth taking time to look at Philosophy's attempt to answer the question in order to discover whether this answer has had any influence on Chaucer's work.

Lady Philosophy declares that the 'miracle' or 'wonder' whereby the good governor appears to allow injustice and undeserved suffering to be 'gretteste of alle thingis that mowen ben axed' (IV.pr6.11–12). Such is the magnitude of the problem that its resolution will involve a discussion of 'the symplicitie of the purveaunce of God, and of the ordre of destyne, and of sodeyn hap, and of the knowynge and predestinacioun devyne, and of the liberte of fre wil' (26–9). Such a preamble might lead one to expect a complex and sophisticated resolution of the problem, but the answer, when it comes, is startling and even disconcerting in its simplicity.

Philosophy distinguishes between the immovable providential order which encompasses all things and destiny, the working out of that order in time, but she recognises a possible objection to the idea that providence turns everything to good:

> 'But thou mayest seyn, "What unreste may ben a worse confuson than that gode men han somtyme adversite and somtyme prosperite, and schrewes also han now thingis that they desiren and now thinges that they haten?"' (IV.pr6.178–83)

Her response to such perceptions of injustice is to question men's understanding and judgement:

> 'Whethir men lyven now in swich holnes of thought (as who seith, ben men now so wyse) that swiche folk as thei demen to ben gode folk or schrewes, that it moste nedes ben that folk ben swiche as thei wenen? But in this manere the domes of men discorden, that thilke men that some folk demen worthy of mede, other folk demen hem worthy of torment.' (183–90)

Even if one concedes 'that som man may wel demen or knowen the good folk and the badde' (191–3), their understanding, Philosophy says, is still not complete:

> 'may he thanne knowen and seen thilke innereste atempraunce of corages as it hath ben wont to be seyd of bodyes?' (193–5)

She goes on to make an analogy between man's 'corage' or inward temper and the health of bodies whose true condition only the physician knows (199–213). In the same way and by a similar 'miracle' or 'mervayle', only God can know men's true 'corage': and he, in accordance with this knowledge, dispenses rewards for good and evil:

> 'But what othir thing semeth hele of corages but bounte and prowesse? And what othir thing semeth maladye of corages but vices? Who is elles kepere of good and dryvere awey of yvel but God, governour and lechere of thoughtes? The whiche God, whan he hath biholden from the hye tour of his purveaunce, he knoweth what is covenable to every wight, and lenyth hem that he woot is convenable to hem. Lo, herof comyth and herof is don this noble miracle of the ordre destynal, whan God, that al knoweth, dooth swich thing of which thing unknowynge folk ben astonyd.' (210–23)

What Philosophy is saying here might indeed cause some astonishment. She responds to the problem of how to reconcile belief in a good governor with unjust suffering by declaring that there is in fact no such thing as unjust suffering: if we could only see through to men's true 'corages', we would see that all the suffering (and likewise all the good fortune) which is ordained by God's providence is after all 'covenable' ('fitting'; cf. Lat. *convenire*) and just. And the principle that providence decrees only what is just and fitting is referred to several times in the course of Book V of *Boece.* In her discussion of free will in Book V, *prosa* 2, for example, Philosophy postulates the idea that men are authors of their own destiny: the closer they are to God, the source of all goodness, the freer they are; the more they yield to corporeal passion, the less free. '. . . in this manere,' she says, 'thei ben caytifs fro hir propre liberte' (V.pr2.26–43). But beyond this measure of self-determination, there is in operation an external law which dispenses appropriate rewards and punishments:

> 'The whiche thingis natheles the lokynge of the devyne purveaunce seth, that alle thingis byholdeth and seeth fro eterne, and ordeyneth hem everiche in hire merites as thei ben predestinat' (43–7)

Again, in Book V, *prosa* 6, at the conclusion of her discussion of free will and divine foreknowledge, right at the end of the work, returning to the question from which this entire discussion arose, Philosophy refers unambiguously to the divine 'lawes' which propose just rewards and punishments to men, according to their deserts:

> 'And syn that thise thinges ben thus (that is to seyn, syn that necessite nis nat in thynges by the divine presience), thanne is ther fredom of arbitrie, that duelleth hool and unwemmed to mortal men; ne the lawes ne purposen nat wikkidly medes and peynes to the willynges of men that ben unbownden and quyt of alle necessite' (286–93)

She concludes:

> 'and God, byholdere and forwytre of alle thingis, duelleth above, and the present eternite of his sighte renneth alwey with the diverse qualite of our dedes, dispensynge and ordeynynge medes to gode men and tormentz to wikkide men.' (293–8)

Such then is the—in my view—quite extraordinary teaching of Boethius on the problem of how to reconcile apparently unjust suffering with the idea of a God-centred and love-guided universe. Such suffering only appears to be unjust as a consequence of our human ignorance; in fact, insofar as it is always decreed by providential 'lawes', it is always 'covenable' and just. While Boethius' teaching on this matter may be bound up with and even dependent upon complex ideas of free will, divine foreknowledge, and so on, it is, in the last analysis, remarkably close to the popular and simple medieval belief an imminent justice whereby God is seen to intervene directly in the affairs of men, dispensing rewards for virtue and punishment for vice. However that may be, it is clear that a truly Boethian reading of the *Knight's Tale* would have to go beyond the by now familiar recognition of, say, Arcite's imperfect grasp of the Boethian concepts of fortune and providence, or his and Palamon's un-Boethian belief in an earthly love as the greatest good, to a full recognition that his death, while it may appear to be grossly unjust, has in fact been ordained by a God who, in the full knowledge of Arcite's 'corage', deemed it to be 'covenable' for him, and is therefore deserved and, consequently, just. Such a reading seems, on the face of it, perverse and impossible; it would appear that Boethius' teaching on the question of human suffering has no place in the *Knight's Tale*. Yet I believe the influence of this teaching may indeed be felt, albeit at a rather obscure level of the tale.

V

Edward C. Schweitzer, in an important article,[30] has brought evidence, chiefly from the medical treatises of the period, to show a series of suggestive correspondences between the 'loveris maladye | Of Heroes' from which Arcite suffers in the first half of the tale and his fatal injury in the second—correspondences which, he believes, 'show that Arcite's death is not only just but poetically inevitable.' The most significant of these correspondence, in my view, is that, just as Chaucer explicitly tells us that Arcite suffers from the advanced form of *amor hereos* called 'manye' (1374), so we are told he is struck down by a 'furie infernal' (2684). (Boccaccio, by comparison, calls his fury by name, *Erinis* (*Teseida*, IX. 4, 6).) Schweitzer points to a tradition going back to Isidore's *Etymologies* in accordance with which Arnald of Villanova calls *amor hereos* a *furia*, and, he notes, Chaucer's younger contemporary, the physician Valescus of Tarenta, says flatly: *Mania etiam dicitur quaedam furia infernalis*. The correspondence is indeed suggestive and points to a deliberate linking by Chaucer of illness and injury.

Schweitzer sees a whole series of such correspondences, a few more of which are worth recounting. According to Arnald of Villanova, the *amor heroes* causes the estimative power in man to err in thinking the beloved much better than she is, so that reason is subjected to the delusions of the senses. The estimative power, says Arnald, wavers or 'stumbles' (*claudicat*), as Arcite's horse 'foundered' (2684) while leaping sideways, frightened by the fury. There may be significance too in the fact that in Chaucer, unlike Boccaccio, Arcite's horse does not simply rear up at the sight of the fury and fall over backwards onto him, crushing his

30 'Fate and Freedom in *The Knight's Tale*', *Studies in the Age of Chaucer* 3 (1981), 13–45.

chest with its saddle; instead, 'er that Arcite may taken keep' (2688), it first throws him off onto 'the pomel of his heed' (2689)—interally upside down—just as the image of Emelye in Arcite's imagination overthrew his reason: 'turned was al up so doun | Bothe habit and eek disposicioun' (1377–8). Moreover, the fury is summoned by Saturn, just as *hereos* is a variety of Saturnian melancholy—whereas in the *Teseida* it merely comes down from above (IX.7.3). Finally, Schweitzer sees significance in the fact that Arcite dies when 'nature hath no dominacioun', when

> The vertu expulsif, or animal,
> Fro thilke vertu cleped natural
> Ne may the venym voyden ne expelle. (2749–51)

He dies despite the artificial aid of emetics, laxatives and blood-letting, all aimed at removing the corrupted blood from the region around the heart, just as, according to Valescus and Bernard of Gordon, the cure for *hereos* consists in distracting the lover from his obsession, removing the delusive image from his consciousness. 'The loss of rational control and nature's "dominacioun",' says Schweitzer, 'corresponds exactly to the breakdown in the interaction of reason and imagination characterised by *amor hereos*.'[31]

Such, then, are some of the ways in which, according to Schweitzer, Chaucer makes Arcite's injury correspond to his illness. But while I believe the discovery of these correspondences is vitally important for a full understanding of the *Knight's Tale*, I cannot agree with the conclusions Schweitzer draws from them:

> Arcite's downfall enacts the progress of the 'loveris maladye | Of Hereos' from which Arcite suffered in the first half of the tale, as that malady was explained by the medical authorities of Chaucer's time. (. . .) If [Arcite's death] is the symbolic re-enactment of what has gone before, then the conclusion which seemed arbitrary and unpredictable becomes almost inevitable, and if Arcite is responsible for his infatuation with Emelye—and there is no reason to suppose that he is not (. . .)—then, by the logic of poetry, he is responsible, too, for the fury sent by Saturn, and the death he suffers becomes an emblem of the end of those who persist in loving unreasonably.[32]

The objections to this interpretation of Arcite's death are many. For one thing, it is clear from Chaucer's shockingly stark and explicit account of that death that it is not an 'emblem' of anything at all, but rather a harsh

31 'Fate and Freedom', p.28.
32 Ibid., pp. 21, 29.

reality, a literal fact which must somehow be accounted for. Furthermore, while an authority such as Dino del Garbo may explain that 'love can kill by impeding with its vehemenece the operation of the vegetative or vital powers of the soul', and while the prognosis for love-sickness of the kind suffered by Arcite may indeed, as Schweitzer says, be death, the fact remains that Arcite emphatically does not die from *amor hereos* or *mania.* (Indeed, that he has recovered from it and is now only intermittently dejected is wittily brought out in the scene in the grove outside Athens, where Chaucer describes the young lover as being 'Now up, now doun, as boket in a welle' (1533).) Moreover, if Chaucer had truly wished to convey the sense that Arcite's death is, to use Schweitzer's term, the 'poetically inevitable' result of his illness, of the love-sickness which signifies inordinate love for an earthly creature, he could simply have left Mars and Venus as he found them in the *Teseida*, where they signify man's irascible and concupiscible appetites—that is, moral forces acting from within, and in this way, could have pointed unambiguously to Arcite's death as being self-determined. Instead, as Schweitzer himself points out, Chaucer chooses to present them primarily, and Saturn (his own addition to the tale) exclusively, as planets, 'cosmic forces acting from without'. And, in fact, I believe this decision to transform Venus and Mars as well as Saturn into forces which are entirely external to the protagonists provides an important clue to Chaucer's real intention.

Schweitzer declares that 'the *Consolation* makes brilliant sense of the paradox that the planetary gods determine exactly what the protagonists choose', and he invokes a passage from Book V, *prosa* 2 I have already quoted in part, in which Philosophy says that by turning from the light of the sovereign good 'to lowe thingis and derke' and yielding to their passions, men 'hepen and encressen the servage which they han joyned to hemself; and in this manere thei ben caytifs from hir propre liberte.' (1–43). But Schweitzer ignores the fact that Philosophy does not end here: to the notion of self-determinations she adds the idea of external laws which dispense rewards and punishments to good and evil men respectively:

> 'The whiche thingis *natheles* the lokynge of the devyne purveaunce seth, that alle thingis byholdeth and seeth fro eterne, and ordeyneth hem everiche in hire merites as thei ben predestinat' (43–7)

I believe it is less some kind of 'poetic justice' than the operation of such laws that is responsible for Arcite's death. Insofar as Chaucer allows us to perceive a series of correspondences between Arcite's love-sickness and his fatal injury, between his 'manye' and Saturn's 'furie infernal', he is, I would suggest, encouraging us to see the two as being related as cause and effect. But there is no need to invoke 'a paradox of fate and free-will': what happens is that external forces—planetary gods, who are revealed in turn to be agents of the First Mover—inflict on Arcite an injury which corresponds suggestively with his earlier—and, in Boethian terms, morally culpable—love-sickness. The process is, I believe, remarkably similar to Boethius' concept of providential laws 'of mede or peyne' which reward or punish man according to whatever is deemed by God to be appropriate or fitting—'covenable'—for him. The sending of a fury is, after all, as Schweitzer has shown, notably 'covenable' as a punishment for *mania*. And if one accepts that the operation of external forces in the *Knight's Tale*, Saturn's sending of the fury, is indeed analogous to the operation of Boethius' laws 'of mede or peyne', then the description of the advent of this fury as a 'myracle' gains further point. In Book IV, *prosa* 6 of *Boece*, Lady Philosophy, having proved that God beholds all men's doings from 'the hye tour of his purveaunce' and knows thereby 'what is covenable to hem', declares that from this knowing ('hereof') 'is don the noble miracle of the ordre destynal, whan God, that al knoweth, dooth swich thing, of which thing unknowynge folk ben astonyd.' If we read the *Knight's Tale* in a truly Boethian way, then we will see the 'myracle', the advent of the fury, not as an extraordinary event evoking wonder in the onlooker, but simply as part of this 'noble myracle' of destiny according to which God's providence has dispensed what is fitting for Arcite. We may indeed have wondered at the 'myracle' and at Arcite's death, but if we did, it was a sign only of our 'unknowyng'.

This idea may offend our sense of justice, but such a reading is, after all, the only one which truly accords with Boethius' *Consolation*. And if the penalty exacted of Arcite seems wildly inordinate for his offence—he has, after all, been guilty only of falling in love, albeit to the extent of suffering *mania*—it is well to remember that the idea of death as a penalty for a certain kind of love is not without a basis in the *Consolation*. It was noted earlier that Arcite's allusion early in the tale to the proverb, 'who shal yeve a lovere any lawe?' refers back to the *metrum* in *Boece* which told the story of Orpheus and Eurydice, a fable which warns against excessive love for things of the earth (the kind of excessive love which, according to Arnald of Villanova and others, led to *amor hereos*). And the fate Orpheus suffers for his love is death:

> 'Allas! Whanne Orpheus and his wif weren almest at the termes of the nyght Orpheus lokede abakward on Erudyce his wif, and lost her, and was deed.' (III.m12.55–9)

One might object that Troilus was guilty of precisely the same kind of love and his penalty was nothing worse than betrayal—a fate which, as he himself objected, he had not 'deserved'. But it is as if Chaucer, in the *Knight's Tale*, wished to take Boethius at his word, to be true to both the letter and the spirit of the *Consolation*, thereby probing Boethius' philosophy, pushing it to its limits, testing the validity of one of its central tenets and its success as a theodicy.

The Boethian view of Arcite's death is, I admit, barely perceptible in the *Knight's Tale*. It is almost as if Chaucer wished to make it as elusive as possible. Certainly, he could easily have increased its force—perhaps for example by spelling out how the 'loveris maladye | Of Hereos' from which Arcite suffers is evidence that, as the medical authorities had it, the rational power of the lover has been subjected to the delusion of the senses, thereby further 'incriminating' Arcite. But Chaucer neglects any attempt to explain the cause of the *mania*, and that he has chosen not to is, I believe, indicative of his true intention. One cannot simply say, as Schweitzer does, on the evidence of the correspondences between Arcite's injury and his illness, that Chaucer wished to present Arcite's death as being 'just and poetically inevitable'. If one wishes to see how Chaucer might present a death which was unequivocally just, one has only to look at the case of Creon who was, he says,

> . . . of Theseus yserved
> As he that hadde his death ful wel deserved. (963–4)

What I am suggesting is rather that there is a tension between two readings of the tale—the more obvious and primary one which cries out that Arcite's death is manifestly unjust, and the other, contrary, and strictly Boethian one, according to which it is no more than he has deserved. And evidence of a tension of this kind may be found in an otherwise inexplicable passage in Chaucer's account of the Temple of Mars, on the walls of which, he says,

> So was it shewed in that portreiture,
> As is depeynted in the sterres above
> Who shal be slayn or elles deed for love.
> Suffiseth oon ensample in stories olde;
> I may nat rekene hem alle though I wolde. (2036–40)

The distinction between those who are 'slayn' and those who are otherwise 'deed' for love is not an obvious one, but I assume that in the first case the reference is to those who are killed by external forces; in the second, to those whose death is self-inflicted. And in fact these two cases correspond exactly to the two readings of Arcite's death which I have just outlined: the former is the case—Arcite is 'slayn' for love—if one adopts the primary, more obvious reading of the tale and sees Arcite simply as the innocent victim of a malevolent Saturn; the latter applies—he is 'deed for love'—in a Boethian reading, according to which Arcite's death, while accomplished finally by external forces, is caused primarily (and here the debt to Schweitzer must be acknowledged) by the 'loveris maladye | Of Hereos', which itself signifies certain moral failings in Arcite, and is, in that sense, self-inflicted. It is striking that while Chaucer says that 'oon ensample' of these cases must suffice, he then—astonishingly—proceeds to give none. And how is it, if the 'elles' ('otherwise') of 2038 is intended to suggest that the two cases are distinct alternatives, that a single example must suffice for both? Arcite's fate is the only single instance I can think of whose fate exemplifies both alternatives, and so, in the absence of any other explanation, I would suggest that Chaucer intended Arcite, who is after all, Mars' knight, to serve as his 'ensample'.

The obvious inequity of the dénouement of the *Knight's Tale* throws into relief the flaw in Boethius' teachings on providence and justice. Death was deemed 'covenable' for Arcite according to the letter of Boethian law, while Palamon—almost ('migh') out of his mind with love-sickness but not actually 'guilty' of *mania*—was apparently let off on that technicality.

It may of course be objected that no ethos of justice whatever would have been adequate in dealing with the dilemma posed by the tale; that the situation of two young, 'trewe' knights in love with one and the same lady admits of no purely happy solution. Yet I believe that it was precisely this aspect of the plot which he found in Boccaccio's *Teseida* that interested—and in artistic terms delighted—Chaucer. The opening movement of the tale, with its account of how victory for the Athenian ruler necessarily entailed defeat and imprisonment for the Theban cousins, anticipates the tale's dénouement, in which it becomes clear that triumph for one of the young lovers entails tragedy for the other. In considering this aspect of the situation of Palamon and Arcite, the reader may perhaps be reminded of what Aquinas had to say by way of explanation and consolation when called upon to reconcile innocent suffering with 'the perfect goodness of God'—namely, that 'every evil in things of nature is included under the order of something good'; hence, for example, 'the killing of a sheep is the feeding of a wolf, and it follows that, since human acts are subject to divine providence, just as things in nature are, the evil which occurs in human acts must be contained under the order of some good.'[33] If, however, one finds it hard to respond to Arcite's death and Palamon's subsequent joy in quite such an equable fashion, one may be reminded instead of the case of 'Carneades' plank', so beloved of the sceptics. To the question of which of two drowning men deserves the single plank of wood, the answer must be 'both' and 'neither'. To the question of which of the two young lovers deserves Emelye, the answer

33 *Summa Contra Gentiles Book Three*: *Providence*, tr. Vernon J. Bourke (London, 1975), Chapter 140.

must be the same. In such a situation, the order of justice simply cannot hold, and I believe that if it is acknowledged to adumbrate a rejection of Boethius' *Consolation*, the *Knight's Tale* has enormous potential to be read sceptically. John Burrow has said that 'the voice of religious scepticism is never heard in the literature of the English Middle Ages.'[34] It may be true that it is never heard directly, but it seems to me that sceptical ideas come perilously close to articulation here in what is usually considered to be one of the most orthodox of *The Canterbury Tales*.

To conclude: that Chaucer has embedded a strictly Boethian reading of Arcite's death in the *Knight's Tale* at all is evidence that he did not wish to ignore entirely Boethius' teaching concerning apparently unjust suffering and the notion of how to reconcile it with the goodness of God; but that it is felt to be so at odds with a natural reading of the tale is, I would suggest, a measure of the extent to which he wished to dissociate himself from that teaching. And that the limitations—what may even be felt in the *Knight's Tale* as the absurdity—of Boethius' account of the operations of divine justice are not exposed more overtly or more ruthlessly bespeaks not only, I believe, characteristic Chaucerian subtlety, but also a natural reluctance on the part of the poet to reveal the shortcomings of a philosopher to whom he owed such a great debt. *Troilus and Criseyde* is evidence of the magnitude of that debt, but I believe the *Knight's Tale* marks Chaucer's final disengagement from the philosophy of the *Consolation*.

34 John A. Burrow, *Mediaeval Writers and their Work* (Oxford, 1982), p. 86.

Gentle Men, *Lufly* and *Loothly* Ladies, *Aghlich Maysters*

Characterization in *The Wife of Bath's Tale* and *Sir Gawain and the Green Knight*

CATHALIN BUHRMANN FOLKS

A study of character types in the Middle English romances reveals the importance of the type of the ideal knight, a role frequently taken by Gawain, who usually exemplifies a rather simple conception of perfection focused on a single virtue or a generalized idea of chivalry. But there is also considerable precedent, especially in the later romances, for the presentation of the hero as flawed in some significant way, either by sin, as is typical of the alliterative tradition, or by realistically humorous traits, more common in the tail-rhyme romances. The English tradition also gives us a variety of shape-shifting characters, most of whom are ambivalent in nature, who usually test the hero in a novel way and frequently reveal themselves to be the hero's allies rather than adversaries after the successful completion of the tests.[1]

Chaucer and the *Gawain*-poet, while drawing upon these types, seem to have seen beyond conventional characters of romance tradition to the broader possibilities those figures offer for exploring the maturation and development of their young heroes. While using the full range of features from the rather diverse traditions governing the ideal romance knight, the poets also endow their heroes with human failings. Gawain's flaw is relatively minor (though he takes it seriously), while that of the Wife of Bath's knight is far more extreme (so that he must learn to take it seriously). Furthermore, neither poet is content with a purely magical

1 By the English tradition I refer in particular to Breton lays such as *Sir Degaré*, *Sir Launfal*, *Sir Landevale*, and *Sir Orfeo*; to tail-rhyme romances such as *The Jeaste of Syr Gawayne*, *Sir Gawain and the Carl of Carlisle*, *The Turk and Gawain*, and *The Weddynge of Sir Gawen and Dame Ragnell*; to alliterative poems such as *The Awntyrs of Arthure at the Terne Wathelyn*, *Golagros and Gawane*, and the *Morte Arthure*; and to Gower's *Tale of Florent*, a close analogue to *The Wife of Bath's Tale*. See my unpublished doctoral dissertation, 'Chaucer's *Wife of Bath's Tale*, *Sir Gawain and the Green Knight*, and the English Romance Tradition' (Indiana University, 1989), pp. 27–47.

metamorphosis for his shape-shifter. Instead, both turn their versions of these characters to novel uses, especially in illuminating the inward character transformations of their heroes, drawing upon the expectations produced by the later variations on the basic romance types to create characters that are vivid, appealing, often comic, and full of natural vitality.

I

The English tradition offers ample precedent for the idea of a flawed hero, and thus for our two protagonists: Chaucer's bachelor and Sir Gawain. Gawain in the later English tail-rhyme romances was more likely to present a rather tarnished image, though usually accompanied by a humanizing dimension of comedy that had not been present in the more idealistic romances. In the alliterative tradition, Gawain is the best of Arthur's knights, the peacemaker, but still a much less complex character than his counterpart in *Gawain.* One significant similarity between Gawain and Chaucer's bachelor is that both authors draw upon the wide range of expectations, idealistic as well as satiric, available from the late romance tradition to create their unique versions of the romance hero, playing off romantic against antiromantic features, though in very different ways. Whereas the traditional characters were static, Chaucer's knight and Sir Gawain grow more mature through the tests that left the traditional hero relatively unchanged.

Chaucer has stripped his young bachelor of all the positive elements associated with the romance hero, even his name, which would, of course, have traditionally been Gawain. In addition to discouraging the audience from identifying the hero as Gawain, the knight's namelessness suits the Wife's exemplary purposes for her tale. What Chaucer creates is a scheming, opportunistic, but still appealing womanizer with all the worst features, as well as a touch of the charm, of the happy-go-lucky Gawain of the tail-rhyme romances. Only after this impudent young man matures by learning the true meaning of *gentilesse* from his loathly old bride does he behave with the courtesy and dignity expected of a true romance hero. *Gawain* presents the reverse pattern: the poem begins with the exemplary Gawain of epic and courtly romance, a hero whose virtue usually remains intact throughout the trials of his quest. After presenting his hero as an unrivalled paragon of chivalry, the poet surprises the expectations of his audience, no less than those of Gawain himself, by first hinting at the tarnished side of Gawain's traditional reputation, then allowing his hero an all-too-human lapse. Like Chaucer's knight, Gawain will mature, but the lesson is the more painful because it involves learning to accept, rather than overcome, his human weaknesses. As Laura Hibbard Loomis puts it, Gawain is saved 'from a schematic perfection', that of the typical romance hero who never disappoints his own or others' expectations in his quest.[2]

One can hardly discuss Chaucer's bachelor without first noting how many aspects of his character stem from the personal interests and motives of his immediate creator, the Wife of Bath. Her choice of a hero who embodies features of the wanton Gawain of the tail-rhyme tradition humorously reflects the Wife's rather capricious tastes, not only in men but also in literature. The exploits of such a hero may have filled many an hour of her numerous *visitaciouns* to public places of entertainment. Indeed, men and women of the Wife's solidly bourgeois status and upward social aspirations were likely to have formed an important part of the late fourteenth-century audience for popular romances in English, and may also help to account for the genre's acquisition of just those amusingly pragmatic traits that are found in the analogues to our stories.[3] Romances concerned with Gawain's sexual prowess (*Sir Gawain and the Carl of Carlisle*, *The Jeaste of Syr Gawavne*) and lays in which elven knights ravish helpless maidens (*Sir Degaré*) offer appropriate models for the Wife's fantasy hero. Furthermore, the 'bad' fairy knights were akin in temperament to the Wife's 'bad' fifth husband, who may have been the thinly-disguised hero of her tale. Again, an imperfect hero is essential to the Wife's overt thesis, as a deserving subject of feminine dominance. How awkward it would have been to demonstrate her argument with a model hero like Florent (in Gower's *Tale of Florent*), or with a courteous Gawain like the hero of the *Carl of Carlisle* or *Golagros and Gawane*. Instead, her purpose for the tale demands the worst attributes of the popular romance hero, the lechery and rudeness evident in the Gawain of late tail-rhyme romances like *The Turk and Gawain* or *The Jeaste of Syr Gawayne*. The hero's virtues must be allowed to surface only after he has diligently learned his lesson at the hands of his wise old wife.

The humour and naturalism of the details contributed by the Wife's perspective on her hero are an extension of the comic voice of her *Prologue*. She describes the knight with overtones of the same amused indulgence she had given her own husbands, a point-of-view producing a believable character prone to typically masculine evasions when he finds himself in one troublesome predicament after another:

2 '*Gawain and the Green Knight*', *Arthurian Literature in the Middle Ages: A Collaborative History*, ed. Roger Sherman Loomis (Oxford, 1959), pp. 528–40, at 537.

3 See Gisela Guddat-Figge, *Catalogue of Manuscripts Containing Middle English Romances* (Munich, 1976), pp. 47–8.

Wo was this knyght, and sorwefully he siketh;
But what! He may nat do al as hym liketh.
And at the laste he chees hym for to wende
And come agayn, right at the yeres ende,
With swich answere as God wolde hym purveye . . . (III.913–17)[4]

We may recall that in *Dame Ragnell* Arthur, not Gawain, behaved in this manner (165–309).[5] While other versions of the loathly lady tale direct most of their humour at the lady's ugliness and bad manners (*Ragnell* 231–52, 548–621; *Florent* 1672–1702, 1749–65[6]), Chaucer overturns the traditional roles, making his knight's evasions and rudeness the main source of satiric amusement:

This knyght answerde, 'Allas and weylawey!
I woot right wel that swich was my biheste.
For Goddes love, as chees a newe requeste!
Taak al my good and lat my body go.' (III.1058–61)

The adolescence of her hero allows the Wife to bring about this reversal in the direction of the tale, an achievement that would have been impossible with a more admirable hero. The humour and naturalism in the characterization of the knight also help to reinforce another feature of the Wife's thesis: her formula for a happy marriage may seem more applicable to experience if at least one of her characters (the man, of course) exhibits the kind of obstreperous behaviour which usually destroys marital bliss.

Superficially, the methods of characterization used by Chaucer for the knight seem close to those of the typical metrical romances (*Degaré* 57–65[7]; *Landevale* 35–42[8]) with their rather matter-of-fact manner of narrating events and describing characters.[9] This apparently bland style may be seen in the narration of the rape:

4 Line numbers in my text refer to *The Riverside Chaucer*, 3rd ed., ed. Larry D. Benson, Boston, Mass., 1987.

5 *Sources and Analogues of Chaucer's Canterbury Tales*, edd. W.F. Bryan and Germaine Dempster (New York, 1941, rpt. 1958), pp. 242–64, reprinted from Laura Summer's edition, *Smith College Studies in Modern Languages* 5 (1984), 4.

6 *Confessio Amantis* I. 1407–1861 (*The Complete Works of John* Gower, ed. G.C. Macaulay, 4 vols. (Oxford, 1899–1902), I.74–86).

7 *Middle English Metrical Romances*, edd. Walter Hoyt French and Charles Brockway Hale, 2 vols. (New York, 1930), I, 288–320.

8 Thomas Chestre, *Sir Launfal*, ed. A.J. Bliss (London and Edinburgh, 1960), pp. 105–28; references to both *Sir Landevale* and *Sir Launfal* are to this edition.

9 P.M. Kean comments upon Chaucer's use of narrative techniques typical of English romance: see C*haucer and the Making of English Poetry, 2 vols.* (London, 1972), II, 60–71.

And so bifel that this kyng Arthour
Hadde in his hous a lusty bacheler,
That on a day cam ridynge fro ryver,
And happed that, allone as he was born,
He saugh a mayde walkynge hym biforn,
Of which mayde anon, maugree hir heed,
By verray force, he rafte hire maydenhed . . . (III.882–8)

But the effect in *The Wife of Bath's Tale* is ironic rather than merely naïve, in the tale's lack of concern about the inconsistencies of the knight's behaviour with traditions of chivalry. This ironic perspective is conveyed in brief, but crucial, details of the bachelor's unchivalric deportment at appropriate points in the action of the tale:

'My love?' quod he, 'nay, my dampnacioun!
Allas, that any of my nacioun
Sholde evere so foule disparaged be! . . .
Thou art so loothly, and so oold also,
And therto comen of so lough a kynde,
That litel wonder is thogh I walwe and wynde.
So wolde God myn herte wolde breste!' (III.1067–9, 1100–3)

The knight's behaviour provides quite a contrast with Gawain's zealous response to Dame Ragnell, 'I shalle wed her and wed her agayn' (343). Chaucer's flourishes give life to a character who is never fully described nor permitted a lengthy speech, and whose active role is confined to the rape and the frantic quest for the answer to the queen's riddle. In place of the more active role taken by the heroes of the analogues (*Ragnell* 182–98, 342–89; *Florent* 1472–91, 1507–25) and typical of English romance in general, the bachelor must constantly submit himself to the mercy and authority of women. His behaviour comes more and more to resemble that of a helpless damsel, with sighs, pleas, and aimless wandering.[10] Obviously, the Wife of Bath has been careful in limiting her hero's potential for prowess. Yet, while he is less active than the knights of popular romance, his character proves to be far more dynamic.

The growth of the knight's character is an important corollary to the Wife's thesis concerning marriage. She must allow him to prove that he is capable of becoming a good husband out of a genuine change of heart toward his homely wife, and indeed toward women in general, if the idealistic conclusion of her romance is to attain any credibility. Critical opinion

10 See Marc Glasser, 'He Nedes Moste Hire Wedde: The Forced Marriage in the "Wife of Bath's Tale" and Its Middle English Analogues', *Neuphilologische Mitteilungen* 85 (1984), 239–41.

on the degree of development in the young knight's characterization is varied. For Kemp Malone, he is no more than the stock romance hero.[11] Francis G. Townsend, on the other hand, asserts that Chaucer went beyond convention to create a vivid and believable character.[12] P. Verdonk, in one of the most extensive commentaries on the knight, argues that Chaucer's method of characterization is static, that the final irony of the tale lies in the fact that the knight remains a calculating manipulator of women throughout, fooling all the women he encounters into giving him the upper hand.[13] While this view applies to the character of the bachelor in the portions of the tale preceding the lesson on *gentilesse*, one misses the point of the tale by interpreting the knight's acceptance of the still loathly hag as merely another of his manipulative devices. The distinction is crucial, because the tale's ultimate interpretation becomes bitterly anti-romantic under such a reading. There is the temptation, perhaps a result of modern sensibility, to give the most cynical emphasis to the ironic elements in Chaucer, a situation that is frequently paralleled in interpretations of the ending of *Gawain*. There one must also be careful not to overemphasize the rueful response of the hero in blaming women for his failure, a reaction that is valid for Gawain's state of mind at that moment, but which is certainly not the final word on the significance of his adventure. Instead, one must note that both romances hold these more satiric glimpses at their heroes' personalities in tension with more positive perspectives. As we have seen, a conflict between the satirical and idealistic characterization of Gawain and other heroes is inherent in the English romance tradition.

In *The Wife of Bath's Tale* the question of whether the narrator controls her hero or is outwitted by his masculine chicanery has far-reaching implications for the meaning of the tale, our assessment of the Wife, and, ultimately, our view of where Chaucer stands in relation to medieval anti-feminism. However, I do not believe that the precarious ideal of mutuality finally achieved by the knight and his bride has been undermined by cynicism on the knight's part. While an ironic view of his character is applicable to most of the tale and typical of the satiric treatment of heroes in many English romances (cf. Arthur in *Ragnell* or Gawain in the *Turk*), the knight's conversion is genuine and helps to restore to the genre an idealism more like that of the earlier English Breton lays (*Sir Orfeo*, *Sir Landevale*). We may question the Wife's appraisal of the felicity of her fifth marriage after Jankyn's 'conversion', which seems more like his defeat, but in the tale Chaucer is not trying to present bitter reality, but the Wife's dream: Take the most impertinent and manipulative of men

11 *Chapters on Chaucer* (Baltimore, 1951), p. 216.

12 'Chaucer's Nameless Knight', *Modern Language Review* 49 (1954), 1–4.

13 '"Sire knyght, heer forth ne lith no wey": A Reading of Chaucer's *The Wife of Bath's Tale*', *Neuphilologische Mitteilungen* 60 (1976), 306–7.

and marry him to the most unpromising hag of a wife. Even this most inauspicious of marriages can be transformed, along with its partners, by the true *gentilesse* that comes from an unselfish concern for the feelings of others. Only if he adopts this change in attitude with heart-felt sincerity can the bachelor become a truly gentle knight.[14] The moment of harmony is short-lived, being broken by the abrupt intrusion of the Wife herself, yet her tale and the role of its hero make little sense if we fail to acknowledge the earnestness of his statement, made only after heavy deliberation:

> 'My lady and my love, and wyf so deere,
> I put me in youre wise governance;
> Cheseth youreself which may be moost plesance
> And moost honour to yow and me also.
> I do no fors the wheither of the two,
> For as yow liketh, it suffiseth me.' (III.1230–5)

Although the tone of the knight's answer may be somewhat lacking in enthusiasm, there is no suggestion of the sarcasm that marked his previous responses to his loathly bride. The situation is clearly different from that of the other versions, in which the husbands give up making the decision entirely out of frustration at their own inability to choose, rather than out of respect for their wives' wishes (*Ragnell* 667–84; *Florent* 1814–31). Of course, the Wife's thesis demands that her knight's conversion be sincere.

Another point at which critical opinion of the knight's behaviour has gone seriously astray involves the interpretation of the lady's reward to the knight for his reformation. Robert P. Miller has asserted that having his natural inclination for an attractive young bride fulfilled plunges the knight into sinful concupiscence, a deadly 'bath of bliss'.[15] If anything, this particular bath ought to be viewed as a baptism into a new, more virtuous existence, based on the unselfish behaviour of *gentilesse* handed down from Christ himself, rather than as immersion in sin. For the first time, we see this young knight behaving in a manner appropriate to a chivalric hero. Rather than plunging him into sin, the change has helped to release him from his former sinful ways, an act of purification. He has become more like the true romance knight, redeemed from the unsavoury and ludicrous associations that the hero of several of the later English romances (*Launfal*, *Ragnell*, *Carl*, *Turk*, *Jeaste*) had acquired. The happy ending of *The Wife of Bath's Tale* precludes any further discussion of the

14 See Joseph F. Ropollo, 'The Converted Knight in Chaucer's *Wife of Bath's Tale*', *College English* 12 (1951), 263–9.

15 '*The Wife of Bath's Tale* and Mediaeval Exempla', *English Literary History* 32 (1965), 454–6, at see also Bernard S. Levy, 'The Wife of Bath's *Queynte Fantasye*', *Chaucer Review* 4 (1969–70), 106–22, at 121–2.

logical consistency of the accommodation the couple has reached, an outcome wholly in the spirit of the early Breton lays (*Orfeo*, *Landevale*). Chaucer echoes traditions of flawed knighthood from the late English tail-rhyme romances in his portrait of this knight, but incorporates characteristics of the hero from more idealistic romances as well.

II

Whereas Chaucer's bachelor finally emerges from his churlishness into *gentilesse*, in *Gawain* the hero begins his adventure already 'voyded of vche vylany', so that he resembles refined gold. Although the earlier English romances might require only that such a hero prove his prowess in one or more trials, usually involving combat (*Degaré*) or sexual temptation (*Landevale*), from which he would reappear even more perfect than he began, the tail-rhyme romances (*Launfal*, *Ragnell*, *Carl*, *Turk*, *Jeaste*) provide examples of heroes flawed by realistic or humorous foibles.[16] Still, one might wonder how Gawain could, before his quest is ended, come to resemble Chaucer's knight in any significant way, since the idealistic hero seems so remote from the comic and sexual connotations of his namesake in the tail-rhyme tradition. Yet Gawain does change in significant ways as a result of his quest, just as we have seen Chaucer's knight undergo a metamorphosis of character that is as striking as the physical metamorphosis of his bride. The transformation in character for Gawain is in the opposite direction from the bachelor's, for his quest and the testing he experiences at Bertilak's castle lead him inevitably into the unfamiliar territory of human imperfection. Through fear of the Green Knight's blow, Gawain learns a dishonourable mode of behaviour that tarnishes, if only so slightly, the purity of his image. His opportunistic action in accepting the lace places him in one respect at least in the same category as Chaucer's bachelor, the category of ordinary human beings who resort to practical, if not entirely honourable, means of dealing with the overwhelming threat of death. There is, of course, a vast difference in degree of participation in this opportunism, for Gawain is still a 'perle' and Chaucer's knight must surely fall into the category of the 'þe quite pese'. Gawain's painful alteration is, like the bachelor's, a process of spiritual growth that all imperfect human beings must undergo to become truly mature.

Gawain's entrance in the opening scene of the poem is marked by his superlative show of noble manners, the polar opposite of the opening-scene behaviour of Chaucer's knight. The young courtier is so deferential

16 See John Finlayson, 'The Expectations of Romance in *Sir Gawain and the Green Knight*', *Genre* 12 (1979), 1–24, at 7, 9–11, 15–17, 21.

to his lord and lady that he will not even rise from his seat beside the queen to take up the Green Knight's challenge without first politely asking permission. In traditional romance, Gawain nearly always makes his initial appearance in a way designed to illustrate his matchless courtesy, usually in contrast with Kay's rudeness:

> Than spak schir Gawane the gay, gratious and gude:
> "Schir, ye knaw that schir Kay is crabbit of kynde;
> I rede ye mak furth ane man, mekar of mude,
> That will with fairnes fraist frendschip to fynd."
> (*Golagros*[17] 118–21)

The *Gawain*-poet gives a polished version of this typical scene, in which the natural insolence of Kay is replaced by the calculated rudeness of the Green Knight. After lavishing almost extravagant praise on the noble company of Camelot, the poet must take additional care to find a means of differentiating his hero's unique excellence; this is done by understating, rather than heightening, Gawain's response to the Green Knight's threat to Arthur.[18] Gawain responds to the crisis with modest circumlocution and adroit humility, qualities which extend the sophistication of his manners beyond the plainer versions of courtesy of the other English Gawains (cf. *The Awntyrs off Arthure at the Terne Wathelyn*[19] 464–8; the Alliterative *Morte Arthure*[20] 2638–45). The contrast between Arthur's angry and direct acceptance of the challenge—'Haþel, by heuen, þyn askyng is nys' (323)[21]—and Gawain's polished and apologetic tone accentuates the hero's most famous attribute in an original way:

> 'Wolde ȝe, worþilych lorde,' quoþ Wawan to þe kyng,
> 'Bid me boȝe fro þis benche, and stonde by yow þere,
> Þat I wythoute vylanye myȝt voyde þis table,
> And þat my legge lady lyked not ille,
> I wolde com to your counseyl bifore your cort ryche.' (343–7)

While Gawain's character will later be defined in terms of the complex perfection of the pentangle, the first view of the hero highlights his almost excessive modesty and politeness.

17 *Scottish Alliterative Poems*, ed. F.J. Amours (Edinburgh, 1897), pp. 1–46.
18 On the use of romance methods of characterization in Gawain's speech, see John Stevens, *Medieval Romance: Themes and Approaches* (London, 1973), p. 174.
19 Ed. Ralph Hanna III, Manchester, 1974.
20 Ed. Valerie Krishna, New York, 1976.
21 Line numbers in my text refer to *Sir Gawain and the Green Knight*, edd. J.R.R. Tolkien and E.V. Gordon, 2nd ed. rev. Norman Davis, Oxford, 1967.

After emphasizing Gawain's courtesy as well as his courage in his acceptance of the challenge, the poet reserves a more complete description of his hero for the scene of arming for his 'anious vyage'. At that point, the knight's inner *þewez* find elaboration, when the worldly splendour of his arms is superceded by the pentangle and its symbolism (619–65). The completion of Gawain's qualities as a chivalric hero through the addition of this new device leads, as has frequently been pointed out, to a much more idealistic and specifically Christian interpretation of his character than is true of any of the other incarnations of Gawain (cf. *Morte*, *Awntyrs*, *Golagros*).[22] Spiritual considerations are also emphasized more than traditional quest motifs in Gawain's winter journey. While the marvelously detailed descriptions of the winter landscape and his physical hardships are typical of alliterative poems as far back as *Beowulf*, the poet's abstention from narrating the typical fights with giants and dragons runs directly counter to alliterative convention, where such material was usually over- rather than under-developed, as in the giant-killing episode of the *Morte* (840–1197). Thus, one catches only a glimpse of Gawain the perfect warrior, but the poet demonstrates instead the worthlessness of his hero's armour against the cold. The spiritual expectations of the pentangle are, on the other hand, more fully realized, for the narrator concludes: 'Nade he ben duȝty and dryȝe, and Dryȝtyn had serued, | Douteles he hade ben ded and dreped ful ofte' (724–5).

As with Chaucer's knight, whose quest consists of the humdrum business of having to interview women of all classes and ages, this poem's account of Gawain's journey disappoints romance expectations by being largely concerned with mundane matters of personal discomfort, the more dramatic events—battles with *wormez*, *wodwos*, and *etaynez*—being mentioned only incidentally (720–3). The experiences which get the most attention are no more noble than the hardships suffered by the poorest of peasants every winter—endurance of the elemental forces of nature, which have begun their assault on the hero: 'For werre wrathed hym not so much þat wynter nas wors' (726). But, although Gawain is steadfast against these obvious manifestations of experience, even the virtues represented by the pentangle will eventually prove inadequate against the assault awaiting him at the castle.

The introduction of decidedly non-heroic issues into the characterization of Gawain tests the hero in ways closer to the tests in *The Wife of*

22 See Larry D. Benson, *Art and Tradition in Sir Gawain and the Green Knight* (New Brunswick, N. J., 1965), pp. 95–6, 101–4; J.A. Burrow, *A Reading of Sir Gawain and the Green Knight* (London, 1966), p. 50; Ann Derrickson, 'The Pentangle: Guiding Star for the *Gawain*-Poet', *Comitatus* 11 (1980), 10–19; Stephanie J. Hollis, 'The Pentangle Knight: *Sir Gawain and the Green Knight*', *Chaucer Review* 15 (1980–1), 273–9.

Bath's Tale, where the knight was faced for the first time with obstacles to his brash self-confidence, initially by the riddle and then by the forced marriage to the hag. Like Chaucer's bachelor, who tried to evade his problems by improvising his usual manipulative techniques against women, Gawain will, upon his arrival at Bertilak's castle, be thrust into a situation in which he must try to outmanoeuvre a clever lady in a battle of wits that is far removed from his own heroic expectations for the quest. He is deceived by the cheerfulness of Hautdesert into believing he is once again in a milieu perfectly suited to the exercise of his more courtly virtues. Even when he becomes aware of danger amid the festive life of the castle, his understanding of the situation is too muddled for him to see how thoroughly his chivalry is being assailed (1476–1557). The poem's audience is more clear-sighted, both as a result of hints about the nature of the attempted seduction (1281, 1549–50, 1733–41, 1767–72) and through knowledge of traditions associating Gawain with the arts of the bedroom (*Carl*[23] 406–14, 462–95; *Ragnell* 638–9, 706–36, 805–10; *Jeaste*[24] 1–10, 124–30). By repeatedly asking the hero if he is really Gawain and thus slyly referring to the reputation that is so apparent in the tail-thyme tradition, the lady manages at the same time to disarm her opponent and dramatically reveal his human and comic side (1226, 1248–55, 1291–3, 1481–6). In response to her ever-changing barrage of tactics, Gawain's behaviour comes more and more to resemble the tribulations of Chaucer's bachelor trying to escape his female tormentors: 'And as ho stod, ho stonyed hym wyth ful stor wordez' (1291). To give Gawain his due, he is more successful than Chaucer's knight in avoiding both discourtesy toward womankind and the lady's sexual advances. However, he still manages to look rather foolish in the process of evading the lady's advances, as her *bourdez* suggest: 'Now ar ȝe tan as-tyt! Bot true vus may schape, | I schal bynde yow in your bedde, þat be ȝe trayst' (1210–11). The humour of his all-too-human predicament is underlined by the implied comparisons with his host's prey: timid deer, resolute boar, and cunning fox,[25] heightened by the fact that Gawain hides under the bedcovers rather than in the woods:

23 Sir Gawain and the Carl of Carlisle *in Two Versions*, ed. Auvo Kurvinen, Helsinki, 1951 (Annales Academiae Scientiarum Fennicae); line numbers refer to the A version, MS. Porkington 10.

24 *Syr Gawayne*, ed. Frederic Madden (London, 1839, rpt. New York, 1971), pp. 207–23.

25 See H. L. Savage, 'The Significance of the Hunting Scenes in *Sir Gawain and the Green Knight*', *Journal of English and Germanic Philology* 27 (1928), 1–15, and *The* Gawain-*Poet: Studies in His Personality and Background* (Chapel Hill, 1956), pp. 31–48.

And he heuez vp his hed out of þe cloþes,
A corner of þe cortyn he caȝt vp a lyttel,
And waytez warly þiderwarde quat hit be myȝt. (1184–6)

Gawain's circumstances force him to react in a self-protective and impulsive manner that will eventually lead to his acceptance of the lace as a charm to save him from the Green Knight's axe:

Þen kest þe knyȝt, and hit come to his hert
Hit were a juel for þe joparde þat hym iugged were:
When he acheued to þe chapel his chek for to fech,
Myȝt he haf slypped to be vnslayn, þe sleȝt were noble. (1855–8)

Pursued and dominated by Bertilak's wife, Gawain fails to realize how much his actions at this critical juncture will affect the outcome of his quest, nor does he see that behind the seeming sincerity of a young wife's desire lies the malicious cunning of an older, more sinister woman, the traditionally evil Morgan. The allusions of Bertilak's wife to Gawain's reputation as a womanizer (1226, 1248–55, 1291–3, 1481–6) ensure that the more effort he throws into the preservation of his chastity, the more comic he will appear, especially in the contrast with his amorous behaviour in romances like the *Carl*, *Ragnell*, and the *Jeaste*. The fact that his courtesy precludes a hasty retreat leaves him in the dangerous predicament of having to go along with even the lady's more treacherous courtly-sexual games (1757–65). However, no matter what delusions Gawain may have about the lady's feelings for him, he is still only acting out a comic travesty of the classic games of *fin amour*. For this reason, his great exertion to maintain courtesy is almost as amusing as the effort of Chaucer's bachelor to avoid it:

For þat prynces of pris depresed hym so þikke,
Nurned hym so neȝe þe þred, bat nede hym bihoued
Oþer lach þer hir luf, oþer lodly refuse. (1770–2)

As was the case with Chaucer's hero and, to a lesser extent, Florent, Gawain's undoing results from a rash promise made with no thought for the consequences, because the promiser's attention is riveted on the more pressing matter of saving his own life.[26] In addition, Gawain's relief at having finally ended his hostess's attempts at seduction produces the same effect that the comfort of a correct answer to his question did on

26 J. F. Kiteley sees this feature as traditional for Gawain ('The Knight Who Cared for His Life', *Anglia*, 79 (1962), 131–7).

Chaucer's knight, causing him to relax his guard and respond without due consideration of the consequences. Perhaps Gawain is just as unconscious of the difficulty caused by his promise to conceal the lace, at least at the moment he makes it, if not also when he actually refrains from giving it to his host. The narrator's unwillingness to mention any outward manifestation of guilt and the hero's absolute astonishment when he learns the truth seem to imply that Gawain manages to keep the significance of his retention of the lace as well hidden from his own consciousness as he keeps the object itself hidden from his host's sight.

As Gawain arms to meet the Green Knight, his careful donning of the lace (2030–5) accentuates the change that has taken place in his character since the previous arming.[27] That earlier stage of Gawain's journey seems to be echoed as he stoically faces the terror of his rendezvous with the Green Knight against the background of another bleak winter landscape, except that this time the encounter with the adversary has been brought centre-stage. The guide's cowardly warning, the sinister appearance of the Green Chapel, and the blood-curdling whirr of blade against grindstone put Gawain back into the context of an alliterative hero like Arthur at Mont-Saint-Michel, whose guide had also warned him against going any farther (*Morte* 955–73). But, once again, this time much more emphatically, Gawain is undermined at the very moment of rejoicing at the opportunity for heroic action. The sight of his amused opponent leaning against the axe, coupled with the humiliating news that his foe knows all about the lady's love-lace, deflates Gawain's only show of bravado in an instant. The stalwart military hero is suddenly overwhelmed with confusion: 'Alle þe blode of his brest blende in his face, | Þat al he schrank for schome þat þe schalk talked' (2371–2). Once again, moments of humiliation for Chaucer's knight (III.1046–72) and for such romance heroes as Launfal (211–16) and Gawain in the *Carl* (403–17) and in the *Turk*[28] (86–8) come to mind.

Only during this most vulnerably human of moments does Gawain lapse from his identity as the most courteous of Arthur's knights, as he delivers his anti-feminist apology to Sir Bertilak (2411–28).[29] This passage demonstrates how profoundly the hero's identity has been shaken by the recognition of his error. Although he has just confessed his fault to the Green Knight and been thoroughly forgiven, the pain evident as Gawain

27 Hollis, 'Pentangle Knight', p. 275; see also Stoddard Malarkey and J. Barre Toelken, 'Gawain and the Green Girdle', *Journal of English and Germanic Philology* 63 (1964), 14–20.

28 *Bishop Percy's Folio Manuscript*, edd. J.W. Hales and Frederick J. Furnivall (London, 1867), pp. 90–102.

29 On Gawain's anti-feminism, see Mary Dove, 'Gawain and the Blasme des Femmes Tradition', *Medium Ævum* 41 (1972), 20–6; John Eadie, 'Sir Gawain and the Ladies of Ill-Repute', *Annuale Mediaeviale* 20 (1981), 52–66.

attempts to exonerate himself, through references to Solomon and other Old-Testament heroes led astray by women, suggests that the hero's struggle to come to terms with his imperfection has just begun. Only the long penitential journey back to Camelot and the healing of his wound will bring Gawain closer to a reluctant acceptance of his new identity. The bend sinister of the lace completes the redefinition of Gawain's identity, symbolizing the flawed nature now recognized by the hero. The poet has completed his humanization of Gawain by showing us a hero who is not only capable of failure, but behaves in a predictably human fashion by trying to excuse himself, though in doing so he places himself in the best of company. But the final picture that emerges of Gawain is comic only in the sense that the hero completes the circular route of his journey, to be given the traditional festive welcome at Camelot. For Gawain, the journey has another meaning: it is the pilgrimage of a penitent wearing his badge of shame, and the reunion is a public confession of his guilt.[30] Arthur and his *meny* try gallantly, if somewhat obtusely, to bring Gawain back into the companionship of the Round Table, a tradition for a knight who had successfully completed a quest or other triumph, as had been the case for Gawain at the end of *Golagros*, the *Awntyrs*, the *Carl*, or *Ragnell*. But the hero remains in the isolation of his discomfort, unable to forgive himself as cheerfully as do the other knights. The uneasy tension of our final glimpse of the hero's distress with the honour accorded him by his companions jars against romance expectations for the triumph and reconciliation that usually conclude the knight's quest.[31]

Starting from opposite points on a continuum of Gawain's attributes in the English romances, Chaucer and the *Gawain*-poet avail themselves of many of the same possibilities in terms of expectations concerning their heroes' heterogeneous background. In the process, both have created subtle and complex ironies, setting off features of the 'good Gawain' tradition against Gawain's humorous, often licentious conduct in the tail-rhyme romances. Before he learns *gentilesse* from a most unlikely old hag, the Wife of Bath's lusty and churlish young protagonist may have reminded Chaucer's audience of all the worst peccadillos of the tail-rhyme knights. Indeed, the bachelor's lechery and rudeness surpass Gawain's antics in *Ragnell* and the *Carl*, and approach his ill-breeding in the *Jeaste*, where he is at his most boorish in the English romances. *Gawain* begins on the reverse side of the coin, with a version of the hero who has been refined of all impurities, resembling the noble Gawain of other alliterative

30 Robert L. Kindrick sees in Gawain's guilt the conflict between romance values and Christian chivalry ('Gawain's Ethics: Shame and Guilt in Sir Gawain and the Green Knight', *Annuale Mediaeviale* 20 (1981), 5–32).

31 See Edmund Wilson, *The* Gawain-*Poet* (Leiden, 1976), pp. 129–30.

poems, only more perfect. Yet, as both heroes travel, in opposite directions, the circular route from Camelot to the wilderness and back, each exhibits traits ranging widely within the conflicting expectations raised by traditional portrayals of Gawain, from the most ideal to the most ironically realistic. Chaucer's knight finally acquires the courtesy and willingness to defer to the needs of others that romance audiences would expect from a hero. Gawain, through fear of the Green Knight's blow, learns some of the compromises characteristic of Chaucer's knight, as well as of the more satiric versions of his namesake in the late tail-rhyme romances, who exhibit unrestrained lust (*Carl*, 406–14), frequently accompanied by bad manners (*Jeaste, passim*). Although a reversal takes place in each character, both also seem to have grown into a more mature, human wisdom born of their willingness to accept life's great compromises in order to exist in harmony among the society of their fallible companions.

III

In the *Wife of Bath's Tale* and *Gawain*, courtesy and a forgiving attitude are also evident in the characters derived from types normally antagonistic to gentle society: the loathly ladies, churlish knights and evil temptresses of romance tradition. Chaucer's hag and the host and hostess of Hautdesert exceed the traditional expectations for their roles as the adversaries of the hero, taking on more affable traits, though there are some precedents for this development in the English tradition, for example, the agreeable Carl of Carlisle and the ugly, but good-natured Dame Ragnell. The effect is to bring the polarities of good and evil closer together. Only one character in the two poems remains thoroughly within the tradition of the evil type: Morgan le Fay, the *dea ex machina* who serves as a convenient scapegoat for the treachery at Hautdesert, allowing the poet to exonerate the good-natured host and his lovely wife.[32] Like the heroes of the two poems, the feminine characters share a number of similarities which are most striking within the frame of reference of their predecessors in romance. The identity of the types drawn upon in both works is brought home by W. A. Davenport in his discussion of the passage in which Gawain first sees the hostess and Morgan; Davenport contends that the paired descriptions may have suggested to an audience familiar with the loathly-lady tale 'that the two women are really one, present both in her young and old guises'.[33]

32 Whether this explanation is convincing is another matter; Albert B. Friedman refers to Morgan as a *deus ex machina* in 'Morgan le Fay in *Sir Gawain and the Green Knight*', *Speculum* 35 (1960), 260–74.

33 *The Art of the* Gawain-*Poet* (London, 1978), p.160.

The English romances tended to polarize expectations for female types into utterly evil villainesses (Guinevere in *Landevale*) and blandly virtuous heroines (Degaré's *leman*), with the exception of the more lively characterization of the fairy mistress (as in *Landevale*). The tail-rhyme romances, on the other hand, present vulgarly comic, but not particularly flattering, versions of the loathly-lady type (Dame Ragnell). However, the alliterative tradition tends either to ignore (most of *Morte* and all of *Golagros*) or vilify (ending of *Morte*, the ghost in *Awntyrs*) feminine characters, that is, ignore most virtuous women and provide anti-feminist portraits of the wicked ones, though, in all fairness, one alliterative romance provides a clear picture of a traditional temptress trying to behave virtuously (Guinevere in the *Awntyrs*). But, for the most part, only a few examples among the many feminine types of the English tradition emerge as both positive and well-developed characters.

As might be expected, the Wife of Bath reverses the traditional roles of Gawain and his loathly bride: Gawain's shape-shifting adversary becomes the embodiment of true *gentilesse*, while his stand-in, the young knight, must outgrow a churlishness unbecoming to his noble ancestry. The Wife's feminist interests are evident in the elevation of her loathly lady to a status far above that of her English sisters, one which restores to her some of the dignity of her venerable ancestor in an earlier analogue of the tale, the Sovereignty of Ireland.[34] As one would expect, the Wife presents her feminine representative in the best possible light, tactfully omitting the physically repugnant details given in the other versions (*Ragnell* and *Florent*) and enhancing her heroine's qualities of wisdom and inner worth to match the principle of *gentilesse* expounded in the pillow lesson. The reasons for these changes should, of course, be obvious. The Wife of Bath could hardly have been expected to dwell upon her alter ego's horrendous deformities, a frightening prospect indeed for a middle-aged woman planning to sell her bran to the last mote. As a consolation for the inevitability of her own aging, the Wife offers a heroine who, despite her age and lack of physical endowments, possesses the charm and wit to win over a most recalcitrant husband. Furthermore, the Wife's sagacious old lady refutes the evidence of anti-feminism by being a model of wisdom, reason, and courtesy, while her husband is emotional, impulsive, and headstrong until converted by her teaching.

34 Ériu, the Sovereignty of Ireland, was a loathly lady of Irish historical legend. Potential kings faced the test of accepting marriage or love with the lady in her hideous form to determine their fitness for the difficult task of ruling Ireland, with her beauty as the reward for their courage in accepting her. See G. H. Maynadier, *The Wife of Bath's Tale: Its Sources and Analogues* (London, 1901; rpt. New York, 1972), pp. 25–42; Sigmund Eisner, *A Tale of Wonder: A Source Study of The Wife of Bath's Tale* (Wexford, 1957; rpt. New York, 1969), pp. 31–44; Meredith Cary, 'Sovereignty and Old Wife', *Papers in Language and Literature* 5 (1969), 375–88.

The first glimpse of Chaucer's heroine suggests, at least to someone more astute than the young bachelor, the loathly lady's shape-shifting ability and links her with the fairy mistress of the Breton lays. The fairy dance of four and twenty ladies, of which she, presumably, is one, is an addition to the tale that shows her in a much more favourable light than her counterparts in *Ragnell* and *Florent*, who dwell alone and are intimidating, rather than attractive, to passers-by. The lady's sudden appearance is an indication of her control over the situation, suggesting that she herself has chosen her hideous phase as the appropriate antidote to the hero's infamous eagerness for encounters with attractive young damsels alone in the forest. By implying the voluntary nature of the hag's later metamorphosis, this scene also helps to remove doubt about the validity of the hero's conversion. Rather than being tricked by her husband into the final bargain, this wise old wife has the power to discern the knight's fitness for the reward. The suggestion that the lady is in control is reinforced by the appearance of dignity she emanates, in strong contrast with the foolish antics of her immediate literary kin, Ragnell and Florent's hag. She assumes a grandmotherly tone, a blend of gentle chiding and helpfulness, made-to-order for the hero's immaturity and his predicament as he seeks the answer to the queen's question, for he is obviously lost in the woods and in need of a mature guide:

> Agayn the knyght this olde wyf gan ryse,
> And seyde, 'Sire knyght, heer forth ne lith no wey.
> Tel me what that ye seken, by youre fey!
> Paraventure it may the bettre be;
> Thise olde folk kan muchel thyng,' quod she. (III.1000–4)

By portraying her heroine as a wise guide for the young knight, the Wife of Bath has set the stage for our acceptance of her role as his instructor in the bedroom scene. The lady immediately lets the bachelor know that she wants him to reform his ways and show her some respect when she insists he plight his *trouthe* to do what she requires (1000–12). She is, furthermore, a good deal shrewder than the other loathly ladies, who state the price of their answers directly (*Ragnell* 253–90; *Florent* 1551–60). Her strategy is perfectly suited to the bachelor, a real opportunist who might have evaded the marriage if he had known about it in advance. She keeps the secret of her price for the answer to herself, lulling the knight into thinking he has once again used his charm to get what he wants from a woman. She is determined to let him learn his lesson in a way he won't easily forget, so she waits until the dramatic moment when he thinks he is in the clear to reveal her demand. Then, as soon as the knight has delivered the correct answer to the queen and court of ladies, the hag shocks him with her claim, demanding not only marriage, but love:

'For thogh that I be foul, and oold, and poore
I nolde for al the metal, ne for oore
That under erthe is grave or lith above,
But if thy wyf I were, and eek thy love.' (III.1063–6)

In her *Prologue* the Wife of Bath had demonstrated a saving ability to laugh, without bitterness, at her own misfortunes, a quality which makes one forgive her equal predilection for laughing at her husbands' miseries. The same generous sense of humour saves her heroine from the appalling fate suffered by the hags in *Ragnell* and *Florent*. The Wife sympathetically deflects the misogynistic and obscene ridicule traditionally accorded the hags, allowing her audience to laugh with, but not at her heroine, whose knowing smile replaces the leering countenances of her English sisters. While the hags and churls of the English tradition voiced a rather incoherent protest against the lack of *gentilesse* with which they were treated by some of the Round Table knights, Chaucer increases the audience's sympathy with his loathly lady by carefully avoiding all mention of unflattering details of her appearance and behaviour. For instance, Chaucer tactfully leaves out all the traditional jollity over the hag's appearance and manners at the wedding feast, leaving only this dignified summary of the event: 'I seye ther nas no joye ne feeste at al; | Ther nas but hevynesse and muche sorwe' (III.1078–9). In place of the outrageous sexual aggressiveness of the other loathly ladies, Chaucer's hag displays a demure and subtle wit, as she wryly parodies the conventions of *fin amour* in attempting to woo her reluctant mate:

'O deere housbonde, benedicitee!
Fareth every knyght thus with his wyf as ye?
Is this the lawe of kyng Arthures hous?
Is every knyght of his so dangerous?' (III.1087–90)

Her appeal to her husband's reputation as one of Arthur's knights should bring to mind the tactics of another lady in a similar situation, namely, the hostess as she tries to tempt Gawain.

While humour dominates the loathly lady's response to her husband's *danger* in bed, there is also an underlying earnestness, most evident as her query over her husband's rejection takes up the subject of her own inner worth:

I am your owene love and youre wyf;
I am she which that saved hath your lyf,
And, certes, yet ne dide I yow nevere unright;
Why fare ye thus with me this firste nyght? (III.1091–4)

At this point the lady makes a delicate transition from humorous parody of *fin amour* (1089–90) into a serious exploration of the nature of truly *gentil* behaviour (1109–1216). This careful transition and the coherence and authority of her lesson ensure the credibility of the loathly lady.[35] Her high purpose is also reflected in the more challenging dilemma she offers her spouse (1219–27), in replacing the easy fairy-tale riddle of the other romances, fair by night or day (*Ragnell* 656–66; *Florent* 1810–13), with a choice between inner and outer beauty in order to test the bachelor's understanding of her lesson.[36] As in her previous tactics, she remains severe with her recalcitrant young husband (1104) until he finally takes her teaching to heart (1228–35). Nor does she want simple submission from her knight. Her standards are much higher. He must convince her that he has truly begun to consider the feelings of another person—a woman, in particular—as more important than his own immediate desires (1236–8). By making her fairer self slightly more *dangerous* than did the other loathly ladies (1106–8) and by being firmly in control of the circumstances surrounding her transformation (1239–49), the Wife of Bath's *alter ego* manages to fulfil her husband's desires without cheating the Wife of her central thesis of feminine sovereignty (1235–6). In the end, this wise heroine succeeds in bringing the knight up to her level without stooping to conquer, a feat which, more than the simple fact of dominance, is the inner wish of the tale's narrator.

IV

Chaucer elevates his heroine far above her counterparts in the English tradition in order to satisfy the feminine interests of the tale's narrator, but the motives behind the *Gawain*-poet's attractive portrait of the lady of Hautdesert remain somewhat more obscure. Whatever the reasons, the hostess is largely free of the taint attaching to the type of the evil temptress (cf. Guinevere in *Launfal* and the *Morte*). In place of the inner-outer duality typical of that character type, the poet gives his seductress a perfect scapegoat, Morgan le Fay, allowing the ancient miscreant to embody all the unattractive features normally associated with the unmasked temptress, including guilt for the temptation itself, since the lady is only carrying out Morgan's orders, as communicated to her by

35 The loathly lady's argumentative method is in this respect antithetical to the argumentative methods of the Wife of Bath herself, as seen in her *Prologue* and acknowledged in the Pardoner's comment that she is a 'noble prechour in this cas' (WBPro III.165).

36 See Alfred David, *The Strumpet Muse: Art and Morals in Chaucer's Poetry* (Bloomington, 1976), pp. 155–6.

Bertilak. This unusual approach leaves the lady in a curiously ambivalent situation. In all fairness, she should be held no more to blame than her husband, against whom Gawain holds no grudge, yet one cannot help but share a little of the hero's chagrin over the shock of her duplicity.

The paired and contrasted descriptions of Morgan and the lady make the dualism of their roles apparent from the start:

> Bot vnlyke on to loke þo ladyes were,
> For if þe ȝonge watz ȝep, ȝolȝe watz þat oþer;
> Riche red on þat on rayled ayquere,
> Rugh ronkled chekez þat oþer on rolled . . . (950–3)

The older woman's features, 'naked lyppez . . . soure to se and sellyly blered' (962–3), might have been taken from a description of Dame Ragnell, 'Her lyppes laye lumpred on her chyn; | Nek forsothe on her was none i-seen' (554–5), or Gower's hag, whose cheeks are 'rivelen as an emty skyn | Hangende doun unto the chin' (1681–2). By contrast, her companion resembles an idealized romance heroine, evoking the beguiling charm of the traditional fairy mistress of *Launfal* (286–360) or *Thomas of Erceldoune*[37] (30–130). The narrator does not hesitate in expressing his revulsion toward the older woman and enthusiasm for the younger.

Because the names of the residents of Hautdesert are a part of Bertilak's secret, one little suspects the identity of the *mensk* old woman, although she clearly wields a good deal of power, particularly over her younger companion (946–9).[38] Like the non-Chaucerian loathly ladies, Morgan attempts rather unsuccessfully to cover her foulness, but her *gorger* and veils only give her a peculiar appearance:

> Ðat oþer wyth a gorger watz gered ouer þe swyre,
> Chymbled ouer hir blake chyn with chalkquyte vayles,
> Hir frount folden in sylk, enfoubled ayquere,
> Toreted and treleted with tryflez aboute . . . (957–60)

In fact, Morgan has been described with language oddly similar to that describing Bertilak's castle: 'Towres telded bytwene, trochet ful þik' (795); 'Chalkwhyt chymnees' (798); 'So mony pynakle payntet watz poudred ayquere' (800). The narrator's distaste for her becomes more apparent at the conclusion of her description, where any attempt to be tactful is abandoned with the blunt list of defects in the wheel:

37 Ed. Ingeborg Nixon, 2 vols., Copenhagen, 1980; line numbers refer to the Thornton MS version.
38 Davenport, *Art of the* Gawain-*Poet*, p. 160.

Hir body watz schort and þik,
Hir buttokez balȝ and brode,
More lykkerwys on to lyk
Watz þat scho hade on lode. (966–9)

One cannot help but notice the rather unseemly sexual overtones in this description of the older lady's body, a technique which echoes traditional descriptions of romance hags (cf. *Ragnell* 241–2; *Florent* 1687–91), as well as deliberately contrasting with her younger companion's allure. Nor does the narrator apologize for the fact that Gawain shows a similar response to the ladies, offering a much warmer greeting to the younger (972–6). His instinctive feeling about the older woman appears in this case to be valid, for Morgan is indeed a menacing character, as Gawain learns later.

The portrait of the younger lady is presented with a contrasting eagerness and enthusiasm; however, the narrator's admiration for her freshness and *joie de vivre* have already been somewhat qualified by her intimacy with the older woman. The complex ambivalence of the lady's characterization will continue to be developed as the ironies of the temptation scenes unfold. Among other techniques, one is kept guessing about which character-type best fits the lady: alluring, but sullied? siren, or charming ingenue? She seems too thoroughly vital to be a mere mask for sin and destruction, but too calculating to be exempt from guilt. The sinister insinuations of the bedroom scenes are further reinforced by their juxtaposition with the dangers of the hunts. In addition, the image with which the lady flatters Gawain, that of the married romance heroine who, like Guinevere or Isolde, falls hopelessly in love with another man, is undercut by the detached artfulness of her stratagems.

Several factors tend to obscure Gawain's perceptions of the lady's true nature. One problem arises from traditional romance expectation that characters, feminine in particular, will usually fit a particular simple, polarized type. This expectation is defeated, at least in part, by the fact that the lady, a consummate actress, convincingly plays a bewildering variety of roles during the course of the three days' temptations: impetuous love-lorn maiden (1248–55, 1268–75, 1733–5, 1764–72, 1779–84, 1792–1800), witty comedy of manners hostess (1208–12, 1222–36, 1495–7), haughty courtly mistress (1291–3, 1481–6, 1509–34), and devious vixen (1187–94, 1281–9, 1549–50, 1846–54, 1736–41, 1862). Her subtle acting makes it impossible for Gawain to place her within any one of this complex set of expectations, though there are hints throughout the wooing of a scheme behind her apparent infatuation: 'And ay þe lady *let lyk as* hym loued mych' (1281); 'Ne þe purpose to payre þat pyȝt in hir hert' (1734). While the narrative insinuates to readers that the true nature of her motivation is devious, her temptation of Gawain depends on convincing him that her love is spontaneous and genuine. For example, it is difficult to know how to read the description of the gloriously seductive attire the lady dons on the third morning:

> In a mery mantyle, mete to be erþe,
> Ðat watz furred ful fyne with fellez wel pured,
> No hwez goud on hir hede bot þe haȝer stones
> Trased aboute hir tressour be twenty in clusteres;
> Hir þryuen face and hir þrote þrowen al naked,
> Hir brest bare bifore, and bihinde eke. (1736–41)

This apparel seems a little too artful and contrived to be an impetuous show of affection by one who is rushing from her bed to Gawain's chamber (1735). Yet the lady seems to be thoroughly caught up in her various roles, enjoying the game for its own sake, playfully rather than maliciously. In this respect, she is similar to her fun-loving husband, who is also greatly entertained by Gawain's winnings each day.

All this is confusing for the modern reader trained to look for some kind of consistent, underlying psychological motivation in a character. The details of the lady's behaviour are presented with wonderful verisimilitude, so that she seems the image of a realistically believable character, yet the picture turns out to be an illusion, a surface reflection that vanishes when one tries to plumb its depths. Why, then, did the poet outdo himself in making the hostess of Hautdesert such an appealing character?[39]

The poet's use of Morgan to explicate the temptation suddenly casts the lady into the unsuspected role of an obedient wife who will go to any length, even infidelity, to carry out her husband's command or some other trouthe-plighted tenet. Griselda and Dorigen are exemplars of this familiar medieval character type. The beautiful wife in the *Carl of Carlisle* also acts out this role when she obeys her husband's command to let Gawain kiss her in bed (449–65). Although Bertilak's wife has been Gawain's 'enmy kene' in following her assigned task so adroitly, she is technically free of guilt under this peculiar system of thinking, in which a wife's obedience to her husband supersedes all other moral principles, including fidelity and motherhood. The fact that the lady is only doing her duty makes Gawain's humiliation even more bitter than if she had been either truly in love with him or borne him actual malice.

39 Richard R. Griffith points out that the wife of Bertolais/Bertelak in the Vulgate *Merlin* and *Lancelot* is the false Guinevere, illegitimate half-sister of Guinevere, who schemes with her husband for revenge against the Round Table; the terrible fate of the False Guinevere makes the beauty and vitality of the lady in *Gawain* the more poignant. See 'Bertilak's Lady: The French Background of *Sir Gawain and the Green Knight*', *Annals of the New York Academy of Sciences* 314 (1978), 257–63.

The author's attempt to exonerate the lady has the agreeable side-effect of allowing the reader to enjoy the lady's wit and *joie de vivre* without sinning against the poem's basic moral values. The exuberance shown by the poem's narrator for the wooing scenes turns them into elegant games played with consummate skill. The delight in the *solace* of these well-played games seems spontaneous, almost as if the poet himself may have fallen a little in love with his lovely creation, for he describes her in terms that seem more wholesome than her role demands, as when she breathes in the intense beauty of the clear winter's morning of Gawain's last day at Hautdesert:

> Ho comez withinne þe chambre dore, and closes hit hir after,
> Wayuez vp a wyndow, and on þe wyȝe callez,
> And radly þus rehayted hym with hir riche wordes,
> with chere:
> 'A! mon, how may þou slepe,
> Þis morning is so clere?' (1742–7)

The *Gawain*-poet has broken with traditions of romance, especially alliterative romance, by making the lady so delightfully energetic. Her vitality contrasts dramatically with the passivity of a heroine/villainess like Guinevere in the *Morte*, whose infidelity seems more a matter of submission to Mordred (3550–2, 3575–6), though the poet shows so little interest in her that we cannot be too sure about her motivation. Even the conniving Guinevere in *Launfal* (661–720) seems drab and inept in comparison with Bertilak's wife. In place of the villainy usually attributed to such seductresses, the Gawain-poet provides a *dea ex machina*, Morgan le Fay, to help explain how the lady can behave as she does without being deeply implicated in the immorality of her role or being condemned more openly.

The technique illustrated by the *Gawain*-poet's characterization of the lady has an underlying similarity with Chaucer's approach to characterization, most notably that of the Wife of Bath herself. There is a similar sense of enjoyment of both characters' vitality, humour, and even foibles, all in terms that make them seem humanly approachable, without ever thoroughly resolving their inherent contradictions. I have pointed out the manner in which Chaucer allows the Wife to project her better, more idealistic (though submerged) qualities into her *alter ego*, making the loathly lady a model for true *gentilesse*. This technique reflects favourably upon the Wife of Bath's personality, if not upon her *praktike*. A comparable interest in creating a character who is compelling as well as forgiveable in her own right seems also to be among the concerns of the *Gawain*-poet in his brilliant, innovative characterization of the lady.

V

While Bertilak's wife resembles the Wife of Bath in her *likerous* youth, Bertilak himself possesses the comfortable and forgiving wisdom of the mature Wife. He also has a great deal in common with her loathly lady, including the ability to shift shape, an omniscient view of the action of the story, and a sympathetic interest in testing the story's hero under the most rigorous conditions possible, yet without the least bit of malice. Also intriguing is the fact that both poets selected such homely, home-grown types, akin to the shape-shifters of the lowliest tail-rhyme romances (Dame Ragnell and the Carl of Carlisle), as the spokespersons for major statements on the subject of chivalric *gentilesse*.

As the good host of the castle Bertilak still manages to evoke some of the associations of an uncourtly churl in his mannerisms, particularly in his enthusiastic responses to Gawain's presence.[40] The humorous excess of Bertilak's courtesy toward Gawain might be compared with the more loutish courtesy of the Carl of Carlisle, who apologizes for his own churlishness and entertains his guests by ordering increasingly huge cups of wine (276–97). However, a look at the churlish knights of the English tradition reveals that this character type may not always have stood simply for opposition to courtliness, but for a slightly more complex, though poorly articulated, protest against the *surquidry* of the Round Table for its lack of *gentilesse* to those it considered to be worthy only of exploitation through conquest and rude subjugation. The English popular romances invite comparison between the deliberate haughtiness of Arthur and his knights (Gawain excepted) and the outrageous appearance and manners of the churls or hags, who were, nevertheless, doing their best to practise 'carllus corttessy' (278). In both the alliterative and metrical English romances, the type of the churlish knight suggests a questioning on the part of solid, non-courtly gentles of the value of elaborate chivalric ritual and aristocratic pride. In the light of this consistently non-aristocratic bias in the English tradition, the *Gawain*-poet may have been quick to seize upon the opportunity the churlish knight character-type presents for a corrective to the extreme delicacy of Gawain's

40 Cf. Benson, *Art and Tradition*, especially pp. 62–3. Benson's study of the literary antecedents of the Green Knight, based mainly upon examples from French romance, finds a dualism in the Green Knight, attributed to the combination of two types: the green man and the wild man. The green man provides the Green Knight's more attractive features of dress and physique, while his uncouth fierceness and other monstrous qualities belong to the tradition of the wild man, a type usually shown as totally antagonistic to the values of chivalry. I am not sure this dualism holds up under close scrutiny of either the Green Knight or the types I have surveyed in the English tradition, in which several 'wild men' also possess attractive features or undergo transformations which render them attractive.

definition of courtesy, which is much more in line with the fastidious etiquette of a French *chevalier* than the simple good manners of an ordinary English knight.

The Green Knight's extraordinary appearance and the desolation of the Green Chapel suggest a strong affinity with the monsters of other English romances. For instance, in the *Morte*, a tremendous suspense builds up as Arthur approaches the domain of the giant of Mont-Saint-Michel, ironically compared with the locale's famous saint. The ambience of this scene parallels the tone of Gawain's jests about the Green Chapel: 'Wel bisemez þe wyȝe wruxled in grene | Dele here his deuocioun on þe deuelez wyse' (2191–2). Despite the terrifying aspects of the Green Knight, Bertilak, the good host, embodies a far more positive image, closer to the standard for the heroic knight of alliterative tradition, such as Golagros, Arthur (*Morte*), or even Gawain himself (*Morte* and *Golagros*)—a stalwart and big-hearted lord who shows a genuine interest in the well-being of his guest, as well as possessing an infectious sense of humour. Despite hints of Bertilak's role in the conspiracy, the poet goes out of his way to establish his audience's trust in this powerful lord with his huge stature and beaver-hued beard. The eagerness with which the host and his retinue welcome the opportunity for contact with a representative of Camelot may have been a witty commentary on the isolation of a country demesne from London court society, yet there is also a sense of confidence in this self-sufficient way of life, as well as a feeling that, wonderful as they are, the ultra-refined manners of the more fashionable courtiers of Camelot are a bit supercilious and impractical for a lord who spends most of his time hunting. The *Gawain*-poet is careful to surround Bertilak's less temperate traits with a reassuring humour. His frenetic energy seems safely channelled into festive Christmas games, his excessive interest in Gawain assumes the guise of the provincial's bountiful hospitality, and his physical combativeness is wholly given over to the hunting (or so the reader assumes). By leaving the more treacherous elements of Gawain's trial up to the lady, the poet manages to suppress the host's more menacing side. Of course, the alert reader will still notice hints of the huge lord's identity with the Green Knight but, if anything, these will serve to make that character's sudden about-face more acceptable. Although the Green Knight's use of Morgan as scapegoat seems awkward and inadequately-prepared for, we are relieved by any excuse that will mitigate his role in the conspiracy. Furthermore, a contemporary audience might have been more comfortable with accepting the notorious enchantress as the root of all evil in the poem, since an evil enchanter or enchantress lies behind the churlish appearance and behaviour of most of the shape-shifters in the English tradition (as in *Ragnell*, *Florent*, and the *Carl*). The preparation of the audience for the acceptance of the host's basically good intentions toward Gawain also prepares for the Green Knight's role as spokesman for one interpretation, the comic, pragmatic, sympathetic view of Gawain's performance in the test:

> 'I sende hir to asay þe, and sothly me þynkkez
> On þe fautlest freke þat euer on fote ȝede . . .
> Bot here yow lakked a lyttel, sir, and lewte yow wonted;
> Bot þat watz for no wylyde werke, ne wowyng nauþer,
> Bot for ȝe lufed your lyf; þe lasse I yow blame.' (2362–3, 2366–8)

In his role as instructor to young Gawain, Bertilak bears a close resemblance to the old wife of the Chaucerian tale. For instance, he relies on many of the same techniques to convey his message as emphatically as possible. In *The Wife of Bath's Tale* the old wife allowed her knight to believe he was taking advantage of her before astonishing him with her demand of marriage and love (III.1054–9). In much the same fashion, Bertilak waits until the precise moment when Gawain thinks he has been saved to reveal his embarrassing secret. Yet the poet is careful to make it clear that no ill-will is behind this humbling method of disclosure:

> The haþel heldet hym fro, and on his ax rested,
> Sette þe schaft vpon schore, and to þe scharp lened,
> And loked to þe leude þat on þe launde ȝede,
> How þat doȝty, dredles, deruely þer stondez
> Armed, ful aȝlez: in hert hit hym lykez. (2331–5)

Bertilak's attitude toward the young hero is that of an amused, yet admiring father who wishes his son to learn by experience. Consistent with this approach, Bertilak refrains from preaching to Gawain about his fault, offering only a concise and objective explanation for the significance of his three blows.[41] While Chaucer's lady is more of a sermonizer, she also has the good sense to know when to abbreviate her lecture and turn to experience as a more effective teaching technique. When Gawain's self-accusation threatens to turn the scene from comic recognition to tragedy, Bertilak tries to intervene on behalf of a more compassionate view of the hero's failure. Gawain is not ready to accept the lace as a sign of honour, though Bertilak's suggestion that it be treated as such adumbrates the final resolution at Camelot, when Gawain reluctantly allows himself to be recruited into the order created to honour his achievement.

41 For one possible significance see Victoria L. Weiss, 'The Medieval Knighting Ceremony in *Sir Gawain and the Green Knight*', *Chaucer Review* 12 (1977–8), 183–9.

Chaucer's loathly lady was most concerned with teaching her imperfect young spouse to recognize the inner worth hidden under her ugliness, a theme illustrated by the concerns of the hags in English romances like *Ragnell* and *Florent*. Bertilak, whose incredible appearance as the Green Knight is also revealed to be illusory, wishes Gawain to see beyond his own flaw to his basic worth and, by extension, the worth of all imperfect humanity, a concern which emerges in rudimentary form in romances like the *Carl*. Both Chaucer's young knight and Gawain set themselves on a different level from the rest of humanity and in so doing echo the behaviour of Arthur or his other knights (but not Gawain) in *Ragnell* and the *Carl*. Chaucer's bachelor keeps insisting that somehow, in absolute terms, he is better than the women he has tried to dominate, his loathly bride in particular. Gawain's self-condemnation is an essential first step in his penance for having taken and concealed the lace and is followed by a continuing realization of the gravity of his sin. His reaction may seem excessive by modern standards, but the continuing sense of sinfulness is entirely in accordance with medieval standards of piety. But we should not expect the perspective of the penitent sinner to be shared by either the Green Knight or Arthur's courtiers. From their point of view, Gawain's response is, to put it in modern terms, a psychologically consistent one for a young idealist up against life's first major disappointment. Gawain's recognition of his human sinfulness is so painful a process precisely because he has come so close in his own conduct to realizing those ideals. That is why his more sober interpretation of his adventure pulls as strongly upon the reader's sympathy as the more lighthearted, but no less judicious, reactions of Bertilak and Arthur's court.

King Arthur at the Crossroads to Rome*

LESLEY JOHNSON

Today's visitor to Modena in Northern Italy may well be jolted out of a sense of cultural *dépaysement* when he or she sees, sculpted on the archivolt over the north doorway, an Arthurian frieze depicting the rescue of Winlogee by Artus, Galvaginus, and Che, which dates from the early twelfth century.[1] The subject of this essay, however, is not the journey which takes Arthurian material from Britain to Modena but the journey of Arthur, Britain's legendary king, to Rome. Its focal point is the late fourteenth-century/early fifteenth-century Middle English narrative known as the alliterative *Morte Arthure*, a text concerned with both the theory and practice of King Arthur's campaign against the Romans.[2] The alliterative *Morte Arthure* traces Arthur's Roman campaign

* This essay was originally given as a paper to the Medieval Society, University of Leeds, in December 1988.

1 For the Modena archivolt see R. S. Loomis, 'The Oral Diffusion of the Arthurian legend' in *Arthurian Literature in the Middle Ages*, ed. R. S. Loomis (Oxford 1959), pp. 52–63, esp. 60–1; Rita Lejeune and Jacques Stiénnon, 'La légende arthurienne dans la sculpture de la cathédrale de Modène', *Cahiers de Civilisation Médiévales* 6 (1963), 281–96.

2 All references to the text of the *Morte Arthure* (*MA*), including quotations, will be taken from the excellent edition by Mary Hamel (New York and London, 1984) and will be cited by line number in my text. I have also consulted the editions by Valerie Krishna, *The Alliterative Morte Arthure* (New York, 1976); Larry Benson, *King Arthur's Death* (Indianapolis, 1974); Erik Björkman (Heidelburg, 1915); Edmund Brock, *Morte Arthure*, London, 1865 (Early English Text Society 8), and the abridged selection edited by John Finlayson (London, 1967). The date of the *Morte Arthure* is the subject of some critical debate, as is the case with many of the poems of the so-called 'Alliterative Revival'; a phenomenon generally considered to be of the second half of the fourteenth century, although most of the texts which might be classified as its products are preserved in manuscripts which date from the fifteenth century (even the sixteenth and seventeenth centuries), as I. Doyle has pointed out in 'The Manuscripts' in *Middle English Alliterative Poetry*, ed. D. Lawton (Woodbridge, 1982), pp. 88–100, at 88. The manuscript which contains the single extant text of the *Morte Arthure*, Lincoln, Cathedral Library 91, was copied sometime between 1422–50. For a facsimile and description of the Lincoln manuscript and its contents see *The Thornton Manuscript, Lincoln Cathedral MS 91*, introduced by D. S. Brewer and A. E. B. Owen, rev. ed., London, 1977. George Keiser discusses the date of the manuscript and the identity of its scribe, Robert Thornton, in 'Lincoln Cathedral

and its aftermath in considerable detail: it charts Arthur's progress to Rome through France, Luxembourg, to Metz, down the Rhine to Lucerne, over the Alps through the Mount Gottard Pass, and thence through the Northern Italian states, via a series of battles, sieges and chevauchées. This route is of interest for several reasons. As George Parks has observed, the *Morte Arthure* offers an unprecedented account of Arthur's campaigns in Italy and contains the earliest recorded reference in England to the Mount Gottard Pass across the Alps (made practicable in 1230).[3] The topical appeal of Arthurian history in the *Morte Arthure* is certainly enhanced by updated details of this kind.[4] But the representation of the roads to Rome in this narrative is of greater significance than this alone. In the *Morte Arthure* the narrative of King Arthur's campaign against Rome is radically reworked so that two routes to Rome cross on the outskirts of Viterbo as King Arthur, the leader of a military campaign to Rome which has all the makings of a crusade, meets Craddoke, a former member of his court, who has left Britain to undertake a pilgrimage to Rome (*MA* 3456–3590). This crossing of pilgrim

Library MS 91: Life and Milieu of the Scribe', *Studies in Bibliography* 32 (1979), 158–79; 'More light on the Life and Milieu of Robert Thornton', *Studies in Bibliography* 36 (1983), 111–19. See also John Thompson's discussion in *Robert Thornton and the London Thornton Manuscript* (London, 1987). A compositional date of *c.*1375 for the poem has been favoured by some critics (on the basis of apparent contemporary allusions to events in the reign of Edward III); however, I am persuaded by the arguments of John Finlayson and George Keiser against a mid fourteenth-century date for the poem, and by those of Larry Benson for a date *c.*1399–1402. For Finlayson's discussion see '*Morte Arthure*: the Date and a Source for Contemporary References', *Speculum* 42 (1967), 624–38; for Keiser's discussion see 'Edward III and the Alliterative *Morte Arthure*', *Speculum* 48 (1973), 37–51; for Benson's argument see 'The Date of the Alliterative *Morte Arthure*' in *Medieval Studies Presented to Lillian Herlands Hornstein*, edd. Jess B. Bessinger Jr. and Robert Raymo (New York, 1976), pp. 19–40.

3 'King Arthur and the Roads to Rome', *Journal of English and German Philology* 45 (1946), 164–70. Some of Parks' comments on Italian place-names are based on contested textual readings: see Larry Benson, 'The Date of the Alliterative *Morte Arthure*' (cited above, n. 2), and Mary Hamel's discussion in the introduction to her edition, pp. 36–8, and the notes to the lines she lists there. Parks' claim that the *Morte Arthure* is the first narrative in English 'to bring Arthur to Italy' (p. 164) requires some qualification as will be clear from my later comments on Robert Mannyng's treatment of this episode.

4 For more detailed discussions of the topical resonances of the representation of Arthurian society, its rituals of diplomacy and warfaring, and its topography, in the *Morte Arthure* see Larry Benson, 'The Date of the Alliterative *Morte Arthure*' and John Finlayson '*Morte Arthure*: The Date and the Source for Contemporary References' (cited above in n. 2); Juliet Vale, 'Law and Diplomacy in the Alliterative *Morte Arthure*', *Nottingham Medieval Studies* 23 (1979), 31–46; Henry Harder, 'Feasting in the Alliterative *Morte Arthure*', *Chivalric Literature*, edd. Larry Benson and J. Leyerle (Kalamazoo, 1980), pp. 49–62.

and crusading paths reflects tensions figured in the narrative as a whole between the various ways of justifying action according to Christian and chivalric ethics, both individual and collective. However, before moving on to explore the significance of these crossroads to Rome in the *Morte Arthure*, I will place this narrative of Arthur's campaign for Rome in a broader historiographical context and trace the form and function of this episode in the earlier Galfredian tradition of British history, to which it is indebted.

I

As modern readers have long recognised, the alliterative *Morte Arthure* reworks material from the tradition of Arthurian narrative which derives from Geoffrey of Monmouth's account of the Kings of Britain, *History of the Kings of Britain* (*Historia Regum Britannie*), in circulation by 1139, and probably written about 1138.[5] Geoffrey of Monmouth made history in several respects with this text, which provided a new perspective on British history and endowed the history of the island and its most famous king, Arthur, with an aura of classical prestige and status. The new slant offered by the *History of the Kings of Britain* is obvious when it is compared with the accounts of British history compiled by other early twelfth-century insular historiographers, notably William of Malmesbury

5 See the introduction to Hamel's edition of the *Morte Arthure*, pp. 59–60, for an overview of the possible source texts in Latin, French, and English, and her comments on pp. 34–8 for a summary of the texts' debts to the 'chronicle' tradition of Arthurian narrative. Neil Wright discusses the probable date of the composition of Geoffrey of Monmouth's narrative in the introduction to his edition, *The Historia Regum Britannie of Geoffrey of Monmouth.* I: *Bern Burgerbibliothek MS. 568* (Cambridge, 1985), pp. x-xvi. All quotations will be taken from this edition and cited by paragraph number in my text. I will also cite parallel passages (in Roman numerals) from *The History of the Kings of Britain* translated by Lewis Thorpe (Harmondsworth, 1966). The popularity of the Galfredian version of British history is indicated by the large numbers of Latin texts extant (leaving aside the numerous vernacular reworkings) which have now been catalogued by Julia Crick, *The Historia Regum Britannie of Geoffrey of Monmouth.* III: *A Summary Catalogue of the Manuscripts*, Cambridge, 1989.

The textual 'condition' of the *Historia Regum Britannie* (*HRB*) is very complex: it appears that shortly after its appearance (in the so-called 'Vulgate' version), a revised version was made which moderated some of the more provocative features of the 'Vulgate' narrative. Neil Wright considers the relationship between the Vulgate and variant texts, reviews past scholarship on the issue, and discusses the possible date of the variant version in the introduction to his edition of *The Historia Regum Britannie of Geoffrey of Monmouth.* II: *First Variant Version*, Cambridge, 1988. See also Julia Crick's discussion in *The Historia Regum Brittanie of Geoffrey of Monmouth.* IV: *Dissemination and Reception in the Later Middle Ages* (Cambridge, 1991), pp. 3–6.

and Henry of Huntingdon, who in the *Gesta Regum Anglorum* and the *Historia Anglorum* tackle the subject of British history as part of their larger scale projects to retrieve a continuous political history of England.[6] Their accounts of British history, which draw on material provided by Bede and Gildas amongst others, represent it as a relatively ill-documented and inglorious period of the history of the island. Although Geoffrey of Monmouth aligns his narrative to this tradition of insular historiography by opening the *History of the Kings of Britain* with a description of the island modelled on that of Henry of Huntingdon, Bede, and Gildas, he goes on to disrupt that tradition by offering an account of British history, from Britain's foundation by Brutus to its domination by the Saxons, in which the hegemony of the Britons is both temporally extended and qualitatively enhanced.[7] The transition from British to Saxon dominion over the central parts of Britain occurs much later in the *History of the Kings of Britain* than in any other insular histories, and the representation of a unified British kingdom as a great international power (above all in the time of King Arthur) has no precedent in any of the recognised historical authorities which precede the *History of the Kings of Britain*.[8]

6 For the *Gesta Regum Anglorum*, which first appeared in 1125, and which records events up to 1120, see *Willelmi Malmesbirensis Monachi de Gestis Regum Anglorum Libri Quinque*, ed. W. Stubbs, 2 vols., London, 1887, 1889 (Rolls Series 90). William revised the *Gesta Regum Anglorum* in 1135 and was at work on its continuation, the *Historia Novella*, in 1140. The standard edition of Henry of Huntingdon's work is still that by Thomas Arnold, *Henrici Archdiaconi Huntendunensis Historia Anglorum*, London, 1879 (Rolls Series 74), but Diana Greenway is currently preparing another. Henry's work first appeared c. 1129 but was subsequently revised on several occasions. See Diana Greenway's helpful discussion of the successive editions and revisions of this text in 'Henry of Huntingdon and the manuscripts of the *Historia Anglorum*', *Anglo-Norman Studies* 9 (1986), 103–26. For general discussions of twelfth-century Anglo-Norman historiography see Antonia Gransden, *Historical Writing in England*, I, London, 1974; Nancy Partner, *Serious Entertainments: The Writing of History in Twelfth Century England* (Chicago and London, 1977), esp. pp. 194–211; Marjorie Chibnall, 'The Historian and his World', *The World of Orderic Vitalis* (Oxford, 1984), pp. 169–220; D Tillmann-Bartylla, 'Hofische Welt und Geschichtsbedürfnis: die anglonormannischen Verschroniken des XII. Jahrhunderts', *Grundriss der romanischen Literaturen des Mittelalters*, II: *La littérature historiographique des origines à 1500*, edd. Hans Ulrich Gumbrecht *et al.* (Heidelberg, 1986–7), pp. 313–50.

7 Robert Hanning discusses Geoffrey of Monmouth's contribution to, and disruption of, traditions of insular historiography in his important study, *The Vision of History in Early Britain* (New York, 1966); Neil Wright discusses the sources for Geoffrey of Monmouth's opening description of Britain in 'Geoffrey of Monmouth and Gildas', *Arthurian Literature* 2 (1982), 1–40, esp. 5–7.

8 Robert Hanning discusses the imperialist cast of Geoffrey's historical narrative in *The Vision of History in Early Britain* (cited above n. 7). See also J.S.P. Tatlock, *The Legendary History of Britain* (Berkeley and Los Angeles, 1950), pp. 305–20. R. William Leckie Jr. discusses the innovative periodization of British history in

The notion that Britain was founded by the Trojan, Brutus (great grandson of Aeneas), is not, of course, the invention of Geoffrey of Monmouth.[9] However Geoffrey of Monmouth elaborates on the consequences of this founding act to an unprecedented extent and thereby endows British history with a new design and greater status. The topos of *translatio imperii* is realised in the *History of the Kings of Britain* as the narrative traces the process by which Britain finally lives up to the standards of its classical heritage and becomes an island of great power and prestige. This naturalisation of the classical roots of British society is established by Brutus's act of foundation: he names the New-Found-Island after himself and builds a New Troy (*Troiam Nouam*) on the banks of the Thames (*HRB*, 22; I,17). The Trojan (or 'crooked Greek') dialect spoken by these founding fathers becomes known as British too (*HRB*, 21; I,16):[10] British, it appears, is a classical language. But there is a complication in the realization of this pattern in British history. Britain is not the only civilisation that rises up out of the ashes of Troy, and Britain's competitive relationship with Rome forms a larger, structural *leitmotiv* within the *History of the Kings of Britain* as a whole. Geoffrey of Monmouth gives a new edge to British history, indeed makes British history, by reassessing and reworking the history of political relationships between Britain and the Roman Empire.

In the historical narratives of William of Malmesbury, Bede, and Gildas, the Roman occupation of Britain seems to have the status of a founding act; in Geoffrey of Monmouth's text, in contrast, the Roman occupation is framed by a wider context of Romano-British relations.

the Vulgate version of the *Historia Regum Brittanie* in *The Passage of Dominion: Geoffrey of Monmouth and the Periodization of British History in the Twelfth Century* (Toronto, 1981).

9 The historical compilation, the *Historia Brittonum*, which survives in over forty medieval manuscripts and dates from the ninth century, contains a version of the Trojan 'origin story' of Britain. See Hanning's discussion of this compilation in *The Vision of British History*, pp. 91–120; D. Dumville's critique of its attribution to Nennius, 'Nennius and the *Historia Brittonum*', *Studia Celtica*, 10–11 (1975–6), 78–95, and his more general article, 'The Historical Value of the *Historia Brittonum*', *Arthurian Literature*, 6 (1986), 1–26. Dumville's work qualifies some of John Morris' points in his edition and translation, *Nennius: British History and The Welsh Annals*, Chichester, 1980. For a more general discussion of the function and popularity of Trojan origin stories in circulation in early medieval Europe see Susan Reynolds, 'Medieval *Origines Gentium* and the Community of the Realm', *History* 65 (1983), 375–90. Henry of Huntingdon evidently had access to some version of the *Historia Brittonum* and included details of a Trojan 'origin story' for Britain in his *Historia Anglorum*, I. 9.

10 T.D. Crawford discusses the phenomenon of 'crooked Greek' and other linguistic issues in his article, 'On the Linguistic Competence of Geoffrey of Monmouth', *Medium Aevum* 51 (1982), 152–62, esp. p. 155. The variant version offers an abbreviated account of these linguistic processes (see Wright's edition, p. 21).

Long before Julius Caesar conquers Britain, Rome itself has been conquered by the forces of the British king, Belinus, and his brother, Brennius (*HRB*, 35–44; III.1–10). During the troubled period of the Roman occupation itself, British prestige is recovered partially when Constantine, the son of a Romano-British union, becomes Emperor of Rome and overlord of the whole world (*HRB*, 78–80; V.6–8). But it is after the Roman withdrawal that British society most fully lives up to its classical heritage and overshadows Rome martially, culturally, and materially, and this happens in Arthur's reign. Both William of Malmesbury and Henry of Huntingdon acknowledge that after the Roman withdrawal a figure called Arthur leads a British resurgence and, temporarily, quells the Saxon threat to British hegemony.[11] But Geoffrey of Monmouth makes Arthur into a national and international leader: a figure who not only brings relief from the Saxon invaders but, in the words of Merlin's prophecy, is feared by the House of Romulus (*HRB*, 112 [2]; VII.3). There is no trace in any of the histories that precede Geoffrey of such an illustrious period of British history, nor is there any record of the Roman empire itself being in such good imperial shape as it evidently is in the time of Arthur. Arthur's Roman antagonists represent the power of the Roman Empire at its height; in fighting against Arthur, the Romans rally support from fourteen countries in the Orient and the East.[12]

The first part of Arthurian history in the *History of the Kings of Britain* recounts how Arthur deals with an internal Saxon threat to

11 In *Gesta Regum Anglorum*, I, §8, William notes that King Ambrosius, a survivor of the Roman race, helped the Britons fight back against the Angles, after the death of Vortigern, and was aided by Arthur, a battle leader who had a great reputation amongst the British, at the battle of Mount Badon. Nothing more is said about Arthur until much later when William recounts the discovery of 'Walwen's tomb' in Wales and notes, briefly, that Arthur's tomb is nowhere to be found—a mystery which fuels stories about Arthur's return (III, §287). Henry of Huntingdon fills in more information about Arthur, whom he represents as a king, and describes his twelve battles (drawn from material in the *Historia Brittonum*) in his *Historia Anglorum*, II, §18. On the pre-Geoffrey notices of Arthur see E. K. Chambers *Arthur of Britain* (London, 1927); T. Jones, 'The Early Evolution of the Legend of Arthur', *Nottingham Medieval Studies* 8 (1964), 3–21.

12 The levels of anachrony and syncretism built into the text of the *Historia Regum Britannie* are discussed by J. S. P. Tatlock in his study of *The Legendary History of Britain*. Tatlock specifically discusses the anachronistic representation of the Roman Empire in Arthur's time in the *Historia Regum Britannie* in 'Contemporaneous Matters in Geoffrey of Monmouth', *Speculum* 6 (1931), 206–24. At this stage in their histories, both the British and the Romans have been converted to Christianity, and yet the portrait of Roman power which Geoffrey of Monmouth presents at this stage is that of a great imperial power. The difficulties of dealing with the double significance of Rome, in its imperial and spiritual dimensions, are avoided in Geoffrey's narrative by re-routing Arthur's campaign back to Britain, before it nears Rome itself.

British control over the island, and charts the progress of his campaigns in the Northern islands, Norway, and Gaul (*HRB*, 143–55; IX.1-11). The second part recounts Arthur's campaign against the Roman forces, his decisive engagement with the Roman side in Burgundy, and the circumstances which interrupt that campaign and prevent a British attack on Rome itself: the British king is forced to return to the island to campaign against his nephew, Mordred, who has seized the throne and mobilised Saxon forces to support his position (*HRB*, 157–78; IX.13–XI.2). The account of Arthur's coronation ceremony at Carleon serves as a transitional sequence between these two periods and is the occasion for a monumental summary of the power and prestige of the British kingdom at this point in its history as the narrator's comments emphasise:

> Ad tantum etenim statum dignitatis Britannia tunc reducta erat quod co‹pi›a diuiciarum, luxu ornamentorum, facecia incolarum cetera regna exellebat. (*HRB*, 157)
>
> By this time Britain had reached such a standard of sophistication that it excelled all other kingdoms in its general affluence, the richness of its decorations and the courteous behaviour of its inhabitants. (IX.13)

Ironically, it is at this moment when the nation appears to be preeminent (Rome-like in its power, Troy-like in its cultural prestige), that the celebrations are interrupted by the arrival of twelve ambassadors from Rome who carry a message from the Roman procurator, rebuking Arthur for his conquest of Gaul and demanding British payment of tribute to Rome. This demand is the trigger for Arthur's campaign for control over Rome itself. But the omens for British success appear to be good,[13] and subsequently the British side defeat the Roman forces in Burgundy. However, King Arthur does not get beyond the Alpine passes in his campaign for Rome itself: Mordred's usurpation requires the King to return to Britain (*HRB*, 176; XI.13). The clash between Britain and Rome in Arthur's reign, the highpoint of British history in the *History of the Kings of Britain*, is represented as the clash between competing impe-

13 Hoel supports Arthur's plan to campaign against Rome by citing a Sybilline prophecy which predicts that there should be three British emperors of Rome (HRB, 160; XI.17) and Arthur also has a dream, *en route* for the Continent, which also seems to presage his success (*HRB*, 164; X.2). His companions interpret this dream (in which a mighty dragon defeats a great bear) as a sign of his success against some giant; Arthur himself prefers to interpret it as a sign of his future victory over the Roman procurator Lucius (*HRB*, 164; X.2). In the event it could refer to both: Arthur's first action in Brittany is to kill the Giant who has raped Hoel's daughter, and the British side later defeat the Romans at Saussy.

rial powers, who both use the evidence of historical precedents (Belinus/Brennius, Julius Caesar, Constantine) to back up the justice of their claims to lordship over the other (*HRB*, 158–9; IX.15–16). The contest is thereby placed within the larger web of Romano-British relations which has partly structured the representation of British history up to this point in the *History of the Kings of Britain*. Given that the Roman side is supported by a markedly larger contingent of pagan allies, it would be possible for Arthur's campaign against the Romans to evoke crusading associations and thus to be linked to the other structuring *leitmotiv* of British history, the growth and consolidation of the Christian faith in Britain. But although King Arthur claims a religious motivation for his battles against the pagan Saxons, he makes no such claim for his contest against the Romans, nor does the narrator who interprets Arthur's victory over the Roman army as a sign of divine support for the justice of the *political* cause of the British (*HRB*, 175; XI.12). In the *Morte Arthure* this complex of potentially spiritual and overtly imperial-political motivations is much developed. At the same time, however, the latent paradoxes of the syncretic portrait of the Roman antagonists become much more obvious.

In the *Morte Arthure*, the sequence from King Arthur's Northern conquests to his death in his campaign against Mordred has been disengaged from its place in the larger sweep of the Galfredian version of British history and is made the central focus of this narrative.[14] Imperial and religious motivations are explicitly claimed and amplified, and Rome itself is represented as both the centre of an imperial power structure and the spiritual capital of the West.[15] Arthur's forces get much closer to Rome in

14 Some contextualisation for Arthur's Roman campaign is provided by the long list of Arthur's conquests in lines 26–47, which economically gives an impression of the dimensions of Arthur's realm geographically and historically (and, to some extent, modernise the terms of reference). There is no precedent in any of the sources for such a long list of conquests. In gaining control of these regions Arthur, it appears, has regained his heritage (*MA* 26–9): this reference to Arthur's heritage is one of a number added in the *Morte Arthure* which support Arthur's claims not only to these areas but also to Rome itself (*MA* 521; 640–3; 1309–10). For references to other periods of British history cited in this text see lines 275–87; 1694–9; 3403–5; 3541–3545; 4207–8. It is clear that the compiler of the *Morte Arthure* is acquainted with a much wider sweep of British history than the Arthurian sections alone from the way in which certain sections of the narrative are informed implicitly, rather than explicitly, by material drawn from other periods of British history. See the discussion of the *Morte Arthure* in my unpublished Ph.D. thesis 'Commemorating the Past' (London University, 1990), pp. 390–97.

15 In the council scene in which Arthur consults his closest advisors about campaigning for Rome, council members vow to Christ and the 'holy Vernacle' to wreak vengeance on the Romans (*MA* 297–303; 308–315; 346–56; 386–394). One of the grievances of the Welsh King is that his earlier pilgrimage had been disrupted by the Viscount of Rome at Pontremoli (*MA* 324–29). Mary Hamel

this version of events, but, at the same time, judgements on the ethics of his campaign become more complicated by the nexus of political, chivalric and Christian values which the participants claim both motivates and determines their action. The *Morte Arthure* follows the Galfredian framework of events, from the arrival of the Roman ambassadors to the death of the Roman emperor Lucius (*MA* 78–2370), but then continues with an account of the British encounter with the Duke of Lorraine (one of Lucius's allies), King Arthur's journey down to the Northern Italian states, and his ravaging campaigns through Tuscany to Spoleto to Viterbo, where he awaits a response to his campaign from the Roman senators (*MA* 2371–3175).[16] It is here that Arthur is visited by the wisest cardinal from Rome, who prays Arthur to have pity on the Pope and proposes that the British King be crowned as the sovereign of that City in a ceremony a week later (*MA* 3176–90). It is here that Arthur formulates his plan to embark on a further crusade, over the sea to Jerusalem, to 'reuenge the Renke that on the Rode dyede' (*MA* 3217); and it is here, too, that Arthur has his second dream of the narrative, in which the shape and pattern of his history is reviewed and Mordred's betrayal is anticipated (*MA* 3227–455). It is from here in Viterbo that Arthur walks out of his camp, having heard his advisor's interpretation of his dream, and meets Craddoke, a former member of his court, on a pilgrimage to Rome (*MA* 3456–522). Craddoke brings the news of Mordred's treason, which forces Arthur to leave Italy before he can receive the imperial crown, and from this point on the narrative returns to follow the Galfredian frame for its account of Arthur's demise (albeit with some amplification and modification). Altogether, around 1,000 lines are taken up with this extended account of King Arthur's journey Rome-wards in the *Morte Arthure*: in a narrative of 4346 lines this addition evidently constitutes a sequence of importance and consequence.

Some of the material used to amplify Arthur's Roman campaign in the *Morte Arthure* derives from episodes in other narrative traditions of classical and Christian history, more specifically those which recount Alexander's and Charlemagne's imperial and/or crusading ventures.[17] But vernacular reworkings of Galfredian British history seem to have offered further prompts for the amplification of Arthur's campaign for Rome too. The most tangible debt of the compiler(s) of the *Morte Arthure* is not to the Latin versions of the *History of the Kings of Britain*, but rather to two vernacular reworkings: Wace's *Roman de Brut* (finished in 1155)

discusses the syncretic qualities of Arthur's antagonists in 'The Christening of Sir Priamus in the Alliterative *Morte Arthure*', *Viator* 13 (1982), 295–307, esp. 299.

16 Lucius is a 'procurator' in Geoffrey of Monmouth's narrative; for his representation as the emperor of Rome in vernacular reworkings which precede the *Morte Arthure* see Hamel's note to *MA* 86–7.

and Robert Mannyng of Brunne's *Chronicle* (written about 1338).[18] Mannyng's narrative is a compilation of two earlier French narratives: Wace's poem and Pierre de Langtoft's version of British/English history, which follows the history of the kings of the island up to 1307 and was probably written fairly soon after this date.[19] Basically, Mannyng's account of Arthurian history follows Wace's account of British history, but in recounting the history of Arthur's Roman campaign he adds a significant detail from Langtoft's text: in Mannyng's narrative, Arthur gets as far as Pavia before learning of Mordred's rebellion.[20]

17 The Priamus episode in particular (*MA* 2501–2716) is made up from narrative motifs drawn from histories of Alexander and Charlemagne. Indeed Priamus claims to be a descendant of Alexander and prophecies that Arthur will be Alexander's heir (*MA* 2595–2605; 2633–5). Hamel surveys the debt to the narrative traditions concerning Alexander and Charlemagne in the introduction to her edition (pp. 38 ff.) and supplies further bibliographical references.

18 *Le Roman de Brut de Wace*, ed. Ivor Arnold, 2 vols, Paris, 1938, 1940 (Societé des anciens textes français). *The Story of England by Robert Mannyng of Brunne*, ed. Frederick J. Furnival, 2 vols., London, 1887 (Rolls Series 87). All quotations from these works will be drawn from these editions and cited in my text. Furnival's edition covers only the pre-Saxon section of Mannyng's narrative. See Hamel's comments on the versions of British history that seem to be reworked in the *Morte Arthure* in the introduction to her edition, pp. 34–8. Not all the evidence cited by Mary Hamel to support her views on the poem's sources is equally persuasive. I have briefly considered the equivocal evidence for the *direct* use of the *History of the Kings of Britain* and Laȝamon's *Brut* in the appendix to my thesis 'Commemorating the Past'. There is little doubt that Wace's *Roman de Brut* provided an important textual resource for the *Morte Arthure*, as John Finlayson showed in his unpublished Ph.D thesis 'The Sources, Use of Sources, and Poetic Techniques of the 14th Century *Alliterative Morte Arthure*' (Cambridge University, 1962), but Finlayson does not fully recognize the debts of the *Morte Arthure* to Mannyng's historical narrative too.

19 For a recent discussion of Mannyng's *Chronicle* see Thorlac Turville-Petre, 'Politics and Poetry in the Early Fourteenth Century: The Case of Robert Mannyng's *Chronicle*', *Review of English Studies* 39 (1988), 1–28. The *Chronicle* of Pierre de Langtoft has been edited by Thomas Wright, 2 vols., London, 1866, 1868 (Rolls Series 47). It is not clear whether the composer of the *Morte Arthure* had direct access to Langtoft's narrative, although there are several points of connection between their respective versions of Arthurian history. These borrowings of distinctive details from Langtoft's narrative could be drawn from Mannyng's composite text.

20 For Langtoft's account see his *Chronicle*, p. 216 (there are no line numbers in Wright's edition); for Mannyng, see Furnivall's edition, 14025–6. Although the prompt to develop Arthur's campaign for Rome in the *Morte Arthure* may have come from Mannyng's narrative (and possibly Langtoft's text), there is no doubt that in the Galfredian tradition of Arthurian history, Arthur *intends* to journey on to Rome after Saussy. There is no suggestion that Arthur's campaign has somehow finished after the death of Lucius, as some critics seem to imply when they discuss the amplified campaign after Saussy in the *Morte Arthure* as if it were an unnecessary expedition. It is simply that in the *History*

Although Arthur's journey towards Rome is extended in Mannyng's version of events, no details are provided of either the route or the campaign. However, the narratives of both Wace and Mannyng do provide a more detailed account of an earlier British campaign which reached Rome. This is the campaign undertaken by Arthur's ancestors, Belinus and Brennius, who journey to Rome using the Mount Bernard and Cernis passes and then head Rome-wards on a similar route to that taken by Arthur in the *Morte Arthure*. This amplification of Belinius's and Brennius's campaign seems to have been Wace's responsibility and it seems likely that he drew on a pilgrim itinerary for his information.[21] As George Parks has suggested, the *Morte Arthure* composer seems to have taken this earlier Roman campaign (recounted in detail in the texts of Wace and Mannyng) as the model for the development of Arthur's journey down to Rome. However, in the *Morte Arthure* the details of the campaign route have been 'modernized' (Arthur travels over the Mount Gottard pass) and the very notion of a pilgrimage route to Rome is both literalized, and made to be of thematic significance in the narrative. The idea of a pilgrimage route to Rome which both coincides with, and yet is potentially separate from, Arthur's route to Rome is dramatized in the King's meeting with Sir Craddoke the pilgrim at the crossroads outside Viterbo. This meeting draws attention to the status of Rome as a spiritual centre and to the potential incongruity of Arthur's mode of approach. It literalises one of the thematic interests of the narrative as a whole: there are, as Chaucer points out, 'diverse pathes' that 'leden diverse folk the . . . way to Rome', but do they all lead the right way?[22]

II

In the *Morte Arthure*, then, King Arthur gets closer to Rome than in any of the previous versions of Galfredian history. But, in the Galfredian tradition of Arthurian history, Rome is represented as both the centre of an imperial power and as the base for the Pope, and the paradoxes latent in this highly syncretic representation are more developed in the *Morte*

of the Kings of Britain and in Wace's *Roman de Brut* Arthur is called back to Britain before he can get much closer to Rome.

21 For discussions of the amplified campaign route of Brennius and Belinus in the *Roman de Brut* see R. Blenner-Hassett and F. P. Magoun, 'The Italian Campaign of Belin and Brenne in the *Bruts* of Wace and of Lawman', *Philological Quarterly* 21 (1942), 385–90, George Parks, 'King Arthur and the Roads to Rome', and Mary Hamel's discussion in the introduction to her edition, pp. 36–8.

22 *A Treatise on the Astrolable,* Preface (*The Riverside Chaucer*, ed. Larry D. Benson (Oxford, 1988), p. 662.39–40).

Arthure, as are the tensions between the aims, means, and ends of Arthur's campaign for Rome, which are figured in the King's encounter with Craddoke at Viterbo. However, if pilgrimage and crusading routes to Rome cross in Arthur's meeting with Craddoke, this is not the first time such routes have been brought into significant alignment in the *Morte Arthure*. Indeed, in the very first incident in Arthur's campaign, as he lands in Brittany and fights a giant, the action is developed in a way which enhances the pilgrimage and crusading associations of the encounter.[23] In the *Morte Arthure*, Arthur's fight with the giant becomes a highly idealised, unproblematic example of martial action which may serve Christian and imperial ends (*MA* 840–1221). As such, this episode anticipates the larger contest between the British and Roman forces, but it also provides a point of contrast with the large-scale campaign. The ethics of fighting giants are much simpler than those involved in the grand Christian-imperial venture, and if, at Viterbo, pilgrimage and crusade routes are made to cross, in the earlier incident on Mont St Michel they are allowed to coincide. Material from a range of sources has been reworked and compressed in the giant-killing episode in the *Morte Arthure*, but the compiler of the text has given this incident a distinctive edge by exploiting the associations of its setting.[24] When Arthur takes on the giant, he does so in the guise of making a pilgrimage to the Mount to pay his respects to its Saint (*MA* 888–9) and is accompanied to the base of the Mount by only Kay and Bedevere. When Arthur returns from his 'pilgrimage' by tumbling down the Mount, locked in the embrace of the

23 Prior to this episode, the spiritual motivation of Arthur's side has been suggested by the vows made by Arthur's chief supporters in the council scene (*MA* 289–394). The Welsh King, indeed, vows that his performance in the campaign against Rome will avenge the Viscount of Rome's interference in his earlier pilgrimage (*MA* 320–36). This vowing sequence has no precedent in the Galfredian sources: as Mary Hamel notes, the 'Vernacle' on which the oaths are sworn is a symbol of pilgrimage to Rome (see the introduction to her edition, pp. 41–6, and her note to lines 296–7).

24 Material already present in the parallel sections of the Galfredian source narratives has been substantially reworked in this scene as John Finlayson has shown in his detailed analysis of this episode, 'Arthur and the Giant of St Michael's Mount', *Medium Ævum* 33 (1964), 112–20. As Finlayson notes, the grotesque portrait of the giant was perhaps inspired by the Wild Herdsman who appears in Chrétien de Troyes' *Yvain*. I would argue that a few descriptive details for this scene in the *Morte Arthure* have also been taken from the earlier sections of the Brut narratives in which Corineus fights Gomagog, particularly that of the giant breaking three of the hero's ribs (*Roman de Brut* 1111–68; Mannyng, 1803–48); Wace and Manning, following Geoffrey of Monmouth (HRB, 165; X.3), note that the Mount on which Arthur encounters the giant is now called St Michael's Mount (*Roman de Brut* 11293; Mannyng, 12159), but in the *Morte Arthure* this place-name plays an important part in the action in Arthur's time and determines the King's approach to the episode as a whole.

giant whom he manages to stab, Kay and Bedivere's initial shock and horror are soon replaced by jokes about God's unlikely taste in saints (*MA* 1162–9). This is Christian comedy, and in this episode a clear opposition is established between Arthur, the Christian hero who is fighting as a representative of his people, and his monstrous, anti-Christian opponent, who rapes well-born women, eats children for breakfast, and collects the beards of kings (and thus poses an imperial threat too). More complex oppositions, and more complex ethical issues, are involved in Arthur's large-scale Christian-imperial venture against the Romans.

There is no doubt that great pains have been taken to legitimize the actions of the British side in their campaign against Rome in the *Morte Arthure*. Not only are the pagan affiliations of Lucius's allies reinforced and the Christian motivations of the British side developed, but also in the account of the continued campaign, after Lucius's death, the British appear to scrupulously abide by the laws of war as they besiege and fight against the Roman allies.[25] Yet if the representation of the British action in this narrative seems to have an exemplary cast, attention is drawn, at the same time, to problematic features of the campaign. The issues at stake in the antagonism between the British and the Romans do not fall into neat white and black patterns: the campaign has complex political and religious motivations and has evident Christian costs. The Romans themselves are not pagans; some of their allies are schismatics.[26] The

25 John Finlayson was one of the first critics to note the detailed interest in the 'laws of war' in the *Morte Arthure* in 'The Concept of the Hero in the *Morte Arthure*', *Chaucer und seine Zeit: Symposium für Walter C. Schirmer*, ed. by Arno Esch (Tubingen, 1967), pp. 249–74. More recently, Juliet Vale has considered how the concept of the law of arms features in the narrative (in general and specific ways) in 'Law and Diplomacy in the alliterative *Morte Arthure*', *Nottingham Medieval Studies* 23 (1979), 31–46. She concludes that 'By the standards of the laws of arms which the poet seems to have had in mind, Arthur is very far from the cruel and covetous tyrant that he has been held to be [by some modern critics]' (p. 39). Vale's conclusion has been supported by the more detailed discussion of Elizabeth Porter, 'Chaucer's Knight, the Alliterative *Morte Arthure* and Medieval Laws of War: a Reconsideration', *Nottingham Medieval Studies* 27 (1983), 56–78. Porter specifically argues against Finlayson's division of Arthur's Roman campaign into just/unjust sections and concludes that the martial encounters which follow Lucius's death are devised 'in part at least, to show Arthur as the ideal king and conqueror' (p. 72). References to more general studies of the notion of a 'just' war and the laws of war are cited in Porter's study.

26 Mary Hamel discusses the significance of the representation of Priamus and the Duchess of Lorraine as schismatics in 'The Christening of Sir Priamus in the Alliterative *Morte Arthure*', *Chaucer Review* 14 (1980), 298–312. Hamel argues that the Priamus episode presents a variation on the 'conversion of the infidel' topos which reflects a more complicated situation of opposition between Christians, which arises out of the split *between* the Eastern and Western churches. The fact that the symbol of the dragon is associated with both the British and Roman forces in the *Morte Arthure* is another example of the way

miseries caused by Arthur's campaign, the destruction of churches in Metz (*MA* 3036–43), the ravages of the British forces in Tuscany (*MA* 3150–61) are vividly described. Moreover, although Arthur may command his men to 'spare the spirituell' so that they might speed the better (*MA* 2414), the Pope is evidently oppressed by the British campaign (*MA* 3176–80). Arthur's proximity to Rome in the *Morte Arthure* heightens both the tensions, and the triumphs, of his enterprise. The problem of assessing the British campaign for Rome in general, and the actions of King Arthur in particular, are made evident in the dream vision sequence which precedes the crossing of paths between King Arthur and Sir Craddoke, a crusader and a pilgrim, both *en route* for Rome. The dream sequence, in fact, provides the pre-text for the crossing of the roads to Rome.[27]

When Arthur recounts his dream experience to his 'phylosophers' at Viterbo (*MA* 3226), he tells them how his dream began with a nightmare vision of wild animals menacing the king and lapping the blood of his knights (*MA* 3227–35); from here the king escapes to a *locus amoenus*, in which he meets a beautiful woman spinning a wheel (*MA* 3236–61). On the outer rim of the wheel are six kings who collectively and individually lament the heedlessness of their conduct on earth; two more kings are

in which their opposition cannot be represented in terms of a neat binary pattern (and again signals some innovations in the version of Arthurian history presented in the *Morte Arthure*). Mary Hamel comments on the use of dragon-symbolism in the text on pp. 46–50 of her edition.

27 There are no precedents for this second dream experience in the narratives of Geoffrey of Monmouth, Wace or Mannyng, though the composer of the *Morte Arthure* is not the first to contrive another dream sequence which might balance that which precedes Arthur's battle against the giant of Brittany (*HRB* 164; X.3). In Laȝamon's *Brut* a second dream sequence is inserted into the narrative which anticipates the news of Mordred's treachery and Arthur's return journey across the Channel. Hamel suggests that Laȝamon's narrative provided some inspiration for this sequence in the *Morte Arthure*, in addition to a wide range of other source texts, including the Vulgate *Mort Artu* and Dante. See the introduction to her edition, pp. 42–4, and 'The Dream of a King: The Alliterative *Morte Arthure* and Dante', *Chaucer Review* 14 (1980), 298–312. I am less convinced of the link between the *Morte Arthure* and Laȝamon's *Brut*: although the timing of the dreams is similar in both texts, the dreams themselves have quite different forms and functions. Whereas Arthur's dream in Laȝamon's *Brut* provides a vehicle for the mediation of unthinkable news and an opportunity for a meditation on the consequences of Mordred's crime, Arthur's dream in the *Morte Arthure* is much more concerned with the shaping of Arthurian history and how it may be assessed and interpreted. The fact that both dreams in the *Brut* and in the *Morte Arthure* make use of symbolic animals (in different ways) seems more likely to be the result of traditional conventions of dream representation than evidence of Laȝamon's influence on the *Morte Arthure*.

climbing up the wheel as they speak (*MA* 3262–337). Arthur himself is lifted up to the top seat on the wheel by the lady who claims credit for all his achievements, presents him with the symbols of worldly power, makes the trees bow down and offer their fruit to him and brings him wine to drink from a well (*MA* 3338–81). Then about midday she changes her mood, spins her wheel, and crushes Arthur under its rim (*MA* 3382–91); and Arthur awakes.

The philosopher who interprets Arthur's dream identifies the figures round the rim of the wheel of Fortune as members of the Nine Worthies—the heroic elite of all time composed of nine great figures from the Old Testament, classical, and New Testament ages, whose ranks Arthur is to join.[28] The notion of co-ordinating one of the most commonly stylised representations of the movement of history, the wheel of Fortune, with the motif of the Nine Worthies seems to have been the innovation of the *Morte Arthure* poet.[29] This compounding of the two motifs expands the temporal and moral frameworks of the narrative, but it also raises questions about which are the most appropriate 'patterns' to extract from Arthurian history, and which are the most appropriate terms in which it should be judged. Although the dream and its interpretation may appear to offer an insight into the 'prime mover(s)' behind Arthurian history, the episode is more puzzling on closer inspection. The problems may be illustrated, most simply, by considering the incompatible lessons which the philosopher draws from the King's dream experience. Three different readings of Arthur's dream can be identified in the philosopher's commentary, each of which imply a different view of Arthurian history: the philosopher tells Arthur how to save his soul; how his history will be remembered and celebrated for all time on earth; how his realm of Britain is under immediate threat.[30]

28 The best surveys of the motif of the Nine Worthies are by H. Schroeder, *Der Topos der Nine Worthies in Literatur und bildendur Kunst* (Göttingen, 1971) — see pp. 309–18 for a discussion of the *Morte Arthure*—and by K. J. Höltgen, 'Die "Nine Worthies"', *Anglia* 77 (1959), 279–309. Maurice Keen provides a brief history of the motif in *Chivalry* (New Haven and London, 1984), pp. 102–24. Mary Hamel discusses the motif and the possible use of a Middle English alliterative dream-vision poem, *The Parlement of the Thre Ages*, as a source text in her introduction, pp. 42–4.

29 See Hamel's discussion of this innovative configuration in her introduction, p. 43, and in 'The Dream of a King: The Alliterative *Morte Arthure* and Dante'.

30 My discussion of this dream sequence is much indebted to the work of Mary Hamel (especially 'The Dream of a King') and to Lee Patterson's important study, 'The historiography of romance and the Alliterative *Morte Arthure*', *Journal of Medieval and Renaissance Studies* 13 (1983), 1–32, which has been revised and reprinted as 'The History of Romance and the Alliterative *Morte Arthure*' in Patterson's book, *Negotiating the Past* (Madison, Wisconsin, 1987), pp. 197–230.

The lesson of the dream for Arthur's life as a Christian frames the philosopher's dream reading. The philosopher suggests that Arthur has been given a warning of his fall (which seems synonymous with his death); the imperative now is for Arthur to take heed of the warning, to repent of the sins he has inevitably committed as a king and conqueror; to do penance for them, and thus to prepare his soul for its after-life:

> Thow has schedde myche blode,   and schalkes distroyede,
> Sakeles, in cirquytrie,   in sere kynges landis.
> Schryfe the of thy schame   and schape for thyn ende!
> Thow has a schewynge, sir Kynge,   take kepe ȝif the lyke,
> For thow sall fersely fall   within fyve wynters.
> Fownde abbayes in Fraunce —   Þe froytez are theyn awen! /—
> Fore Froill and for [his] fernet,   and for thir ferse knyghttis
> That thowe fremydly in Fraunce   has faye beleuede.
> Take kepe ȝitte of oÞer kynges,   and kaste in thyne herte,
> That were conquerours kydde   and crownnede in erthe: . . .
> I rede thow rekkyn and reherse   vnresonable dedis,
> Ore the repenttes full rathe   al thi rewthe werkes;
> Mane, amende thy mode   or thow myshappen,
> And mekely aske mercy   for mede of thy saule! (3398–455)

From this moralized perspective Arthur appears as a kind of Everyman-figure who has been given a timely reminder of his mortality and must straighten his account before confronting his end.

Many of the recent readings of the *Morte Arthure* have tended to view the philosopher's statement that Arthur 'has schedde myche blode, and schalkes distroyede, | Sakeles, in cirquytrie, in sere kynges landis' (*MA* 3398–9) as the interpretative key to the causal sequence of the narrative: it is because Arthur has sinned that he falls.[31] There is more critical

31 Since the publication of William Matthews' study, *The Tragedy of Arthur* (Berkeley and Los Angeles, 1960) a critical orthodoxy has arisen amongst the modern, 'public', audience of the *Morte Arthure*: the most common line of argument, following Matthews, is that the *Morte Arthure* promotes a reading of Arthurian history in which Arthur's spiritual and moral degeneration, which is reflected in his ultimately 'unjust' war against Rome, is causally linked to his downfall. The continuing influence of Matthews' controversial (and contestable) reading of the poem on recent readers can be seen in the essay collection edited by Karl Heinz Goller, *The Alliterative Morte Arthure: A Reassessment of the Poem* (Cambridge, 1981), in which the 'tragedy of Arthur' seems to have been accepted as an interpretative premise by all the contributors (so the volume is rather less of a 'reassessment' than its title claims). For critics who have challenged the interpretative paradigm of Matthews, see J. Eadie, 'The Alliterative *Morte Arthure*: Structure and Meaning', *English Studies* 63 (1982), 1–12, and Lee Patterson's discussion (cited above, n. 30).

debate, however, about where to locate this 'sinning'. Is Arthur in this state from the beginning of his Roman campaign, or is this 'sinning' something which happens at a specific point in the campaign, perhaps when he goes too far along the road to Rome? In the moralising section of his commentary, however, the philosopher alludes to events which predate the *Morte Arthure* narrative (specifically Arthur's victory over Frollo, *MA* 3404–5): it appears that if Arthur has sinned, this is not simply as a consequence of his campaign in Germany and Italy, as Finlayson and Hamel have argued.[32]

The second lesson of the dream, paradoxically, is to confirm Arthur's membership of the trans-historical elite of the Nine Worthies and his everlasting fame. Although the philosopher begins by signalling the admonitory value of the collection of kings and conquerors arranged round the rim of the wheel, his remarks also suggest that membership of this group, and indeed Arthur's future fame, have a positive value:

> Forethy Fortune þe fetches to fulfill the nowmbrye,
> Alls nynne of þe nobileste namede in erthe.
> This sall in romance be redde with ryall knyghttes,
> Rekkenede and renownde with ryotous kynges,
> And demyd one Domesdaye for dedis of armes
> For þe doughtyeste þat euer was duelland in erthe—
> So many clerkis and kynges sall karpe of ȝoure dedis
> And kepe ȝoure conquestez in cronycle for euer! (3438–45)

The Doomsday reference suggests that ultimately Arthur's heroic achievements will be judged favourably. As Mary Hamel has pointed out, the philosopher's interpretation here appears to ignore the contents of the Worthies's laments, yet it also draws attention to a fundamental premise of the motif of the Nine Worthies. The motif is one which can be used both to undermine and yet to validate the idea of historical enterprise: the power of the Worthies as moral *exempla* (illustrating transience and mortality) paradoxically derives from their status as the most memorable figures of history, a status which is both proven and perpetuated by the writers of romances and chronicles. On one level, then, Arthur's

32 John Finlayson and Mary Hamel offer a refinement on Matthews' reading of the *Morte Arthure*: in their view the downturn in Arthur's moral and spiritual profile occurs only after he has defeated Lucius. See John Finlayson's argument in 'The Concept of the Hero in the *Morte Arthure*' for a brief summary of his views developed at length elsewhere, especially p. 265. For Hamel's discussion of the turning point in Arthur's campaign see her introduction, pp. 37–8, 42, and her more detailed exposition in 'The Dream of a King: The Alliterative *Morte Arthure* and Dante', esp. pp. 307–9.

membership of this group validates his history, for his story will be remembered, recalled, and reworked (as the *Morte Arthure* itself proves) for all future time.

The transhistorical perspective on Arthur's history gives a different dimension to the question of Arthur's 'after-life' which the philosopher had raised. But juxtaposed with these perspectives is a view of Arthurian history *in medias res*, for the dream also appears to contain a warning of the present demands on Arthur and the dangers affecting his realm. Arthur's opening vision of himself threatened by wild animals and lions lapping the blood of his knights is interpreted by the philosopher as a sign that Britain itself is under immediate threat:

> Bot the wolfes in the wode and the whilde bestes
> Are some wikkyd men that werrayes thy rewmes,
> Es entirde in thyn absence to werraye thy pople,
> And alyenys and ostes of vncouthe landis:
> Thow getis tydandis, I trowe, within ten dayes,
> That some torfere es tydde sen thow fro home turnede.
> (3446–51)

The philosopher's interpretation falls into three sections, then, according to the different temporal views which are taken on Arthurian history. But there is of course a fundamental link between these readings: Mordred's usurpation provides the circumstances in which Arthur is to meet his end (and the spiritual consequences of his life), which itself is to form part of his story for all time. Yet there are radical points of tension between the philosophical interpretation of the dream and the nature of the advice/warning/insight it provides for Arthur. How can Arthur withdraw, amend, repent, and respond to the imperative to act on Britain's behalf? As Lee Patterson has observed:

> If Arthur does 'amende [his] mode', as the philosopher enjoins, 'And mekely aske mercy for mede of his sawle' (3454–5), then who will free Britain from Mordred's barbarism, whose atrocities Cradoke is soon vividly to detail (3523–56)? . . . Participation in the historical world is simultaneously proscribed and required, both revealed as without value and imposed as a duty.[33]

The subject of Arthur's dream has been his history, but the difficulty of extracting *sens* from this *histoire* is demonstrated in the tensions between the dream and the interpretation, and from the tensions in the philosopher's dream reading itself. The interpretation of the dream has

33 'The Romance of History', p. 227.

created a kind of narrative hiatus since it has made action an ethical problem seemingly without resolution.

The resolution of the ethical and narrative problem is impressive: Arthur does not verbally reply to the impossible lessons of his philosopher, rather he dresses and walks away from the camp only to meet up with the pilgrim Sir Craddoke and, thereby, to confront the tensions of his history in a more direct way.[34] Arthur, the crusader for Rome, meets an exiled member of his own household on a pilgrimage to Rome and learns how Britain has fared in his absence. His plan to embark on a crusade for Jerusalem (*MA* 3212–17) is displaced by the necessity of saving Britain. The mysterious meeting between Arthur and Craddoke at the crossroads is represented in a way which recalls and restates the moral problems about Arthur's action which have been isolated in the dream episode, while it literally provides the means for the narrative to move forward. Arthur has taken the road to Rome as a crusader; he has undertaken a campaign of conquest for which he claims divine support and which he claims is in the service of God. The way in which the campaign is represented in the narrative supports the justice of its cause, to some extent, but also draws attention to its cost. Craddoke, in contrast, takes the road to Rome as an individual, private, gesture of penance. His action corresponds to the kind recommended by Arthur's philosopher in the lesson which frames his dream reading: withdraw, repent, amend. But if Craddoke's pilgrimage implicitly raises questions about the validity of Arthur's crusade, it also demonstrates that Arthur does not have the opportunity to turn aside from his public role in defending his land and his faith. The imperative is now to crusade for Britain:

. . . there es sir Childrike   a cheftayne holdyn,
That ilke cheualrous man;   he chargges thy pople.
They robbe thy religeous   and ravische thi nonnes,
And redy ryddis with his rowtte   to rawnsone þe pouere.
(3537–40)

34 George Keiser has noted the parallels between Arthur's preparations to meet the giant of St Michael's Mount (*MA* 900–19) and his 'dressing up' (*MA* 3456–65) before he walks off and unexpectedly meets Craddoke, but Keiser interprets Arthur's action as a sign of his refusal to submit to the philosopher's teaching. See 'The Theme of Justice in the Alliterative *Morte Arthure*', *Annuale Mediaevale* 16 (1975), 94–109, esp. p. 103. But the resonances of this scene may be more teasing than this. The writer seems to be playing on, and varying, the conventions of the arming motif in describing Arthur's dressing here. The arming motif usually signals the imminence of an epic encounter; but what is provided here is an epic encounter of an unusual kind. At St Michael's Mount, the King had donned martial gear to undertake a 'pilgrimage': in this episode he dons rich travelling gear and meets a pilgrim at the crossroads. The range of meanings in this scene is allowed to resonate: direct narratorial commentary, as such, is not provided.

The episode with Craddoke, then, both reformulates the moral problems of earthly achievement and Christian service posed by Arthur's dream, but also suggests a way in which Arthur's public action may be reconciled again with service of God: Arthur can rightly claim to be fighting for the faith in campaigning against Mordred.[35]

What happens in the rest of the narrative is partly epic commonplace: the fight against Mordred is one against the odds.[36] Yet, even in the those last bloody stages of Arthurian history, questions continue to be raised about the compatibility of heroic ethics with the ethics of those in governance and with the ethics of Christian conduct by the way the action is represented in this text. In the sequence which culminates in the death of Gawain, for example, a tension arises between the terms in which Gawain formulates his mission to attack Mordred's forces against the odds (which he represents as an experience of religious martyrdom for himself and his men—*MA* 3795–812), and the terms used to describe Gawain's death (in which it is represented as the result of a suicidal descent into a bestial, bloody frenzy—*MA* 3813–38). Characteristically, there is no moderating judgement on the scene in the narrator's voice, apart from the observation, 'Iche a wy may be warre be wreke of anoþer' (*MA* 3839). On the blood-soaked battlefield, Arthur asks God why he has not been destined to die so that his men might be saved (*MA* 4155–60). God does not reply. There are no miraculous interventions in this text which offer a final judgement on the action and either confirm or deny Arthur's claim to be acting in the service of God. Nor, characteristically, are any offered in the voice of the narrator. The final outcome, the victory over Mordred, may be interpreted as a providential one, but its great cost is evident too. The achievements of King Arthur are celebrated in the *Morte Arthure* at the same time as the resonant juxtaposition of episodes in this text draws

35 Although I am suggesting that here Craddoke's pilgrimage throws Arthur's crusading enterprise into relief, I am not implying, therefore, that pilgrimages and crusades are consequently to be interpreted as inherently incompatible activities (either within the boundaries of this text or outside it). Much crusading propaganda was concerned to prove the essential compatibility of these two modes of Christian errantry. Yet it seems to me that the narrative organisation of the *Morte Arthure* draws attention to the areas of contradiction, as well as compatibility, between making pilgrimages and crusades, as indeed to that between the ethics of individual chivalric endeavour and the codes of behaviour which are appropriate to those in governance. Elizabeth Porter discusses the topicality of crusading ideals in the late fourteenth century in 'Chaucer's Knight, the Alliterative *Morte Arthure* and the Medieval Laws of War: a Reconsideration', pp. 73–7. For a more general discussion of the secular and religious ethics of chivalry see Maurice Keen, 'Chivalry, the Church, and the Crusade', *Chivalry,* pp. 44–63.

36 Unlike the Galfredian narratives, Arthur's army is greatly outnumbered by Mordred's forces in the *Morte Arthure* and this is one of several features of the narrative which seems to have been inspired by the Vulgate *Mort Artu*, as Hamel observes in her notes to lines 4031–2.

attention to the complications, compromises, and costly consequences of this sequence of British history.

III

Various kinds of history writing are brought together in the *Morte Arthure*: history writing as a record of past deeds; history writing as an act of commemoration, a celebration of achievements of the past for the present; history writing as an exemplary and moralising activity in which actions of the past may be used as a guide to determine actions in the present, in which the actions of the past may be used as a moralising mirror that enables writers and audiences to play God and see the connections between beginnings and ends; history writing as the occasion for reflection on the opaque nature of any higher designs when judged from a mundane perspective. In the *Morte Arthure*, as Lee Patterson has so eloquently argued, the encounter with the past becomes a matter of negotiation. In this narrative, the process by which figures from the past are used to measure the accomplishments of more recent figures from the near-present is inverted.[37] Whereas in Pierre de Langtoft's narrative, for example, the representation of Edward I is clearly modelled on that of King Arthur, or in Froissart's narrative Edward III is compared with King Arthur, topical historical and cultural resonances are built into the text of Arthurian history itself in the *Morte Arthure*.[38] In this narrative Arthurian history is used

37 As Maurice Keen has observed, the 'references to past heroes put more recent deeds and enterprises into perspective, showing what was important and what was worthy of being remembered' ('Chivalry, heralds, and history', *The Writing of History in the Middle Ages*, edd. R.H.C. Davis and J.M. Wallace Hadrill (London, 1981), pp. 393–414, at 400). Diane Tyson surveys the use of the figure of Arthur as a comparative measure in French vernacular historiography in 'King Arthur as a Literary Device in French Vernacular History Writing in the Fourteenth Century', *Bulletin Bibliographique de la Société Internationale Arthurienne* 33 (1981), 237–57.

38 Larry Benson and Mary Hamel have considerably refined the discussion of the range of topical allusions in the *Morte Arthure* in their respective articles on 'The Date of the Alliterative *Morte Arthure*' (see above, n. 2), and 'The Christening of Sir Priamus' (n. 26). See also the articles by Juliet Vale and Elizabeth Porter listed above (n. 25). But if there is general critical consensus on the topical quality of this reworking of Arthurian history, there is much less sense of agreement on the specific relations between this text and fourteenth-century history. At various stages in the modern critical reception of the *Morte Arthure*, it has been suggested that Arthur's representation recalls Edward III, the Black Prince, and Henry IV. John Finlayson's contribution to this issue in '*Morte Arthure*: the Date and a Source for a Contemporary Reference', *Speculum* 42 (1967), 624–38, suggests how complex the levels of temporal

as a site for investigating the practice of history making, and for exploring how the ethics of chivalry and those of Christianity may be both mutually enhancing and at odds; and it does so, in part, by exploiting the complicated temporal perspectives of its inherited material: in encountering his antagonists on his relatively modern road to Rome, King Arthur is confronting twelfth-century images of pagans and representations of fourteenth-century allies of the Holy Roman Empire too.[39] Allusions to some of the topical religious and political issues of the late fourteenth century (including those of crusading ethics themselves) are refracted through the narrative of Arthur's war. The result is a narrative which, by considering the implications of the different routes to Rome, addresses the question of how deeds of 'elders of alde tym' (*MA* 13) may be 'Plesande and profitabill to the pople þat them heres' (*MA* 11), as the narrator prays in the introductory sections of the text.

We have little information about the author of the *Morte Arthure*, but rather more about the scribe, and by implication one of the readers, of the single extant copy of the text, Robert Thornton.[40] From

layering might be in this narrative. Arguing against William Matthews' influential assertion of a synchronous relationship between the events of Edward III's reign and the composition of the *Morte Arthure*, Finlayson suggests that aura of Edwardian influence in the text might derive from the composer's use of a historical narrative such as Chandos Herald's *Vie de Prince Noir*. Arthurian history is thus made more topical by being associated with a more recent 'Golden Age'.

39 As Mary Hamel observes, 'the poet, writing in about the year 1400, tells a story that occurred in "Arthurian times", that is in the late fifth and sixth century; his major source for those times was the twelfth-century account of Geoffrey of Monmouth and the French translation of Wace. Thus Arthur's forces [in the *Morte Arthure*] fight not only the pagan Saxons and Picts that they faced in history, but also the twelfth-century Saracens (e.g. the kings of Syria and Libya) of Geoffrey's version, allied with the Roman army of Lucius. The Duke of Lorraine's army, even more contemporary, is composed primarily of elements from the Holy Roman Empire: Saxons, Westphalians, Lombards, Prussians, men of Lorraine and of Dauphiné' ('The Christening of Sir Priamus', p. 200).

40 Mary Hamel builds up a profile of the composer of the text from evidence provided by its evident interests and sources on pp. 59–62 of the introduction to her edition. Evidently its writer had an informed acquaintance with the politics of Milan in the late fourteenth century (see Larry Benson's study, 'The Date of the Alliterative *Morte Arthure*') and, according to Juliet Vale, 'the poet's expertise in legal and diplomatic aspects of current military practice is an indication of the milieu in which we should seek him' ('Law and Diplomacy in the Alliterative *Morte Arthure*', p. 31). Hamel's profile broadly accords with Elizabeth Salter's account of the probable context for the production of poems such as the *Morte Arthure* and the works of the Gawain poet. Such poems, in Salter's view, 'tell us of the likely interaction of two things: an aristocracy able to offer conditions and material for the labour of poets, and a class of authors, possibly of mobile class

this, and other limited signs of the poem's later readers, we can begin to reconstruct some image of the public of the *Morte Arthure* in the fifteenth century, although hardly enough to build up a picture of the receptive context of this work in any detail. However, if it is also possible to build an image of the public of the *Morte Arthure* from an analysis of the text's distinctive interests and concerns, then it seems to me that it shares certain of the features which Anne Middleton has identified in the audience and in the public of *Piers Plowman*.[41] Middleton has noted how often copies of *Piers Plowman* are found in manuscript collections which also contain historiographical narratives of various kinds, on classical and Christian subjects and copies of compendia of works of religious instruction too. Middleton suggests that from the contextual associations of *Piers Plowman* 'one may see its readers' sense of the mode of its compendiousness, and its utility. It makes particularly heavy demands on its readers' ethical reflection upon, and engagement with, contemporary communal life, on what one may call their practical historical imaginations'.[42] Middleton also suggests that this capacity is not only exercised by reading *Piers Plowman*, but also by the reading of 'historical romance in most of its major late medieval aspects'.[43] Middleton's analysis of how such narratives engage this capacity is worth quoting in some detail, since it seems so relevant to the kind of engagement required by the version of Arthurian history presented in the *Morte Arthure*. In Middleton's view:

origin, but perhaps also of minor gentry status, in the employ of, or closely associated with, the aristocracy' (*Fourteenth-Century English Poetry: Contexts and Readings* (Oxford, 1983), pp. 45–6). Angus McIntosh analyses the eastern Lincolnshire provenance of Robert Thornton's exempla in 'The Textual Transmission of the Alliterative *Morte Arthure*', *English and Medieval Studies Presented to J.R.R. Tolkein*, edd. Norman Davis and C.L. Wrenn (London, 1962), pp. 231–40. References to the detailed studies on the work and milieu of Robert Thornton are listed above in n. 2. Other 'readers' of the *Morte Arthure* include the composer of the *Awntyrs off Arthure*, possibly John Hardyng, and certainly Sir Thomas Malory.

41 Anne Middleton, 'The Audience and Public of *Piers Plowman*' *Middle English Alliterative Poetry and Its Literary Background*, ed. David Lawton (Woodbridge, 1982), pp. 101–23, at 101–2. All further references to this essay will be cited by page number in my text. Middleton works with a distinction between the 'audience' of a work (the historically documented consumers or owners of the text) and its 'public' (that is the receptive context signalled by the text itself), although she recognises that the distinction is a difficult one to maintain (and, indeed, uses the term 'readers' in a way which elides any differentiation between the two categories). Jutta Wurster uses a similar distinction in 'The Audience' (*The Alliterative Morte Arthure: A Reassessment of the Poem*, ed. K. H. Goller, pp. 44–56), but in comparison Middleton's essay seems much more suggestive.

42 *Ibid.*, p. 109.

43 *Ibid.*

> These narratives comprise a kind of mythography of rule, a legendary for 'possessioners', lay and ecclesiastical. Whether at the level of catechetical dialogue (between ruler and philosopher, prophet and unjust judge, Saracen or pagan king and apostle) or war between the traditional culture-bearing powers of the West and the opposing culture it will in the long process of time supplant (Greece and Troy, Rome and Jerusalem), these works present in a compendious historical mirror man's confrontations with spiritual dangers, and the rationale of large communal enterprises. They do so for the benefit, and from the viewpoint, of those who are situated to reflect on these enterprises and their consequences: the nobles, knights, burgesses and clerics who advised, judged, acted in them by virtue of 'possessioun'—their responsibilities and powers devolve from what they hold and from whom . . . For a significant part of its early audience whose testimony survives, *Piers* belongs amongst works in which the quest for salvation and the examination of the foundations of possession and authority were mutually metonymic.[44]

The *Morte Arthure* is not amongst the works which form part of the manuscript context of *Piers Plowman*, although there is some overlap between some of the subject material of the narratives in the Thornton anthologies and those found in manuscripts of *Piers Plowman*.[45] But in all other respects the distinctive interests and concerns of this alliterative poem would fit those Middleton identifies in *Piers Plowman* and the his-

44 *Ibid.*, pp. 109–10.

45 The *Siege of Jerusalem* is included in the London Thornton manuscript and appears in two other manuscripts which also contain copies of *Piers Plowman*; it appears with a copy of a B-text in Huntingdon (Calif.), Huntingdon Library 128, and with a copy of the C-text in Oxford, Bodleian Library 1059 (Land Misc. 656). Narratives about Troy and Alexander are also found in manuscripts containing copies of *Piers Plowman*: the 'holster book', London, Lincoln's Inn Library, Hale 150, contains a copy of the *Siege of Troy, Arthour and Merlin, Kyng Alisaunder*, and an A-text of *Piers Plowman* (see Middleton, p. 103); in the 'Liber Glastoniensis' (Cambridge, University Library, Dd 1. 17), copies of many important Latin insular historiographical texts (including material from Henry of Huntingdon and a copy of the *Historia Regum Britannie*), a copy of the Pseudo-Turpin life of Charlemagne, and Guido de Columnis's *Historia Destructionis Troiae* (among other texts), precede a copy of the B-text. It seems preferable to call such texts as the *Siege of Troy*, *Kyng Alisaunder*, the *Siege of Jerusalem* vernacular historical narratives rather than historical romances since they do not exhibit the structural pattern of a romance narrative (such as *Sir Gawain and the Green Knight* or *Sir Percyvelle of Galles*); similarly, although the *Morte Arthure* contains certain episodes which are structured in ways which recall those of romances (notably Arthur's confrontation with the giant of St Michael's Mount and Gawain's encounter with Priamus), this narrative is not structured overall as a romance.

torical romances and narratives which provide its manuscript context. The *Morte Arthure* offers an excellent example of a text which questions whether, and how far, the quest for an empire is compatible with that for salvation. Indeed, the range of references encoded in the text of the *Morte Arthure* would suggest that the issues raised by this narrative have an important topical appeal for the 'possessioners' amongst its public and would, indeed, exercise their practical historical imaginations.

This account of the narrative traditions which take Arthur towards Rome is far from complete: I have simply tried to track some of the stages in the depiction of Arthur's journey in Geoffrey of Monmouth's version of British history and in the *Morte Arthure*, and to suggest some of the implications of the meeting between King Arthur and Craddoke in this later text. But the Middle English poem is not the last stage of the history of Arthur's journey to Rome. The next obvious step would be to consider Thomas Malory's fifteenth-century reworking of the *Morte Arthure* in his epic prose compilation of Arthurian narrative. In Malory's text, at a relatively early stage in Arthurian history, Arthur actually reaches Rome and is crowned Emperor.[46] In Malory's text, however, there is no crossing of paths between pilgrim and crusader; Arthur succeeds as an imperial conqueror and his success in Rome is not the prelude to his final campaign against Mordred, but the beginning of a world of Arthurian adventure in which the ethics of action continue to be investigated through the actions of individual knights and their stories. At this stage in Malory's narrative, there is but one road to Rome.

46 See the text and notes of 'The Tale of the Noble King Arthur and the Emperor Lucius' in *The Works of Sir Thomas Malory*, ed. E. Vinaver, 3rd ed. rev. P.J.C. Field, 3 vols., Oxford, 1990. Vinaver argues that 'Malory altered his source so as to make Arthur's journey across the Continent resemble Henry V's itinerary' (p. 1368). Mary Hamel provides the text of this 'Tale' in her edition of the *Morte Arthure* and also, unlike previous editors of the alliterative poem, makes textual emendations on the basis of some of the readings in the Winchester manuscript. See pp. 4–14 of her edition for her discussion of the importance of the Winchester version of the narrative. The 'Tale' is reproduced as Book V in Caxton's edition of Malory's narrative. As has long been recognised, Caxton's version is a substantially revised version of Malory's text (as represented in the Winchester manuscript). For a comparative discussion of the Caxton and Winchester versions, and the implications for the emendation of the text of the *Morte Arthure*, see E. V. Gordon and Eugene Vinaver, 'New Light on the Text of the Alliterative *Morte Arthure*', *Medium Aevum* 6 (1937), 81–98. Malory, though, is not the first to celebrate Arthur's coronation in Rome: this seems to be John Hardyng's innovation in his *Chronicle*, ed. Henry Ellis (London, 1812), which, in its first version, dates from *c.*1440–57. For a recent discussion of Hardyng's *Chronicle* and a survey of Hardyng bibliography to date, see Edward Donald Kennedy in *A Manual of Writings in Middle English 1050–1500*, ed. A.E. Harting, in progress (New Haven, 1967–), VIII, 2644–7, 2836–45.

Burlesque Romance and the Bourgeoisie

DAVID SCOTT-MACNAB

I

We can be reasonably certain that the mediaeval English romances, in their heyday, were produced for audiences that were both noble and courtly. Some of the later romances, however, contain features that have been taken to suggest that audiences of the genre were becoming less courtly than they had been before. In the late fourteenth-century *Gamelyn*,[1] for instance, there are traces of an apparent lowering of minstrel respect in the apostrophe, 'Litheþ, and lestneþ and holdeþ ȝoure tonge, | And ȝe shul heere gamen of Gamelyn þe ȝonge' (341–2), which is very similar to one of the calls imitated by Chaucer in his *Tale of Sir Thopas*, 'Now holde youre mouth, *par charitee*, | Bothe knyght and lady free' (*CT*, VII.891–2).[2] Details such as these are frequently cited as evidence for the theory that some literature, from about the middle of the fourteenth century, was being produced for a new class of literary consumer: the bourgeois urbanite. Quite why a middle-class audience, rather than any other, should tolerate minstrel impertinence is never explained. Nevertheless, the idea remains tenacious, and one of its corollaries is the belief that burlesques of romance and other chivalric literature, particularly those of the fifteenth century, reflect the impatience of the urban middle classes with what they perceived to be the anachronisms of chivalry in both literature and reality. The well-known *Tournament of Tottenham* (hereafter *Tottenham*) has for some time now been cited as evidence of such attitudes, its absurd peasant tournament offered as proof that the poem ridicules both chivalry and peasantry, so that 'about the only people who must have laughed at it were medieval urbanites'.[3]

But there are several problems with this view. In the first place, although there can be no cause for doubting that a class of urban-

1 *Middle English Metrical Romances*, edd. Walter Hoyt French and Charles Brockway Hales, 2 vols. (New York, 1930, rept. 1964), I, 209–35.

2 *The Riverside Chaucer*, 3rd ed., ed. Larry D. Benson, Oxford, 1988. On romance audiences see A.C. Baugh, 'The Middle English romance: some questions of creation, presentation, and preservation', *Speculum* 42 (1967), 1-31, at 10–18).

3 *Middle English Verse Romances*, ed. Donald B. Sands (New York, 1966), p. 314; see also L.C. Ramsey, *Chivalric Romances* (Bloomington, 1983), p. 214; G.F. Jones, 'The tournaments of Tottenham and Lappenhausen', *PMLA* 66 (1951), 1123–40.

bourgeois reader was developing and growing throughout the later Middle Ages, we possess little substantive empirical evidence about its literary consumption and tastes. Surviving records indicate that the libraries of fifteenth-century merchants and other wealthy townspeople tended, in general, to be quite small, and both conventional and devotional in their contents. Equally orthodox are the books known or suspected to have been commissioned or patronised by wealthy and influential merchants.[4] In contrast, no burlesque romance, or anything like it, is documented as having been enjoyed, commissioned, or owned by the medieval English bourgeoisie. Nor is there good reason to suppose that contempt for chivalry and romance is necessarily characteristic of the middle classes, a group who, after all, were well known for their aspirations to gentility, and from whose ranks came Caxton himself—a burgess with strong personal belief in the ethos of chivalry.[5]

In fact, most of the evidence that is submitted for seeing the burlesque romances as satires for the amusement of middle-class urbanites is internal to these works, and, as I intend to show, leads to this interpretation only as a consequence of two fundamental mistakes. The first relates to the basic issue of how to read burlesque, and how to interpret what John Burrow calls the 'direction' of the comedy of any given burlesque: that is, what it is 'aimed' at.[6] For what has happened is that the vehicle of the comedy of burlesque romance has been confused with its 'targets', and the vehicle misidentified *as* the target. In more concrete terms, the worlds of chivalry and romance, which provide the machinery for the comedy of these works, have been mistakenly judged to be the objects of their ridicule. Yet, underlying this misapprehension, there is an even more serious problem in the treatment of burlesque as if it were satire. I shall return to this point later, observing for the present that conflation of the two genres not only impoverishes our perception of literary variety, but imposes a wearisome burden on burlesque generally, and on medieval burlesque in particular. For burlesque is a form of comedy in which the desire to provoke amusement is the primary goal, and even, sometimes, an end in itself. Some critics seem reluctant to accept this and force burlesque to do more serious work, usually of a satirical nature, and often with significant socio-

4 See S.L. Thrupp, *The Merchant Class of Medieval London* (Chicago, 1962), pp. 161–3, 247–9; V.J. Scattergood, 'Literary culture at the court of Richard II', *English Court Culture in the Later Middle Ages* edd. V.J. Scattergood and J.W. Sherborne (London, 1983), pp. 29–43, at 42–3; N.F. Blake, *Caxton and his World* (London, 1969), pp. 87–8, 90–7.

5 See *Caxton's Book of the Ordre of Chyualry*, ed. A.T.P. Byles, London, 1926, (Early English Text Society 168), pp. xxxviii–ix, 121–4; Blake, *Caxton*, pp. 64–78, 129; Thrupp, *Merchant Class*, pp. 234 ff.

6 J.A. Burrow, 'Chaucer's *Sir Thopas* and *La Prise de Nuevile*', *Yearbook of English Studies* 14 (1984), 44–55, at 48.

historical implications (such as providing evidence of middle-class contempt for old, heroic values). There is perhaps an element of critical *apologia* here: for broad or low comedy may be made more reputable and appears to have more consequence if it can be shown to contain some serious matter.

But critical motivation is tangential to my main point, which is that the burlesque romances of the fifteenth century need to be delivered from widely accepted interpretations that deny them their quintessential qualities as burlesques and compel their comedy to operate in quite the wrong direction. (Many of the points I have made and shall make apply with equal force to medieval English burlesque generally, but restrictions of space constrain me to treating fifteenth-century burlesque romance as a special case in point.) I therefore propose to examine three burlesque romances, rivals to their serious compatriot and approximate contemporary, Malory's *Le Morte Darthur*. *Tottenham* is perhaps the best known of them, but the other two—*The Hunting of the Hare* (hereafter *Hunting*) and *The Felon Sew* ('sow')—deserve to be equally well known.

These three poems form rather a disparate group; they represent a variety of burlesque techniques, and although they are all deeply dependent on serious literary models, they vary markedly in the explicitness with which they allude to them. Nevertheless, they comprise a useful group in that each poem draws on, and makes play with, a different, prominent theme in chivalric literature: tourneying, hunting, and confronting a major animal adversary. These themes of chivalric endeavour provide what I have called the 'vehicle' of the comedy in these poems; they supply and sustain the means of making a joke, but without themselves being derided or belittled. (Which is not to say that the vehicle of comedy cannot also be its object; only that in these poems it is not.) In spite of their differences, *Tottenham*, *Hunting* and *The Felon Sew* are mutually revealing and provide a combined testimony that I believe contradicts much received opinion regarding burlesque romance. Rather than showing middle-class contempt, these poems are, I shall argue, unlikely to have been intended for the amusement of any groups other than the nobility and aristocracy, the devotees of chivalry, and the appreciators of romance.

II

I shall open this discussion with *The Felon Sew*, a late fifteenth-century burlesque written in the familiar tail-rhyme stanzas of the popular romances.[7] The poem is a sustained mock-heroic parody (in the widest,

7 All references are to the critical edition by G.H. Cowling, 'The Felon Sew', *Essays and Studies* 8 (1922), 70–89.

most neutral sense of the term: that of calculated, comic imitation), based on the romance theme of knightly combat with a fearsome animal. Everything about it suggests the work of a highly literate author, who may have had in mind parts of *The Avowing of Arthur*, as John Robson first suggested.[8] However, no individual model is really necessary because the theme of valiant battle with an animal, especially a boar, is so common in mediaeval romance.[9]

The opening three stanzas present the grand, heroic style and tone which are sustained throughout the poem:

> Ye men that will of Aunters mene
> That lately in this Land hath bene,
>   Of one I will you tell;
> Of a Sew at was Sea Strang —
> Alas at ever She lived Sea Lang,
>   For Fell folke did She wheell. (1–6)

There is a possible note of discord in the statement that the poem's subject, its monster, is a sow (4), but this is easily overlooked amid all the grandiose rhetoric, which continues to assert its serious purpose by observing that: 'She was mare then other three, | The Griesliest Beast at ever might be, | Her Head was great and Graye' (7–9). With stanza four, however, the poet reveals that the whole enterprise is actually mock-heroic by announcing that the sow was really a farmyard animal which, 'Ralph of Rokeby with full good will, | The friers of Richmond gave her till | Full well to gar them fare' (19–21).

The Felon Sew thus employs the familiar burlesque device of structural incongruity between manner and matter: it uses high, epic-heroic style and the well-established 'fierce-animal' theme to describe the low world of farmyard butchery, and makes this even more amusing by having events go disastrously wrong for the butchers. For the felonious sow has no intention of cooperating in her own slaughter and immediately sets about routing Friar Middleton and the 'Wight men two' (25) who arrive to collect her for the friary. The fray is described in appropriately heroic terms, with the friar soon believing that the sow is a fiend of Hell, whom he must command '. . . to go againe | Where thou was wont to Dwell' (80–1); though neither this injunction nor John's Gospel have any effect: 'The Sew

8 *Three Early English Metrical Romances*, ed. J. Robson, London, 1842 (Camden Society 18), pp. 105–10. C. Brown and R.H. Robbins are certainly mistaken when they suggest that *The Felon Sew* is a parody of *The Awntyrs off Arthure*: (*The Index of Middle English Verse* (New York, 1943), No. 4252).

9 See M. Thiébaux, 'The mouth of the boar as a symbol in medieval literature', *Romance Philology* 22 (1969), 281–99, at 287–91.

Sho would not Latin heare, | But only loked at the Freer, | That blenked all his Blee' (85–7).

The unhappy friars then summon two ostensibly professional warriors, 'Gilbert Griffins Son' and 'a Bastard Son of Spaine' (160–8), to despatch the sow. They solemnly pledge themselves to their task and in return receive promises that if they should die in their duty the friars and all their successors should sing masses for them 'Till Doomesday' (166–80). Heroic death at first seems quite likely because, as in the first confrontation, the sow behaves exactly as her more famous romance counterparts would do, roaring, snapping swords and shields, and even threatening Adonis' fate: 'Sho would have riven his privy geare . . .' (199). In the final show-down, romance and epic hyperbole are taken to their limits in the account of Gilbert's struggle:

> He Strave so Stiffely in that Stour,
> That thorough all his rich armore,
> The Blood ran out at Last.
> Then Gilbert grieved was Sea Seare,
> That he rave off both Hide and Hayre,
> The flesh came fro the Beane. (208–13)

This is all the more ridiculous because between these two engagements the sow had returned home to be fed as a meek farmyard animal by her mistress (124–9). Inevitably, the warriors achieve their conquest and deliver the 'Beast of prise' (224) to the friars, who merrily sing *Te Deum* in gratitude, leaving the poet to praise this success in the best romance tradition: 'There did man never yet more manly, | Knight Marcus nor yet Sir Guye, | Nor Gother or Gawaine' (226–8).

Lines such as these affirm time and again that literary models and themes provide the poem with much of its material. Other material—the action itself—may have been furnished by historical events, as was suggested by Ralph Rokeby, the poem's first known scribe and putative grandson of the 'Ralph of Rokeby' of line 19.[10] Rokeby surmises that *The Felon Sew* deals with events in his grandfather's day and, interestingly, rejects an ancient allegorical interpretation by 'Some Silly Paraphrasting Frier of Newburgh' that the sow represents lechery and Rokeby senior the Church.[11] The younger Rokeby's historical conjecture seems both plausible and likely, and may usefully account for some of the poem's eccentric details (e.g. 49–50, 124–6) and its consistent use of highly

10 R. Rokeby, *Œconomia Rokebiorum*, ed. A.W.C. Hallen, *Northern Notes and Queries*, 1, Supplement (1887), 13, 17. On the history of this text see Cowling, 'The Felon Sew', pp. 71–3.

11 Rokeby, *Œconomia*, p. 17.

specific place- and personal names, from which it derives a strong sense of historical occasion. If the heroes were in reality a couple of known butchers or farmhands who had been sent to collar a miscreant sow, their depiction as valiant knights must have seemed an excellent joke when the poem was composed. Unfortunately, such tantalising possibilities cannot lead very far: apart from Rokeby himself, we now have no evidence as to who or what the various characters in the poem might have been. The most concrete material we have to work with are the poem's essential features and events—among them, the fearsome animal, its ritual exorcism, descriptions of the heroes, the ceremonies for indenture to military service, and the priestly promises of prayers should the fighters fail and die. These are all respectable themes in serious romance literature, and are here undermined by the single, simple fact that the hysteria and chaos are caused, not by a Calydonian monster, but by a misbehaved sow which was bred and reared for the table.

The fact that these themes are used thus for humorous effect is taken by Robert Kindrick as proof that *The Felon Sew* is an 'outstanding' example of what he calls 'anti-romance'; that is, a tale that 'use[s] romance conventions for the purposes of satire'—by which he means an 'attack' on romance.[12] Interestingly, Kindrick proffers this interpretation in contradiction of any view of the poem as a satire on chivalry, knighthood, or feudalism. However, there is little point in examining Kindrick's argument in detail because its analysis and terms of reference are so shallow, and many of its statements so absurd, that little would be gained.[13] Still, the general tenor of Kindrick's view of the poem needs to be tackled because it represents an approach to burlesque in general, and late medieval burlesque in particular, which is both widespread and, as I have argued, essentially misguided.

In the first place, this view evinces the fundamental mistake, already briefly discussed, of classifying burlesque as satire. The two genres are not the same, and the distinction between them is an important one that deserves emphasising. For upon it depends our perception and understanding of crucial issues of motivation, intention, method, and tone. Of course, there is the added complication of the appropriateness of the term *satire* to literature of this period, since the very notion of medieval satire is itself deeply problematic. As R.H. Robbins has observed, 'Of what may be

12 R.L. Kindrick, 'The beast of great renown: anti-chivalric satire and anti-romance in *The Felon Sew*', *Satire Newsletter* 10 (1973), 6–11, at 6.

13 Kindrick, for example, confuses Rokeby, the scribe, with the poet (*ibid.*, p. 7); he believes that the tail-rhyme stanza indicates 'satire', so that 'the meter establishes humor by incongruous contrast with the pompous tone' (*ibid.*); and he pursues an absurd analogy between *The Felon Sew* and *The Awntyrs of Arthur*, reasoning that, 'The battle between the friars and the sow would then be a parody of the appearance of the ghost of Guinevere's mother . . . ' (*ibid.*, p. 10).

called satire in the limited sense of the term, there is little in English before the sixteenth century. Yet extant from the fourteenth century are a number of English writings that deal with contemporary diseases, abuses, or ill conduct with an ultimate objective of correction.'[14] Such writings are, of course, properly classified as 'complaint', which *The Felon Sew* indubitably is not. Medieval 'satirical' complaint is generally little given to expressing humour or to using comic devices.[15] By contrast, the overriding geniality and comical wit of *The Felon Sew* are unmistakable and speak across the centuries, emphasising that the poem is also not satire 'in the limited sense of the term'. Burlesque, as I have suggested, is characterised by having as its principal goal the intention to provoke amusement. Which is not to say that entertainment need be the *only* aim of burlesque (though it often is), merely its foremost aim. Consequently, a burlesque may legitimately seek to deflate seriousness, even to mock some 'target', by way of its humour. But it will not employ humour for some *other* leading purpose, such as heaping ridicule, or casting irony or censure; such intentions belong, not to burlesque, but to travesty or satire, or something of that nature. The distinction may depend on little more than a subtle variation of tone, but is no less worthwhile for that.

It is difficult to believe that anyone reading *The Felon Sew* could doubt that it is motivated by anything other than a light-hearted and essentially good-natured sense of fun. Its jocularity emerges readily as its primary intention, rather than as something tacked on to some other, more serious, or mocking, purpose. And this highlights Kindrick's second mistake, which is to confuse the device(s) or means used for creating humour with the object(s) or 'targets' of that humour. In *The Felon Sew*, the device used is that of mock-heroic, structural incongruity (high style for a low world); the objects of its comedy are the events (and, if Rokeby junior is correct, the characters) it describes. But there is nothing in this poem to indicate that the heroic literature it uses for showing up the absurdity of its events is itself the butt of any joke. The themes and formulae of serious literary models are certainly used in a ludicrous manner, but only in terms of their application to an inappropriate subject. And it is important to see that their being used for a ridiculous purpose need not—and here, does not—mean that they are themselves made ridiculous.

It is too easy to assume that everything that appears in a burlesque is the object of derision. On the other hand, suggesting refinements of interpretation at this distance in time is a tricky business. Few things are as

14 R.H. Robbins in *A Manual of the Writings in Middle English, 1050–1500*, ed. A.E. Harting, in progress (New Haven, 1967–), V, 1432.

15 See J. Peter, *Complaint and Satire in Early English Literature* (Oxford, 1956), pp. 1–13.

difficult to gauge as the humour of a past age; even modern jokes can lose their nuances within a few months or miles of composition. Nevertheless, I suggest that there needs to be some definite sign that the high world of romance and epic-heroic endeavour is derided—something more than merely its association with the low world of the poem's events. John Burrow has dealt with precisely this issue in his comparative analysis of the thirteenth-century French burlesque *La Prise de Nuevile* and Chaucer's *Sir Thopas*.[16] His method and conclusions are immensely valuable, for he shows convincingly how in *La Prise*, the high world of the *chanson de geste* remains inviolate while being used to deride the low world of Flemish cloth-workers and would-be *chevaliers*; and how in *Sir Thopas*, Chaucer deliberately imitates, comically exaggerates, and disfigures many features of the style and diction of the popular romances precisely in order to make fun of their general style and methods of versification.

Burrow's criteria can be equally well applied to *The Felon Sew*, which, like *La Prise*, derives its comedy from essentially the same device of incongruity between contrasting elements, and which similarly shows no signs of stylistic 'cacology' (as occurs in *Sir Thopas*) or anything else that would betray mockery of the high world of literature. The heroic themes and formulae that appear in *The Felon Sew* are certainly used tongue-in-cheek, as is necessary for the mock-heroic technique, but they are not otherwise exaggerated or disfigured. And this, it should be seen, accentuates the disparity between high and low worlds, and so highlights the poem's comedy of incongruity. No motive is needed for such comedy, though perhaps it was inspired by recent events on the Rokeby estate. Either way, the mock-heroic method does not of itself necessarily represent derision of its literary sources, and neither do other forms of 'parody'. Ezra Pound's *Winter is icummen in*, for example, imitates its serious model for comic effect without debunking, sending-up, or criticising it.

The argument so far has been rather abstract, at least partly because Kindrick makes no attempt to explain for whom the poem, as an attack on romance, might have been written, or in what social or intellectual climate it might have been inspired. These matters have, however, been discussed by G.F. Jones in relation to *Tottenham*, which he interprets in much the same way as Kindrick does *The Felon Sew*. So it is to *Tottenham* that I shall now turn.

III

Like most burlesque, *The Tournament of Tottenham* relies on a simple plot. Amid the merriment of a festival at Tottenham, Perkyn the Potter

16 'Chaucer's *Sir Thopas*', pp. 48–55.

asks Randolf the Reeve whom he considers most worthy to marry his daughter, Tyb. Randolf quells the hubbub of rival claims that immediately ensues by asserting that Tyb will marry the victor of a tournament to be held a week hence. The prospective suitors prepare their 'armour', and on the appointed day ride to battle taunting each other with boasts and vows of success. They then fight with gusto until Perkyn triumphs and wins the prize. The fallen are dragged home (many by their wives!), but reappear at the wedding feast which reunites the embattled community.

The mainspring of *Tottenham's* action—the 'tournament' for discovering a meritorious husband for Tyb—is clearly inspired by the romance tournament, such as we find in *Ipomadon* and *Guy of Warwick*, called for the purpose of finding the worthiest suitor for a lady.[17] In fact, the world of chivalric romance suffuses the poem; it can be seen in numerous details, such as the accounts of the peasants' armour, crests, and boasts, and it is immediately and explicitly evoked in the flourish of the poem's opening lines:

> Of all þes kene conquerours to carpe it were kynde:
> Of fele feȝtyng-folk ferly we fynde;
> The Turnament of Totenham haue we in mynde:
> It were harme syche hardynes were holden byhynde,
> In story as we rede. (1–5)[18]

The style, language, and alliterative rhythm belong to the high world of romance, but the expectations they arouse are immediately undercut by the intrusion of the low world to which the poem's 'kene conquerours'—Hawkyn, Herry, Tomkyn, and Terry (6–7)—properly belong. For a moment the poet plays with this incongruity by pretending that there has been no let-down, referring to these bumpkins as 'þem þat were dughty | And stalworth in dede' (8 9). However, this tension of elements is not maintained long, for with the second stanza we enter the peasant world entirely, so that its antithesis to the chivalric world, evoked in the course of the introduction, becomes wholly implicit (except for an occasional epic-heroic descriptive phrase). Romance thus provides the poem with its events and details, but these are distorted (as in *La Prise*) by their association with low-world characters. This provides an interesting contrast with *The Felon Sew*, which persists throughout in describing its events in proper epic-heroic terms. Clearly, the mock-heroic technique is supple and capable of intriguing variety.

17 *Medieval English Romances* edd. A.V.C. Schmidt and Nicholas Jacobs, 2 vols. (London, 1980), II, 196–239; *The Romance of Guy of Warwick*, ed. J. Zupitza, London, 1875 (Early English Text Society, Extra Series 25, 26) 557–674.

18 All references are to the edition of French and Hale, *Middle English Metrical Romances*, II, 990–8.

This mock-heroic opening indicates plainly the mechanics of the poem's comedy of incongruity: the pretence of dealing with worthy fighting men and their deeds, which is belied by the quaintness of the actors and, later, by the grossness of their actions. The peasants of *Tottenham* are themselves conventional stereotypes of a particular sort common in burlesque literature. They occur also in *Hunting*, and are distinguished by such qualities as arrogance, coarseness, cowardice, brutish aggression, and ridiculous pretentiousness. Such characters are exploited, particularly, for their propensity for fighting, which is what they do best in both *Tottenham* and *Hunting*, in events that constitute the recognised theme of 'the peasant brawl'. This theme, and the characters it depends upon, are further exemplified by two fifteenth-century Scots poems, *Christis Kirk on the Grene* and *Peblis to the Play*, both possibly written by James I of Scotland.[19] These poems show considerable scorn for their protagonists, and in both a happy rustic event turns into a disastrous brawl, to which they devote comprehensive attention as they elaborate the comedy of the peasants' murderous assaults on one another. A fairly robust sense of humour is needed to appreciate these brawls, for (as in *Hunting*) the description of wounds is an important element of the jest, with special emphasis given to the uncontrollable voiding of wind (or worse) and the infliction of permanent incontinence.[20] Nevertheless, the emphasis, as in *Tottenham*, is on the peasants' complete incompetence with everything but agricultural implements (most of the arrows they shoot miss by far). And although some of the terms used in *Christis Kirk* might indicate a more rural and unsophisticated audience than is likely to have enjoyed either *Tottenham* or *Hunting*,[21] it is clear that all four poems use the same basic theme peopled by the same stereotyped characters.

In *Tottenham*, however, the brawl theme is partly subsumed and disguised by another theme, that of the peasant tournament, or the mock tournament, a rarity in British literature, and unique in this poem in its combination with the brawl.[22] A similar admixture occurs in the colossal

19 *The Maitland Folio Manuscript*, ed. W.A. Craigie, 2 vols., Edinburgh and London, 1919, 1927 (Scottish Text Society, New Series 7), I, 149–55, 176–83. Both poems are examined by G.F. Jones, '*Christis Kirk*, *Peblis to the Play*, and the German peasant brawl', *PMLA* 68 (1953), 1101–25, and by A.H. MacLaine, 'The *Christis Kirk* tradition: its evolution in Scots poetry to Burns', *Studies in Scottish Literature* 2 (1964–5), 3–18.

20 Dunbar also uses this idea in his mock battles: *Schir Thomas Norny* 46–8, and 'The Turnament' (*Fasternis Evin in Hell* 121–228) 154–6, 190–2, 205–7 (*The Poems of William Dunbar*, ed. J. Kinsley (Oxford, 1979), Nos 27, 52B).

21 For example, lines 197–8: 'Quhill bludie barkit was þair berd | As thay had worreit lambis'.

22 MacLaine, 'The *Christis Kirk* tradition', pp. 16–17, is mistaken in describing Dunbar's 'Turnament' as a mixture of these two themes; it contains a mock tournament, but no brawl.

tournament-brawl which opens Heinrich Wittenwiler's *Ring* (*c.*1420), and, as G.F. Jones has shown, the peasant tournament is fairly common in a variety of fifteenth- and sixteenth-century German writings, particularly in association with Shrovetide festivities.[23] Interestingly, real mock tournaments fought by 'peasants' dressed in tarred jackets stuffed with straw, and armed with ridiculous implements, seem to have been a widespread form of entertainment in medieval Germany, though Jones argues that they were probably not enacted by actual peasants or villagers, but by the urban bourgeoisie disguised as foolish rustics.[24] Jones concludes that such comical events must have been satirical in intention, and that they ridiculed both genteel tournaments, which naturally excluded burghers by birth, and country bumpkins. Finally, he argues that the literary versions of such tournaments must have had the same purpose, and that *Tottenham* is therefore a middle-class lampoon of contemporary knightly tournaments, of the chivalric literature which celebrated such events, and of the universally despised peasantry.[25]

This interpretation of *Tottenham*, as I have mentioned already, has been highly influential. Yet there are many peculiarities in it, not the least of which is that Jones's evidence does not point consistently towards the conclusions that he is so eager to draw. Jones himself points out, for example, that some mock tournaments clearly did not satirise their chivalric models; as when, in 1491, the Emperor Maximilian financed one at the Diet of Nuremberg to follow a real joust for princes.[26] Moreover, Jones merely assumes that other mock tournaments were explicitly derisory: he offers no substantive proof. Finally, it is not at all apparent that Jones's continental sources are relevant to English attitudes or appropriate for interpreting English practices or literature. Indeed, there is good reason to believe that they are not. Jones quotes, for instance, the condemnation of Shrovetide tournaments in Sebastian Brant's *Narrenschiff* ('Ship of Fools') of 1494. Yet, in Alexander Barclay's English translation of this work (1509), there are clear indications that Barclay did not understand the references to these customs in his source: English Lenten celebrations were obviously different from those on the Continent.[27]

In fact, there is no evidence of Englishmen dressing up like the peasants in *Tottenham* or the *Narrenschiff* at Lent or any other time. Yet, many forms of mock tournament (in the widest sense of *mock*, as in *mock turtle*) were enjoyed in England, often by townsmen, without any indication that they expressed disdain for anyone or anything. One of these

23 Jones, 'The tournaments', pp. 1126–8.

24 *Ibid.*, pp. 1126–7; 1128.

25 *Ibid.*, p. 1139.

26 *Ibid.*, pp. 1126–7.

27 See A. Pompen, *The English Versions of the Ship of Fools* (London, 1925), pp. 252–8.

substitutes was the sport of running at a quintain, or 'peacock'. As early as 1253, according to Matthew Paris, some attendants of the royal household took exception to young Londoners enjoying this sport at Lent, and proceeded to insult and challenge them, only to be soundly beaten in the fracas that followed.[28] Significantly, Paris gives no hint of there being ridicule in the Londoners' game, and it would appear that the royal attendants reacted purely from a sense of righteous superiority. Indeed, the quintain became popular with the nobility, and was widely used as a training game for tyros and knights alike. As the antiquarian Joseph Strutt observes, the warlike sports of the nobility 'attracted the common mind in a very powerful manner', and, though they were excluded from these activities by birth, commoners imitated them as best they could.[29] In England there were other imitations of the joust, such as skaters rushing at each other with poles, and 'knights' jousting on fast-moving boats (a development of aquatic quintain, first recorded by William FitzStephen in the twelfth century).[30] And, rather than any of these sports being seen as insulting, they were often performed by townsmen specifically for the amusement of nobles and royalty.[31] Thus, the evidence of English practices does not support Jones's contention that imitation or 'mock' tournaments necessarily derided their serious models. Far from being insolent, these sports could be the sincerest form of flattery.

There is another reason that the peasant tournament in *Tottenham* could not have been intended as a satire of contemporary chivalric practices: its form, which is that of the *mêlée*, had by the fifteenth century been long out of date. The *mêlée*, or massed encounter, was the original form of the tournament, and is virtually synonymous with it in much chivalric literature. In its heyday, in the twelfth and thirteenth centuries, the *mêlée* was often almost indistinguishable from real warfare, especially when it was fought *à outrance*, or with sharp, not blunted, weapons. Large companies of knights would charge each other and fight complicated tactical battles across great swathes of countryside, often supported by infantry. Gradually, however, this *imago belli* was replaced by the joust, in which two knights fought each other within a fenced-off

28 *Chronica Majora*, ed. H.R. Luard, 7 vols., London, 1872–84 (Rolls Series 57), V, 367–8.

29 J. Strutt, *Sports and Pastimes of the People of England* (London, 1810), pp. 132–3.

30 *Descriptio Noblissimae Ciuitatis Londoniae* (1174), in John Stow, *A Survey of London*, ed. C.L. Kingsford, 3 vols. (Oxford, 1908–27), II, 219–29, at 225–9.

31 See Stow, *Survey of London*, I, 91–9; J. Nichols, *The Progresses and Public Processions of Queen Elizabeth*, 4 vols. (London, 1788–1821), I, 54–6 (for 1573). See also J.R. Barker, *The Tournament in England, 1100–1400* (Woodbridge, 1986), pp. 149–52, for a fuller account of the quintain and other imitative sports. In France there were more debauched mock tournaments held by burgesses, but these again were not deliberately derisory; see F.H. Cripps-Day, *The History of the Tournament in England and in France* (London, 1918), pp. 21–2.

area. Such jousting—closely related to notions of judicial combat—could also be very dangerous when fought *à outrance*. There was thus no dishonour in the joust, and it became increasingly popular, at least partly because it offered greater spectator pleasure than the *mêlée*. Finally, though, even the free joust gave way to a more controlled encounter: that between two knights separated by a barrier (introduced in the 1420's).[32]

It is to some such contemporary form of individual joust that Dunbar alludes in his bizarre account of a Lenten tournament in Hell.[33] Which is why it seems extraordinary that, if *Tottenham* were a middle-class assault on contemporary chivalric practices, it should depict a form of tournament that had, by the fifteenth century, been long obsolete (the last great *mêlée* tournament in England was held at Dunstable in 1342).[34] The external evidence simply does not support Jones's view of this poem, and nor, I suggest, does any internal evidence. For Jones has made the same mistake as Kindrick in confusing the vehicle of the comedy—the tournament and other themes of chivalric literature—with its object: the bumbling peasants. There is no denying that the tournament in *Tottenham* is farcical, but only in conformity with the farcicality of its stock characters, who aspire to a sport inappropriate to their situation. The jest therefore depends on the recognition that this is a *peasant* tournament; it is absurd, not because the poet considered tournaments to be absurd, but because the peasants necessarily make it so.

There is no reason why the tournament, as it is presented, should not have appealed to the humour of the most ardent supporter of the joust or the old heroic *mêlée*. This should be clear from a comparison with what is truly satirical treatment of knightly combat in the fifteenth-century French dramatic farce, *l'Aventureux*.[35] This is an authentic anti-chivalric piece whose protagonists are not bumbling peasants, but a pair of elderly, yet still boastful knights, and their sons, who urge them to do battle over some trivial dispute. The knights reluctantly accede, but they are most strongly armed at their backs, and their battle, which never gets beyond shouts and imprecations, is dropped at the first opportunity. Knighthood and chivalry are plainly depicted in this play as preposterous, outmoded vanities, and there is a strong sense in other contemporary

32 For a fuller discussion of these developments see Barker, *The Tournament*, pp. 4–19, 137–61; also, N. Denholm-Young, 'The tournament in the thirteenth century', *Studies in Medieval History Presented to Frederick Maurice Powicke* edd. R.W. Hunt and others, Oxford, 1948, pp. 240–68, at 241–2; A.B. Ferguson, *The Indian Summer of English Chivalry* (Durham, N.C., 1960), pp. 15–17; R.L. Kilgour, *The Decline of Chivalry* (Cambridge, Mass., 1937), pp. 37–9.

33 'The Turnament', in *Fasternis Evin in Hell*. See above, p. 122, n. 20.

34 See Barker, *The Tournament*, p. 139.

35 See Kilgour, *Decline of Chivalry*, pp. 369-72.

French writings of deep frustration, disillusionment, and even contempt for knights and their deeds. (Such attitudes were probably engendered in large part by the long-term suffering inflicted on ordinary people by the increasingly brutal and self-interested armies of knights fighting the Hundred Years War, whose depredations are described in graphic detail by, among others, Jean Juvénal des Ursins in his *Complainte* to Charles VII (1440).)[36] But there is nothing like *l'Aventureux* and similar satirical pieces in English literature of this period. As A.B. Ferguson has observed, 'England produced no such critics of chivalry as appeared in France. Malory no doubt understood only too well what the French original of his Sir Dinadan meant, and chose wherever possible to remove the barbs from his shafts of satirical common sense.'[37]

Tottenham is quite different from *l'Aventureux*, most obviously in the fact that its protagonists are peasants who get everything wrong. Consequently, their mock tournament belongs properly to *their* low world, serving to show up *their* absurdities, while not in itself becoming an object of ridicule. The chivalric sport is distorted by association with them, rather than by the exaggeration or exposure of any inherent absurdities. Distortion or grotesquerie of this sort is a common device in burlesque, where its purpose is to reinforce the lowness of the world presented. We see it in *Sir Thopas*, for example, in the more absurd details of Chaucer's description such as Thopas's rose-red lips, his 'semely nose', and latten helmet, and also in Chaucer's comic exaggeration of the style and diction of the popular romances. And it is an obvious feature of *La Prise*, where it serves to make the world of incompetent Flemish combatants lower than strictly necessary: an aspiring *chevalier* knocks himself out on his own gateway before even joining his fellows, and another has his feet tied together beneath his horse so that he and his horse must fall either together or not at all.[38] It is by means of such exaggeration that the world of the Flemings, and the versification of the distant, fictional author of *Sir Thopas* are made and kept low. Similarly, the quaint and hopeless antics of the peasants in *Tottenham* emphasize *their* inadequacy—not that of the world they ape.

This world is present, not only in the tournament itself, but also in the lengthy section devoted to a series of themes that are often a prelude to combat, both sportive and martial, in literature. *Tottenham*'s description of the peasants' armour, weapons, rustic coats of arms, and warrior-vows patently evokes similar accounts in serious chivalric literature. In each case, what is revealed is the ludicrousness of the peasants and their pitiful

36 *Ibid.*, pp. 315-74, esp. 333 ff., 373–4.
37 Ferguson, *Indian Summer*, p. 22.
38 See Burrow, 'Chaucer's *Sir Thopas*', pp. 46, 51, 49–52.

imitation of high chivalry: the daftness of the translation of the chivalric world into a rustic equivalent. Hence the description of Hud's 'armes . . . so clere', containing agricultural implements, a burning dragon, and three sections of a cake (104–8), does not mock heraldry, but its yokel simulacrum. So too with the contenders' vows, which are redolent of the vows made by knights as a spur to achievement both in literature and history.[39] Although it would seem that such flamboyant gestures became themselves the subject of aristocratic humour through extravagant exaggeration,[40] that is not the joke in *Tottenham*. Here it is the quaint homeliness of the vows—as if the speakers were children—and the substitution of rural for courtly terminology that creates the comedy:

> 'I vow to God', quod Perkyn, 'þou spekis of cold rost!
> I schal wyrch wyselyer, withouten any bost:
> V of þe best capullys þat ar in þys ost,
> I wot i schal þaym wynne, and bryng þaym to my cost.' (136–9)

Likewise, the peasants' armour is appropriate to them in a way that does not disparage real or literary knights. Interestingly, their sheepskins, mats, and bowls (59–72) are very like the armour that another author mockingly assigns to a Flemish contingent after its defeat at Gravelines in 1436. The Flemings are described as being armed:

> With messis, & meskins, & eke with side Iakes
> Doun vnto mydde þe leg of kanuas, lyke to sakes,
> Stoppid al with hempen tawe, and þat in straunge wise,
> Stiched like a matrace al of þe newe gyse.[41]

Of course, this may be an accurate portrait of the Flemish soldiers, but the similarity of their accoutrement to the panoplies in *Tottenham* suggests that there may have been established conventions for describing contemptible or risible combatants.

There is no need to labour the point, for it should be obvious that at every turn it is not tournaments that are derided, but the peasants' version of them—'Þer was clynkyng of cart-sadellys and clattiryng of cannes; | Of fele frekis in þe feld, brokyn were þer fannes' (163–4)—the

39 *The Avowing of Arthur*, ed. C. Brockhouse, Copenhagen, 1968 (Anglistica 15), pp. 113–45, see also [John Barbour,] *The Avowis of Alexander* (*The Buik of Alexander*, ed. R.L.G. Ritchie, 4 vols., Edinburgh and London, 1921–9 (Scottish Text Society, New Series 12, 17, 21, 25), III, 248–351) 5171–912.

40 See J. Huizinga, *The Waning of the Middle Ages* (London, 1924), pp. 74–81; also, B.J. Whiting, 'The vows of the heron', *Speculum* 20 (1945), 261–78.

41 *Historical Poems of the XIVth and XVth Centuries*, ed. Rossell Hope Robbins (New York, 1959), No. 29, 11–14.

comedy of which is made the more trenchant by the occasional interjection of an epic-descriptive phrase: 'Sych anoþer gadryng haue i not sene oft!' (73); 'I wot it ys no chylder-game when þay togedyr met!' (154).[42] A middle-class audience might well have appreciated such humour, but how much more likely is it not to have appealed to the aristocracy and nobility—the classes most steeped in chivalric literature and values, and so most likely to have appreciated every nuance and allusion in the burlesque? The problem is that we know so little about *Tottenham*, its authorship, provenance, and conditions of reception.[43] In any case, the weight of evidence, both internal and external, contradicts the view of Jones and others that the poem expresses a middle-class, anti-chivalric, satirical point of view. And if my characterisation of burlesque, and of this poem in particular, is correct, an audience comprised of admirers of romance and adherents of chivalry would make perfect sense.[44]

IV

To support this argument I shall turn, finally, to the evidence of my third burlesque, the little-known *Hunting of the Hare*, an anonymous poem in a northern-English dialect of the mid-fifteenth century.[45] *Hunting* deploys the broadest comedy of the three poems considered here, and is arguably a borderline specimen of burlesque romance. It has the feel of a ballad in its homeliness of tone—'A letyll tale Y wyll yow tell' (1)—and it contains no explicit mimicry or evocation of the world of romance, which means that it creates no mock-heroic tensions: no obvious formal incongruity between matter and manner, subject and style, high and low worlds. Nevertheless, romance is what provides the poem with its inspiration, its action, its tail-rhyme stanza, and some of its techniques of delivery—for example, the calls for audience attention (7, 118, 127), and the half-revelation, at the beginning of the second fitt, of the climax of the tale. Furthermore, as I shall argue, *Hunting* relies on a precise knowledge of upper-class literature and sporting practices for its humour to be fully understood. Therefore, although the poem's

42 Cf. *Octavian* (*Six Middle English Romances*, ed. M. Mills (London, 1973), pp. 75–124) 966, 1038.

43 For a summary of the debate about these issues see M.G. Frampton, 'Gilbert Pilkington once more', *PMLA* 47 (1932), 622–35.

44 MacLaine, 'The *Christis Kirk* tradition', pp. 11–13, is similarly in no doubt that the Scots peasant-brawl burlesques could have been written only for the amusement of the upper classes.

45 *Metrical Romances of the thirteenth, fourteenth and fifteenth centuries*, ed. H. Weber, 3 vols. (Edinburgh, 1810), III, 279–90; this is the only printed edition.

comedy is primarily a farce of plot and action, within this is an implicit high-world antithesis that gives the humour a particular trenchancy. And it is the very tacitness of this high-world exemplar that best indicates the upper-class origins of this burlesque.

Hunting is similar in many ways to *Tottenham*: it employs the same stereotypical peasant characters—even the name Parkyn the Potter reappears—who embark on an activity that appertains properly to the upper classes, only to end up thrashing one another into the ground. The institution which here provides the opportunity for showing up the inadequacies of over-ambitious churls is a hunt, or, more accurately, coursing a hare. In contrast with *Tottenham*, however, the travesty which the peasants make of this sport (before everything backfires) is not as obvious, at least partly because coursing does not have as large a place in chivalric literature as tourneying or other forms of hunting, and is, accordingly, to us a little obscure. This is complicated by the fact that the poet relies quite heavily on his audience's recognition of the disparity between what should happen and what does. Nevertheless, once again, the noble institution which provides the mechanics of the comedy remains itself inviolate, for it is shown to fail only when undertaken by oafish incompetents instead of its proper votaries: expert, noble enthusiasts. Like *Tottenham*, *Hunting* is pure comic burlesque, and even if its stock figures and their actions appear less amusing today than when it was written, its tone and intentions are unmistakably light.

The plot is very simple, with events working with fateful inexorability towards a single cataclysm: an unexpected battle or brawl. Yet in some ways this disaster is not wholly unsurprising. Within the logic of the poem it is arguably the inevitable outcome of the villein-protagonists' presumption; more precisely, their arrogant belief that they need none of the specialised knowledge or the hounds developed and refined by noblemen over centuries for coursing the hare.[46] A yeoman has found one sitting in fallow land and has ridden to town, where he asks Honkyn of the Halle,

> 'Dwelles ther ony gentyllmon here,
> Gud mon, as God thè save?
> Yonder Y have fond a hare syttyng:
> Yf ye have ony grehowndes hom with yow to bryng,
> A cours ther schall ye have.' (20–4)

Honkyn's reply spells the disaster that is to come: 'What nedys that? . . . | Ychon of hus hase a dogge or too; | For grehowndes have thou no care' (25–7). For, when the dogs are catalogued (28–54), they are nightmare-

46 These were matters of jealous pride to the nobility and its fringe emulators, as Chaucer's description of his Monk testifies (*CT*, I, 189–92).

opposites of the fine, highly trained hounds appreciated by all hunters and coursers throughout history. The essence of the humour of the descriptions that follow goes deeper than the obviously motley appearance of the assembled crowd of churls and their mongrels: it depends on an implicit contrast between them and the noble company that usually gathered to hunt the hare, 'the kyng of alle venery', as the animal is described by Edward of York in his hunting treatise, *The Master of Game* (*c*.1406–13).[47] To appreciate this one needs to know a little about coursing, probably the oldest form of hunting as pure sport, and about medieval hunting generally.

Hare-coursing is first mentioned in Western literature by Xenophon (*c*.430–*c*.354 B.C.), who must have observed the use of gazehounds in Asia Minor.[48] The first full account, however, comes some centuries later from another Greek, Flavius Arrianus, also known as 'Xenophon the Younger' (*c*.96–*c*.180 A.D.), who provides the first description of a European greyhound—the Celtic breed which he calls 'Vertragus'—and its use.[49] Arrian shows great enthusiasm for the sport, which, he emphasises, is run purely by sight (that is, using gazehounds, not scenting hounds), and is undertaken by men whose primary interest is not to kill the hare, or even to see it caught. Rather, '. . . those who are truly hunting men do not take out the hounds to catch the little beast, but for the competition of the race and as a contest. They are well pleased if the hare succeeds in coming through safely.'[50]

In the Middle Ages, coursing disappears somewhat from our view. Chaucer's description of the Monk, as a man who hunts from horseback and with greyhounds, suggests strongly that he is a coursing man (*CT*, I, 165–92). Yet the sport is hardly mentioned in the English and French hunting treatises as these reflect the dominant French methods of hunting, which relied principally on scenting hounds. Gazehounds, generally referred to by the (then) generic terms *greyhound* or *lévrier*, formed no small part of such hunting practices.[51] They are described in the manuals and in imaginative literature, and are shown in contemporary illustrations, pursuing a variety of quarries, but not in a way that could be called coursing as such. Most sources show greyhounds being used in relays,

47 Ed. W.A. and F. Baillie-Grohman, (London, 1904), p. 103. Cf. also *The Boke of St. Albans*, 1486 (*English Hawking and Hunting in 'The Boke of St. Albans'*, ed. Rachel Hands (London, 1975), pp 3–87, at 61.1327–8).

48 Xenophon describes hare-coursing in *Cyropaedia* I. 6, 40, as part of a discussion of how hunting techniques may be applied to war.

49 See Arrian, *Cynegeticus* III. 6–7 (*Hounds and Hunting in Ancient Greece,* ed. and tr. D.B. Hull (Chicago and London, 1964), pp. 161–84).

50 Arrian, *Cynegeticus* XVI. 4.

51 These terms could indicate any one of a variety of dogs, from the large Irish wolfhound to the *petit lévrier pour lièvre*, united by the single attribute of hunting by sight; see Baillie-Grohman, *Master of Game*, pp. 142–5, s.v. *Greyhound.*

often in combination with scenting hounds, and for such functional purposes as heading-off or pulling-down quarries, usually deer.[52] In the poem *Summer Sunday*, for example, the narrator witnesses a deer-hunt employing 'kenettes' (small scenting hounds) and 'grehoundes', and in *Sir Gawain and the Green Knight*, greyhounds are used together with beaters and bowmen in the form of hunt known as the 'battue'.[53]

In spite of the lack of evidence, coursing must, nevertheless, have remained popular, for when George Gascoigne translated Jacques du Fouilloux's *La Vénerie* in 1576, he felt it necessary to fill a lacuna in his source by providing a chapter of his own on the sport.[54] Gascoigne observes that '. . . we here in England do make great account of such pastime as is to be seen in coursing with Greyhoundes at Deare, Hare, Fox, or suche like . . . when there are neyther [scenting] houndes hunting, nor other meane to help them', and it is interesting to see that his account of hare-coursing, in particular, differens little from that of Arrian.[55]

It should also be remembered that by the late Middle Ages all forms of hunting (except snaring and trapping) had become the jealously guarded privilege of the upper classes, who, as they secured hegemony over the hunt, extended their sense of their own worth to it and encompassed it within growing conceptions of courtly, courteous, and chivalric behaviour. As an elaborate etiquette and ceremony accrued to the hunt among its noble and aristocratic followers, the sport came to be seen as an activity both belonging to the nobility and proving the nobility of its devotees. Time and again, in literature and the handbooks, emphasis is given to doing everything properly, as the *Gawain*-poet hints when the deer are cut up 'as þe dede askez' (1327).[56]

52 See, for example, the illustrations in Gaston de Foix's *Le Livre de Chasse*, ed. G. Tilander, Karlshamn, 1971 (Cynegetica 18), pp. 193, 216, 222; also, the tapestries known as the 'Devonshire *Hunts*' (D. King, 'The Devonshire *Hunts*: art and sport in the fifteenth century', *Connoisseur* 196 (1977), 246–53), and Edward of York, *Master of Game*, pp. 18, 26, 36–7.

53 *Summer Sunday*, (Robbins, *Historical Poems*, No. 38), 5, 10, 19; *Sir Gawain and the Green Knight*, edd. J.R.R. Tolkien and E.V. Gordon, 2nd ed. rev. Norman Davis (Oxford, 1967), 1150–73. The battue is described by Edward of York, *Master of Game*, pp. 107–12.

54 *Turbervile's Booke of Hunting, 1576,* Oxford, 1908 (Tudor & Stuart Library), pp. 246–50. Gascoigne's treatise, which is now properly referred to as *The Noble Arte of Venerie or Hunting*, used to be attributed to George Turbervile; see, however, C. and R. Prouty, 'George Gascoigne, *The Noble Arte of Venerie*, and Queen Elizabeth at Kenilworth', *Joseph Quincy Adams Memorial Studies*, edd. J.G. McManaway and others (Washington, 1948), pp. 639–64.

55 Gascoigne, *Noble Arte*, p. 246.

56 These notions are more fully examined by M. Thiébaux, 'The medieval chase', *Speculum* 42 (1967), 260–74, at 260–3, 267, and *The Stag of Love* (Ithaca and London, 1974), pp. 26–7.

It is this entire world that Honkyn spurns with his 'What nedys that?', but it provides an implicit, antithetical standard against which the poem's events and characters must be judged. It provides, for example, a measure for the dogs. Jac Wade's dog that will hold a bull 'ston-styll' (40–2), and Hob Andrew's dog that will bring a sow 'to the cowtte' (43–5), are all very well, but they are indubitably not coursing dogs. Nor are Parkyn the Potter's three hounds, described as having 'Short schonkes and neuer a tayll; | No kalfe so greyt, as Y wene' (50–1). Such brutes, chosen over the greyhound for a hare-course, would have had the most horrifying resonances for any noble sportsman. We know from Froissart that Gaston (Phoebus) de Foix, a legend among hunters even in his own day, loved all (fine) dogs, and his *Livre de Chasse* shows that he was deeply knowledgeable about them; so it is interesting to see Gaston accept for his treatise a proverbial, poetic description of the greyhound.[57] A few details from Edward of York's translation will suffice to indicate the sort of dog that the peasants have chosen to spurn:

> . . . here eynne shuld be reed or blak as of a sparhauke, þe eerys smal and hie in þe maner of a serpent, þe neke grete and longe bowed as a swannes nek, his paas [chest] greet and opyn, þe heere vndir his chyn wel hangyng adoun in þe maner of a lyon, hey shuldres as a roo buk . . .[58]

The lengthy portrait of the assembly of churls, dogs, and their various accoutrements (76–90), must indicate the heart of the poem's humour. For the peasants, armed with clubs 'Syche as thei betyn clottys withall' (91–2), get everything wrong and are obviously not about to undertake Gascoigne's 'gallant sport' (*Noble Arte*, p. 248) or Arrian's sporting run. Instead, on getting to the field, they try to head-off and surround the hare with shouts that betray their aggressive boorishness. Gascoigne specifies that only two shouts (both very much in keeping with the spirit of earlier manuals) are appropriate: 'sa How', on finding the hare, and 'up pusse up', to start her running.[59] By contrast, the yokels of *Hunting* bellow, '". . . Hy, hy!" all at ones | "Kyll! kyll! for kockes bownes! | Bewar lest sche schape owte"' (136–8). This little scene powerfully confirms the validity of the lament of a hare in the poem known as *The*

57 J. Froissart, *Les Chroniques*, ed. J. Buchon (Paris, 1838–40), III. 13, IV. 23 (II, 399; III, 119). See Gaston de Foix, *Livre de Chasse*, ed. Gunnar Tilander, Karlshamn, 1971, chapters 15–24, esp. ch. 18.

58 Edward of York, *Master of Game*, p. 62; I have made small corrections to the editors' punctuation to allow this passage to make better sense.

59 *Noble Arte*, p. 248. The earlier treatises describe only hunting with scenting hounds, for which more elaborate calls (including 'So how') were needed; see, for example, Edward of York, *Master of Game*, pp. 103–6.

Hunted Hare that she is mercilessly pursued by all, and given a sporting chance (and little enough of that!) only by the gentleman.[60]

In this poem, however, the hare has her just requital in a strikingly bizarre peripeteia in which the tables are turned on her tormentors as they try to brain her:

> The hare thoght che wold owt wyn,
> And hit Jac Wade apon the schyn,
> That he fell apon the backe.
> 'Owt! owte!' quoth Jac, and 'alas!
> That euer this batell begonen was!
> This is a sorè note.'
> Jac Wade was neuer so ferd,
> As when the hare trade on his berd,
> Lest sche wold have pult owt his throwt. (142–50)

Such eccentricity is rare, even in burlesque, but it is not unknown. It is of approximately the same order as the flying monks in *The Land of Cokaygne*, and may be compared, in particular, to the flight of a tormented piglet from his would-be slaughterers, a harlot and her outrageous company, in the Scots poem *Colkelbie's Sow*.[61] In that burlesque, the hubbub of the pursuit leads bystanders to think there is some festivity, and a country dance ensues. In *Hunting*, the escape of the hare is similarly almost incidental to the action, for, as we learn, the dogs had not even noticed her (154–6), being more interested in savaging one another (157–61), so that:

> Men myght se the dogges ren,
> Sum the guttes out-drayn,
> Sum on thei backes thei lay,
> Sum wer pynchyd by the haunche,
> And sum pulled owt the panche,
> And thus thei scheyd hur whay. (162–8)

And yet the behaviour of the dogs is only a premonition of their masters' actions, which quickly precipitate a connoisseur's peasant brawl of quite startling brutality. The causes and rapid escalation of the violence are perfectly simple:

60 See *Secular Lyrics of the XIVth and XVth Centuries,* ed. Rossell Hope Robbins, (London, 1952), No. 119, lines 61–8.

61 For *Cokaygne* see Robbins, *Historical Poems*, No. 48, esp. lines 121–66. For *Colkelbie's Sow* see *The Bannatyne Manuscript*, ed. W.T. Ritchie, 4 vols., Edinburgh and London, 1928–34 (Scottish Text Society, New Series 26) IV, 279–308, esp. 282–96.

Jac Wade was war his dogge was down,
And he hit Jac Grym dog on the crown,
That bothe his een start owt.
Jac Gryme swere then full sone,
He swere be God that syttes in trone,
And radly raght hym a clowte.
. . . . . .
Jac of Bonam he was constabull,
He seyd, 'Yow to arese Y am full abull,
All that ben olde or yong.'
Anon won brake his necke wel ny,
That euer after he lokud awry,
And hongyd owt the tonge. (169–74, 193–8)

And thus it continues for ten of the poem's forty-five stanzas, with men and dogs fighting it out separately (223–5). Only when all are either incapacitated or exhausted do they stop, to be brought home in carts and, as in *Tottenham*, wheelbarrows by wives and friends (241–52).

The dominant themes that I have identified so far are the hunt and the peasant brawl. But the author of *Hunting* may also have had in mind another convention in which *hunting* and fighting are felicitously combined: the romance motif of the hunt that leads directly to a battle, as occurs in *Guy of Warwick*, *Sir Tristrem*, and *Sir Eglamour of Artois*.[62] This is also the pattern of action on a grander scale in the Border ballad, *The Hunting of the Cheviot*.[63] In fact, the similarity of the action of *Hunting* and *Cheviot* is noteworthy in several respects, as is their technique of battle description. *Hunting*'s rhyme scheme is sufficiently different from *Cheviot*'s for it to be unlikely that the ballad was its direct inspiration, but it is possible that a similar poem, using the same association of ideas, was, and that *Hunting*'s literary antecendents were once better established than is now apparent.

In conclusion, it should be clear that burlesque romance need not denigrate its serious literary models, but may use them to make fun of other, usually readily identifiable, targets. For, to make fun *with*, or by means of, something is not the same as making fun *of* that thing. In *The Felon Sew*, *Tottenham*, and *Hunting*, perfectly sober literary styles, themes, and devices provide the means to the comedy; fun is made with them, but not of them. This need not have been the case. Chaucer's *Sir Thopas* is the foremost example of a burlesque that makes play both with and of the same thing,

62 *Guy of Warwick*, 6409 ff.; *Sir Tristrem*, ed. G.P. McNeill, Edinburgh, 1886 (Scottish Text Society), 2718 ff.; *Sir Eglamour of Artois*, ed. F.E. Richardson, London, 1965 (Early English Text Society 256), 259–336.

63 *English Verse 1300–1500*, ed. J.A. Burrow (London, 1977), No. 32.

which, usefully for this enquiry, happens to be popular romance. But in *Sir Thopas*, as in all these burlesques, the impulse that lies behind such 'ridicule' is quite different from that which motivates the ridicule of satire. In burlesque, comedy and jest are paramount; denigration—of which there may be much, as in the case of the grotesquely stereotyped peasants—is secondary, and usually merely an instrument for the comedy.

The comedy of *The Felon Sew* is directed at a farmyard misadventure, and that of *Tottenham* and *Hunting* at a ready-made straw man, the pretentious, belligerent peasant. In none of these poems does the ridicule reflect back on the means—chivalric practices and literature—used for creating it. And for this reason, if no other, the notion of a contemptuous, urban-bourgeois audience may be dismissed as erroneous and irrelevant to these burlesques.

Author, Scribe, and Reader in Malory

The Case of Harleuse and Peryne

P.J.C. FIELD

I

According to Eugène Vinaver's standard edition, Harleuse le Berbuse and Peryne de la Mountayne appear twice in Malory's *Morte Darthur*, first in the story of Balin in his first tale, in which he gave their names to characters who were anonymous in his source, the Post-Vulgate *Suite de Merlin*, and second, some hundreds of pages later, in his story of Alexander the Orphan, where Malory took the actions and the names of both characters from the Alexander story in the French prose *Tristan*.[1] Malory often gives names from one source to anonymous characters in another,[2] and the earlier appearance of Harleuse and Peryne might have escaped particular comment had it not been that both are immediately killed. This naturally creates interpretative problems for their later appearance.

Such problems are not unique. There are other instances in the *Morte Darthur* where a character apparently takes part in the action after his death or before his birth. No single solution will resolve all these anomalies, and most of the scholars who have commented on them have put forward, with varying degrees of conviction, one permutation or other of three critical responses.[3] Inconsistencies have sometimes simply been accepted as authorial error, fractures in the aesthetic coherence of

1 Sir Thomas Malory, *Works*, ed. Eugène Vinaver, 3 vols. (Oxford, 1973), pp. 79–81, 646–7, 1666–7. As this essay takes issue with some of Vinaver's opinions, I cite this edition, the last he controlled, rather than the subsequent one (Oxford, 1990) revised by myself. I am obliged to Dr. Thomas Corns, Miss Linda Gowans, and Dr. Steven Price for helpful suggestions.

2 Robert H. Wilson, 'Malory's Naming of Minor Characters', *Journal of English and Germanic Philology* 42 (1943), 364–385; 'Addenda on Malory's Minor Characters', *Journal of English and Germanic Philology* 55 (1956), 563–87.

3 Charles Moorman, 'Internal Chronology in Malory's *Morte Darthur*', *Journal of English and Germanic Philology* 60 (1961), 240–9; Ellyn Olefsky, 'Chronology, Factual Consistency, and the Problem of Unity in Malory', *Journal of English and Germanic Philology* 68 (1969), 57–73; Robert H. Wilson, 'Chronology in Malory', *Studies in the Language, Literature, and Culture of the Middle Ages and Later* [= *Studies for Rudolph Willard*], edd. E. Bagby Atwood and Archibald A. Hill (Austin, Texas, 1969), pp. 324–34.

Malory's book. At other times, they have been taken to involve different characters of the same name. At other times again, complicated chronologies have been proposed to put the events of the story into a more acceptable order. Vinaver's much-controverted theory that the eight tales making up the *Morte Darthur* are independent literary works[4] can be taken as an extreme version of this last response, the different tales being in effect different universes between which there is no connection, and therefore no possibility of contradiction.

However, although the problem of characters who live after they die was conspicuous among the evidence on which Vinaver based his theory, and although a strong form of that theory, for someone willing to pay the aesthetic price that it exacts elsewhere, would have solved the problem completely, Vinaver did not invoke it or any other literary-critical response. Instead, he argued that, unless Malory (less probably) had the prose *Tristan* open in front of him when he composed the earlier passage, the names of Harleuse and Peryne must (more probably) have been inserted by a scribe, perhaps a rubricator, working back from the later passage.[5] These alternatives, however, do not exhaust the possibilities: plainly, the two names in the earlier passage could have been supplied either by a scribe or by Malory, either from the later passage or the prose *Tristan*.

These complications can be reduced, because a re-examination of the evidence will show that the standard edition was wrong about the names in the prose *Tristan*. The character corresponding to Malory's Harleuse has a name corresponding to Harleuse, but the character corresponding to Peryne is, in all surviving manuscripts containing that part of Malory's source, an anonymous knight *de merveilleuse proesse*.[6] The French phrase may well have triggered Peryne's name, in a way characteristic of Malory:

*de m*erveilleuse *p*roesse > *de* la *m*ountayne *p*eryne.

Nevertheless, it is clear that neither Malory nor any of his scribes could have taken Peryne's name from a copy of the *Tristan* open in front of

4 *Works*, pp. xxxv-li. For one overview of the controversy, see R.M. Lumiansky, 'Sir Thomas Malory's *Le Morte Darthur* 1947–87: Author, Title, Text', *Speculum* 62 (1987), 878–98.

5 *Works*, pp. 1502 (note to 646.5) and 1666–7.

6 I have consulted St. Petersburg, M.E. Saltykov-Shchedrin State Public Library, fr. F. v. XV-2, fol. 220; New York, Pierpont Morgan Library, M41, fol. 82; and Paris, Bibliothèque Nationale, fr. 99, fol. 383, and assume, on the authority of *Works* p. 1498, that Chantilly, Musée Condé 646 is identical with B.N. fr. 99. A fifth manuscript (not known to Vinaver) gives the same reading: Cologny-Geneva, Bibliotheca Bodmeriana, Codex Bodmer 164, fol. 385. Vinaver's mistake seems to derive from misreading E. Löseth *Le Roman de Tristan en prose, analyse critique* (Paris, 1890), p. 194 n. (Wilson 'Addenda', p. 582).

him. If we can rule out as too complicated the hypothesis that either Malory when composing or a scribe when copying the earlier episode looked forward to the *Tristan* for Harleuse's name, invented Peryne's, brought both names back to the earlier passage, and then, when composing or copying out the later episode, remembered to bring Peryne's forward again for the *Tristan*'s anonymous knight, then either Malory or a scribe must have brought both names back from the later episode in the *Morte Darthur* to the earlier one.

Vinaver preferred the hypothesis that a scribe did so, and Robert H. Wilson's authoritative examination of Malory's minor characters gave that hypothesis cautious support.[7] Although none of the inconsistencies in the careers of any of the other characters in the *Morte Darthur* has ever been attributed to anyone but Malory, there is some force in this. An author would have had to have been grossly careless to fail to notice, while inserting the two names in the earlier passage, that he was killing off two characters who would later be needed alive in the very passage from which he was copying the names. Scribes, on the other hand, in general know their copy less well than authors, so some kinds of inconsistency are classic symptoms of unauthorised scribal 'improvement'. Vinaver's hypothesis has the further advantage that it should eradicate the inconsistency that is its subject: scribal interpolations have no place in an author's text, so the interpolated names should be removed, so the inconsistency would cease to exist. Why Vinaver did not remove them from his own editions he never explained.

However, since all the evidence elsewhere points to Malory rather than his scribes having given names to anonymous minor characters, the possibility that he himself might have amplified the earlier passage from the later one is not to be dismissed without examination, which Vinaver did not give it. Malory could have made the change either during the writing of the *Morte Darthur* or after its completion, the latter alternative fitting neatly into the pattern of his life in the late 1460's. The imprisonment during which he wrote the *Morte Darthur* probably begin in June 1468, but although he had completed the book by March 1470, it seems unlikely that he was released from prison until the Lancastrian *coup d'état* of October 1470.[8] What more natural than that he should use the time hanging heavily on a prisoner's hands to reread the book on which he had spent so much time earlier, and doing so, make small revisions here and there? Among such revisions, he would certainly have found giving names to anonymous minor characters both congenial and easily done.

7 Wilson, 'Addenda', p. 566.

8 P.J.C. Field, 'The Last Years of Sir Thomas Malory', *Bulletin of the John Rylands Library* 61 (1981–2), 433–56.

It seems likely that Malory interpolated the names of other minor characters into passages he had already written, although proof is difficult, for two reasons. First, although it is natural to assume that Malory wrote the tales making up the *Morte Darthur* in the order in which they now stand, it is remarkably difficult to prove it.[9] Second, since he seems to have known most of his sources before he started work on any of them,[10] it is also difficult to distinguish revision from anticipation. (Happily, neither difficulty applies with Harleuse and Peryne,[11] which makes enables us to make assertions about them with fewer reservations than with practically any other of Malory's minor characters.) If the relevant parts of the *Morte Darthur* were written in their present order, one of the characters most likely to have had his name retrospectively inserted in an earlier episode is Sir Malagryne. Malagryne, like Harleuse, was translated from the Alexander story in the French prose *Tristan* into the corresponding story in Malory's fifth tale, and from there apparently introduced into the fourth.[12] No-one has suggested that any part of that process was the work of a scribe; but if Malory introduced Malagryne's name retropectively into the fourth tale, it must increase the probability that he did the same with Harleuse and Peryne in the first.

Moreover, it can be shown that the hypothesis of scribal interpolation is untenable for one of their names, and therefore presumably for both. Demonstration depends on the variant forms of the name in question, but it is worthwhile to consider all the forms of both names in both texts of the *Morte Darthur*.

Harleuse's name appears twice (in successive sentences) in the text of the earlier passage and once in the later one, a total of six appearances in the two texts. On four of those occasions, and also in a marginal rubric

9 Malory scholars have shown no enthusiasm for Vinaver's theory that Malory's second tale was written before his first, or Terence McCarthy's that the tales were written in order of increasing distance from their sources (*Works*, pp. lii–iv; McCarthy, 'Order of Composition in the *Morte Darthur*', *Yearbook of English Studies* 1 (1971), 18–29); cf. Edward D. Kennedy 'Malory and His English Sources,' *Aspects of Malory*, edd. Toshiyuki Takamiya and others (Cambridge 1981), pp. 28–39. Professor Takamiya has suggested persuasively that the fourth tale was written after the second ("Wade", "dryvande" and "Gotelake": Three Notes on Order of Composition in the *Morte Darthur*', *Studies in English Literature* (1974), 131–48), but his first two points would be weakened if the fourth tale had an English source, and his third if Gotelake's name was introduced during revision. Cf. also below, note 11.

10 Robert H. Wilson, 'Malory's Early Knowledge of Arthurian Romance', *University of Texas Studies in English* 29 (1950), 33–50.

11 For the earlier Harleuse and Peryne episode being the product of revision rather than anticipation, see above; for a passage near the first episode having been written before one near the second, see *Works*, pp. 1308–9 (note to 72.6).

12 Wilson, 'Addenda', pp. 568–69.

alongside its first appearance in the manuscript text, it is given as *Harleuse le Berbuse* or as a form equivalent to that in fifteenth-century orthography. On the first occasion in the manuscript text, however, it appears simply as *Berbuse*. Since the corresponding passage in the Caxton passage and the adjacent marginal rubric have the full form, we may infer a scribal omission (presumably by homoeoteleuton) at a copying stage subsequent to the archetype from which both known texts derive.[13] On the last occasion in the Caxton text, *Harleuse* becomes *Harsouse*, presumably by a scribe misreading *le* as *so* with a long *s*. When Caxton's was the only known text of the *Morte Darthur*, the *Harsouse* of the later episode could be taken to represent a character different from the *Harleuse* of the earlier one,[14] but the agreement between the manuscript text and the source at this point shows that *Harsouse* too is a post-archetypal scribal error. The faint ghost of a character called Harsouse le Berbuse should therefore be exorcized from the places where it still lingers in current Malory scholarship.[15] There is every reason to assume that at every point at which Harleuse's name appeared, the archetype of the two extant texts read *Harleuse le Berbuse*. That uniformity should be helpful to editors of the *Morte Darthur*, whichever text they base their editions on, but it tells us nothing about who first supplied the names of Harleuse and Peryne to the earlier of the two episodes in which they appear, or why.

The variants in Peryne's name fall into a very different pattern. In both texts the later episode gives the name as *Peryne de la Mountayne* and the earlier one, including a marginal rubric in the manuscript text, as *Peryne de Mounte Belyarde*. Since the two texts agree, the variation must have been in their archetype, and so must be due to an early scribe or to Malory himself. The different name-forms have always been given separate entries in name-indexes,[16] implying or seeming to imply that they represent different characters. Whether they do or not, however, can only be decided after deciding who supplied Peryne's name to the earlier passage, a matter best addressed by considering the surprising fact that the derived name-form in the earlier episode is the more specific. One would expect a derived form either to reproduce its original, like Harleuse's, or to become less specific, like *Bryaunte de la Foreyste Saveage* at the beginning of the first tale, which produced *Bryan of the Foreyste* seventy pages

13 I thought this through too late to emend the 1990 Oxford text at this point.

14 They are given separate entries in the Index of Names in *Le Morte Darthur*, ed. H.O. Sommer (London, 1889–91), II, 147–83; and cf. Wilson, 'Minor Characters', pp. 372, 382.

15 See *Caxton's Malory*, ed. J.W. Spisak (Berkeley, Calif., 1983), pp. 705–6 (note to 335.4).

16 See the name-indexes in the editions of Vinaver, Sommer, and Spisak above, and R.W. Ackerman, *An Index of the Arthurian Names in Middle English*, Stanford, Calif., 1952.

later.[17] The varying of Peryne's name cannot be attributed to any discomfort felt by Malory or his scribes for appellations like *de la Mountayne*: the *Morte Darthur* has four other characters with that addition or a very similar one, three of which Malory apparently also invented.[18] The only explanation for *de Mounte Belyarde* that has been offered until now is that it was inspired by the source's *une tour fort et haut qui seoit a une marescherie*.[19] Vinaver, surely rightly, found that unconvincing, but could offer no alternative. An alternative, however, exists. Allowing for the variations normal when Malory puts French names into English, his *Mounte Belyarde* is identical with a name of some importance in the history of the Arthurian legend, a name from the earliest cycle of Arthurian romances, that by Robert de Boron. Robert's two verse romances, *Joseph d'Arimathie* and *Merlin*, survive (the latter incomplete) in a single manuscript; and at the end of the *Joseph*, Robert says that he composed it for a certain Gautier de Montbéliard. The unique manuscript spells the place *Mont Belyal*, but the identification is not disputed.[20]

Given the rarity of Robert's poems, it is unlikely that Malory knew them; but from them the name of Robert's patron made its way into at least some manuscripts of other, more widely read Arthurian romances. Not long after they were composed, Robert's two poems were turned into prose romances with the same titles, and one of the two manuscript families of the prose *Joseph d'Arimathie* mentions Gautier de Montbéliard.[21] The sixteen manuscripts of the prose *Joseph* divide into two families of eight, but because of lacunae in two manuscripts, Gautier's name actually appears in six manuscripts, in all cases, as in its verse original, at the end.[22] Two manuscripts, however, contain a second reference, in one case (the best manuscript of all) much earlier, in the other (a related manuscript) a few lines earlier. In these manuscripts Gautier's domicile is spelt *Mon(t)beliart*, and he is always spoken of as Robert's patron.

That does not complete the tally. There is a reference to *Gauter de Montbeliart*, again as Robert de Boron's patron, in a single manuscript of

17 *Works*, pp. 36.7, 104.27.

18 See the index of names in *Works*, pp. 1667–1701, *s.vv.* Garnyshe of the Mownte, Hew de la Mountayne, Madok de la Mountayne, and Mellyon of the Mountayne.

19 *Works*, p. 1313 (note to 81.9).

20 *Arthurian Literature in the Middle Ages*, ed. Roger Sherman Loomis (Oxford, 1959), pp. 252–3; Louis-Fernand Flutre, *Table des noms propres avec toutes leur variantes figurant dans les romans du moyen âge* (Poitiers, 1962), *s.v.* Mont Belyal; G.D. West, *An Index of Proper Names in French Arthurian Verse Romances* (Toronto, 1969), *ditto.*

21 R. O'Gorman, 'La tradition manuscrite du *Joseph d'Arimathie* de Robert de Boron,' *Revue d'Histoire des Textes* 1 (1971), 145–81, esp. 164–5.

22 Bibliothèque nationale fr. 748 gives no Christian name, calling him simply *le preu conte de Monbeliard.*

the prose version of Robert's second romance, the prose *Merlin*.[23] This is plainly a very isolated phenomenon: none of the other 46 classifiable prose *Merlin* manuscripts that contain that passage names Gautier, and no other such reference is known in any prose *Merlin* manuscript.[24] It should be noticed, however, that one other manuscript names Robert de Boron at that point without naming his patron, that the manuscript that names Robert alone is the best manuscript of the prose *Merlin*, and that that which names Robert and Gautier is the manuscript closest to it.[25]

The prose *Joseph* and *Merlin* with a third prose romance, the Didot *Perceval*, which may also be based on a lost poem of Robert's, make up a complete cycle of Arthurian romances.[26] That cycle inspired, directly and indirectly, the two other major cycles of Arthurian romance, the Vulgate and Post-Vulgate cycles. A manuscript of the the Vulgate cycle should begin with adapted versions of the two romances, and one of the Post-Vulgate (oddly) with the unmodified versions. The first of the *Morte Darthur*'s eight tales comes from a prose *Merlin* that was followed by a Post-Vulgate *Suite*, which suggests a preceding unmodified prose *Joseph*. In practice, of course, manuscript tradition can be very complicated: of the two known French manuscripts containing a prose *Merlin* and a Post-Vulgate *Suite*, one begins with the unmodified prose *Joseph* and the other with the adapted Joseph (i.e. the Vulgate *Estoire del Saint Graal*). On the other hand, at least four other manuscripts of the *Merlin* are

23 H.O. Sommer, 'An Interesting Find in the Bibliothèque Nationale, Paris,' *Athenaeum* (1906), 243–44, citing British Library, Add. 32125, 214r, the relevant passage from which Sommer later published in the apparatus criticus to his *Vulgate Version of the Arthurian Romances* (Washington, D.C., 1909–16), II, 20.12.

24 Cf. *Merlin*, ed. G. Paris and J. Ulrich, 2 vols, (Paris, 1886), I, 33; *Vulgate Romances, ibid., Merlin*, ed. A. Micha (Geneva, 1979), p. 76; their indexes of names; Flutre, *Table des noms propres*; and G.D. West, *An Index of Proper Names in French Arthurian Prose Romances*, Toronto, 1978. For the classification of the manuscripts, see Micha, 'Les manuscrits du Merlin en prose de Robert de Boron,' *Romania* 79 (1958), 78–94, 145–74. Of the fragments unknown to Micha, St. Petersburg and Hanover should contain the passage, Iowa City and Modena do not: P. Colin, *Romania* 88 (1967) 113–32; H. Suchier, *Romanische Studien* 1 (1875), 373; R. O'Gorman, *Romania* 84 (1963), 251–5; F. Bogdanow, *Romania* 90 (1969), 371–81. St. Petersburg is textually remote from the manuscript that names Gautier; Hanover has not been classified. Paris, Archives de France, MS. AB XIX 1734, dossier Moselle, is listed as a *Merlin* manuscript in Brian Woledge, *Bibliographie des romans, Supplement* (Geneva, 1974), p. 52, but appears in fact to be a lost portion of the *Livre d'Artus*: see 'A New Episode from the *Livre d'Artus*', *Bibliographical Bulletin of the International Arthuran Society* 43 (1991), 253–6. I am obliged to M. Favier, Director-General of the Archives, who supplied me with photographs of this fragment.

25 See Micha's essay and edition, above, n. 24.

26 See most recently, Linda Gowans, 'New Perspectives on the Didot-*Perceval*', *Arthurian Literature* 7 (1981), 1–22.

preceded by parts both of the *Joseph* and of the *Estoire*. It is difficult to estimate probabilities, but there is plainly a possibility that, although Malory began his book at a point well after the reference to Gautier, he looked back into an earlier part of the *Merlin*, or into a preceding *Joseph*, and found one of the references mentioned above, or a different one.

Such a hypothesis, however, provides no explanation why Malory used the name of Robert's patron's domicile where he did. There is an alternative hypothesis that does: that Malory's *Mounte Belyarde* was inspired by a lost reference to Robert's patron in the *Suite du Merlin*. At a point almost corresponding to Malory's reference to Mounte Belyarde, the *Suite* has a reference to Robert, a reference much discussed in other contexts, which says that Robert divided the *livre* of which the *Suite* is part (i.e. the Post-Vulgate Cycle) into *parties* of equal length. The two known manuscripts of the *Suite* that include the episode that Malory used both include the reference to Robert.[27] Neither mentions Gautier, but there is a good deal of evidence elsewhere that the manuscript Malory used was fuller and more authentic than either of them.[28] We may suppose it fuller and more authentic at this point too, naming Gautier as Robert's patron in a form of words like that used in the *Joseph* and *Merlin* romances. Of the possible explanations of the origin of the name Peryne de Mounte *Belyarde*, this is the one that accounts for the largest number of factors. Peryne's name can then be seen to be a conflation of the name of Robert de Boron's patron from the *Suite du Merlin* with the name Peryne of the Mountayne from later in the *Morte Darthur*.

It is very hard to believe that a scribe was responsible for this. The scribes who copied medieval vernacular prose romances were much given to making small changes *en passant* to improve the language and sense of their copy, but rarely to changes across hundreds of pages. In France, the scribes who copied Arthurian romances seem to have had a tradition of more wide-ranging emendations than most, and sometimes to have emended under the stimulus of passages hundreds of pages away, occasionally even consulting other manuscripts for information, but the purpose of their interventions was overwhelmingly to resolve contradictions, not, as it is here, to add material.[29] Malory's scribes made the usual

27 British Library, Add. 38117 (the Huth manuscript), 123 vols, published in Paris and Ulrich, *Merlin,* I. 280, and *Le Roman de Balain*, ed. M.D. Legge (Manchester 1942), p. 47; Cambridge University Library MS. Add. 7071, 264ra.

28 *Works*, p. 1281; cf. Vinaver's observation about the name *Brastias* (*Works,* p. 1294, note to 35.35–36.24) and Wilson's that Arthur's half-sister *Elayne* (*Works*, p. 10.7), who has no counterpart in the French manuscripts, has one called *Elena* in the corresponding Spanish romance, the *Baladro del Sabio Merlin* ('Addenda', p. 565).

29 Elspeth Kennedy, 'The Scribe as Editor', *Mélanges de langue et de littérature du moyen âge et de la renaissance offerts à Jean Frappier*, 2 vols. (Geneva 1970), I, 522–31.

'improvements' to their copy *en passant*, but there is no sign that they attempted to resolve far-flung contradictions with or without Malory's sources, or that they knew what his sources were, or had access to them.

The only way to salvage the hypothesis of scribal origins is to postulate that when Malory wrote the earlier passage he gave the second character a name that included the phrase *de Mounte Belyarde*, and that a later scribe introduced the names of Harleuse and Peryne. That still attributes to a scribe an implausible interest in inserting the names of minor characters in a passage hundreds of pages from the point where he found them. There is no sign elsewhere in the *Morte Darthur* of any scribe wanting to do this, and nothing about this passage to explain why a scribe who did not tamper elsewhere should have done so here. Moreover, although an author who failed to notice the difficulties caused by giving characters who promptly died the names of characters who were alive later in his book would no doubt be grossly careless, a scribe who did the same would have to be thought just as careless. Such a scribe would have been acting as an author, and the well-understood factors about the rhythm and mechanics of copying manuscripts that explain the usual kinds of scribal carelessness would do nothing to explain the kind of error that he would have committed.

This scribe begins to look like the scribe Richard Bentley thought had corrupted *Paradise Lost*, but whom later scholarship has unanimously seen as a figment of Bentley's imagination, the ludicrous product of over-confidence and inability to accept the uncongenial aspects of a great book.[30] The alternative candidate, however, Malory himself, altered characters' names often enough to make the *Morte Darthur* an appreciably different kind of book,[31] and in doing so created some of the inconsistencies that have so exercised his modern critics. He must be assumed to have made these alterations too, in one way or another. We may picture him either naming from the later passage and the source of the earlier passage together two characters who were anonymous in his first draft, or renaming from the later passage alone two characters, the second of whom already had a name that included *de Mounte Belyarde*. Many people might feel that the second was the more natural picture, but either requires us to assume that it was Malory, working back from his story of Alexander the Orphan, who introduced Harleuse's and Peryne's names into the first tale in the *Morte Darthur*.

30 J.W. Mackail, 'Bentley's Milton,' *Proceedings of the British Academy* 11 (1924), 55–73; cf. A.E. Housman, 'Introductory Lecture', *Selected Prose*, ed. John Carter (Cambridge, 1961), p. 1–22, at 12–13.

31 See Wilson, 'Naming', *ad fin.*

II

We can now ask whether we should think of Harleuse and Peryne as two characters, or three, or four. The various name-indexes naturally appear to imply three, but one Harleuse consorting with two different Perynes makes an unlikely picture. Two and four, however, seem at first sight equally plausible: there are plenty of cases in the *Morte Darthur* both of one name representing two characters and of two representing one.[32] That fact at least means that the problem could be solved if we could establish a case either way for either name, because if there were certainly two Perynes, we could assume two Harleuses, and if one Harleuse, we could take the Peryne name-forms as variants, as is generally assumed of *Bryaunte de la Foreyste Saveage* and *Bryan of the Foreyste.*[33] Vinaver's eight-tale theory could be read to provide a simple answer, but Malory scholarship has decisively rejected that theory, and even Vinaver himself did not assert it consistently when discussing Malory's minor characters. In the introduction to his Index of Names, he set out as his fundamental principle that when a name occurred in the same form in two or more passages anywhere in the *Morte Darthur* it was to be taken to refer to the same person unless Malory's text provided clear evidence to the contrary.[34]

That the same name should refer to the same person might seem self-evident once the eight-tale theory is rejected, but Wilson's comprehensive account of Malory's minor characters entered a subtle caveat against it.[35] He suggested that, except with a few favourite characters and with the name-lists in the later tales, Malory's repetition of the names of minor characters from one tale to another was unconscious, the product of a wish to increase the amount of personal action in his book. When he used a name for a second time, he would have forgotten the existence as well as the attributes of the character to whom he had given it before. Since Malory would have had no intention either that the name-form should represent one character or that it should represent two, his reader must determine the question from the remainder of the *Morte Darthur*, including its sources insofar as they are implied in and consistent with it. Wilson's caveat would change the criteria for deciding how many characters Harleuse and Peryne's names represent. Decisions about identity and difference would no longer require 'clear evidence' to override the normal presumption that the same name

32 *Works*, pp. 1665–6.
33 So Vinaver, Spisak, and Ackerman's name-indexes.
34 *Works*, p. 1665. 'Anywhere in the *Morte Darthur*' is not explicit, but is implied by the entire Index.
35 Wilson, 'Addenda', pp. 574–7 and *passim.*

implies the same character, but could properly be distinguished on the basis of the smallest details.[36]

Wilson's caveat is plainly closer to the realities of authorship than theories that see Malory as in total simultaneous command of each of the 343,000 words of the *Morte Darthur* in relation to all the others, and to every word of his sources as well. It is also sophisticated in the way it allows for possible differences between author's intention and reader's response. However, it appears to envisage, apart from the exceptions Wilson himself allows, a mental process of summoning names out of a limbo of memory to apply them *at random* to any anonymous character, a process that would surely have created many more discrepancies in Malory's book than any scholar has found. Certainty is unattainable, and the notion of the unconscious mind is a difficult one, but the very substantial consistency of Malory's characterisation strongly suggests that he named his minor characters by what we would normally think of as a conscious process. Such a process (which might well include written notes, systematic revision, and suggestions from people other than the author, as well as many unconscious operations of memory) normally implies that all occurrences of the same name-form denote the same person. Only when assuming this produces a character of whom, in Wilson's crisp phrase, not all that is asserted could be true simultaneously[37] should we look to Wilson's caveat or other explanations to resolve inconsistencies.

Because it comes close to the realities of the mind and of writing, Wilson's caveat may help resolve some problems that he formally excluded from its scope, such as whether *Bryaunte de la Foreyste Saveage* and *Bryan of the Foreyste* in the first tale should be thought of as one person or two. Other cases, however, which it was intended to deal with, are much more difficult. Even when Wilson's description of the mental process by which Malory produced incompatible statements about minor characters is convincing, the response that he suggests may not be. He proposed, for instance, that the names of Bryan de les Iles and Collgrevaunce of Goore should each be taken as representing no fewer than four distinct characters. There is something absurd about that degree of multiplication of characters with such small rôles and such distinctive names. Fortunately, however, another response is possible, to which I shall return shortly.

Harleuse and Peryne are particularly difficult to explain in Wilson's terms because the combination of their complicated and distinctive names[38] and the fact that there are two of them points decisively to

36 *Ibid.*, pp. 576.

37 *Ibid.*

38 The *Morte Darthur* includes no other Peryne, no other Harleuse, and no other character called le Berbuse.

Malory having put them into the Balin story by a conscious act—indeed, to his having done so with the passage in which they appear in the Alexander story open before him. Fitting their two names to a pair of anonymous or differently named knights-errant in his first draft does not look at all like Malory's unconscious operating at random. Rather, it looks like a small-scale version of something that Wilson showed was characteristic of Malory's work as early as his fourth tale, the systematic use of lists of names to create complicated consistent action in tournaments and other ceremonial occasions.[39]

If Malory transferred the two names consciously from one passage to the other, he must have intended either that each character should be the same person in each passage or that he should not, and in the former case he must have envisaged the first incident as taking place after the second. Even though his intentions may turn out not to be a sufficient guide to the response proper to an informed reader, we must next enquire what they were.

Because there are two Peryne name-forms, the problem presents itself more clearly with Harleuse. Malory found Harleuse le Berbuse as a knight errant with a tiny part in the Alexander story and deliberately gave his very distinctive name to an anonymous knight errant with a tiny part in his first tale. It is natural to assume that when he used that name again, he meant the same person by it, yet the episode into which he had introduced it relates the knight's death. He cannot have overlooked that death: on both occasions when he put Harleuse's name into the earlier episode he put it next to and made it the obvious subject of the verb *was slayne*. He may even have composed the marginal rubric at that point in the manuscript text: 'Here Garlonde that went invisyble slew Harlews le Barbeus under the conduyt of Balyn.' These things could be interpreted as a pointer intended by Malory to show that the Harleuse in the earlier episode was a different character from his namesake in the later one. Malory's normal practice with names, however, suggests quite the opposite.

There are some 454 named characters in the *Morte Darthur*, of whom at least 168 seem to have had their names supplied by Malory for all or some of their appearances.[40] The combination of what Malory changed and what he left unaltered show him taking great pains to distinguish different characters by different names. His practice with simple names consisting of a single word is different from his practice with compound

39 'Addenda', pp. 569–70.

40 See *Works*, Index of Names, above, n. 18; Wilson, 'Addenda', pp. 583–7. These figures exclude the occasions on which Malory gave the name of a *major* character to someone anonymous in his source: cf. *Works*, p. 1484 (note to 571.9–18).

names such as *Bryan de Lystenoyse*. He sometimes deliberately gives a simple name to more than one character if their circumstances distinguish them clearly. So we find an Edward in the army that Arthur takes to the Roman war, and another Edward in the opposing army. We find five Elaynes, clearly distinguished as the wives of Kings Nentres and Ban, the daughters of King Pelles and Barnard of Astolat, and the son of Sir Bors. Once Malory makes such a distinction in his own person as narrator: when a second Sir Marhalte appears in the story, he carefully explains who he is and how he is related to his namesake.[41] There are a dozen cases in which he distinguishes a pair of characters by one having a simple name and the other adding an appellation to it, and another dozen in which he distinguishes pairs by different appellations added to the same simple name.[42]

There is, however, no sign that Malory ever deliberately gave more than one character the same compound name. He may sometimes, under the circumstances Wilson describes, have done so by mistake— and we have noticed in the cases of Bryan de les Iles and Coll grevaunce of Goore the absurdity that that can produce—but here we are not concerned with his mistakes, but with his intentions. The totality of his naming practice entitles us to impute to Malory even in the case of unconscious repetitions a virtual intention that any one compound name should represent one character, and in the absence of clear evidence to the contrary from his text, we should interpret that text in the light of that virtual intention.[43] However, in the case of Harleuse, we need not invoke any such intention. Since, as we have seen, Malory consciously transferred Harleuse's compound name, we may assume that he consciously intended the same person at both points, and so that he meant the Harleuse le Berbuse who dies in his first tale to be the same person as the Harleuse le Berbuse in his story of Alexander the Orphan.

41 *Works*, p. 729.28. The source has a similar explanation (cf. Löseth, *Roman de Tristan,* pp. 271, 342).

42 See the index of names in *Works*, *s.vv.* Arnolde, Bedyvere, Blamoure, Breuse (cf. Wilson, 'Addenda', p. 577; *Works*, p. 659), Carados, Elyas, Galahalte, Harry, Kay, Myles, Persydes, Phelot, Pynnel, and Sadok; and Blamoure, Bryan, Edwarde, Felotte/Phelot, Hervis/Hervyse, Hew, Isode, Ladinas/Ladynas, Melyot, Playne, Uwayne, and Vale. Some cases are disputable (the two Pynnels, for instance, may be the same person), but the principles are not.

43 For authorial 'final intention', see Jerome J. McGann, *A Critique of Modern Textual Criticism*, Chicago, 1983.

III

Malory's intentions, however, are not the end of the matter. Modern critical theory warns us against assuming that a work of art expresses the whole of its creator's intentions and nothing else, and urges us to discover the meaning of the work from the work itself.[44] It follows from this that when a part of the text is ambiguous, its meaning should be decided by interpretative norms derived from the remainder of the text rather than by *a priori* probabilities drawn from authorial intention or lack of it, or from literature in general (although we may expect that in many cases all three criteria will support the same conclusion). If this proposition seems radical, it is at least much less radical than the universally accepted process of supplying medieval texts with modern punctuation.[45] The totality of character-naming in the *Morte Darthur*, therefore, is more than evidence for Malory's intentions: it is the basis for an interpretative norm that can be stated as one compound name one character.

Bryan de les Iles will provide an example of how that norm can be applied. If we accept Wilson's hypothesis that Malory had no intentions as to the number of characters implied by Bryan's name, this norm and the text of the four episodes in which he appears both point not, as Wilson suggested, to four characters, but to either two or one. The knight-errant whose brother-in-arms promises to bring him to Arthur's court in the first tale will be the same person as Arthur's retainer in the war in the second tale, and the 'noble knight' who sides against Arthur in the tournament in the fourth tale will be the same person as the 'noble man and grete enemy to kynge Arthure' deprived of his lands in the fifth.[46] One of Malory's sources provides additional support for identifying the second

44 The classic statement is W.K. Wimsatt Jr., 'The Intentional Fallacy', *The Verbal Icon* (Lexington, Kentucky, 1954), pp. 3–18. For other views see E.D. Hirsch, Jr., *Validity in Interpretation* (New Haven, 1967), pp. 1–67; René Wellek and Austin Warren, *Theory of Literature* (Harmondsworth, 1973), pp. 142–57; and Janis L. Pallister and Ramona Cormer, 'Authorial Intention and the Literary Work', *Poetica* (Tokyo) 17 (1986), 71–83.

45 Consider as representative P.L. Heyworth, 'The Punctuation of Middle English Texts', *Medieval Studies for J.A.W. Bennett*, ed. P.L. Hayworth (Oxford, 1981), pp. 139–57, which, after observing that mediaeval vernacular manuscripts are almost always punctuated unsystematically and in ways unhelpful to elucidating the text, recommends an editor (1) to restore the text to a state that represents that which the author originally wrote, and (2) to punctuate ambiguous passages so as to bring out clearly the sense the editor sees as satisfactory. Since there are no grounds for supposing that mediaeval authors in general punctuated better than their scribes, this strategy cannot be thought of as restoring the author's punctuation or supplying its modern equivalent: it is at best an act of interpretation, based on other (presumably the more narrowly verbal) aspects of the text.

46 *Works*, pp. 117, 212, 343, 469, 476.

pair with each other: although source evidence has to be used with circumspection, since Malory often gives us what he evidently feels his sources should have said rather than what they did say,[47] both the second pair of figures surely in some sense 'are' the only other Bryan de les Iles in Arthurian literature, Arthur's enemy in *Perlesvaus*, and so the two figures, being equivalent to a third thing, must be equivalent to each other.

Whether there are two Bryans or one is a matter of whether the *Morte Darthur*'s lexical norms allow us to read the narrator's final words about Bryan, that he 'wolde never' be one of Arthur's retainers, in a sufficiently restricted sense (one, say, confined to future intention) to allow for his having been Arthur's retainer in the second tale, and whether the narrative norms of the *Morte Darthur* allow us to postulate something like an unrecorded quarrel between Arthur and Bryan between the second and third episode. If, as seems likely, both questions can be answered affirmatively, there is no impediment to believing that all the episodes in which Bryan's name appears describe the same person; and if there is no impediment, the rest of the *Morte Darthur* requires us to do so.

In Harleuse's case, however, there is a serious impediment that no chronological ingenuity can remove: his death. We need not here arbitrate between the common reader's view of the chronology of the *Morte Darthur* as more or less successive (with perhaps a substantial retrospective section at the beginning of the fifth tale) and the more complicated chronologies proposed by Moorman and others. None of them is compatible with any chronology that would put the deaths of Harleuse and Peryne at the end of their lives.

We must conclude that Malory attempted something that would have increased the unity of the *Morte Darthur*, and failed. In the debate over unity, the attempt will not please one party nor the failure the other, but Malory's two statements cannot be reconciled with each other. He presumably somehow came to think of Harleuse's appearance in the story of Alexander the Orphan as taking place before his appearance in the story of Balin. One can see how this might have happened. Although, as the best account of the chronology of the *Morte Darthur* has argued, Malory did not sustain any chronological scheme consistently, the closing words of his first tale show he had a notion of an 'objective' Arthurian time-scheme external to his book.[48] Some of the events in the *Morte Darthur* suggested that the Alexander story took place very early indeed in that time-scheme. For instance, Malory gave Alexander a son (unknown to any French source) called Bellingere le Beuse, and made Bellingere one of Lancelot's regular comrades in arms in the last part of the *Morte Darthur*. Any of the numerous occasions when Malory named Bellingere could have reminded

47 Wilson, 'Malory's French Book Again', *Comparative Literature* 2 (1950), 172–81.
48 Olefsky, 'Chronology', pp. 63–4; *Works*, p. 180.18–19.

him of Bellingere's dead father, whose youth would have been a notional generation earlier, and which Malory could then, forgetting irreconcileable statements he had made elsewhere, have imagined as contemporary with Arthur's own youth, and so with the beginning of the *Morte Darthur*. That may explain how the inconsistency arose, but does not resolve it; and any chronology that attempted to do so would create many more inconsistencies.

If chronology cannot resolve that inconsistency, we could resort to another of the traditional expedients, distinguishing two knights of the same name, to resolve it and the comparable cases of Collgrevaunce of Goore, Dinadan, and Uwayne les Avoutres, all of whom are said to be killed in the quest for the Holy Grail, then listed among the knights who attempt to heal Sir Urry in the following tale.[49] Wilson recommends this expedient, even for cases in which the mental processes producing the original error might not be those described in his caveat.[50] He argues that where it is necessary to multiply characters to make sense of the facts of Malory's story, that need must take precedence over his own and anyone else's view of Malory's intentions. He also recommends it to deal with inconsistencies like those between Aladuke and Priamus in the Roman War story and their namesakes in the Urry list.[51] We could invoke it too over the duplication, on almost successive pages of the Urry list, of the name of Constantine son of Cador, postulating presumably a different father called Cador of Cornwayle for each of the two Constantines.[52] A process that produced seven doppelgängers in three pages might be absurd, but at least it would not be self-contradictory.

There is however a further difficulty. The *Morte Darthur* presents other problems of factual consistency similar in their apparent pyschological origin and in the effect they have on the narrative to the problems with minor characters that we have been considering. Nearly fifty are listed in an appendix to Ellyn Olefsky's excellent account of Malory's chronology, and there are others—one group, for instance, involving the chronological relationship between the *Morte Darthur* and the external history of Christendom.[53] It would contribute nothing to solving most of these

49 *Works*, pp. 973, 615, 945, 1148.

50 Wilson, 'Addenda', p. 576.

51 *Ibid.*, pp. 578, 581. These two cases recall Harleuse: Wilson demonstrates of both that Malory consciously intended the character in the later episode to be the same person as his earlier namesake.

52 *Works*, pp. 1147.26, 1149.14.

53 Olefsky, 'Chronology'; P.J.C. Field, 'Time and Elayne of Astolat', *Studies in Malory*, ed. James W. Spisak (Kalamazoo, Michigan, 1985), pp. 231–6. Some of Dr Olefsky's examples involve minor characters like those considered above, but to those that do not one could add Ironside's duplicated first appearance at Arthur's court, Malory's unfulfilled promise to relate the death of Kayhidins, and his assertion that 110 knights attempt to heal Sir Urry (*Works*, pp. 326 and 336,

further problems if we imagined a complete set of new characters on every page. There is something unsatisfying about a solution that can cope with an unlimited number of problems of one type but gives no hint of how to cope with others of obviously related types.

Given these two difficulties, it is worth considering more seriously than usual the third of the traditional expedients, which at least offers the prospect of coping (in some sense) with every possible kind of inconsistencies: that is, that we should simply accept them as errors. Such errors are of course not deviations from fact, since the *Morte Darthur* is written, as Sidney said, not affirmatively but allegorically; nor failures to agree with a French source, as Vinaver sometimes implies;[54] nor (except figuratively) deviations from a purer version of the story found elsewhere, as Victorian critics sometimes suggested. An error in the *Morte Darthur* must be an internal contradiction: the element in the contradiction that harmonises better with the rest of the Malory's book will be 'true', the other 'false'. Such a definition allows, and it is to be hoped will even encourage, readers to look for the most harmonious reading of the book. That in principle will mean considering not only the other two expedients, but also identifiable scribal corruption and any other factor that could reduce the number of 'errors', and may, if all the factors involved are evenly balanced, mean adopting one set of interpretations on the grounds that it leaves the smallest residue of error.[55] At the end of any such process, however, errors will still remain, and they should be treated like errors in a non-fictional work. So, for instance, in any index of the characters in the *Morte Darthur*, Harleuse and Peryne would have a single entry apiece, with (if the index admitted annotation) a note that one of the episodes in which the character appeared was in error. As in a non-fictional work, though for different reasons, it might be unnecessary or even impossible to say which episode was erroneous.

Any such error in a work of fiction must by definition be a fracture in the book's aesthetic coherence. Since aesthetic coherence has been fundamental to literary theory since Aristotle,[56] it is hardly surprising that critics of the *Morte Darthur* have been reluctant to admit that it contained errors.

493, and 1150). There are various errors in both texts affecting the total number of knights, and editors disagree about correcting them, but no combination of proposed corrections or refusals to correct will bring the number up to 110.

54 Sir Philip Sidney, 'A Defence of Poetry', *Miscellaneous Prose*, edd. K. Duncan-Jones and Jan van Dorsten (Oxford, 1973), p. 103; *Works*, e.g. p. 1461 (note to 404.16–18).

55 The possibility that the reader's final interpretative act might be opting on the basis of his own preferences between otherwise equally attractive interpretations does not make the process advocated here one of 'deconstruction'. Cf. Roland Barthes, 'Theory of the Text', *Untying the Text*, ed. Robert Young (Boston, Mass., 1981), pp. 31–47.

56 See Malcolm Heath, *Unity in Greek Poetics*, Oxford, 1989.

Error may sometimes, as we have seen in the present essay, be valuable to the literary historian or textual critic in pursuit of sources or authorial intentions; but to the literary critic as such it is anathema. Even good critics have been reluctant to accept apparent errors, despite the fact that the difficulties presented by any other hypothesis that aims to deal comprehensively with the minor characters plainly become even more unmanageable as those characters become less minor, cease to be interchangeable embodiments of chivalric behaviour and begin to acquire individuality.[57] Critics have sometimes tried to attribute apparent errors to scribes more out of a concern for Malory's good name than on the evidence, and when that was impossible, have only been able to suggest that, since the *Morte Darthur* is big and the errors are small, it may be able, like Whitman, to contain them.[58] That is both true and important, but it would be agreeable to be able to do a little more for the *Morte Darthur* than that.

It may be possible to do so, because some errors at least may compensate for the damage they do to the story of *Morte Darthur* by helping to characterise the book in a striking and effective way. What makes this possible is the *Morte Darthur*'s unusual narrator. Chaucer's *Canterbury Tales* and More's *Utopia*, for instance, give us signals that we are to take the narrator of the story as one of its characters, with limitations that the author uses to entertain and instruct us. In the absence of such signals, critics normally assume by default the omniscient narrator conventional in western literature, and particularly in its dominant modern form, the novel. Such a narrator functions as a god within the fiction, and for him to co-exist with error is to contradict himself, inducing in the reader literary atheism, nihilism, and paranoia. However, although Malory gives us none of the signals we get from Chaucer or More, neither does he assert the conventional narrator's omniscience. On the contrary, he presents himself, as I have argued at length elsewhere,[59] as distinctly fallible. Among the signs of fallibility that concern us here are, for instance, his confession that he has lost part of a source; and on another occasion his putting forward something his sources have told him but which he seems unable to endorse, as if, although he was dubious about it, he could do

57 So with Wilson's hypothesis that the Priamus baptised by Tristram must be a new character rather than a confusing of the Priamus baptised by Gawain with Palomides baptised by Tristram (*Works*, pp. 1149.19, 241.4, 842–5). A second discrepancy over Priamus that Wilson points out may be illusory. It is, as Wilson says, unlikely that the earlier Priamus, who is from the Levant, would be, as the later Priamus is said to be, the brother of two British knights; but *brother* can mean 'brother-in-arms': *Middle English Dictionary*, s.v. *brother* n., 4 (a). On brotherhood in arms, cf. K.B. McFarlane, 'A Business-partnership in War and Administration', *English Historical Review* 78 (1963), 290–310.

58 Cf. Wilson, 'Chronology', pp. 332–4; Olefsky, 'Chronology', p. 67; Field, 'Time and Elayne,' p. 233.

59 P.J.C. Field, *Romance and Chronicle* (London, 1971), pp. 142–59.

no better.[60] Again, although he appears to have searched conscientiously for the true story of Arthur's death, his very emphasis raises the possibility that he might have failed to find it.[61]

It is entirely in keeping that such a man should himself sometimes make mistakes; and in such a man, readers can tolerate errors that they could not in an omniscient narrator, provided the errors are in the strict sense negligible, as those ennumerated above are. Malory's character as narrator allows us to understand those errors as having been committed by a narrator who cares about fact, who has tried to find the 'auctorysed' version of his story, who, if he had noticed an error in his story would have put it right, not merely (as Thackeray did in comparable circumstances)[62] apologised for it; but who in the last analysis is writing about something other than factual consistency. His subject is the nobility of King Arthur and his knights of the Round Table, that when they were together there was ever an hundred and fifty. It is significant that the last words of the *Morte Darthur* get that number wrong.[63] The error may well be scribal, but even if it is not, the attentive reader will not be much disturbed, because Malory gets the nobility right.

60 *Works*, pp. 1154.12–14, 1257.27–8.

61 *Works*, p. 1242.

62 At the end of *Pendennis*, Thackeray apologises for having killed off the Marquess of Farintoft's mother in one chapter and then having made her beseech him not to marry Blanche Amory in a later one.

63 'Wrong' of course because it is the odd statement out compared with *Works*, pp. 98.10–11, 19–30, 293.25, 942.5, 946.4–16, 1146.33–1147.1; and cf. 1324 (note to p. 98.33).

Malory's Lancelot

J.D. PHEIFER

More than sixty years ago Myrrha Lot-Borodine observed that Tristan and Lancelot represent contrasting views of love as tragic passion and *Frauendienst*, and that Tristan's appeal is therefore more popular and romantic in the ordinary sense, while Lancelot's is restricted chiefly to medievalists:

> Les deux héros qui portent des noms justement célèbres dans notre vieille littérature sont les symboles vivants de l'amour conçu sous cette double forme: la passion tragique et fatale, le service-culte de la dame.
>
> Le premier de ces héros, Tristan, moins attaché à une époque particulière, plus profondément humain, séduit davantage le cœur des foules et l'imagination des poètes; le second, Lancelot du Lac, étroitement lié au milieu courtois qui l'a fait naître, en opposition à son émule, déjà glorieux, attire surtout les esprits curieux des formes d'art et de sentiment passées.[1]

Mme Lot-Borodine was thinking of modern readers, but the history of the two great prose romances with Tristan and Lancelot as their central figures suggest that Tristan was more popular in the Middle Ages as well: it was the Prose *Roman de Tristan*,[2] not the Prose *Lancelot*,[3] though it was first in the field, that was expanded in successive redactions and imitated in later romances like the *Estoire du Graal*[4] and Malory's *Morte*

1 'Tristan et Lancelot', *Medieval Studies in Memory of Gertrude Schoepperle Loomis* (Paris and New York, 1927), pp. 21–47, at 21.

2 *Le Roman de Tristan en prose*, ed. René Curtis, 3 vols., Cambridge, 1985, cited as 'Curtis'; this edition breaks off at the end of Dr. Curtis's copy-text, Charpentras, Bibliothèque municipale 404. For the remainder of the *Tristan* references are to the résumé in E. Löseth, *Le Roman de Tristan, le roman de Palamede et la compilation de Rusticien de Pise*, Paris, 1890 (Bibliothèque de l'École des Hautes Études 82), cited as 'Löseth', and occasionally to microfilm copies of Paris, Bibliothèque nationale, fr. 99 and 334, for which I am indebted to Mme Florence de Lussy and the library authorities. The portions of the Prose *Lancelot* relating to the coming of Galahad that were incorporated in the *Tristan* (Löseth, §388a) are printed in H. Oskar Sommer, 'Galahad and Perceval', *Modern Philology* 5 (1907–8), 55–84, 181–200, 291–341.

3 *Lancelot*, ed. Alexandre Micha, 9 vols., Paris, 1978–83.

4 See below, p. 176 and n. 93, and Fanni Bogdanow, *The Romance of the Grail* (Manchester, 1966), pp. 10–13 and *passim*.

Darthur.[5] In the prose romance, however, Tristan was not so much the tragic lover as a fallible human being his admirers could identify with, who failed to prevent the abduction of Seguradés' wife, his first mistress, because he feared her other lover, King Mark,[6] and tried to console himself for the loss of Isolde of Cornwall with her namesake in Brittany,[7] unlike Lancelot, who never ceased to mourn the loss of Guinevere when he was on the *Isle de Joie* with King Pelles' daughter.[8] This *homme moyen sensuel*, who became a true lover and learnt by trial and error that he could not break off the relationship,[9] is a more attractive and sympathetic figure than the faultless Lancelot.

I

Writing as he did in the late fifteenth century, Malory could hardly avoid being influenced by a literary tradition that was firmly established when its two heroes first met at the *Perron Merlin*.[10] Tristan had long been a hero of Celtic legend,[11] and the main events of his story were already circulating in literary form when the earliest Arthurian romances were written and provided the standard by which their heroes and heroines were measured. In the prologue to *Chevrefoil*, her lay of Tristan and Isolde, Marie de France mentions oral tales and an *escrit* which contained a *Liebestod* like that in Thomas's *Roman de Tristan*, probably the oldest surviving Tristan romance:[12]

5 Sir Thomas Malory, *Le Morte Darthur*, ed. H. Oskar Sommer, 3 vols., London, 1889–91 (reprinted from Caxton's edition); *The Works of Sir Thomas Malory*, ed. Eugène Vinaver, 2nd ed., 3 vols. paged continuously, Oxford, 1967 (a critical edition of London, British Library, Add. 59678), cited as '*Works*'. Quotations are from Vinaver's text unless otherwise indicated.

6 Curtis, §377. Cf. *Morte Darthur* VIII. 15; *Works*, pp. 396–7.

7 Curtis, §561, condensing Thomas's *Roman de Tristan* (*Les Fragments du Roman de Tristan*, ed. Bartina H. Wind, Geneva and Paris, 1960), Sneyd[1] 1–368. Cf. *Morte Darthur* VIII. 36; *Works*, pp. 434–5.

8 Lancelot, CVII, §§43–6. Cf. *Morte Darthur* XII. 5–6; *Works*, pp. 825–7.

9 Curtis, §568. Cf. *Morte Darthur* VIII. 36; *Works*, pp. 434–5.

10 Löseth, §§202–3. Cf. *Morte Darthur* X. 5; *Works*, pp. 568–70.

11 See Helaine Newstead, 'The Origin and Growth of the Tristan Legend', *Arthurian Literature in the Middle Ages*, ed. Roger Sherman Loomis (Oxford, 1959), pp. 122–33, esp. 124–9.

12 Professor Wind, pp. 16–17, dates Thomas's poem tentatively between 1150 and 1160 on linguistic grounds; see also Frederick Whitehead, 'The Early Tristan Poems', *Arthurian Literature in the Middle Ages*, pp. 134–44, at 135–6.

Plusurs le me unt cunté e dit
E jeo l'ai trové en escrit
De Tristram et de la reïne,
De lur amur que tant fu fine,
Dunt il eurent meinte dolur,
Puis en murerent en un jur.[13]

In *Erec et Enide*, his first Arthurian romance, Chrétien de Troyes, her contemporary, compared Erec's victory over Yder to Tristan's conquest of le Morholt and contrasted Isolde, whose place was taken by Brangwen on her wedding night, with Enide, who needed no substitute;[14] in *Cligés*, his next, Chrétien listed a piece *del roi Marc et d'Ysalt la blonde* among his own works, and Fenice contrasted her relationship with Cligés, the nephew of her husband the Emperor, with Isolde and Tristan's:

'Mialz voldroie estre desmanbree
Que de nos deus fust remanbree
L'amors d'Ysolt et de Tristan,
Don mainte folie dit an,
Et honte en est a reconter.
Ja ne m'i porroie acorder
A la vie qu'Isolz mena.
Amors en li trop vilena,
Que ses cuers fu a un entiers,
Et ses cors fu a deus rentiers.'[15]

In these early romances Arthur and his knights were not even contemporary with Tristan: Thomas's Arthur seems to have belonged to the previous generation,[16] while Fenice implies that Tristan and Isolde were already dead.

Lancelot du Lac, on the other hand, although his sobriquet also implies a mythical origin,[17] made his literary debut in Chrétien's *Erec et Enide* as Arthur's third best knight, after Gawain and Erec,[18] and was

13 *Chevrefoil* (*Lais*, ed. Alfred Ewert (Oxford, 1944), pp.123–6) 6–11. Cf. *Roman de Tristan*, Douce 1017–1815 + Sneyd² 783–819. In Douce 835–84 Thomas refers to conflicting accounts of Tristan's fatal wound, alternate versions of which are still to be found in the Prose *Tristan* (Löseth, §§540a–4a, 546–9).

14 Chrétien de Troyes, *Erec et Enide*, ed. Mario Roques (Paris, 1973), 1241–4, 2021–3. Cf. Thomas, *Roman de Tristan*, Douce 2–25.

15 Chrétien de Troyes, *Cligés*, ed. Alexandre Micha (Paris, 1970), 3105–14.

16 The giant Tristan killed in Spain was the nephew of Orgillos, whom Arthur had slain (*Roman de Tristan*, Sneyd¹ 662–728).

17 See Jean Frappier, 'Chrétien de Troyes', *Arthurian Literature in the Middle Ages*, pp. 157–91, at 178.

18 *Erec* 1674.

the second knight Cligés overthrew at the tournament of Oxford;[19] in the *Chevalier de la Charrete*, however, he was abruptly promoted from this subaltern role to Guinevere's paramour and the chief exponent of courtly love as it was interpreted by Chrétien's patroness, the Countess of Champagne:

> Del CHEVALIER DE LA CHARRETE
> comance Crestïens son livre;
> matiere et san li done et livre
> la contesse, et il s'antremet
> de panser, que gueres n'i met
> fors sa painne et s'antancïon[20]

Lancelot and Guinevere's grand passion, like that of Cligés and Fenice, was probably inspired by Tristan and Isolde's,[21] but their relationship was very different. Guinevere's will, however capricious, was Lancelot's command: he submitted *a meniere de fin amant* without a word when she dismissed him from her presence after all his efforts to find her,[22] he let himself be beaten at the tournament of Pomelegoi when she gave the word.[23] In part, at least, this difference was sociological. Lancelot was not the sovereign's nephew like Tristan and Cligés, or even (in Chrétien) a foreign king's son like Erec; he was merely one of Arthur's household knights, involved in the classic 'courtly love' situation described by C.S. Lewis:

> We must picture a castle which is a little island of comparative leisure and luxury, and therefore at least of possible refinement, in a barbarous country-side. There are many men in it, and very few women—the lady and her damsels. Around these throng the whole male *meiny*, the inferior nobles. the landless knights. the squires, and the pages—haughty creatures enough in relation to the peasantry beyond the walls, but feudally inferior to the lady as to her lord—her 'men' as feudal language had it.[24]

Lancelot's social position explains his obsequiousness to Giunevere and the humility which was to become his distinctive virtue. In other respects, however, the *Chevalier de la Charette* is not so different from Chrétien's

19 *Cligés* 4710–45.
20 *Le Chevalier de la Charrete*, ed. Mario Roques (Paris, 1974), 24–9.
21 See Frappier, 'Chrétien de Troyes', p. 178; Roger Sherman Loomis, *Arthurian Tradition and Chrétien de Troyes* (New York, 1939), pp. 251–2.
22 *Charrete* 3960–4. Cf. *Lancelot*, XXXIX, §20.
23 *Charrete* 5636–758, 5829–67. Cf. *Lancelot*, LXI, §10.
24 *The Allegory of Love* (Oxford, 1936), p.12.

other late romances, *Yvain*[25] and *Perceval*.[26] In each Gawain, Arthur's best knight, who had fought Cligés to a draw after he overcame Lancelot and Perceval,[27] became a foil to set off the achievements of the hero, a technique that was to be applied more widely in the prose romances: his mistress Lunete and his niece and his nephews were saved by Yvain, who then defended the younger daughter of the *Sire de la Noire Espine* against the wicked elder daughter he championed;[28] he refused to mount the cart with Lancelot and nearly drowned when he slipped off the *Pont soz Eve* after Lancelot successfully negotiated the *Pont de l'Espee*;[29] he was caught making love to the king of Escavalon's sister while Perceval enjoyed his child-like idyll with Blancheflor.[30]

II

There is no evidence that Chrétien's Guinevere had an affair with Lancelot before he rescued her, but it was broadly hinted (in the concluding section by Godefroi de Laigny) that she meant their relationship to continue although she prudently hid her feelings when he returned from Meleagant's prison:

> Por ce reisons anferme et lie
> son fol cuer, et son fol pansé;
> si l'a un petit racenssé
> et a mis la chose an respit
> jusque tant que voie et espit
> un boen leu et un plus privé,
> ou il soient mialz arivé
> que il or ne sont a ceste ore.[31]

25 *Yvain* (*le Chevalier du Lion*), ed. T.B.W. Reid, Manchester, 1942; *Ywain and Gawain*, edd. Albert B. Friedman and Norman T. Harrington, London, 1964 (Early English Text Society 254).

26 *Le Roman de Perceval ou le Conte du Graal*, ed. William Roach, Geneva and Paris, 1959.

27 *Cligés* 4705–919.

28 *Yvain* 3485–4575, 4703–5106, 5810–6509; *Ywain and Gawain* 2059–645, 2743–930, 3359–828.

29 Charrete 314–94, 3003–123, 5105–28. Cf. *Lancelot*, XXXVI, §§24–5

30 *Perceval* 1935–2069, 2354–63, 2574–7, 5788–873. Cf. Frappier, 'Chrétien de Troyes', p. 189. *Perceval* 2067–9 *Tant li fist la nuit de solas | Que bouche a boche, bra a bra, | Dormirent tant qu'il ajorna* makes it clear that Perceval and Blancheflor's lovemaking stopped short of intercourse. The child-lovers Flores and Blancheflor also enjoyed hugging and kissing (*Le Conte de Floire et Blancheflor*, ed. Jean-Luc Leclanche (Paris, 1980), 241–2b).

31 *Charrete* 6846–53.

Whether or not this was Chrétien's intention, in the early thirteenth-century prose romances Lancelot, now the son of King Ban of Benoïc, was both the queen's faithful lover and a leading seeker of the Holy Grail, a dual role that even he could not fill successfully. In *Perlesvaus*, a prose continuation of *Perceval* that apparently antedated the Prose *Lancelot* in its present form, in which Galahad, not Perceval, was destined to achieve the Holy Grail,[32] Lancelot was warned by a damsel at the outset of his quest that '*Li Graax ne s'apert pas a si amoreus chevalier com vos estes, car vos amez la roïne, la fame le roi Artu vostre saignor*',[33] and he later told the Hermit King that he would rather see Guinevere than the Holy Grail:

> Li rois Hermites li demanda s'il avoit veü le Graal, et Lanceloz li dit que non. 'Je sé bien,' fet li rois, 'por coi ce fu. Se vos fussiez en si grand desierier longuement de voer le Graal conme vos estes de la roïne, vos l'eüssiez veü.' 'Sire,' fet Lanceloz, 'la roïne desir je molt a voer, por apenre sens et cortoisie et valor. Ausi doivent fere tuit li chevalier, car ele a totes les enors en soi que dame puist avoir.'[34]

Here Lancelot, the exponent of courtly love, touches on its ennobling effect, a parody of the Christian doctrine of Grace he developed more fully in the Prose *Lancelot* when Guinevere reproached herself after hearing that the 'son of the dolorous queen' (whom she recognized as Lancelot) would never achieve the Grail because of his lechery:[35]

> 'Dame,' fait Lanceloz, 'vos dites mal. Sachiez que je ja ne fusse venuz a si grant hautesce com je sui, se vos ne fussiez, car je n'eusse mie cuer par moi au conmancement de ma chevalerie d'amprandre les choses que li autre laissoient par defaute de pooir. Mais ce que je

32 *Le Haut Livre du Graal Perlesvaus*, edd. William A. Nitze, T. Atkinson Jenkins, and others, 2 vols., Chicago, 1932, 1937, cited by the line numbers in this edition; for its date see Nitze's introduction, II, 73–89. Nitze considers the Prose *Lancelot* 'in its earliest form antecedent to P[erlesvaus]' (*ibid.*, II, 335), a view consistent with the textual evidence of its first branch (Micha's vols. VII–VIII): 17 of the 30 manuscripts that contain *Lancelot*, VIIIa, §8 *Galaat, celui qui vit apertement les grans mervelles del graal et acompli le siege perillous de la Table Reonde et mena a fin les aventures del roialmes perelleus et aventureus, che fu li roialmes de Logres* read *Perceval* instead of *Galaat* (*Lancelot*, vol. VII, pp. 462–76). See further *Lancelot do Lac*, ed. Elsbeth Kennedy , 2 vols. (Oxford, 1980), II, 89–90 and *passim.*

33 *Perlesvaus* 2793–5.

34 *Ibid.*, 3861–7.

35 *Lancelot*, LXXXV, §2. Cf. *ibid.*, LXV, §§25, 32, LXXXIV, §72. Lancelot's mother was known as *la Roïne as Grans Dolors* because she lost her land, her husband, and her son on the same day (*ibid.*, IIIa, §§4–8, 10, IV, §40).

baoie a vos et a vostre grant biauté mist mon cuer en l'orgueil ou j'estoie si que je ne poïsse trouver aventure que je ne menasse a chief; car je savoie bien, se je ne pooie les aventures passer par prouesce, que a vos ne vandroie je ja, et il m'i couvenoit avenir ou morir. Dont je vos di vraiement que ce fu la chose qui plus acroissoit mes vertuz.'[36]

The page-heading in Micha's edition rightly calls his profession *le magnifique amour de Lancelot*, but a careful reader will note that in its scale of values Pride becomes a virtue, and his next speech reveals the central paradox of his career, that the very thing which made him worthy to achieve the Grail kept him from doing it:

'Je cuit que ja ne fusse venus a la grant prouesce ou je sui se par vos ne fust, car je estoie jones anfes et nices et fors de mon païs et sanz grant prouesce ne poïsse je mie mener a fin ceste chose dont vos parlez, ne n'an feisse riens, se je ne fusse de vos si bien come je sui.'[37]

This paradox was also anticipated by the Hermit King when he explained to Perceval, who was *chastes et virges de son cors*,[38] why Gawain and Lancelot could not enter the Grail Castle with him: '*car il sont li mellor chevalier dou monde, s'il ne fusent luxurios*.'[39]

The conflict between human and divine love was therefore thematic in *Perlesvaus*, as it was to be in the *Queste del Saint Graal*,[40] and the second and third branches of the *Lancelot* were structured to pave the way for this theme of the *Queste*. At the beginning of the second branch Lancelot's friend Galehot was told that the leopard in his dream, which represented Lancelot, would not achieve the Grail, occupy the Seige Perilous, or bring to an end the adventures of Britain,[41] and contact with the wonders of the Grail began in the middle of the same branch when the voice of Symeu from the burning tomb at the *Gaste Chapele* told Lancelot that he was

36 *Ibid.*, LXXXV, §3.

37 *Ibid.*

38 *Perlesvaus* 16. According to his sister, *Il a le chief d'or e regart de lion e noumblil de virge pucele e cuer de valeur e teches sanz vilenie* (*Perlesvaus* 910–12; repeated in Virgil's prophesy, 5791–2); the strange beast that symbolized the Grail Knight in Merlin's prophesy was also destined to have *rains et nonbril de pucele virge enterrine* (*Lancelot*, IV, §38; 'Galahad and Perceval', p. 336). Unlike Galahad, however, Perceval was not exempt from concupiscence, as he had already proved with Blancheflor (above, p. 161 and n. 30) and was to show again in the *Queste* (pp. 104–10).

39 *Perlesvaus* 6047–8.

40 *La Queste del Saint Graal*, ed. Albert Pauphilet, Paris, 1923.

41 *Lancelot*, II, §10; IV, §§33–42. For the adventures of Britain see below, pp. 173–4 and n. 104.

not 'the best of the good' who was destined to release him;[42] near the end of the second branch Gawain met King Pelles' son Eliezar, who carried the broken sword destined to be mended by the Grail Knight,[43] saw the inscriptions at the *Gaste Chapele* that upset Gwenevere, and visited Corbenic;[44] early in the third branch, before Gawain had reported his adventures, Lancelot visited Corbenic and begot Galahad,[45] and later in that branch he saw the boiling fountain and the white stag in the Perilous Forest;[46] Bors then visited Corbenic, and finally, near the end of the third branch, the Grail healed Perceval and Hector's wounds and cured Lancelot's madness,[47] prefiguring his spiritual regeneration on the Grail Quest. These cures belong to the last section of the *Lancelot*, which begins with the visit of Galahad and his mother to Camelot and is devoted exclusively to its consequences: Lancelot's banishment, the quest in search of him, his crazed wanderings which led him back to Corbenic, and his sojourn with Galahad's mother on the *Isle de Joie*, where he was found by Ector and Perceval, who brought him home again to Camelot;[48] the whole romance ends on the vigil of Pentecost, the day King Pelles' damsel summoned Lancelot to knight Galahad at the beginning of the *Queste*.[49]

Thus, little by little, the vast complexity of its 'polyphonic' narrative[50] was narrowed down until the Grail came to dominate the Prose *Lancelot* in preparation for its sequel; but the Grail theme was simultaneously

42 *Lancelot*, XXXVII, §§37–40. Cf. *Queste*, pp. 264–5; *Morte Darthur* XVII. 19; *Works*, p. 1026.

43 *Lancelot*, LXI, §§3–34. Cf. *Queste*, p. 266; *Morte Darthur* XVII. 19; *Works*, p. 1027.

44 *Ibid*, LXV, §§25, 32–3, LXI, §§ 3–34, LXV, §§24–33, LXVI, §§4–32.

45 *Lancelot*, LXXVIII, §43–LXXIX, §4. Cf. 'Galahad and Perceval', pp. 60–6; *Morte Darthur* XI. 1–3; *Works*, pp. 791–6.

46 *Lancelot*, XCIII, §§1–6, 26–7, XCVI, §§1–3. Lancelot never discovered where the stag and the lions went, for this too was an adventure reserved for Galahad: cf. *ibid.*, CI, §3; *Queste*, pp. 234–5; *Morte Darthur* XVII. 9; *Works*, pp. 998–9.

47 *Lancelot*, XCVIII, §§13–50, CVI, §§41–5; CVII, §§28–31. Cf. 'Galahad and Perceval,' pp. 66–78, 191–2, 322–3; *Morte Darthur* XI. 4–6, 14, XII. 4–5; *Works*, pp. 797–802, 816–17, 824–5.

48 *Lancelot*, CV, §31–CVIII, §14. Cf. 'Galahad and Perceval', pp. 78–84, 181–200, 322–36; *Morte Darthur* XI. 7–XII. 10; *Works*, pp. 802–33.

49 *Lancelot*, CVIII, §15–16; *Queste*, p. 1. Cf. 'Galahad and Perceval', pp. 336–7; *Morte Darthur* XIII. 1; *Works*, p. 853.

50 'Interwoven or Polyphonic narrative' is C.S. Lewis's term for the characteristic structural pattern of Arthurian prose romances in which two or more stories are told simultaneously in alternating episodes, so that one story repeatedly interrupts and is interrupted by another ('The English Prose *Morte*', *Essays on Malory*, ed. J.A.W. Bennett (Oxford, 1963), pp. 7–28, at 7, 13–14); Vinaver compared it with the technique of tapestry-making (*Works*, pp. l–li). This pattern is already found in *Perlesvaus*, but the technique was fully developed only in the second branch of *Lancelot*, which then became the model for later romance writers. See further Rosamond Tuve, *Allegorical Imagery* (Princeton, 1966), pp. 360–9.

combined with another that paved the way in turn for the *Mort Artu*.[51] When Lancelot and Gawain and his companions recounted their adventures after Gawain and the others had returned from the quest for Lancelot which began late in the second branch,[52] Arthur tactlessly remarked that Lancelot alone had gained more honour for the Round Table than all his other knights, causing them to hate Lancelot in secret until they saw their chance to be revenged:

> De cele parole que li rois Artus dist furent si atorné cil de la Table Reonde que il en haïrent puis touz dis Lancelot de mortel haine, ne onques samblant n'en voldrent faire devant que li mesfez de lui et de la roine fu prouvez, quant il furent trové nu a nu par Agravain qui espiez les avoit.[53]

Arthur's own fate was first mentioned at the beginning of that same quest when Mordred was introduced as *li plus joules des freres mon seignor Gauvain, celui que li roi Artus ses oncles meismes occist puis de ses mains a cele bataille ou li rois fu navrés a mort*, and referred to again when Lancelot recounted his adventures after his return to court and Arthur had them recorded separately *si que des fez et des ovres trova l'an .I. grant livre en l'aumaire le roi Artu aprés ce qu'il fu navrez a mort en la bataille Mordret*.[54] Lancelot learnt of it shortly before Bors' visit to Corbenic, when a hermit told Mordred of Arthur's dream the night he begot him, in which he killed a serpent that devastated his realm '*et ne porquant si fort ert envenimé que il l'an couvenoit a morir*';[55] Mordred killed the hermit before he could reveal more, but a paper Lancelot found in the corpse's hand added that Arthur would smite Mordred through the body '*si durement que aprés le cop passera li rais dou souleil*', and would never be seen in the flesh again himself because of his knights' sinful pride:

> 'Et ceste merveille mosterra Diex seulement en toi et lors abaissera li granz orguiex de la chevalerie de la Grant Bretaingne, car aprés cel jor ne sera nus qui li rois Artus voie se ce n'est en songe.'[56]

Gawain and his companions' poor showing in their quest for Lancelot foreshadows the Round Table's failure to achieve the Grail, represented

51 *La Mort le Roi Artu*, ed. Jean Frappier, Geneva and Paris, 1936, cited as '*Mort Artu*'.
52 *Lancelot*, LXXXIV, §§68–73. Cf. *ibid.*, LX, §11-LXXXIV, §4.
53 *Ibid.*, LXXXIV, §73.
54 *Ibid.*, LX, §12, LXXXIV, §72.
55 *Ibid.*, XCVI, §24.
56 *Ibid.*, XCVI, §28.

allegorically in the *Queste* by Gawain's dream of the spotted bulls, only a minority of whom returned to their pasture *si megre et si las qu'a peines se pooient il tenir en estant*[57] due to their pride and envy, as the hermit Nasciens told Gawain and Hector:

> 'Et vos, qui toz jorz chevaucheroiz le grant destrier, ce est a dire qui toz jors seroiz en pechié mortel, et en orgueil et en envie et en maint autre vice, iroiz forsvoiant ça et la, tant que vos vendroiz a la meson au Riche Pescheor, la ou li preudome, li verai chevalier tendront lor feste de la haute troveure qu'il avront trovee. Et quant vos vendroiz la et vos cuideroiz enz entrer, li rois vos dira qu'il n'a cure d'ome qui si haut soit montez come vos estes, ce est a dire qui gise en pecié mortel et en orgueil. Et quant vos orroiz ce, si retorneroiz a Kamaalot, sanz ce que vos n'avroiz gueres fet de vostre preu en cest Queste.'[58]

Nasciens refused to interpret the last sentence in Gawain's account of his dream, *Et quant il estoient venu au rastelier, si montoit entr'ax un tel estrif que la viande lor failloit et les covenoit departir li un ça et li autre la*,[59] which referred to the break-up of the Round Table into warring factions after their return to Camelot, prefigured by Gawain's slaying of Ywain immediately after his dream and again by Lionel's slaying of Calogrenant and Gawain's slaying of Bagdamagus later in the quest.[60]

III

The grand design of the *Lancelot-Queste-Mort* cycle determined the pattern of later 'Arthuriads' such as the *Estoire du Graal* and Malory's *Morte Darthur*, modified, however, by the influence of the Prose *Tristan*, which effectively transformed the romance of Tristan and Isolde into an alternate version of the cycle. The traditional story merged into the wider world of Arthurian chivalry after Tristan's marriage to Isolde of Brittany when he returned to Cornwall with his brother-in law Kehedin, who fell helplessly in love with Isolde of Cornwall; Tristan, thinking himself betrayed, went mad with jealousy, was cured by Isolde, and, banished by Mark, went to Logres, met Lancelot at the *Perron Merlin* and accompanied him to court, where he was made a knight of the Round Table,

57 *Queste*, p. 149.25–6. Cf. *Morte Darthur* XVI. 1; *Works*, p. 942.12–13.

58 *Queste*, pp. 159.24–160. 1. Cf. Hector's arrival at Corbenic, *montez sur un grant cheval* (*ibid*., pp. 259–61).

59 *Queste*, pp. 149.23–5, and 157. Cf. *Morte Darthur* XVI. 1; *Works*, p. 942. 15–18. Malory's version of *si montoit entr'ax un tel estrif*, 'there rose up a grete crye', suggests that he read *escris* for *estrif*.

60 *Queste*, pp. 152–4, 190–2, 261–2. Cf. *Morte Darthur* XVI. 2–3, 15–16, XVII. 17; *Works*, pp. 943–5, 971–3, 1020.

taking the seat of his old adversary, Le Morholt.[61] His metamorphosis from tragic lover to knight-errant was foreshadowed, however, like the Grail Quest in *Lancelot*, by introducing Arthurian characters into earlier episodes: Merlin rescued the infant Tristan and his father;[62] Gareth accompanied le Morholt to Cornwall and recognized Tristan when he saw him at the Irish court before the tournament of *Chastel des Landes*, which was also attented by Gawain and other knights of the Round Table;[63] Blioberis abducted Seguradés' wife, and Tristan encountered Sagremor and Dodinel when he pursued him;[64] Tristan, diverted to Logres on his way to fetch Isolde from Ireland, defended King Anguin against Blanor, overcame several more of Arthur's knights, and forced Breuz sanz Pitié to return the magic shield that the Lady of the Lake's damsel was bringing to Guinevere, then fought with Galehot in the *Loignteignes Isles* on his return journey;[65] Lambeguet, Bors' old tutor, who had defended him from King Claudas, tried to rescue Isolde from Palamedes;[66] Lamorat diverted to Mark the magic horn Morgan le Fay sent Arthur;[67] Lancelot and the damsel who was carrying Guinevere's letter to Isolde visited the *Chastel Felon*, where Perceval's sister was to perish in the *Queste*.[68] The last episode in the traditional part of the story, Tristan's madness, although it incorporates elements from earlier Tristan romances, was modelled on the madness of Lancelot,[69] who, like Tristan, wandered off into the forest

61 Curtis, §§829–940 + Löseth, §§95–206. Cf. *Morte Darthur* IX. 17–X. 6; *Works*, pp. 492–572.

62 Curtis, §§232–9. Cf. *Morte Darthur* VIII. 1–2; *Works*, pp. 371–3.

63 Curtis, §§287, 316–25. Cf. *Morte Darthur* VIII. 9–10; *Works*, pp. 386–7.

64 Curtis, §§374–94. Cf. *Morte Darthur* VIII. 15–18; *Works*, pp. 396–403. Seguradés later tried to force himself on the lady of Roestoc, who was championed by Gawain (Curtis, §374; *Lancelot*, LVIa).

65 Curtis, §§400–32, 457–82. Cf. *Morte Darthur* VIII. 19–27; *Works*, pp. 403–18; *Lancelot*, XXXVa, §6, XXXVIIa, XXXIXa, §§1–7, XLIa, §§3–5, LVIIIa, §§13–17, LXXa, §35, LXXXIa, §§6–9. 'The Browne Knyght wythoute Pyté', who escaped Lancelot and Tristan (Löseth, §§96, 195), was slain by Malory's Gareth (*Morte Darthur* VII, 33, 36, IX. 26; *Works*, pp. 355–6, 362, 512–13).

66 Curtis, §§499–501. Cf. *Morte Darthur* VIII. 30; *Works*, pp. 422; Lancelot, XVIIa, §§22–37.

67 Curtis, §§526–31. Cf. *Morte Darthur* VIII. 34; *Works*, pp. 429–30. The story of the magic horn sent to Arthur's court to test Guinevere's chastity is found in Robert Biket's *Lai du Cor* and the *Livre de Carados* (*The Anglo-Norman Text of 'Le lai du Cor'*, ed. C.T. Erickson, Oxford, 1973 (Anglo-Norman Text Society 24); *The Continuations of the Old French 'Perceval'*, ed. William Roach, vols. 1–3 (Philadelphia, 1949–52), I, 232–8, II, 370–7, III, 195–203).

68 Curtis, §575. Cf. *Queste*, pp. 236–43; *Morte Darthur* XVII. 9–11; *Works*, pp. 1000–4.

69 Curtis, §§852–940 + Löseth, §§95–104. Cf. *Morte Darthur* IX. 18–22; *Works*, pp. 495–502; Curtis, *Roman de Tristan en prose*, III, xi–xii and nn. 2–4. The hermit who fed Tristan in the forest (Löseth, §101; *Morte Darthur* IX. 20; *Works*, p. 499) came from *Yvain* 2827–91, as Löseth pointed out (*Le Roman*

calling on death to come quickly: '*Mort, mort, haste toi devenir a moi, car je sui de vivre touz rasasiez.*'[70] From an early stage the narrative was interrupted by episodes unconnected with the original romance that gave it an increasingly cyclic character before Tristan's exile to Logres—the visit of Tristan and Isolde to the *Loignteignes Isles*,[71] the adventures of Tristan and Lamorat in the *Païs de Servaige* and Lamorat's further adventures,[72] the tale of Brun le Noir, *li chevaliers a la Cote Mautailliee*, in which Lancelot played a leading role,[73] and Tristan and Kehedin's visit to the *Forest d'Arvances* on their way back to Cornwall.[74]

Incidental allusions strengthened the chronological link between the *Lancelot* and the *Tristan* forged by the episode of the magic shield: Arthur had recently begun his reign when Le Morholt came to demand the tribute;[75] Galehot was ill and Lancelot a new-made knight when the tournament was held at the *Chastel des Landes*;[76] Gawain and the damsel he met at the *Chastel des Landes* were both seeking the unknown knight (Lancelot) who had conquered Dolorous Garde;[77] Galehot's sister found him searching for Lancelot, who had returned to Morgan le Fay's prison after freeing Gawain from Carados of the Dolorous Tower, and he died

en prose de Tristan, p. xxv; cf. *Ywain and Gawain* 1671–1709). His recognition by the hound Houdenc (Löseth, §104; *Morte Darthur* IX. 21; *Works*, pp. 501–2) took place in different circumstances in Beroul's *Tristan* and the *Folie Tristan* poems (Beroul, *The Romance of Tristan*, ed. A. Ewert, 2 vols. (Oxford, 1939, 1970), 1540–8; *Les Deux Poèmes de la Folie Tristan*, ed. Joseph Bédier, Paris, 1907 (Société des anciens textes français), Oxford 909–18, Berne 510–18).

70 *Lancelot*, CV, §38. Cf. Curtis, §852, lines 29–30: '*Ha! morz, haste toi de venir. Oste moi de ceste dolor ou j'ai assez plus demoré que mestier ne me fust sanz faille.*'

71 See above, p. 167 and note 65. The lethal beauty contest between Isolde and Galehot's mother was modelled on the sparrow-hawk episodes in *Erec et Enide* and the 'Fair Unknown' romances (*Erec* 691–1076; Renault de Beaujeu, *Le Bel Inconnu*, ed. G. Perrie Williams (Paris, 1929), 1497–1869; *Lybeaus Desconus*, ed. M. Mills, London, 1969 (Early English Text Society 261), 700–999).

72 Curtis, §§583–635. Cf. *Morte Darthur* VIII. 37–41; *Works*, pp. 441–51.

73 Curtis, §§636–776. Cf. *Morte Darthur* IX. 1–9; *Works*, pp. 459–476. 144 lines survive from an early metrical version of the story (Paul Meyer and Gaston Paris, 'Fragment du *Vallet a la cote mal tailliee*', *Romania* 26 (1897), 276–80). Dr. Curtis regards the excursion to the *Païs de Servaige* and the adventures of Lamorat and Brun as early interpolations (*Roman de Tristan*, II, 31–2, III, xxviii), but Lamorat and Brun's paths crossed again shortly before Lamorat's death, when Brun handed Gawain over to his *amie*, whose brother Gawain had murdered, and Lamorat delivered him from her prison (Löseth, §§303–5).

74 Curtis, §§780–830. Cf. *Morte Darthur* XI. 10–16; *Works*, pp. 481–92.

75 Curtis, §287. Cf. *Morte Darthur* VIII. 4; *Works*, pp. 376–7.

76 Curtis, §324. Cf. *Morte Darthur* VIII. 9–10; *Works*, pp. 385–7. In the *Lancelot* Galehot's health did not begin to fail until he and Lancelot returned to Sorelois at the beginning of the second branch (IV, §§12–13.)

77 Curtis, §§337–9. Cf. *Morte Darthur* VIII. 10; *Works*, pp. 388–9; *Lancelot*, XXXIa, XXXIIIa, §§1–3, XXXIVa–Va, XXXVIIa, XLIa–IIa.

shortly after his battle with Tristan;[78] Lancelot was out of his mind with grief after failing to find him at Sorelois when Gwenevere received the letter that Tristan wrote to her before he left the *Loignteignes Isles*:

> Asez est la roïne liee de ces noveles; et encores le fust ele plus se ne fust ce que a la cort ne savoit l'en nules noveles de Lancelot. Il estoit sanz faille a celi point issuz del sens. Et ce fu devant celi tens bien deus anz entiers que Meliaganz, li filz au roi Bademaguz, venist quant il conquist el conduit de Kex le Senechal, la roïne Genevre, et l'en mena en prison el reaume de Gorre. Et puis la suï Lancelot et la conquist vers Meliagant, et la ramena el reaume de Logres.[79]

Thus the history of Arthur's reign down to the middle of the *Lancelot* was squeezed into the space between Tristan's battle with Le Morholt and his return to Cornwall with Isolde, but a two-year gap then opened between Lancelot's madness and Guinevere's abduction by Meleagant, which were narrated consecutively in the *Lancelot*, presumably to allow time for the adventures of Tristan and Isolde in Cornwall, his marriage to Isolde of the White Hands in Brittany, the adventures of Tristan, Isode of Brittany, and Kehedin with Seguardés and Lamorat in the *Païs de Servaige*, Lamorat's subsequent adventures,[80] and Tristan and Kehedin's visit to the *Forest d'Arvances*,[81] where Meleagant himself made an appearance.[82] The abduction, however, was not mentioned again, nor was any further attempt was made to synchronize the *Tristan* and the *Lancelot* until they converged in the visit of Galahad and his mother to Camelot, Lancelot's madness, the quest for him by Gawain and his companions, and Perceval's coming to court.[83] The final phase of Tristan's history was then synchronized with the last part of the *Lancelot* and the *Queste*: after leaving court, Perceval released Tristan from the *Chastel du Pin*, Tristan and Isolde

78 Curtis, §§467–8, 481. Cf. *Morte Darthur* VIII. 28; *Works*, pp. 418–19; *Lancelot*, IX, §52–X, §8, XXIV, §§38–48, XXVI, §§1– 9, XXVIII, §1–23, XXXV,§§1–3. Galehot was recalled to life in the Tournement of Sorelois episode found in some manuscripts of the *Tristan* (B.N. fr. 99, 384rb–397vb; Löseth, §282de; *Morte Darthur* X. 40–50; *Works*, pp. 653–70, 675).

79 Curtis §482.13–19. Cf. *Lancelot*, XXXIV, XXXVI–XLII. In the *Lancelot*, however, Lancelot did not bring the queen back to Logres; he was in Meleagant's prison when she returned (XXXIX, §46–XL, §6; cf. *Charrete* 5044–358).

80 Curtis, §§483–635. Cf. *Morte Darthur* VIII. 28–41; *Works*, pp. 418–51.

81 Curtis, §§781–830. Cf. *Morte Darthur* IX. 10–17; *Works*, pp. 481–92.

82 Curtis, §§796–8, 801–8. Cf. *Morte Darthur* IX. 12–14; *Works*, pp. 485–7. Meleagant also reappeared at the Tournament of Sorelois (B.N. fr. 99, 384vab, 386vab, 387vb–388ra, 397vb; Löseth, §282de; *Morte Darthur* X. 41–3; *Works*, pp. 654–5, 657–8).

83 Löseth, §§300–1, 308–11; *Lancelot*, CV, §31-CVI, §28. Cf. 'Galahad and Perceval', pp. 78–84, 181–6; *Morte Darthur* X. 23, XI. 7–11; *Works*, pp. 610–11, 802–12,

stayed at Joyous Garde with Lancelot until he and Tristan went to Camelot for the feast of Pentecost at which the Grail Quest began, and Tristan's death was reported to the court a few days after Lancelot returned from it.[84] The earlier, 'non-cyclic' version of the *Tristan* ended at this point.

The structural transformation which began with Tristan and Isolde's visit to the *Loignteignes Isles* was paralleled thematically in the letter Tristan wrote to Guinevere before they left, which concluded with the declaration that Lancelot and he were the only two knights in the world, and Guinevere and Isolde the only two ladies:

> En la fin des letres li manda qu'il avoit en cest monde deus chevaliers et deus dames, 'ne plus n'en i puis veoir. En ces deus dames est tote la biauté dou monde, et je ne sai la quele est la plus belle. Et es deus chevaliers est tote la chevalerie dou monde, ne ne porroie en nule fin lor parel trover de chevalerie, ne je ne sai li quiex de ces deus est li plus puissanz d'armes.' Aprés escrit quatre nons: Lancelot dou Lac; Tristan, le neveu le roi Marc de Cornoaille; la roine Genevre; Yselt la Bloe.[85]

Not long after Isolde sent Palamedes to Guinevere with the same message;[86] but their supremacy was soon challenged by Lamorat, who boasted that his lady, the dowager queen of Orkney, was *la plus bele dame del monde*.[87] Lamorat himself would himself have equalled or surpassed Lancelot, Tristan, and Palamedes, the three best knights in the world, had he not succumbed to the emnity of Gawain and his brothers:

> Non auoit il a celui temps fors Trystram et Lancelot du Lac et Palamedes; ces .iii. sanz nule faille estoient meilleurs cheualiers de lui. Mes la haute cheualerie que il auoit encommenciee et le grant cuer que il auoit dedenz le uentre li fesoit mener a la fin honnoureement tout ce que il entreprenoit. Se il eust longuement uescu, bien peust l'en dire que il ateinsist touz les bons cheualiers du monde ou passast; mes il mourut plus tost que mestier ne fust a cheualerie, et de cele mort fu monseingnour Gauuayn trop durement blasmez, car uileinement en mesprist.[88]

84 Löseth, §§314–18, 344–51, 389–97, 546–51, 568–70. Cf. 'Galahad and Perceval', pp. 337–41; *Queste*, pp. 1–25, 261–2; *Morte Darthur* XII. 11–XIII. 8; *Works*, pp. 839–72.

85 Curtis, §482.3–10.

86 *Ibid.*, §511.21–3. Cf. *Morte Darthur* VIII. 31; *Works*, p. 425.

87 Curtis, §521.28.

88 B.N. fr. 334, 330rb-va (Löseth, §250). This passage was anticipated almost verbatim in 328vab (Löseth, §246): *Ne demora mie puis gramment de temps que monseingnour Gauuayn ocist Lamorat assez vileinement, dont ce fu grant douleur,*

The paths of these four crossed in the *Forest d'Arvances*, where Tristan encountered Lamorat and forgave him for diverting the magic horn,[89] the *chevaliers à la beste glatissant* (Palamedes) overthrew them both,[90] and Lamorat met Gawain, who declared his mortal hatred, and Meleagant and Lancelot, with whom he again disputed the primacy of his lady.[91] The *Forest d'Arvances* episode thus anticipates the polyphonic narrative structure which developed after Tristan's removal to Logres and the themes of his friendship with, and Gawain's hatred of, Lamorat, which were the leitmotifs of its earlier part. In this way the Prose *Tristan* was changed from a romance of plot to a romance of characters that matched Tristan with the three other 'best knights', Lancelot, Palamedes, and Lamorat, in a narrative which was loosely constructed, to say the least, especially in its later, 'cyclic' version, where two crucial events apparently happened twice: Gawain's killing of Lamorat, which took place during their quest for Lancelot in the first version, was described as imminent at an earlier stage, and Perceval's coming to court, which followed it, was actually narrated in both places.[92]

car l'estoire de nostre liure tesmoingne que se Lamorat eust vescu grant aage de cheualier, bien eust ateint de bonte et de cheualerie ou passez tous les preudeshommes qui au temps le roy Artus portoient armes. Mes il mourut assez plus tost que mestier ne fust a cheualerie, et a celui iour que il mourut n'auoit il encore acompliz que .xxvj. ans et .ii. mois d'aage. Arthur's court had pronounced Lancelot, Tristan, and Palamedes the best knights in the world when Lamorat reported Tristan's victory over Nabon le Noir: *il dient tout comunement*: '*Il n'a orandroit en tot le monde que deus chevaliers qui de proesce aient passé toz autres preudomes: Lanceloz dou Lac en est li uns, et Tristanz, li niés le roi Marc de Cournouailles, li autres, et qui le tiers voudroit avec eus acompaignier si i mete Palamedes, le chevalier a la Beste Glatissant; cil est bons chevaliers parfez de bonté et de chevalerie. Je croi sanz faille que ce sont li nonper de toz ces que nos sachiens el monde*' (Curtis, §636.14–19). Tristan implied that Lamorat had already reached the first class when he described Palamedes as one of the *four* best knights after the tournament at the *Chastel des Pucelles*: '*se les .iiii. meillours cheualiers qui soient orendroit en ce monde estoient meintenant caiens, celui si en seroit li uns*' (B.N. fr. 334, 252ra; cf. Löseth, §148; *Morte Darthur* IX. 36; *Works*, p. 536).

89 Curtis, §§784–7. Cf. *Morte Darthur* IX. 10–11; *Works*, pp. 481–3. This episode is inconsistent with Trintan's earlier message to Lamorat: '*se il un po mesprist vers moi quant il envoia le cor au roi Marc, por ce ne le hé je mie, car trop est bons chevaliers de son aaige*' (Curtis, §551.18–20). Malory's Tristan had also forgiven Lamorat on the Isle of Servage (*Morte Darthur* VIII. 38; *Works* pp. 443–4), as the latter reminded him in IX. 11 (p. 483).

90 Curtis, §§790–1. Cf. *Morte Darthur* IX. 12; *Works*, p. 484. Brun le Noire and the *demoisele mesdisant* also saw the Beast before they met with Palamedes (Curtis, §§664–5; *Morte Darthur* IX. 3; *Works*, p. 463).

91 Curtis, §§793–808. Cf. *Morte Darthur* IX. 12–14; *Works*, pp. 485–7.

92 Löseth, §§246, 254, 306–11. Malory's accounts of Lamorat's death and Perceval's coming to court (*Morte Darthur* X. 21, 23–4, 54, 58; *Works*; pp. 608, 610–11, 687–9) correspond to Löseth, §§ 246, 250, 254, which are peculiar to the later version, but he also gave a modified version of Agloval's bringing Perceval to

IV

The *Tristan*'s impact on Arthurian tradition can be seen in the *Suite du Merlin*,[93] the central part of the *Estoire du Graal*, the latest of the great French prose romances, which brought the creative phase of the French tradition to its end. The *Suite*, as its name implies, is a continuation designed to link the Prose *Merlin*[94] with adaptations of the *Queste* and the *Mort Artu*,[95] by-passing the *Lancelot* because its size would have distorted the *Estoire's* tripartite structure, as its author carefully explained.[96] The Suite is in fact related to the *Lancelot* in the same way as the *Tristan*, which was really the *Suite's* chief model, although Tristan himself does not appear in its surviving portions. Gawain is the same proud, vengeful character in the *Suite* as he was in the *Tristan*, and his feud with Pellinor and Lamorat is also a leading theme of the *Suite*. Its first episode, after the

Camelot corresponding to Löseth, §§308–9 in his redaction of the 'coming of Galahad' sections of the *Lancelot*, which were incorporated in some manuscripts of the later version of the *Tristan* (*Morte Darthur* IX. 10–11; *Works*, pp. 809–12; 'Galahad and Perceval', pp. 181–7).

93 For the *Suite du Merlin* and its relationship with the Prose *Tristan* see Bogdanow, *Romance of the Grail*, chapter III and *passim.* The surviving portions of the *Suite* are found in *Merlin, roman en prose du XIIIe siècle*, edd. Gaston Paris and Jacob Ulrich, 2 vols., Paris, 1886 (Société des anciens textes français), I, 147–II., 254, cited as '*Merlin*'; *Die Abenteuer Gawains, Yvains und Le Morholts mit den drei Jungfrauen*, ed. H.O. Sommer, Tübingen, 1913 (Beihefte zur Zeitschrift für romanische Philologie 47); *La Folie Lancelot*, ed. Fanni Bogdanow, Tübingen, 1965 (Beihefte zur Zeitschrift für romanische Philologie 109); and Bogdanow, *Romance of the Grail*, pp. 230–49. Paris, Bibliothèque nationale, fr. 12599, one of the two manuscripts containing the *Folie Lancelot*, is a *Tristan* manuscript used by Löseth, whose references to it are cited in the relevant notes. Another manuscript of the first portion, Cambridge, University Library, Add. 7071, referred to by Vinaver and Bogdanow, has not yet been edited.

94 Robert de Boron, *Merlin*, ed. Alexandre Micha (Geneva, 1979), pp. 18–291; the *Estoire du Graal* text is given by Paris and Ulrich, *Merlin*, I, 1–147. This is the prose version of Robert's fragmentary verse romance of the same name (Micha, *Merlin*, pp. 1–17); it also forms the first part of *Lestoire de Merlin*, ed. H.O. Sommer, Washington, 1908 (The Vulgate Version of the Arthurian Romances, II), and *The Didot Perceval*, ed. William Roach, Philadelphia, 1941. See further Pierre le Gentil, 'The Work of Robert de Boron and the Didot Perceval', *Arthurian Literature in the Middle Ages*, pp. 251–62, at 256–7; Alexandre Micha, 'The Vulgate Merlin', *Arthurian Literature in the Middle Ages*, pp. 319–24.

95 Cf. Bogdanow, *Romance of the Grail*, pp. 88–155.

96 After referring to the magic ring that the Lady of the Lake gave Lancelot *si comme le grant hystore de Lancelot le devise* (*Lancelot*, XXIIa, §14), he described the latter as *cele meisme ystoire qui doit estre departie de mon livre, ne mie pour chou qu'il n'i apartiegne et que elle n'en soit traite, mais pour chou qu'il couvient que les trois parties de mon livre soient ingaus, l'une aussi grant coume l'autre, et se je ajoustaisse cele grant ystore la moiene partie de mon livre fust au tresble plus grant que les autres deus* (*Merlin*, II, 57). See further Bogdanow, *Romance of the Grail*, pp. 60–2.

begetting of Mordred,[97] is Arthur's encounter with the *beste glatissant*, pursued by a knight subsequently identified as Pellinor, who was to slay Lot and be slain in turn by Lot's son Gawain,[98] and it concluded with a series of adventures in which Gareth's slaying of his mother, his reconciliation with Lamorat, Erec and Gawain's detention at the *Castel as .x. Chevaliers*, Gawain's slaying of Driant and Lamorat, Perceval's coming to court, and his battle with Gareth[99] are interwoven with the madness of Lancelot, the quest to find him, his cure by the Holy Grail, and his sojourn on the *Isle de Joie*.[100] The further adventures of Erec, Hector, Gareth, and Perceval, which break off after Perceval's meeting with the Fisher King, whom he asked for news of Lancelot,[101] were presumably designed to bring Perceval and Hector to the *Isle de Joie* for their battles with Lancelot, foreshadowed by Gareth's battle with him after parting from Perceval.[102] Thus the main story-lines in the latter part of the *Suite* can be traced back to the death of Lot, whom Arthur's Herod-like attempt to destroy Mordred turned into his mortal enemy,[103] and Balain's Dolorous Stroke, which set in train 'the adventures of

97 *Merlin*, I, 147–8. Cf. *Morte Darthur* I, 19; *Works*, p. 41. Whether or not the portion of the *Estoire de Merlin* narrating Arthur's war with the eleven kings (*Lestoire de Merlin*, pp. 88–128), which follows his coronation in Cambr. Add. 7071, 202vb–30ra, and in Malory's *Tale of King Arthur* (*Morte Darthur* I. 8–18; *Works*, pp. 17–41), but not in British Library, Add. 38117, the manuscript printed by Paris and Ulrich, belongs to the *Estoire du Graal*, as Dr. Bogdanow contends (*Romance of the Grail*, pp. 31–9), the *Suite* proper begins with the begetting of Mordred, a version of which also follows the war with the eleven kings in the *Estoire de Merlin* (pp. 128–9).

98 *Merlin* I, 148–53, 258, 260–1; II, 11–12, 75–6, 129–31, 137–9. Cf. *Morte Darthur* I. 19–20; II. 10, 13; III. 4, 15; *Works*, pp. 42–3, 77–8, 81, 101–2, 119. The pursuit of the *beste glatissant* was *une des aventures dou graal* (*Merlin*, I, 160) and hence appropriate to the father of Perceval. Arthur proved himself in combat by standing up to Pellinor, *li mieudres chevaliers el monde et li plus preudom* (*ibid.*, I, 189–94, II, 11; *Morte Darthur* I. 23–4; *Works*, pp. 48–52). Pellinore also began the custom of challenging passing knights to joust, which was to be the hallmark of Arthurian chivalry (*Merlin*, I, 175–6.).

99 *Folie Lancelot* I. 1–880, III, V, VII–VIII; Löseth, §§283a–4a, 286a, 288a. Cf. Löseth, §§255–7, 306–12, 388a; 'Galahad and Perceval', pp. 181–7; *Lancelot,* CVI, §§10–27; *Morte Darthur* X. 23–4, 54, 58, XI. 10–11; *Works*, pp. 610–13, 687–8, 698–9, 809–12. Erec, who did not appear in the *Lancelot*, was slain by Gawain in the *Tristan* version of the Grail Quest (Löseth, §529).

100 *Folie Lancelot*, I. 880–930, IV, VI; Löseth, §§285a, 287a. Cf. Löseth, §388a; 'Galahad and Perceval', pp. 78–83, 193–200, 322–8; *Lancelot*, CV, §§29–38, CVI, §§ 1–9, CVII; *Morte Darthur* XI. 6–10, XII. 1–7; *Works*, pp. 802–10, 817–27.

101 *Folie Lancelot*, IX–XIV; Löseth, §§ 289a–91a.

102 *Folie Lancelot*, XII. 42–195. Cf. Löseth, §388a; 'Galahad and Perceval', pp. 328–31; *Lancelot*, CVIII, §§1–10; *Morte Darthur* XII. 7–8; *Works*, pp. 827–30.

103 *Merlin*, I, 203–12, 246, 254–5. Cf. *Morte Darthur* I, 28, II, 10; *Works*, pp. 55–6, 77; Bogdanow, *Romance of the Grail*, pp. 75–8, 173–4.

Britain';[104] the version of the *Queste* that followed was substantially identical with the the later version in the *Tristan*.[105]

As the *Tristan* referred in passing to events in the *Lancelot*, so the *Suite* refers to events in the *Lancelot* and the *Tristan*: King Mark was newly crowned when Rions attacked Arthur;[106] Gareth stayed with le Morholt in Ireland until they went to Corwall for the tribute;[107] Arthur made war on King Claudas after Gareth and Hector returned to court.[108] Most of its links with the *Lancelot* and the *Tristan*, however, were provided by Merlin, who put an inscription on Lancer's tomb stating that there Lancelot and Tristan, *li dui plus loial amant que a lour tans soient*, would fight their great battle,[109] and another on the tomb of a knight slain by Garlan stating that there Gawain would kill Pellinor,[110] made the enchanted bed that Gawain saw on the *Isle des Merveilles*,[111] predicted that

104 *Merlin*, I, 231–2, 264, 280, II, 26–31 + Bogdanow, *Romance of the Grail*, pp. 244.118–249.256. Cf. *Morte Darthur* II. 8, 15–16; *Works*, pp. 72–3, 84–6. The first of these adventures was that of the white stag on Arthur's wedding day, as the elder of the two brothers he met when he left Camelot told Gawain: '*Quant nous veismes cest chose nous desimes entre nous que chou estoit des aventures qui estoient coumenchies a avenir en la grant Bretaigne*' (*Merlin*, II, 82). Gawain's adventure was hardly an auspicious beginning, yet when he returned with the body of the lady he had slain, Merlin warned Arthur of worse to come: '*et saichiés que ceste aventure poés vous bien tenir a une des aventures del saint graal, si en verres dès ore souvent avenir de plus crueus et de plus felonnes que ceste n'est*' (*ibid.*, II, 96).

105 Bogdanow, *Romance of the Grail*, pp. 88–120. Cf. Löseth, §§ 390–1, 392a–8a, 399–421, 441–8, 449bc, 458–87, 493–571. Dr. Bogdanow believes that the Grail section in the second version of the *Tristan* was borrowed from that in the *Estoire du Graal* rather than vice versa (*ibid.*, pp. 121–37); both in any case were based on the first version of the *Tristan* (Löseth, §§ 390–490, 492–5, 503–11, 516–51, 568–70).

106 *Merlin*, I, 230. Cf. Curtis, §222; *Morte Darthur* II. 7; *Works*, pp. 71–2. King Rions' demand for Arthur's beard and his invasion of Logres (*Merlin*, I, 202–3, 212–13; 233–44; *Morte Darthur* I, 27, II, 1, 6, 8–9; *Works*, pp. 54–5, 70–5) came near the end of the *Estoire de Merlin* (pp. 409–19), after his war against King Leodegan (*ibid.*, pp. 107, 125, 141, 155–6, 215–36).

107 *Abenteuer Gawains, Ywains und Le Morholts*, pp. 132, 134. Cf. Curtis, §287; *Morte Darthur* VIII. 4; *Works*, p. 376.

108 *Folie Lancelot* I. 880–7; Löseth, §283a. Cf. Löseth, §388a; 'Galahad and Perceval', p. 78; *Lancelot*, CI, §16–CV, §29; *Morte Darthur* XI. 6; *Works*, p. 802.

109 *Merlin*, I, 230–1. Cf. Löseth, §203; *Morte Arthur* II. 8, X. 5; *Works*, pp. 72, 568–70.

110 *Merlin*, II, 11–12. Cf. Curtis, §794, Löseth, §§246a, 302; *Morte Darthur* II. 13; *Works*, p. 81. This prediction was not fulfilled in the surviving portions of the *Suite*, but see below, p. 175, n. 118.

111 *Merlin*, II, 57. Cf. *Lancelot*, CI, §§7–8; *Morte Darthur* II. 19; *Works*, p. 91. Merlin also fitted a new pommel to Balain's sword, with which Lancelot was to kill Gawain, then placed another sword, which Malory confused with Balain's, in a block of marble and made it float to Camelot on the day that Galahad came to court (*Merlin*, II, 58–60; *Queste*, pp. 5–7, 11–12; *Morte Darthur* II. 19, XIII. 2–5; *Works*, pp. 91–2, 855–8, 862–3).

Galehot would submit to Arthur for Lancelot's sake and Arthur would drive Claudas out of Benoic and Gaunes;[112] instituted the custom that knights returning from a quest should report their adventures on oath,[113] and revealed that Tor was Pellinor's son.[114] The exigencies of combining early Arthurian history, already foreshortened in the *Tristan*, with polyphonic narrative were met by a double time-scheme: Gawain, a boy of eleven at King Lot's funeral, shortly before Balain departed in quest of Garlan, was knighted on the eve of Arthur's wedding, soon after Merlin returned from burying Balain on the *Isle des Merveilles*,[115] and Yvain, born after Lot's funeral, was a new-made knight when Arthur defeated the five kings soon after Merlin was entombed by Nineve, the *damoisele chauceresse* at Arthur's wedding feast;[116] the war declared by the Roman ambassadors the day after Arthur's first encounter with Pellinor[117] had not yet begun when Gawain and le Morholt were released from two years' captivity a month before the latter went to Cornwall for the tribute.[118] Thus the chronological inconsistency that overtook the *Tristan* after the *Loignteignes Isles* episode was present in the *Suite* from the start; yet the *Suite* was a 'more homogeneous and closely-knit whole' than the *Estoire de Merlin* or the *Tristan*,[119] and it surpassed them both as a work of the imagination: the adventures of Balain, *le mescheant chevalier* who brought destruction to all he tried to help,[120] and the strange end of Merlin,

112 *Merlin*, II, 61, 144. Cf. *Lancelot*, LIIa, §§61–9, CI, §19–CV, §29; Löseth, §388a; 'Galahad and Perceval', p. 78; *Morte Darthur* XI. 6; *Works*, p. 802.

113 *Merlin*, II, 97–9. The knights' oath was first mentioned in *Lancelot*, LIa, §6, and four clerks were appointed to record their deeds in LXXIa, §48. Cf. *ibid.*, I, §2, IV*, §24, LXXXIV, §§68–73, CI, §§1–11, CVI, §22; *Queste*, pp. 279–80; *Mort Artu*, §2; 'Galahad and Perceval', p. 185; *Morte Darthur* XII. 10, XVII. 23; *Works*, pp. 832, 1036; *Merlin*, II, 113–14, 127–8; *Abenteuer Gawains, Ywains und Le Morholts*, p. 85; *Folie Lancelot* VIII. 336–55.

114 *Merlin*, II, 114–15, 131–3. Cf. Löseth, §§215, 302; *Morte Darthur* III. 3; *Works*, pp. 100–1.

115 *Merlin*, I, 262–3, II, 73–4. Cf. *Morte Darthur* II. 11, III. 4; *Works*, pp. 78, 101.

116 *Merlin*, I, 266, II, 168. Cf. *Morte Darthur* I. 11, III. 13; *Works* , pp. 78, 149–50.

117 *Merlin*, I, 180–1, Cf. *Morte Darthur* I, 23; *Works*, p. 48. The Roman ambassadors appeared near the end of *Estoire de Merlin* (pp. 424–7), and the war began straightaway.

118 *Abenteuer Gawains, Ywains und Le Morholts*, pp. 129–31, 134. Cf. Curtis, §287; *Morte Darthur* VIII. 4; *Works*, pp. 376–7. The lacuna between the two surviving portions of the *Suite* presumably contained some account of the Roman war and the death of Pellinor, which was referred to as already narrated in *Folie Lancelot* VIII. 572–4: *Vous savés bien que messire Gauvain occist de sa main le roy Pellinor, si comme ly comptes l'a ja devisé, et Lamorat et son frere.* Since the Roman war had already been narrated in the *Estoire de Merlin*, the *Suite*'s account of it may have been a summary one, like that of the war with King Claudas (*Folie Lancelot* I. 880–7).

119 Bogdanow, *Romance of the Grail*, p. 199.

120 *Merlin*, I, 213–II, 60. Cf. *Morte Darthur* II; *Works*, pp. 61–92.

which turned his farcical imprisonment in Vivien's love-nest into a nightmare worthy of Edgar Allen Poe,[121] are romantic masterpieces in the truest sense.

V

Between them the *Tristan* and the *Suite* determined the pattern of the first half of the Malory's *Morte Darthur*, which ended when Lancelot brought Tristan to Arthur's court, where he took le Morholt's seat at the Round Table, after their battle at the *perron Merlin*.[122] This was 'the perowne that Merlyon had made tofore, where sir Launceor, that was the kynges son of Irelonde, was slayne by the hondys of sir Balyn', when he prophesied to King Mark 'that in that same place sholde fyght two the beste knyghtes that ever were in kynge Arthurs dayes, and two of the beste lovers':[123]

> 'Here shall be' seyde Merlion, 'in this same place the grettist bateyle betwyxte two knyghtes that ever was or ever shall be, and the trewyst lovers; and yette none of hem shall slee other.' And ther Merlion wrote hir namys uppon the tombe with lettirs of golde, that shall feyght in that place: which namys was Launcelot du Lake and Trystrams.[124]

Merlin's prophesy was the first reference to either Lancelot or Tristan in Malory's *Morte Darthur*, and their names were paired again in the explicit of his first tale, *The Tale of King Arthur*:

> Here endyth this tale, as the Freynshe booke seyth, fro the maryage of kynge Uther unto kyng Arthure that regned aftir hym and ded many batayles.
>
> And this booke endyth whereas sir Launcelot and sir Trystrams com to courte. Who that woll make ony more lette hym seke other bookis of kyynge Arthure or of sir Launcelot or sir Trystrams; for this was drawyn by a knyght presoner, sir Thomas Malleorré, that God sende hym good recover. Amen. Explicit.[125]

121 *Merlin*, II, 191–8. Cf. *Morte Darthur* IV, 1; *Works*, pp. 125–6; *Estoire de Merlin*, pp. 451–2.
122 *Morte Darthur*, X. 5–6; *Works*, pp. 568–72. Cf. Löseth, §§203–6.
123 *Morte Darthur* X. 6; *Works*, p. 572.10–13, 18–20.
124 *Morte Darthur* II. 8; *Works*, p. 72.13–19. Cf. *Merlin*, I, 231.
125 *Works*, p. 180.6–15. Not in Caxton's edition.

Malory's explicit is primarily a claim to literary property, but the reference to Lancelot and Tristan links up with the first sentence of his next tale, *The Noble Tale of King Arthur and the Emperor Lucius*:

> Hyt befelle whan kyng Arthur had wedded quene Gwenyvere and fulfylled the Rounde Table, and so aftir his mervelous knyghtis and he had venquyshed the moste party of his enemyes, than sone aftir com sir Launcelot de Lake unto the courte, and sir Trystrams come that tyme also and than kyng Arthur helde a ryal feeste and Table Rounde.[126]

Although Malory took this tale from the Alliterative *Morte Arthure*,[127] in which Arthur's war with Lucius preceded the *Morte* proper as it did in Geoffrey of Monmouth's *History* and most other versions of the story,[128] he followed the *Estoire de Merlin* (and, by implication, the *Suite*) in placing it at the end of the early part of Arthur's reign, but a little later than the *Estoire*, which concluded before Lancelot came to court.[129] In Malory's version Lancelot, a late-comer with only a small part in the *Morte Arthure* (though he distinguished himself by wounding the emperor),[130] was the hero of the day in the battle on the way to Paris, which thus became his first great exploit in the *Morte Darthur*, as the conquest of Dolorous Garde was in the *Lancelot*: 'Therefore was he honoured dayes of his lyff, for never ere or that day was he proved so well, for he and sir Bors and sir Lyonel was but late afore at an hyghe feste made all three knyghtes.'[131] Tristan (not even mentioned in the *Morte Arthure*) was conspicuous by his absence: 'sir Trystrams at that tyme

126 *Ibid.*, p. 185.1–6. Not in Caxton's edition.

127 *Morte Arthure*, ed. Erik Björkman, Heidelberg and New York, 1915. Although the Alliterative *Morte's* author belonged to the native 'British' school of Geoffrey of Monomouth, Wace, and Laȝamon, his moral perspective was that of French Arthurian tradition, from which he took Arthur's dream of Fortune and her wheel (below, p. 188 and n. 179).

128 Alliterative *Morte Arthure* 26–3217. Cf. *Historia regum Britanniae* (Variant Version, ed. Jacob Hammer, Cambridge, Mass., 1951), IX. 12–X. 14; Wace, *Roman de Brut*, ed. Ivor Arnold, 2 vols., Paris, 1938–40 (Société des anciens textes français), 10621–13015; Laȝamon, *Brut*, edd. G.L. Brook and R.F. Leslie, 2 vols., London, 1963, 1978 (Early English Text Society 250, 277), 12342–13970; *Mort Artu*, §§160–2.

129 *Estoire de Merlin*, pp. 424–41.

130 Alliterative *Morte Arthure* 2073–80. Cf. *Works*, p. 220.15–24 (not in Caxton's edition).

131 *Morte Darthur* V. 7; *Works*, p. 216.24–7. Lancelot was not at the battle according to *Morte Arthure* 1720 'Sir Lancelott sall neuer laughe, þat with þe kyng lengez'. Bors and Lionel accompanied Lancelot when he went to Camelot to be knighted, but they were not knighted themselves until later (*Lancelot*, XXIa, §§24–5, XVIII, §3, XL, §§21–2).

beleft with kynge Marke of Cornuayle for the love of La beale Isode, wherefore sir Launcelot was passyng wrothe.'[132]

At the end of this tale Malory was faced with the same problem as the author of the *Suite* in his *Folie Lancelot* section, how to combine the accounts of Arthurian history given by the *Lancelot* and the *Tristan*, and his solution was to place *The Book of Sir Tristram de Lyones*, which incorporated the final sequence of the *Lancelot*,[133] at the centre of his Arthuriad, before *The Tale of the Sankgreal*, and to preface it with two short tales, *The Noble Tale of Sir Launcelot du Lake* and *The Tale of Sir Gareth of Orkney*, showing Lancelot in the position of Arthur's best knight, which was established in the second paragraph of the first:

> Sone aftir that kynge Arthure was com from Rome into Ingelonde, than all the knyghtys of the Rounde Table resorted unto the kynge and made many joustys and turnementes. And some there were that were but knyghtes encresed in armys and worshyp that passed all other of her felowys in prouesse and noble dedys, and that was well proved on many.
>
> But in especiall hit was prevyd on sir Launcelot de Lake, for in all turnementes, justys, and dedys of armys, both for lyff and deth, he passed all other knyghtes, and at no tyme was he ovircom but yf hit were by treson other inchauntement. So this sir Launcelot encresed so mervaylously in worship and honoure; therefore he is the fyrste knyght that the Freynsh booke makyth mencion of aftir kynge Arthure com frome Rome.[134]

In the adventures that follow, mostly drawn from a long series in the third branch of the *Lancelot*, interwoven with preliminaries of the *Grail Quest*, which began with Lionel's capture by Tarquin and Lancelot's imprisonment by Morgan le Fay and two other sorceress-queens,[135]

132 *Works*, p. 195.11–13. Cf. *Morte Darthur* V. 3 'wherfore syre Launcelot was wrothe for he lefte syre Tristram with kynge marke for the loue of beal Isoulde.'

133 *Morte Darthur* XI. 1–XII. 10; *Works*, pp. 791–833. Cf. Löseth, §388a; 'Galahad and Perceval', pp. 60–84, 181–200, 322–37; *Lancelot*, LXXVIII, §43–LXXIX, §4, XCVIII, §§13–50, CV, §30-CVIII, §16.

134 *Morte Darthur* VI. 1; *Works*, p. 253.1–15.

135 *Lancelot*, LXXVI, §48–LXXVIII, §34: *Morte Darthur* VI. 1–7, *Works*, pp. 253–64; *Lancelot* LXXVIII, §43–LXXIX, §4: *Morte Darthur* XI. 1–3, *Works*, pp. 791–6; *Lancelot*, LXXXIII, §§41–9: *Morte Darthur* VI. 17, *Works*, pp. 284–6; *Lancelot*, LXXXV, §§34–54: *Morte Darthur* VI. 7–9, *Works*, pp. 264–9; LXXXVI, §§7–11: *Morte Darthur* VI. 10–11, *Works*, pp. 269–72; *Lancelot*, XCVIII. §§11–50: *Morte Darthur* XI. 3–6, *Works*, pp. 797–802; *Lancelot*, XCIX, §§12–27: *Morte Darthur* VI. 11–13, *Works*, pp. 272–8; *Lancelot*, C, §§1–32: *Morte Darthur* VI. 18, *Works*, pp. 286–7; *Lancelot*, CV, §30–CVIII, §16: *Morte Darthur* XI. 6–XII. 9, *Works*, pp. 802–33.

Lancelot, already tested in war, displayed his prowess as a super-knight that rescued other knights, like Galahad in the *Queste* or Prince Arthur in the *Faerie Queene*, by releasing his fellows from Tarquin's prison as he had previously rescued Gawain from Dolorous Garde and from the Dolorous Tower of Tarquin's brother Carados,[136] and by setting free the ladies and damsels enslaved by two giants of Tintagel, emulating Yvain's conquest of the *deus fiz de deable* at the *Chastel de Pesme Aventure*,[137] from which Malory presumably took his ladies' description of their sweat-shop (not found in *Lancelot*):

> Than sir Launcelot wente into the halle, and there com afore hym three score of ladyes and damesels, and all kneled unto hym and thanked God and hym of his delyveraunce. 'For,' they seyde, 'the most party of us have bene here this seven yere presoners, and we have worched all maner of sylke workys for oure mete, and we are all grete jentylwomen borne. And blyssed be the tyme, knyght, that ever thou were borne, for thou haste done the moste worshyp that ever ded knyght in this worlde; that woll we beare recorde.'[138]

Yvain's exploit is an episode of great symbolic power, for it also inspired Galahad's conquest of the Castle of Maidens in the *Tale of the Sankgreal*,[139] which signified the Harrowing of Hell, as the hermit told Gawain.[140] The presumption that Malory intended Lancelot's conquest of Tintagel to be read in this way is supported by his subsequent visit to the Chapel Perilous for the sword and piece of cloth with which he healed Meliot's wounds (an adventure borrowed from *Perlesvaus*):[141]

136 *Morte Darthur* VI. 7–9; *Works*, pp. 264–9; *Lancelot*, LXXXV. §§34–54. Cf. *Morte Darthur* VI. 8, VIII. 10, XX. 1, 15; *Works*, pp. 266, 388, 1162, 1198; *Lancelot*, XXIXa–XXXa, XIII, §§2–7, XIV, §§1–8, XXVIII, §§1–24.

137 *Morte Darthur* VI. 10–11; *Works*, pp. 271–2; *Lancelot*, LXXXVI, §§7–11. Cf. *Yvain* 5107–809; *Ywain and Gawain* 2931–3358. The cutting in half of Yvain's horse by the portcullis in *Yvain* 873–952, *Ywain and Gawain* 661–86 is duplicated in *Lancelot* LXXXIII, §§44–6, the source of *Morte Darthur* VI. 17, *Works*, pp. 284–6.

138 *Morte Darthur* VI. 11; *Works*, p. 272.1–10. Cf. *Yvain* 5298–324; *Ywain and Gawain* 3047–60. The *prael* contained *puceles jusqu'a trois çanz* (*Yvain* 5194).

139 *Morte Darthur* XIII. 15; *Works*, pp. 887–90. Cf. *Queste*, pp. 46–51.

140 *Morte Darthur* XIII. 16; *Works*, p. 892. Cf. *Queste*, pp. 55. Professor Tuve discusses the romances' use of typology in *Allegorical Imagery*, pp. 399–436, esp. 430–1. Another three-way example involving Lancelot and Galahad is the girding of the newly-knighted Lancelot with the sword sent by Guinevere and the girding of Arthur and Galahad with swords sent by God (*Lancelot*, XXIIa, §§33, 44–5, XXIIIa, §§15–17; *Queste*, pp. 5–12, Prose *Merlin*, §§83–91; *Morte Darthur* I. 5–7, XIII. 2– 5, XVIII. 7, *Works*, pp. 12–16, 856–63, 1058). Girding with the sword made a new knight *serjans a Nostre Signor* like Galahad, *li Verais Chevaliers* (*Lancelot*, XXIa, §14; *Queste*, p. 77.31).

141 *Morte Darthur* VI. 14–16; *Works*, pp. 278–84. Cf. *Perlesvaus* 8156–250, 8281–380, 8449–92.

> When sir Melyot saw sir Launcelot he kneled uppon his kneis and cryed on hyghte: 'A, lorde, sir Launcelot, helpe me anone!' Than sir Launcelot lepe unto hym and towched his woundys with sir Gylbardys swerde, and than he wyped his woundys with a parte of the bloody cloth that sir Gylbarde was wrapped in; and anone an holer man in his lyff was he never.[142]

Lancelot's charismatic healing power, first displayed when he drew the sword and the truncheons from the *chevalier enferré* on the day he was knighted,[143] was shown once again in *The Book of Sir Launcelot and Queen Guinevere* when he healed Urry, an episode based on the same series of adventures in the *Lancelot* that Malory had used for his *Tale of Sir Launcelot*, in which a knight followed Lancelot on a litter because he could only be healed by the best knight in the world:[144]

> And than sir Launcelot prayde sir Urré to lat hym se hys hede; and than, devoutly knelyng, he ransaked the three woundis, that they bled a lytyll; and forthwithall the woundis fayre heled and semed as they had bene hole a seven yere. And in lyke wyse he serched hys body of othir three woundis, and they heled in lyke wyse. And than the laste of all he serched hys honde, and anone hit fayre healed.[145]

In both places Malory emphasizes the miraculous immediacy of the cure, which was a more gradual process in his sources:

> Lanceloz e la damoisele i atochierent l'espee e le suaire, e eles li sont tantost asoagiees, et dist que il se sent bien or a primes que il n'avra garde de mort. Lanceloz en est molt joiant en son cuer de ce que il voit q'il iert par tens gariz, e ce fust grant domage de sa mort, car il estoit bons chevaliers e sages e loiax.[146]
>
> Et quant Lanceloz voit ce, si a moult grant pitié, si li pardonne volentiers ce qu'il li quiert, puis li prant la saiete qu'il avoit en la cuisse et li errache maintenant. Et quant il se voit delivrés de ce qui

142 *Morte Darthur* VI. 15; *Works*, pp. 281.35–282.5. For the sword with the power of healing the wounds it inflicted see Chaucer, *Squire's Tale* 148–59, 228–34 (*Canterbury Tales*, V. 156–67, 236–42; *The Riverside Chaucer*, edd. Larry D. Benson and others (Oxford, 1988), pp. 171–2).

143 *Lancelot*, XXIIa, §§24–30.

144 *Morte Darthur* XIX. 10–13; *Works*, pp. 1145–53. Cf. *Lancelot*, LXXXVIII, §§7–19, 29–30, XCIII, §§42–3, XCV, §§19– 21.

145 *Morte Darthur* XIX. 12, *Works*, p. 1152.26–32.

146 *Perlesvaus* 8479–83.

> tant li faisoit mal, si dist: 'Ha, sire, de Dieu soiez vos beneoiz, car vos m'avez rendue la vie; et se je eusse mire, je fusse maintenant gariz, car vos m'avez ja tant alegié que je porrai par tans chevauchier.'[147]

Thus by saving and healing Malory's Lancelot, more emphatically than his models, prefigured his son, Galahad the Grail Knight and healer of the Maimed King, who was in turn a figure of Christ the Redeemer,[148] as the *preudons* told him at the White Abbey:

> 'Et cele similitude que li Peres envoia en terre son fil por delivrer son pueple est ore renovelee. Car tout ausi come l'error et la folie s'en foï par la venue de lui et la verité fu lors aparanz et manifestee, autresint vos a Nostre sires esleu sor toz autres chevaliers por envoier par les estranges terres por abatre les grevoses aventures et por fere conoistre comment eles sont avenues. Por quoi len doit vostre venue comparer pres a la venue Jhesucrist, de semblance ne mie de hautece.'

The reason he failed to achieve the Grail himself was also indicated in the second paragraph of the *Tale of Sir Launcelot*:

> Wherefore quene Gwenyvere had hym in grete favoure aboven all other knyghtis, and so he loved the quene agayne aboven all other ladyes dayes of his lyff, and for hir he dud many dedys of armys and saved her from the fyre thorow his noble chevalry.[149]

There his rescue of the queen was described as a deed of gallantry like the juridical combat Yvain fought to save Lunete from burning, but unlike Lunete Guinevere was not falsely accused; she was condemned to the stake for the adultery Merlin foretold when he warned the king 'that Launcelot scholde love hir, and sche hym agayne',[150] and the

147 *Lancelot*, XCV, §20. The *chevalier enferré* also needed a physician to complete his cure: '*Des ore mais,*' *fait li chevaliers*, '*seroie je tous garis, se jou avoie un mire qui s'entremeist de moi garir*' (*ibid.*, XXIIa, §30).

148 *Queste*, p. 38.13–21. The *preudons'* distinction between *semblance* and *hautece* echoes St. Augustine, *De diversis questionibus octoginta tribus*, ed. Almut Mutzenbecher, Turnout, 1985 (Corpus christianorum Series latina 44A), LXXIV *De eo quod scriptum est in epistula Pauli ad Colossenses* (1: 14–15) '*In quo habemus redemtionem remissionem pecatorum, qui est imago dei invisibilis*': *Imago et aequalitas et similitudo distinguenda sunt: quia ubi imago, continuo similitudo non continuo aequalitas.* On the same principle Lancelot, the flower of earthly knighthood, can typify Galahad, a *chevalier celestiel* (*Queste*, pp. 143–4).

149 *Morte Darthur* VI. 1; *Works*, p. 253.15–19. Cf. *Morte Darthur* XX. 1–8; *Works*, pp. 1161–78; *Mort Artu*, §§85–97, Stanzaic *Le Morte Arthur*, ed. J. Douglas Bruce, London, 1903 (Early English Text Society, Extra Series 88), 1672–1965.

150 *Morte Darthur* III. 1; *Works*, p. 97.30–1. Cf. Merlin, II, 61; *Yvain* 3485–769, 4313–575; *Yvain and Gawain* 2059–206, 2507–642.

scandal their relationship caused is referred to twice in this tale, first by the damsel who brought Lancelot to Tarquin's manor, and again by Hallowes, the necrophiliac sorceress of the Chapel Perilous:

> 'But one thyng, sir knyght, methynkes ye lak, ye that ar a knyght wyveles, that ye woll nat love som mayden other jantylwoman. For I cowde never here sey that ever ye loved ony of no maner of degré, and that is grete pyté. But hit is noysed that ye love quene Gwenyvere, and that she hath ordeyned by enchauntemente that ye shall never love none other but hir, nother none other damesell ne lady shall rejoyce you; wherefore there be many in this londe, of hyghe astate and lowe, that make grete sorow.'[151]
>
> 'And, sir Launcelot, now I telle the: I have loved the this seven yere, but ther may no woman have thy love but quene Gwenyver; and sytthen I myght nat rejoyse the nother thy body on lyve, I had kepte no more joy in this worlde but to have thy body dede. Than wolde I have bawmed hit and sered hit, and so to have kepte hit my lyve dayes; and dayly I sholde have clypped the and kyssed the, dispyte of quene Gwenyvere.'[152]

'Jesu preserve me frome your subtyle crauftys' was the only possible reply to Hallowes, but Lancelot's answer to the damsel, 'to be a weddyd man, I thynke hit nat, for than I muste couche with hir and leve armys and turnamentis, batellys and adventures,'[153] is evasive, like his answer to the Maid of Astolat: 'wyte you well, fayre mayden, I myght have bene maryed and I had wolde, but I never applyed me yett to be maryed.'[154] There is no hint of courtly idealism in either speech, and the vehemence with which he condemned the love of paramours in the first betrays an awareness (not found in his prototype) of the moral dilemma that his relationship with Guinevere involved:

> 'And as for to sey to take my pleasaunce with peramours, that woll I refuse: in prencipall for drede of God, for knyghtes that bene adventures sholde nat be avoutrers nothir lecherous, for than they be not happy nother fortunate unto the werrys; for other they shall be overcom with a sympler knyght than they be hemself, other ellys they shall sle by unhappe and hir cursednesse bettir men than they be hemself. And so who that usyth peramours shall be unhappy, and all thynge unhappy that is aboute them.'[155]

151 *Morte Darthur* VI. 10; *Works*, p. 270.22–7.
152 *Morte Darthur* VI. 15; *Works*, p. 281.15–22. Cf. *Perlesvaus* 1444–73, 8338–74.
153 *Works*, pp. 270.29–32, 281.27–8.
154 *Morte Darthur* XVIII. 19; *Works*, p. 1089.26–7. Lancelot gave her the standard courtly lover's reply in *Mort Artu*, §38, Stanzaic *Le Morte Arthur* 201–8.
155 *Morte Darthur* VI. 10; *Works*, pp. 270.32–271.4.

This inner conflict surfaced again in the remorse he expressed to Guinevere for what he would have achieved on the Quest 'if that I had nat had my prevy thoughtis to returne to youre love agayne as I do',[156] and in his bitter words when she apologized for her suspicions after the Maid's death, which expose the darker side of their relationship:

> 'Thys ys nat the firste tyme,' seyde sir Launcelot, 'that ye have ben displese with me causeles. But, madame, ever I must sufir you, but what sorow that I endure, ye take no forse.'[157]

Malory's next work, *The Tale of Sir Gareth of Orkeney*, is a 'Fair Unknown' romance, the sources of which are obscure,[158] but there is nothing to connect the story with Gareth. Malory presumably tailored it to fit him, modelling it mainly on the *Tristan*: Kay gave Gareth an insulting nick-name like the one he gave Brunor 'La Cote Male Tayle', as Lancelot pointed out;[159] although he was Gawain's brother, Gareth asked Lancelot to knight him, as Gawain's squire Hebes had asked Tristan;[160] the Blue Knight told Gareth that Lancelot, Tristan, and Lamorat were the three best knights in the world, whom he would equal if he overcame the Red Knight:

> 'A,' seyde sir Persaunte, 'of a more renomed man myght ye nat be made knyghte of, for of all knyghtes he may be called cheff of knyghthode, and so all the wordle seyth that betwyxte three knyghtes is departed clerely knyghthode, that is sir Launcelot du Lake, sir Trystrams de Lyones and sir Lamerok de Galys. Thes bere now the renowne, yet there be many other noble knyghtis, as sir Palomydes the Saresyn and sir Saphir, his brothir, also sir Bleobrys and sir Blamour de Ganys, his brothir; also sir Bors de Ganys, and sir Ector de Marys, and sir Percivale de Galys. Thes and many mo bene noble knyghtes, but ther be none that bere the name but thes three abovyn seyde. Therefore God spede you well,' seyde sir Persaunte, 'for and ye may macche that Rede Knyght ye shall be called the fourth of the worlde.'[161]

156 *Morte Darthur* XVIII. 1; *Works*, p. 1046.8–9.
157 *Morte Darthur* XVIII. 20; *Works*, p. 1098.5–8.
158 Cf. Claude Luttrell, *The Creation of the First Arthurian Romance* (London, 1974), pp. 120–6, 211–15; Mills, *Lybeaus Desconus*, pp. 48–50. Luttrell and Mills agree that Malory's version of the story was a synthesis of existing literary sources, but opinions will differ as to whether he had a wide enough knowledge of early French romance to have put it together himself.
159 *Morte Darthur* VII. 1–2, IX. 1; *Works*, pp. 294–5, 459. Cf. Curtis, §637.
160 *Morte Darthur* VII. 3–5, VIII. 9–10; *Works*, pp. 297–9, 386–7. Cf. Curtis, §323.
161 *Morte Darthur* VII. 13; *Works*, p. 316.21–35. Cf. above, p.170 and n.88. Gareth's valour was highly praised in the *Lancelot* and in the *Tristan* (*Lancelot*, LXIX,

Here Malory adapted the 'four best knights' formula of the *Tristan* by demoting Palamedes and putting Gareth in place of Lamorat, the young knight who would have rivalled the other three had he not died before his time. The parallel with Hebes is also an ominous one, for Tristan slew Hebes by mistake near the end of his own life as Lancelot was to slay Gareth:

> A l'endemain fist Tristanz de son escuier chevalier; et sachiez qu'il fu mout preudons de son cors et de grant renomee, et compaignon de la Table Reonde, et a la queste del Saint Gaal le fist il mout bien. Mes illec l'ocist Tristanz par grant mescheance, a celi point qu'il sivoit Palamedes, le bon chevalier sarradin, qui tant amoit ma dame Yselt. Et se aucuns me demandoit coment il avoit non, je diroie qu'il amoit non Hebés; et por la proesce de li fu il apelez Hebés li Renomez.[162]

Malory's tales of Lancelot and Gareth justify the peculiar construction of his version of the *Morte Artu*, in which three extraneous episodes, the tournament of Westminster, Gwenevere's abduction by Meleagant, and the healing of Urry, are sandwiched between the stories of the poisoned apple and the Maid of Astolat and the final tragedy.[163] The tournament of Westminster confirmed that Gareth, whom Bors had compared with the three best knights after the tournament at Allhallowmass when he said to Lancelot, 'but if it were you, other the noble knyght sir Trystam, other the good knyght sir Lamorak de Gailis, I saw never knyght bere so many knyghtes and smyte downe in so litill a whyle as ded sir Gareth',[164] was indeed their equal, as the tournament of Surluse had proved that Lamorat was the equal of Lancelot and Tristan:

> And sir Gareth ded such dedys of armys that all men mervayled what knyght he was with the gryne shylde, for he smote downe that day and pulled downe mo than thirty knyghtes. And, as the Freynshe booke sayth, sir Launcelot mervayled, whan he behylde sir Gareth do such dedis, what knyght he myght be. (. . .) And yet

§§2–5; Curtis, §789), and especially in the *Suite*, where the dumb fool told him that he would have surpassed all the knights of the Round Table except two, '*se ne fust la mort de ta mere que tu hasteras par ton pechié*' (*Abenteuer Gawains, Ywains und Le Morholts*, p. 93). Malory overcame this objection by transferring the matricide to his brother Gaheris (*Morte Darthur* X. 23–4; *Works*, pp. 687–8).

162 Curtis, §323.2–9. Cf. Löseth, §§505–7.

163 *Morte Darthur* XVIII. 21–XIX. 13; *Works*, pp. 1103–54. No rubric divides these three episodes from the previous ones, and Malory apparently refers to all five, which comprise Vinaver's *Book of Sir Launcelot and Queen Gwinevere*, as 'the tale of sir Launcelot' (*Works*, p. 1154.13; not in Caxton's edition).

164 *Morte Darthur* XVIII. 18; *Works*, p. 1088.28–32.

> for all thys, sir Launcelot knew nat sir Gareth; for and sir Trystram de Lyones other sir Lamorak de Galys had ben on lyve, sir Launcelot woulde have demed he had bene on of them tweyne.[165]

Gareth's overcoming 'mo than thirty knyghtes' echoes the description Palamedes gave of Lamorat's prowess at Surluse when Hector asked him if any knight besides Lancelot and Tristram had ever been his match:

> 'Yes,' seyde sir Palomydes, 'there was the thirde; as good a knyght as ony of them and of his ayge he was the beste, for yet found I never his pyere. For and he myght have lyved tyll he had bene more of ayge, an hardyer man there lyvith nat than he woulde have bene, and his name was sir Lamorat de Galys. And as he had justed at a turnament, there he overthrewe me and thirty knyghtes mo, and there he wan the gre. And at his departynge there mette hym sir Gawayne and his bretherne, and wyth grete payne they slewe hym felounsly, unto all good knyghtes grete damage.'[166]

Gareth's image was further enhanced at the end of this episode, when Arthur praised his generosity in changing sides to help Lancelot as the pattern of knightly virtue:

> 'For ever hit ys,' seyde kynge Arthure, 'a worshypfull knyghtes dede to helpe and succoure another worshypfull knyght whan he seeth hym in daungere. For ever a worshypfull man woll be lothe to se a worshypfull man shamed, and he that ys of no worshyp and medelyth with cowardise never shall he shew jantilnes nor no maner of goodnes where he seeth a man in daungere, for than woll a cowarde never shew mercy. And allwayes a good man woll do ever to another man as he wolde be done to hymselff.'[167]

Arthus's praise of Gareth is Malory's fullest statement of his belief in chivalry as a moral and religious ideal, and its occasion intensifies the tragedy that was soon to follow.

Guinevere's abduction and the healing of Urry both embody familiar themes anticipated in the *Tale of Sir Launcelot* that foreshadow the *Morte* proper. The abduction begins with a mellifluous comparison of the 'vertuouse love' used in King Arthur's time and 'the love nowadayes' which uses nature imagery reminiscent of *The Floure and the Leafe*, a contemporary love-vision formerly attributed to Chaucer, to evoke a romantic ideal as old as Chrétien's Yvain:

165 *Morte Darthur* VIII. 23; *Works*, p. 1112.3–13.
166 *Morte Darthur* X. 54; *Works*, p. 688.1–10. Cf. B.N. fr. 334, 330rb–va, quoted above, p. 170.
167 *Morte Darthur* XVIII. 24; *Works*, p. 1114.20–32.

For, lyke as wynter rasure dothe allway arace and deface grene summer, so faryth hit by unstable love in man and woman, for in many persones there ys no stabylité: for we may se all day, for a lytyll blaste of wyntres rasure, anone we shall deface and lay aparte trew love, for lytyll or nowght, that coste muche thynge.[168]

This introduction is echoed in the opening of his *Most Piteous Tale of the Morte Arthur*, which employs the same May-Day imagery to introduce the destruction of Arthur and his knights:

In May, whan every harte floryshyth and burgenyth (for, as the season ys lusty to beholde and comfortable, so man and woman rejoysyth and gladith of somer commynge with his freyshe floures, for wynter wyth hys rowghe wyndis and blastis causyth lusty men and women to cowre and to syt by fyres), so thys season hit befelle in the moneth of May a great angur and unhappy that stynted nat tylle the floure of chyïvalry of the worlde was destroyed and slayne.[169]

Malory's version of the *Chevalier de la Charrete*, shorn of its marvels and retold in the naturalistic mode of the *Mort Artu*, ends like the story of the poisoned apple, in which Lancelot also fought a juridicial combat to save Guinevere from the stake, anticipating her rescue in the *Morte*,[170] while the healing of Urry, which concludes the *Book of Sir Launcelot and Queen Guinevere*, recalls the charismatic gift that Lancelot revealed in the *Tale of Sir Launcelot* and dramatizes his sense of his own unworthiness in his finest hour:

168 *Morte Darthur* XVIII. 25; *Works*, p. 1119.14–19. Cf. *The Floure and the Leafe*, ed. D.A. Pearsall (London and Edinburgh, 1962), 547–60; *Yvain* 8–32; *Ywain and Gawain* 33–40.

169 *Morte Darthur* XX. 1; *Works*, p. 1161.1–8. Like the beginning of Chaucer's General Prologue (*Canterbury Tales*, I. 1–18), this opening gives a stock example of digression *a materia ad aliam partem materiae* an original twist: *cum dicendum sit 'Amantes recesserunt ab invicem in tempore veris', prius describendum est tempus veris et postea dicendum 'Tunc recesserunt'* (Geoffroi de Vinsauf, *Documentum de modo et arte dictandi et versificandi*, II. 2, §20 (Edmond Faral, *Les Arts poétiques du XIIe et du XIIIe siècles* (Paris, 1924), pp. 265–320, at 274)).

170 *Morte Darthur* XVIII. 3–8, XIX. 1–9; *Works*, pp. 1048–60, 1120–40. Cf. *Lancelot*, XXXVI, §6–XLII, §12; *Mort Artu*, §§62–3, 67–9, 72, 74–85; Stanzaic *Le Morte Arthur* 832–951, 1168–1671. Guinevere was not condemned to death in the *Lancelot* or in the *Chevalier de la Charrete*; the *Mort Artu* does not say how the queen was to die if she could not find a champion, but she was to be burnt in *Le Morte Arthur* 940–3 and 1318–19 as in Malory. Malory's Tristan also saved his stepmother from the stake, though the manner of her execution was not specified in the *Tristan* (*Morte Darthur* VIII. 2; *Works*, pp. 373–5; Curtis, §§254–6).

> Than kynge Arthur and all the kynges and knyghtes kneled downe and gave thankynges and lovynge unto God and unto Hys Blyssed Modir. And ever sir Launcelote wepte, as he had bene a chylde that had bene beatyn![171]

Here Lancelot's conventionally modest disclaimer to the knight on the litter, '*si an merciez Nostre Signor, car bien saciez que ce est plus par sa volunté et par vos merites que par bonté que ja aie en moi*',[172] is raised to a higher power, yet one that is consistent with his earlier behaviour. From the beginning Malory's Lancelot acted more humanly, and humanely, than his prototype, by staunching the wound of Belleus, the knight who mistook him for his lady, instead of splitting his skull to the teeth;[173] by smiling and saying 'God gyff hym joy that this spere made, for there cam never a bettir in my honde' instead of weeping when, disguised as Kay, he overthrew Sagramor, Hector, Yvain, and Gawain;[174] by apologizing to Lamorat for challenging him when he was weary after his fight with Meleagant;[175] by half disarming himself to give Meleagant a sporting chance in their juridicial combat;[176] and he was to give further proof of his humanity in the *Morte*.

VI

Seen from this angle, the pieces of Malory's Arthurian jigsaw fall into place. Lancelot and Tristan replaced the best knights of Arthur's early days, Balin and Balan, Pellinor, and Le Morholt,[177] and would have been

171 *Morte Darthur* XIX. 12; *Works*, p. 1152.33–6.
172 *Lancelot*, XCV, §20.
173 *Morte Darthur* VI. 4–5, 18; *Works*, pp. 259–60, 287. Cf. Lancelot, LXXVIII, §§15–17.
174 *Morte Darthur* VI. 13; *Works*, p. 278, lines 5–6. Cf. *Lancelot*, XCIX, §§23–7. In the *Lancelot* he smiled earlier, when he encountered the four strange knights who believed he was Kay (*ibid.*, XCIX, §§19–22, at 20; *Morte Darthur* VI. 12; *Works*, pp. 275–7).
175 *Morte Darthur* IX. 13–14; *Works*, pp. 486–7. Cf. Curtis, §§801–8.
176 *Morte Darthur* XIX. 9; *Works*, pp. 1139–40. Cf. *Lancelot*, XLII, §9. Such changes are typical of Malory's technique as C.S. Lewis described it: 'at point after point he adds vividness, throws some figure into bolder relief, cuts away an excrescence, or sweetens some motive that he rightly found odious' ('The English Prose *Morte*', pp. 24–5). The first example of Malory's 'sweetening' occurred when Uther told Igrain 'dismay you not, for I am fader to the child' instead of concealing Arthur's paternity from her in order to make her hand him over to Merlin (*Morte Darthur* I. 3; *Works*, p. 10.29–10; Prose *Merlin*, §§68, 72).
177 *Morte Darthur* I. 18, 22, 24, II. 1–2, 10–11, 19 VIII. 4; *Works*, pp. 40, 46–7, 51–2, 61–4, 77–9, 92, 376. Cf. *Merlin* I, 186, 214–17, 224–5, 231–2, 253–4, 258–9, 265, II, 11–12; Curtis, §287.

replaced in turn by Lamorat and Gareth had they not become victims of the pride and envy of his other knights, as foretold in the *Lancelot* and the *Queste* and personified in the *Tristan* and the *Suite* by Gareth's brothers, the last of whom was Mordred; Arthur's fall thus balances his rise, which began Malory's Arthuriad (unlike its predecessors), and also the sub-tales of Balin and Arthur's wedding.[178] Traditionally the *Morte* exemplified the theme of mutability expressed in Arthur's dream of Fortune's Wheel before his last battle and Lancelot's exclamation when told of his fate, 'Alas! Who may truste thys world?',[179] to which Malory added a contemporary dimension in his apostrophe to the English:

> Lo, ye all Englysshemen, se ye nat what a myschyff her was? For he that was the moste kynge and nobelyst knyght of the worlde, and moste loved the felyshyp of noble knyghtes, and by hym they all were upholdyn, and yet myght nat thes Englyshemen holde them content with hym. Lo thus was the olde custom and usayges of thys londe, and men say that we of thys londe have nat yet loste that custom. Alas! thys ys a greate defaughte of us Englysshemen, for there may no thynge us please no terme.[180]

As in the *Lancelot-Queste-Mort*, however, this secular theme was offset by the spiritual values embodied in a second group of knights, Galahad, Bors, and Perceval, with whom Lancelot, alone among the first group, was associated in the *Tale of the Sankgreal*, and the two themes meet in Galahad's last request to his father, 'remembir of this worlde unstable'.[181]

The transcendental pattern that emerged left no place for Tristan, in spite of Malory's evident regard for 'the chyeff chacer of the worlde and the noblyst blower of an horne of all maner of measures', from whom

> cam all the good termys of venery and of huntynge, and all the syses and mesures of all blowyng wyth an horne; and of hym we had fyrst all the termys of hawkynge, and whyche were bestis of chace and bestis of venery, and whyche were vermyns, and all the blastis that longed to all maner of game; fyrst to the uncoupelynge, to the sekynge, to the fyndynge, to the rechace, to the flyght, to the

178 *Morte Darthur* II. 1, III, 1; *Works*, pp. 61, 97.

179 *Morte Darthur* XXI. 3, 10; *Works*, pp. 1233, 1254.12. Cf. *Mort Artu*, §176; Alliterative *Morte Arthure* 3218–393; Stanzaic *Le Morte Arthur* 3168–91. Lancelot also 'threwe hys armes abrode' as a gesture of renunciation in the Stanzaic *Le Morte Arthur* 3770–85: cf. *Morte Darthur* VIII. 10, IX. 18, X, 80, XXI. 13; *Works*, pp. 388, 496, 762, 1259; Curtis, §§338, 852, 865; Löseth, §381.

180 *Morte Darthur* XXI. 1; *Works*, p. 1229.6–14.

181 *Morte Darthur* XVII. 22; *Works*, p. 1035.11–12. This reminder is not in the corresponding passage in the *Queste* (p. 278.27–8).

> deth, and to strake; and many other blastis and termys, that all maner jantylmen hath cause to the worldes ende to prayse sir Trystram and to pray for his soule.[182]

He was dismissed from the story after his reconciliation with Palamedes on the way to Camelot before the Grail Quest, and his death was only mentioned incidentally in the roll-call of knights at the healing of Urry.[183] The fate of Tristan, like that of Lamorat, was not forgotten in the *Morte* proper, however. When Bors argued with unconscious irony that Lancelot might regain Arthur's favour by restoring Guinevere to him if he rescued her from the stake and kept her at Joyous Garde as Tristan had kept Isolde, Lancelot reminded him of the sequel:

> 'That ys hard for to do,' seyde sir Launcelot, 'for by sir Trystram I may have a warnynge: for whan by meanys of tretyse sir Trystram brought agayne La Beall Isode unto kynge Marke from Joyous Garde, loke ye now what felle on the ende, how shamefully that false traytour kynge Marke slew hym as he sate harpynge afore hys lady, La Beall Isode. Wyth a grounden glayve he threste hym in behynde to the harte, whych grevyth sore me,' seyde sir Launcelot, 'to speke of his dethe, for all the worlde may nat fynde such another knyght.'
>
> 'All thys ys trouthe,' seyde sir Bors, 'but ther ys one thyng shall corrayge you and us all: ye know well that kynge Arthur and kynge Marke were never lyke of condycions, for there was never yet man that ever coude preve kynge Arthur untrew of hys promyse.[184]'

Arthur was certainly no King Mark, but Bors reckoned without Gawain's implacable hostility, which he had already demonstrated by his treatment of Lamorat, as he pointed out himself in the abortive parley at Joyous Garde before the fighting began:

> 'Well, well, sir Launcelot,' seyde sir Gawayne, 'sythyn thou embraydyst me of sir Lamorak, wyte thou well, I shall never leve the

182 *Morte Darthur* X. 52; *Works*, p. 682.26–683.4. Cf. Arthur's greeting when he first came to Camelot: 'For all maner of huntynge thou beryste the pryce, and of all mesures of blowynge thou arte the begynnynge, of all the termys of huntynge and hawkynge ye are the begynner' (*Morte Darthur* X. 6; *Works*, p. 571.29–32).

183 *Morte Darthur* XII. 11–12, XIX. 11; *Works*, pp. 839–46, 1149–50. Cf. Löseth, §§389–90, 546–9; 'Galahad and Perceval', pp. 337–41. In the *Tristan* they were not finally reconciled until Tristan sent Palamedes a greeting from his deathbed which cancelled the return match he had threatened when they met after Hebes' death (Löseth, §§ 508, 549).

184 *Morte Darthur* XX. 6; *Works*, p. 1173.12–25. Cf. *Mort Artu*, §91.

> tyll I have the at such avayle that thou shalt nat ascape my hondis.'
> 'I truste you well inowgh,' seyde sir Launcelot, 'and ye may gete me, I gett but lytyll mercy.'[185]

These backward glances complement the forward looks in the early tales and deepen the resonance of the final movement.

Lancelot, on the other hand, remained at the centre of the pattern as in the *Queste* and the *Mort Artu*, where his role was that of the Everyman-figure in the morality plays, who successively underwent conversion, back-sliding, and repentance.[186] Malory therefore emphasized Lancelot's human weakness in the *Tale of the Sankgreal*. When he heard the birds sing after the voice from heaven admonished him, 'than somwhat he was comforted';[187] after he disembarked from the Ship of Solomon, 'he went to play hym by the watirs syde, for he was somwhat wery of the shippe';[188] and his thanksgiving when he awoke from his trance after seeing the Grail betrayed a hint of complacency echoed in his retort to Guienevere after his return from the quest:

> 'Now I thanke God,' seyde sir Launcelot, 'for Hys grete mercy of that I have sene, for hit suffisith me. For, as I suppose, no man in thys worlde have lyved bettir than I have to enchyeve that I have done.'[189]

> 'I thanke God of Hys grete mercy, and never of my deservynge, that I saw in that my queste as much as ever saw ony synfull man lyvynge, and so was hit told me.'[190]

As his repentance distanced him from Gawain and Hector, so the spiritual limitations shown by Lancelot in these passages distanced him from the sanctity of the Grail Knights, as Naciens made clear to Gawain:

185 *Morte Darthur* XX. 12; *Works*, p. 1190.11–16.

186 Cf. *The Castle of Perseverance*, *Mankind*, *Medwall's Nature*, *The World and the Child*, and the non-dramatic morality *Dowel*, the central part of William Langland's *Piers Plowman* (B-text, passus VIII-XV). This pattern, not Potter's mystery-play sequence of innocence/fall/redemption (Robert Potter, *The English Morality Play* (London, 1975), p. 8), is the one normally experienced by an individual Christian.

187 *Morte Darthur* XVIII. 19; *Works*, p. 896.11. Cf. *Queste*, p. 62.9–19.

188 *Morte Darthur* XVII. 13; *Works*, pp. 1011.31–1012.1. Lancelot did not disembark in the *Queste* (p. 250).

189 *Morte Darthur* XVII. 16; *Works*, p. 1018.3–6. Cf. his words in the *Queste*, p. 258.10–13: '*Et se mes granz pechiez et ma grant maleurtez ne fust, j'eusse encor plus veu, se ne fust que je perdi la veue de mes euz et le pooir dou cors, por la grant desloiauté que Diex avoit veue en moi.*'

190 *Morte Darthur* XVIII. 1; *Works*, p. 1046.5–8.

> 'I shall telle you gladly,' seyde the good man, 'the adventure of the Sankgreall whych be in shewynge now. For hit apperith nat to no synners (wherefore mervayle ye nat though ye fayle thereoff and many othir, for ye bene an untrew knyght and a grete murtherar), and to good men signifieth othir thynges than murthir. For I dare sey, as synfull as ever sir Launcelot hath byn, sith that he wente into the queste of the Sankgreal he slew never man nother nought shall, tylle that he com to Camelot agayne; for he hath takyn upon hym to forsake synne. And nere were that he ys nat stable, but by his thoughte he ys lyckly to turne agayne, he sholde be nexte to encheve hit sauff sir Galahad, hys sonne; but God knowith hys thought and hys unstablenesse. And yett shall he dye ryght an holy man, and no doute he hath no felow of none erthly synfull man lyvyng.'[191]

Malory's Lancelot may have died a holy man like his counterparts in the *Mort Artu* and the Stanzaic *Le Morte Arthure*, but his death, unlike theirs, was not a conventionally saintly one. When he returned to England after Arthur's death to find that Guinevere had retired to a nunnery to do penance for her sins, he renounced the world somewhat theatrically, in a speech that echoes Naciens:

> 'For in the queste of the Sankgreall I had that tyme forsakyn the vanytees of the worlde, had nat youre love bene. And if I had done so at that tyme with my harte, wylle, and thought, I had passed all the knyghtes that ever were in the Sankgreall excepte syr Galahad, my sone. And therefore, lady, sythen ye have taken you to perfeccion, I must nedys take me to perfection, of ryght.'[192]

Though his request for a farewell kiss (which was refused) suggests that his commitment to perfection was as yet insecure, he kept this resolution for six years, living a life of penitential austerity with the bishop of Canterbury, his cousin Bors, and other kinsmen in the hermitage where Arthur was buried,[193] and when he saw the dead Guinevere's face 'he wepte not gretelye, but syghed.'[194] He swooned, however, when she was buried beside her husband, smitten with the belated realization of his responsibility for their deaths, as he explained when the bishop reproved his excessive grief:

191 *Morte Darthur* XVI. 5; *Works*, p. 948.14–28. The corresponding passage in the *Queste*, (pp. 160–1) does not mention Lancelot.

192 *Morte Darthur* XXI. 9; *Works*, p. 1253.13–17. Cf. Stanzaic *Le Morte Arthur* 3696–709; *Mort Artu*, p. 265.56–62.

193 *Morte Darthur* XXI. 10; *Works*, pp. 1253–5. Cf. Stanzaic *Le Morte Arthur* 3712–833; *Mort Artu*, §201. They did kiss in *Mort Artu*, p. 266.70–1.

194 *Morte Darthur* XXI. 11; *Works*, p. 1256.3.

> 'For whan I remembre of hir beaulté and of hir noblesse, that was bothe wyth hyr kyng and wyth hyr, so whan I sawe his corps and hir corps so lye togyders, truly myn herte wold not serve to susteyne my careful body. Also whan I remembre me how by my defaute and myn orgule and my pryde that they were bothe layed ful lowe, that were pereles that ever was lyvyng of Cristen people, wyt you wel,' sayd syr Launcelot, 'this remembred, of their kyndenes and myn unkyndenes, sanke so to myn herte that I myght not susteyne myself.'[195]

Stripped of his last illusion, he became crazed with sorrow and remorse:

> Ever he was lyeng grovelynge on the tombe of kyng Arthur and quene Guenever, and there was no comforte that the Bysshop, nor syr Bors, nor none of his felowes coude make hym, it avaylled not.[196]

No longer a would-be saint but once more the Lancelot of the Joyous Isle, who 'wolde onys every day loke towarde the realme of Logrys, where kynge Arthure and quene Gwenyver was, and than wolde he falle uppon a wepyng as hys harte shulde to-braste',[197] peace came to him only with the last rites, after which Bors and his companions found him dead, 'and he laye as he had smyled, and the swettest savour about hym that ever they felte.'[198]

Malory's Lancelot is a tragic figure in Aristotle's sense, not too bad and not too good but ὅμοιος 'like us', and ὁμαλῶς ἀνώμαλος 'consistently inconsistent' in his 'unstablenesse',[199] which is presumably why his death is more moving than Galahad's. It was therefore right that Hector, the unregenerate brother who had sought him unsuccessfully when he was released from Tarquin's prison, was refused admission to him at Corbenic, and now, having sought him again for seven years, arrived too late to see him alive,[200] should speak his valediction rather than Bors or the bishop:

> 'A, Lancelot!' he sayd, 'thou were hede of al Crysten knyghtes! And now I dare say,' sayd syr Ector, 'thou sir Launcelot, there thou

195 *Ibid.*, lines 29–38.
196 *Morte Darthur* XXI. 12; *Works*, p. 1257.7–11.
197 *Morte Darthur* XII. 6; *Works*, p. 827.10–14. Cf. Lancelot, CVII, §45; 'Galahad and Perceval', p. 327; Löseth, §388a.
198 *Morte Darthur* XXI. 12; *Works*, p. 1258.16–17. Cf. Stanzaic *Le Morte Arthur* 3886–9.
199 Cf. Aristotle, *Poetics*, ed. D.W. Lucas (Oxford, 1968), 1448a 1–6, 1453a 2–7, 1454a 26–8.
200 *Morte Darthur* VI. 2, 9, XVIII. 16–17, XXI. 12–13; *Works*, pp. 254, 268–9, 1019, 1258–9. Cf. *Lancelot*, LXXVII, LXXXV, §§47–53; *Queste*, pp. 259–61; Stanzaic *Le Morte Arthur* 3906–35.

> lyest, that thou were never matched of erthely knyghtes hande. And thou were the curtest knyght that ever bare shelde! And thou were the truest frende to thy lovar that ever bestrade hors, and thou were the trewest lover of a synful man that ever loved woman, and thou were the kyndest man that ever strake wyth swerde. And thou were the godelyest persone that ever cam emonge prees of knyghtes, and thou was the mekest man and the jentyllest that ever ete in halle emonge ladyes, and thou were the sternest knyght to thy mortal foo that ever put spere in the reeste.'[201]

Such was Malory's Lancelot. The *matiere* and the *san* that went into his making were those that Malory received from tradition, as Chrétien had received his from the countess; like Chrétien, he supplied little but care and effort. Yet the result is a profoundly original creation, a *molt bele conjointure* in every sense of that ambiguous phrase.[202] Surely Malory was not 'only the last of the makers of the *Morte*', as Lewis said,[203] but also the greatest.

201 *Morte Darthur* XXI. 13; p. 1259.9–21. Cf. Stanzaic *Le Morte Arthur* 3890–6 (spoken by the bishop).

202 *Erec* 14. Apparently an extention of Horace's *callida iunctura* (*Ars poetica* (Horace, *Epistles Book II and Epistle to the Pisones* ('*Ars Poetica*'), ed. Niall Rudd (Cambridge, 1989), pp. 58–74), 47–8) that can be applied to any aspect of composition; see further Eugène Vinaver, *The Rise of Romance* (Oxford, 1971), pp. 34–7, Luttrell, *Creation of the First Arthurian Romance*, pp. 66–8.

203 'The English Prose *Morte*', pp. 25–6.

Sidney's Political Odyssey

Anti-tyranny themes, Sidney's travels, and *Arcadia*

EILÉAN NÍ CHUILLEANÁIN

I

Sidney's great romance, *The Countess of Pembroke's Arcadia.* has long been recognised as possessing a realistic political dimension. For all its idealised pastoral setting, it is unlike other sixteenth-century pastoralist works such as Sannazzaro's *Arcadia* or the *Diana* of Montemayor and Polo, in presenting an account of the facts of power, reviewing how these operate in differently constituted states, and demonstrating the characteristic dangers of each system. Sidney's narrative strategies, his authorial comments on events and situations, and the ideas expressed by many of his characters exhibit the impact of Renaissance thinking about politics, law, and history, and may, it has been suggested, have been influenced by the special pleading of sixteenth-century political and religious factions. This paper looks at an early phase of his political education, his sojourn in Venice and Padua in 1574, and suggests that this experience marked his romance in ways that have been underestimated by critics and biographers, which are central to its political purpose.

Fulke Greville's *Life* of Sidney early called attention to the political moral of *Arcadia*, but for the succeeding three centuries most commentators preferred to talk of it as an example of the taste for stylish and sentimental fiction. Since the revival of interest in Sidney's works in the twentieth century, their political content has received more notice. His connections with the Huguenots and his reading of Machiavelli attracted comment from, among others, W.D. Briggs and Irving Ribner;[1] more lately, scholars have seen in *Arcadia* a reflection of the Elizabethan political milieu, in its presentation of the class-structure and the distribution of power. Most critics remain preoccupied with the role of the aristocracy in the romance and in sixteenth-century Europe. Two recent articles, by

1 W.D. Briggs, 'Political Ideas in Sidney's *Arcadia*', *Studies in Philology* 28 (1931), 137–61; 'Sidney's Political Ideas', *Studies in Philology* 29 (1932), 534–42; Irving Ribner, 'Machiavelli and Sidney: the *Arcadia* of 1590', *Studies in Philology* 47 (1950), 152–72; 'Sir Philip Sidney on Civil Insurrection' *Journal of the History of Ideas* 13 (1952), 257–65. Cf. *Sir Fulke Greville's Life of Sir Philip Sidney*, ed. Nowell Smith (Oxford, 1907), pp. 11–12.

Robert E. Stillman and Alan Sinfield[2] have directed attention to the ambiguous presentation of aristocratic figures such as the author's *alter ego* Philisides and of the agents of monarchy. Philisides is the narrator of an enigmatic beast-fable about kingship in which tribute is paid to Sidney's mentor, the Huguenot diplomat Hubert Languet; it allegorises the roles of monarch, nobility and people in the state. Stillman reads the allegory, as many critics have done, as an apologia for the nobility; like Sinfield, he develops the theme of Sidney's preoccupation with the part played in national politics by his own class.

II

I should like to take this discussion beyond the area of national politics. The role of aristocracies, still possessed of much real power as well as traditional prestige in a sixteenth-century centralised monarchy, was an explosive issue for Sidney's age all over Europe. The young Philip Sidney's talents and education attracted attention beyond English shores; his destiny was not seen as merely a national one by those who sent him to Europe to study, by the matchmakers who suggested he should marry William of Orange's daughter, by Languet urging this modern knight-errant to take service in Hungary or Germany, or even with the Duke of Alençon. His death as the champion of international Protestant resistance to Spain was the conclusion of a career lived on a European stage, though firmly based in England. If his primary duty was to Queen Elizabeth, the intellectual commitment shown in his writings was to a belief that the English form of government, in which monarch, aristocrats and people all had parts to play, was at once well suited to the English people by tradition, and related to other forms which, by their justice and stability, were exemplary for Europe as a whole. In theoretical terms this amounts to an endorsement of the classic mixed constitution, the best that can be devised to guard against the volatility of the mob and the encroachments of tyranny. When in *Arcadia* he surveys forms of government, subjects them to stress and upheaval from internal and, occasionally, external sources, and shows rebellion, revolution, and the restoration of stability, we see in the fictional mirror a reflection of political ideas evolved through observing analogous systems and their fortunes in the European politics of his day.

2 Robert E. Stillman, 'The Politics of Sidney's Pastoral: Mystification and Mythology in *The Old Arcadia*', *English Literary History* 52 (1985), 795–814; Alan Sinfield, 'Power and Ideology: an Outline Theory and Sidney's Arcadia', *English Literary History* 52 (1985), 259–78. See also Annabel Patterson, 'Under . . . Pretty Tales: Intention in Sidney's *Arcadia*' (*Sir Philip Sidney: An Anthology of Modern Criticism*, ed. Dennis Kay (Oxford, 1987), pp. 265–85).

While most recent critics do not refer to Sidney's evident care to situate his fictional Arcadia in an international context of some complexity, or to the resulting capacity of his political fiction to compare constitutions as well as weighing up the roles of classes and factions, Martin Raitiere pays some attention to the international dimension. Rejecting the notion that Sidney intends the *Arcadia* to plead for the aristocracy as supplying a vital middle force to counterbalance the powers of monarch and people, he finds in it instead a treatise on the necessity for absolutism. He reads Sidney as not only exposing the dangers inherent in the Huguenot notion of the 'subordinate magistrate', who has the right to resist central government, but also as demonstrating the weakness of all constitutions which seek to limit monarchical power. He believes that Hubert Languet was the author of the notorious *Vindiciae contra Tyrannos* with its arguments for tyrannicide and its examples of monarchs deposed by their subjects; but his re-examination of Philisides' tale of the beasts finds in it a rebuttal of Languet's ideas, and he points to the poor showing made in the New Arcadia by the Lacaedemonians, who had enjoyed much prestige as an antique specimen of 'free' government.[3]

Raitiere's argument for Sidney's absolutism needs to be examined in relation to the evidence he adduces, which is not confined to the fable of the beasts. He develops his theory drawing on various episodes in *Arcadia* and on Sidney's other writings and bends the evidence somewhat to make Sidney's opinion of republican government seem lower than it is in fact. He quotes in a truncated form Sidney's remarks in a letter to his brother Robert, pointing to the Venetian mixed constitution with its strong republican element as the only Italian form of polity worth learning about. As this letter is highly relevant to my present theme, I quote the passage in full:

> As for Italy I knowe not what wee have, or can have to doe with them but to buye their scilkes and wynes, and for other provinces (excepting Venice) whose good lawes, & customes wee can hardly proporcion to our selves, because they are quite of a contrarie government, there is little there but tyranous oppression, & servile yeilding to them, that have little or noe rule over them.[4]

These words must surely be read as expressing, rather than the dismissal of aristocratic republicanism which Raitiere finds in them, admiration for the Venetian form of government, seen as an exception to the general

3 Martin N. Raitiere, *Faire Bitts: Sir Philip Sidney and Renaissance Political Theory* (Pittsburgh, 1984), Chapters II–V and Appendix A.

4 *The Complete Works of Sir Philip Sidney*, ed. Albert Feuillerat, 4 vols. (Cambridge, 1912–26), III, p. 127. Cf. *Faire Bitts*, pp. 53–4.

rule of Italian states where tyranny and servility hold sway, admiration compatible with a realistic awareness that the constitution of England can hardly be brought into line with a system so different. Any questioning of the absoluteness of Sidney's agreement with the Huguenots on all points, and especially on the duties and rights of aristocrats, is probably welcome as opening out the discussion of the Arcadian polity. But Raitiere's claims for Sidney's hostility to such mixed constitutions as the Venetians' need to be viewed critically; they have been accepted by one well-known writer on Sidney, and there may thus be some urgency in our need for a re-examination of the question before we are saddled with a new orthodox view of Sidney, the apologist for absolutism.[5] A new look at the nature and reputation of Venetian politics, and the ethos of Sidney's travels, is needed in this context.

Several writers on Sidney's political views have laid emphasis on his association with Huguenot theorists. The arguments of the propagandists who attempt to justify the rebellion of Amphialus in the revised *Arcadia* are certainly reminiscent of some Huguenot thinking, notably that of the *Vindiciae contra Tyrannos*. The question of the lawfulness of rebellion, and the tragic character of Amphialus, important as they are, are not my main subject; my point is that these features have up to now been discussed in too narrow a context. When Sidney included the story of Amphialus in his revised romance, he added other political material as well and gave his entire fiction a new constitutional perspective. He had made his work a modern Odyssey; now he deepened the significance of the heroic voyage by deploying classical ideas to create an international political scene.

Sidney, was, indeed, closely associated with individuals among the group of continental Protestant thinkers which included such Huguenots as Languet, François Hotman, and Philippe Duplessis-Mornay. With them he was concerned for the fate of the Protestants in France, Germany, and the Netherlands, whom they saw as Protestant England's natural allies; and with them he belonged to a network of Protestant, or sympathising, scholars, publishers, cultivated gentlemen, and politicians which functioned partly as a pressure-group, partly as a literary coterie within international aristocratic society.[6] While Sidney's agreement with some of their views on upper-class rebellion against inconvenient monarchs is rightly questioned, there is no doubt of his adherence to their broader tendency of resistance to the encroachment of the Papacy and the King of Spain, seen as tyrannical powers ('the abusers of the world',

5 See Richard McCoy, review of Raitiere, *Faire Bitts*, *Spenser Newsletter* 15 (1984), 65.

6 See Jan Van Dorsten, *Poets, Patrons and Professors,* Leiden 1962; James Osborn, *Young Philip Sidney*, New Haven, 1972.

as Sidney was to call them in a letter dating from the year of his death), resistance by means including the elaboration of political theories which stressed the importance of governments acting legally. In this context, the English legal monarchy appears as the exemplary opposite to tyrannical regimes, and other law-abiding states merit corresponding praise.

As a political being, Sidney's sense of vocation was bound up with his sense of his own high birth. Along with his undoubted talents, this made him, as shown by the work of Osborn and Van Dorsten, a valued member of the international Protestant set. On the other hand, there is no direct evidence of Sidney's reaction to the *Vindiciae contra Tyrannos,* which gave aristocratic lineage a new constitutional implication in the right to rebel in certain circumstances; nor do we know the answers to two other riddles: the authorship of the *Vindiciae*, which has been ascribed at various times to both Languet and Mornay, and the state of Sidney's information about that authorship.

III

Sidney's acquaintance with foreign Protestants, indeed his public career, may be said to have begun with his travels through France (where his political education was spectacularly begun by the St. Bartholomew's Massacre of 1572), the Empire (with periods at Strasbourg with Johann Sturm, at Vienna with Languet, and in Hungary on his own), and northern Italy, then back to Germany, and at last home to England. The general interest taken in his travels and in what it was hoped he would learn from them is attested not only by the letters from Languet, which have been celebrated since their publication in the seventeenth century, but by references in other documents to the hopes and expectations of such observers as the Earl of Leicester and Sir Francis Walsingham.[7] These testify not only to personal interest in Philip Sidney, but also to a position consciously taken on the much debated subject of the desirability of travel for young gentlemen. It was only a few years since the publication, in 1570, of Ascham's *The Schoolmaster* with its bitter attack on the corruptions likely to be brought about by contact with Europe and especially Italy. Sidney's journey was not a private tour; rather, it was a performance, a contribution to the general debate.

A theme in the letter to Robert Sidney quoted above (the earlier of two addressed to him on generally educational topics), inherent in the implications of its genre as a letter of advice to a relative abroad and in the tradition it draws on, is the wisdom to be gained by travel. This first letter to Robert was copied and circulated, no doubt because it was admired as

7 Osborn, *Young Philip Sidney*, pp. 36, 74–5.

an example of a familiar epistle as well as for its moral counsel; Feuillerat lists twelve extant copies, many headed 'touching the direccion of his travayle' or with similar phrases. The seriousness with which they were read can be gauged by the materials associated with them; they rub shoulders in manuscript collections with documents of marked political significance, such as letters from Queen Elizabeth, Robert Cecil, Sir Thomas Egerton, the Earl of Essex, and Sir Robert Cotton. A typical collection at Yale contains, as well as Sidney's letter to Robert, an epistle supposedly by Fulke Greville to his cousin Greville Varney travelling abroad in 1609 but recently shown to be based on a number of earlier letters to travellers. Setting down 'what observacions he thincks fitt for him to make vse of his travells,' the writer—Greville, Bacon, and the Earl of Essex have all been named as possible authors—asserts the utility of the European tour: 'it is a vulgar scandall of travellers that few returne more religious then they went out'; the young man should heedfully study the customs and the military and political condition of the countries he visits.[8]

Sidney's letter, with its less widely circulated successor to Robert, belongs with the letter which he wrote to Edward Denny in 1580 when Denny was setting out to Ireland. All three combine reflections on study, reading, and ethical issues in the context of travel. The *Old*, and especially the *New*, *Arcadia* are indebted to the same tradition, which we may call Odyssean from its earliest example, though for Sidney we need to count Virgil and Xenophon as forerunners along with Homer.

For the Renaissance, Ulysses is an observer of political life, a man who gains wisdom from personal experience, rather than an adventurer. Thomas More's Raphael Hythloday has voyaged, we are told, not like the mariner Palinurus but like Aeneas or Ulysses. He narrates no tales of wonders or monsters, and his hearers too are interested only in prodigies of political wisdom: 'About stale travellers' wonders we were not curious. Scyllas . . . and folk-eating Laestrygones . . . are common enough, but well and wisely-trained citizens are not everywhere to be found.'[9] As Alan Young has pointed out,[10] Sidney's personal motto, *Vix ea nostra voco*, is from Ulysses' speech against Ajax in Ovid's *Metamorphoses* (XI.141); it is a disavowal of the excellence of noble ancestry in favour of individual

8 Fulke Greville, *Certaine learned and Elegant Workes* (London, 1633), sig. Rr4r. See, on the subject of this letter's originality and association with Sidney's letter to Robert in manuscript and printed collections, Norman K. Farmer, Jr., 'Fulke Greville's Letter to a Cousin in France and the Problem of Authorship in Cases of Formula Writing', *Renaissance Quarterly* 22 (1969), 140–7.

9 Thomas More, *Utopia*, edd. and tr., Edward Surtz, S.J. and J.H. Hexter (New Haven, 1965), p. 49.

10 See Alan R. Young, 'Sir Philip Sidney's Tournament Impresas', *Sidney Newsletter* 6, (1985), 3–24, at 22.

wisdom and achievement. The ideal man, like Sidney and Ulysses, is supposed to have both.

Sidney's travels in search of political wisdom entitle him in the letter to Robert to guide his brother on a similar course. He exhorts him, 'Whoe travailes with the eye of Vlisses doth take one of the most excellent waies of worldlie wisdome,' and quotes in illustration Horace's version of Homer's words about Ulysses (a line which appears over and over in this context): *Qui multorum hominum mores cognovit & urbes* (*Ars Poetica* 142). Not content with repeating the line, he comments on the significance of *mores* and *urbes*; the first means not manners merely but ethics, 'the true discerning of men's myndes both in vertuous passions & vices', the second 'the knowing of their religions, pollicies, lawes, bringing upp of their children, disipline both for Warr, and Peace', which are distinguished by being *either* of immediate practical utility, *or* instructive in themselves: 'Nay in the kingdome of China which is almost as farr as our Antipodes from us, their good lawes and customes are to be learned, but to knowe their riches and power is of little purpose for us, since it cann neither advantage us, or hinder us.'[11] Since the period of Robert Sidney's travels coincides with that of the genesis of the *Arcadia*, it is of considerable interest to see Sidney's speculations intermingling myth, practical politics and the comparative study of civilizations however remote. China is as far removed in space, for Sidney, as his Arcadia could be by the barriers of myth and fiction.

The Renaissance faith in the educational efficacy of travel does not oppose a belief in study, but sets out to complement it with the force of example (including that of history); this is fully developed by Sidney in the upbringing and the wanderings of the two heroes of *Arcadia*. Pyrocles and Musidorus are given a first-rate education designed for their class. Later, driven in part by chance, fate, and the malice of enemies, in part by the purpose of reintegrating a family, they pass through a succession of states in Greece and Asia. These adventures provide a plot of episodic variety, and exemplify a variety of political constitutions in the context of peace and normality as well as rebellion and war.

The impact of a tradition of political and ethical theory which derives mainly from Aristotle ('I thinke you have read Aristotle's Ethicks,' he begins his lecture to Robert), and the force of classical and humanist modes of thought on travel as a form of political education, are important not only in the growth of Sidney's political thought but in the expectations of his readers. Political theory and example come together in the letters Sidney wrote to Languet during his sojourn in Venetian territory in 1573/4. In those months in Venice and Padua he had opportunities of studying ancient and modern political philosophers and observing the workings of

11 *Works*, III, p. 126

the Venetian constitution, which differed markedly from that of England, yet showed certain resemblances in the limitations placed on the chief executive power and the involvement of the people in government. The significance of this stage in Sidney's travels and the Aristotelian cast of his political thinking have not been much noticed, though John Buxton wrote persuasively about the importance of the Venetian sojourn in 1954. Walter Davis in 1965 discounted Aristotelian political thought as an influence on Sidney, preferring a scheme of political analysis based on Plato's *Republic*, and was followed in this by Jon S. Lawry in 1972.[12] James Osborn's *Young Philip Sidney*, which covers the period Sidney spent in Italy, hardly pauses to consider the impact of Venice as political exemplar, or the kind of philosophy that was studied at Padua.

The influence of Aristotle and Venice cannot exclude the Huguenot theorists from a discussion of Sidney's political outlook; their ideas too are part of his youthful experiences, as are his reading of Cicero's *De Officiis* at school or the *Cyropaedia* of Xenophon. His travels exposed him to both theoretical discussions and practical demonstrations of the way different states function. Political theorising among the Huguenots originates from the historical experiences of France but derives as well from the intellectual milieu of humanism, which valued ancient authority and the example of successful contemporary political systems (among which Venice enjoyed especially high prestige among Protestants). The humanists believed it possible for an original work to teach wisdom and virtue within the same tradition, to promote, in Sidney's own words in the *Apology for Poetry*, 'the highest end of the mistresse knowledge . . . which stands as I thinke in the knowledge of a man's selfe in the Ethike and Politique consideration, with the end of well doing, and not of well knowing onely.'[13] Not only the ideas discussed in the Arcadia but also its fictional structure show a debt to the humanist faith thus expressed in the *Apology*, as indeed does the pattern of the author's life.

As a heroic adventure-story, *Arcadia* in the original, and even more in the revised, version is modelled on the ancient epics and on Xenophon's *Cyropaedia*. The latter, no doubt because of its educational and didactic content, is mentioned several times in the *Apology for Poetry* as a compelling example of the moral effectiveness of poetic fiction as compared with the reading of mere history. Sidney evidently ranks it, at least in this respect of moral persuasion, with the masterpieces of Homer and Virgil. It seems to fit his literary aims particularly well as an account of the

12 John Buxton, *Sir Philip Sidney and the English Renaissance*, 2nd ed. (London, 1964), pp. 64–76 (see also p. 146); Walter Davis, *A Map of Arcadia*, New Haven, 1965 (Yale Studies in English 158), pp. 137–67; Jon S. Lawry, *Sidney's Two Arcadias, Pattern and Proceeding*, (Ithaca, N.Y., 1972), p. 19.

13 *Works*, III, 11.

education and early adventures of a conquering hero, stressing in its *effigies iusti imperii* the differing ethos of various countries and the evils of tyranny. The heroic models had been invoked as Sidney set out on his journeys, both by him and by his adviser Languet. When he left Vienna in the autumn of 1573 for a brief tour in Hungary, Languet quoted the Homeric programme, as Philip was later to do to Robert: *Laudo quidem generosum illud tuum studium videndi multorum hominum mores & vrbes (vt loquitur poeta) nam ea maxime ratione formatur iudicium.*[14] Some months later Sidney, writing from Venice, asks Languet to pardon his *garrulitas* since Xenophon found it forgiveable *in Cyri iuventute.* In June of 1574 Languet was again quoting Horace/Homer, linked this time with Virgil's lines on the political destiny of Aeneas and of Rome, where the epic emphasis is laid not on war but on the glories of civilization. The literature of the past is helping to form the political hero of the future, Sidney himself: *& memineris ad te pertinere illud Poetae, Tu regere imperio populis, &c & ad eam rem plurimum conferre, hominum multorum, vt ait ille mores, & urbes considerasse.*[16] The shift of perspective which makes education more important than adventure has turned Ulysses, Cyrus, and Aeneas into Sidney's predecessors on the Grand Tour.

Sidney's brief on his travels was to consider the private and public mores of the countries he visited. His sojourn in Venetian territory, though it caused some anxiety to Languet on account of its proximity to the moral, religious, and physical dangers of the Italian peninsula, was a most eligible choice as a stage on his travels, including as it did the passage of several months at the University of Padua. Here many famous Englishmen had studied—and in later years without noticeable damage to their Protestant convictions. They included Francis Walsingham, later to be Sidney's father-in-law and already an admirer of the young man's talents, who had recently been requested by the Earl of Leicester to advise and guide him in his travels.[17] Sir Thomas Smith, Walsingham's diplomatic associate and the author of the (then still unpublished) *De Republica Anglorum*, was another graduate; he had been Elizabeth's ambassador in Paris when Sidney arrived there on the first stage of his travels. Languet himself held a doctorate in laws from Padua; his letters to Sidney show how he differentiates between the Veneto and the rest of Italy, paying tribute to the political virtue of the Venetians and to their reputation for political wisdom, assuring Sidney that the very air of Padua will make him a lawyer.[18] In fact, the young man's tastes seem

14 *Langueti Epistolae*, (Frankfurt, 1633), sig. A1v.

15 *The Correspondence of Sir Philip Sidney and Hubert Languet*, ed. and tr. Stewart A. Pears (London, 1845), p. 214..

16 *Epistolae*, sig. B5v.

17 See above, note 7.

18 *Epistolae*, sig. A11r; Languet jokes about the Aristotelians of Padua at sig. C6v.

directed to ethics and politics rather than law, and to the study of language necessary to read the greatest authority on these subjects, Aristotle himself. And while he plans to equip himself at Padua, centre of Aristotelian studies, to tackle the *Politics* in the original, he writes enthusiastically to Languet about two modern political commentators: Cardinal Contarini and Donato Gianotti on the *Stato di Vinegia*.[19] In later years, writing to Edward Denny on his way to Ireland, he praises Aristotle's *Ethics* as the most advanced treatment of the subject but recommends for Denny's use the book he had studied at Shrewsbury School, Cicero's *De Officiis*. The reason is that Aristotle 'is somethinge darke and hath need of a Logicall examination'.[20] The work he had at least attempted to study at Padua, surrounded by Aristotelian scholars, would be an unsuitable text for Denny to take with him to Ireland, where no such help would be available.

James Osborn in *Young Philip Sidney* assumes that Sidney found Venice unimpressive on the evidence of a letter of Languet's written just after Sidney's arrival in the city.[21] Katherine Duncan-Jones accepts the theory of his 'indifference or even hostility to the splendours of Venice' at first sight; she argues persuasively, however, for the impact on his imagination of the work of the great Venetian painters.[22] Sidney's own letter has been lost, so that there is no direct evidence of what his initial reactions were. We may perhaps assume that, whatever failed to evoke his immediate admiration, the city's government did not seem lacking in interest, since he had been appreciatively reading Contarini's and Gianotti's accounts of it, and since he was later to praise its 'good laws and customs' to his brother Robert. In the Veneto he encountered a society which offered academic education at Padua, and in Venice itself the aesthetic experience of witnessing great painters at work, the intellectual freedom of a major centre of the book trade, and the political spectacle of the Venetian state in operation. He took advantage of all this, studying at Padua but frequently visiting Venice where he bought books, commissioned a picture, and entered into the thriving market for news, scandal, and secrets which existed there by reason of both the geographical and political position of the city.[23] Long a meeting-place of East and West, Venice was by 1574 a listening-post at the junction of Protestant and Catholic Europe. While it remained Catholic, a tradition of independence joined with some considerations of expediency to prevent the admission

19 Osborn, *Young Philip Sidney*, p. 121.
20 Osborn, *ibid.*, p. 538.
21 *Ibid.*, p. 117.
22 K. Duncan-Jones, 'Sidney and Titian', *English Renaissance Studies Presented to Dame Helen Gardner in honour of her Seventieth Birthday*, ed. John Carey (Oxford, 1980), pp.1–2; *Sir Philip Sidney: Courtier Poet* (London, 1991), p. 74.
23 Osborn, *Young Philip Sidney*, pp. 174–8, 180–1, 183–4.

of the Inquisition in its full vigour on Venetian territory. Bold printers and Greek Orthodox immigrants in Venice, Protestant foreign students and innovative scientific researchers in Padua were for the most part safe from the ecclesiastical police.[24] A less serious correspondent than Languet alludes to another notorious freedom of the city; he hopes to see Sidney back in Vienna soon, but adds *ie nay que peur que Ces belles Courtizannes ne vous retiennent.*[25] Political news, compliments, and gossip about friends and acquaintances are the main burden of the letters which testify to the continuation of Sidney's connection with the Veneto for years after his stay there.

From Venice Sidney set out on a further Italian expedition which would seem to have confirmed him in his low opinion of the rest of the country. After moving back to Germany in the autumn of 1574 he kept up his Venetian contacts, for example ordering Carlo Sigonio's history of Italy, which had been printed at Venice in 1574 but not authorised for sale until 1575. Sidney's host at Frankfort when he wrote off for Sigonio's book was the printer Andreas Wechel who issued his own edition of the work later in that same year, complete with a newly prepared index which directed the reader to material showing the papacy in a bad light. The twenty-year-old Sidney was thus connected with an anti-papal campaign of scholarship which made use of the work of independently-minded Italian scholars like Sigonio whose work could only be printed in Venice; Wechel was later to publish and dedicate to Sidney the posthumous *Commentaries* of Petrus Ramus, murdered in the St Bartholomew's massacre.[26]

Aristotelian philosophy flourished in the Veneto. Accused of Averroism in the later middle ages, the metaphysicians might still have been open to charges of heresy from Catholics and Protestants alike. While Sidney's avowed interest was in Aristotle's ethical and political works, his acquaintance with the *Poetics* and the numerous commentaries on it is also likely to date from this period. Many of the commentaries emanate from Venice and Padua; their influence is everywhere in the *Apology for Poetry*. The great vogue of Aristotle's *Ethics* among general readers all over Europe[27]

24 *Ibid.*, p. 152; cf. also William J. Bouwsma, *Venice and the Defense of Republican Liberty*, Berkeley and Los Angeles, 1968.

25 Yale, MS. Osborn f.a.14, letter 5. Osborn's book, *Young Philip Sidney*, is based on and describes this collection of letters to Sidney from his continental correspondents, dating from the years 1573–6, which came to light in 1967; the writers became known to Sidney on his European tour and some of them corresponded with him after his return to England.

26 Carolus Sigonius, *De Regno Ituliae*, Frankfurt, 1575; for correspondence about the publication of Ramus's *Commentaries* see Osborn, *Young Philip Sidney*, pp. 321, 360, 402–3.

27 See Charles B. Schmitt, 'Aristotle's Ethics in the Sixteenth Century', *The Aristotelian Tradition and Renaissance Universities* (London, 1984), pp. 65–112, at 95–6.

may already have touched Sidney on his travels; his resolution to study it and the *Politics* in Padua reflects an appreciation of the city as a centre of Greek language and philosophy, and a conviction that ethics and politics must lie at the centre of his studies. In England the highest vogue of ethical works deriving from Aristotle was yet to come; it was to coincide with the period of composition of the *Arcadia* and the planning of Spenser's *Faerie Queene* in a circle much influenced by Sidney, and to include translations of Italian ethical works by George Pettie and Lodowick Bryskett. The latter had accompanied Sidney to Italy in the 1570s; both had stayed in Strasbourg at the house of Johann Sturm, the great editor of the *Ethics*, who was later to act as tutor to Robert Sidney on his travels. Sidney and Sturm remained in touch through correspondents who reported on the young man's progress. Lodowick Bryskett stayed in Venice after Sidney and engaged in dealings on his behalf into 1575. Bryskett and Sidney were probably in contact again in the early 1580s; his *Discourse of Civil Life* (1602), which purports to describe conversations in Dublin in 1582, features Spenser as an interlocutor, who announces the composition of a great ethical poem.[28]

By contrast with these writers, Sidney's interests appear much more directly political, embracing, as well as Aristotelian theory, commentaries on actual states such as Contarini's and Gianotti's, and general analyses such as Machiavelli's. His copy of Guicciardini's *Histories*, bought in Padua in 1574, survives to suggest that he also studied the historical background to the theorists' work. For these writers, any consideration of politics must take account of the authority of antiquity. Sidney, like them, includes in his Odyssean survey of the manners of men and cities the actuality of politics in his own time as well as the views of the most notable ancient and modern theorists. Venice was the subject of many commentaries; a tradition of praise of the wise Venetians, especially for their commitment to the active life of politics rather than religious contemplation, for their balanced constitution, and for their abhorrence of tyranny, is reflected in Languet's letters and can be traced through such writers as Contarini, Gianotti, Ugoni, and Paruta: a philosophy recommending them to foreigners of anti-papal views. Philip Melanchthon praised them already in 1539: *Cumque unica sit urbs vestra in toto orbe terrarum, in qua vera est aristocratia tot seculis conservata, quae semper inimica fuit Tyrannidi, maxime decet in eo loco esse libera bonorum iuditia* (. . .)[29] The Scottish Protestant Buchanan (a correspondent of Sidney's in

28 Osborn, *Young Philip Sidney*, p. 541; *The Life and Correspondence of Lodowick Bryskett*, edd. Henry R. Plomer and Tom Peete Cross (Chicago, 1927), pp. 13, 78; *A Discourse of Civill Life*, ed. Thomas E. Wright (Northridge, Calif., 1970), pp. 21–2.

29 Philip Melanchthon, letter printed with *Ad Vniuersos Germaniae Principes* (Basle, 1544), sig. A4v.

1579),[30] recorded his admiration in *De Jure Regni apud Scotos*, where a speaker observes to the author:

> 'You seem somewhat injurious to kings, and this very thing I did suspect in you frequently before, whilst I often heard you so profusely commend the Ancient Common-wealths, and the city of *Venice*.'[31]

Contarini's *De Republica Venetorum* (1543) remained a classic, often reprinted in Venice, mostly in Italian translation, and frequently accompanied by other treatises, notably that by Contarini's disciple Donato Gianotti. Since Sidney mentions both authors together and quotes the title in Italian, not Latin, he probably read such an edition. Contarini was translated into other languages too; the English version of 1599 was by Lewes Lewkenor, who dedicated it to the widow of Sidney's uncle the Earl of Warwick, in recognition of 'the dutie our family oweth vnto that noble house wherein you matched'. As a George Lewknor is mentioned as passing on messages from Sidney and Bryskett to an Italian correspondent,[32] the connection between the Lewkenors and the Dudleys may have been through Sidney's Italian journey. The 1599 translation of Contarini is furnished with several commendatory sonnets (by Spenser, among others), all praising the Venetians for their policy, justice, and liberty, which makes them proof against the assaults of 'tyrants haulty'.

Contarini's book is the work of an eminent representative of a family distinguished in the Venetian public service and counting several Doges among its members. His part in the attempts to reconcile the Roman church to some Reformation ideas had brought him into contact with Protestants; Sturm pays tribute to his learning in a polemical reply to the conciliatory *De emendenda ecclesia* in 1538.[33] His account of his own city glows with patriotism and with that pride in Venice's unique tradition which is so often found in the writings of his countrymen. It combines regard for liberty with aristocratic confidence in the competence of the upper class to govern, pride in a modern state with deference to classical principles. Early in his work Contarini concedes that (as Aristotle has said) kingship may well be the highest form of government; he goes on, however, to follow Aristotle's own classification of states and their comparative ranking by pointing out

30 See James E. Phillips, 'George Buchanan and the Sidney Circle', *Huntingdon Library Quarterly* 12 (1948–9), 23–55.

31 George Buchanan, *The due Privilege of the Scotch Government*, tr. 'Philalethes' (London, 1689), p. 12.

32 Lewes Lewkenor, *The Commonwealth and Government of Venice* (London, 1599), sig. *2v; Osborn, *Young Philip Sidney*, p. 387.

33 Printed in Contarini, *De Emendenda Ecclesia* (Strasbourg, 1538), sig. C4rv.

that monarchy suffers from the danger of falling into the worst kind of corrupt rule, which is tyranny.[34] The avoidance of tyranny is a recurring theme among writers about Venice; Gianotti, for example (a republican refugee from Medicean Florence) distinguishes between the honours paid to a Doge and those exacted by tyrants; the former are decreed by the laws. Venice is compared with the ancient, free states of the Romans and Lacaedemonians.[35] The Venetians took over the Terrafirma because the little cities of the Veneto could no longer bear the tyranny of their petty rulers. In the sixteenth century almost all the Italian cities which were ruled by democracies or nobles have fallen into tyranny; the mixed constitution of the Venetians saved them from such a fate.[36] Contarini makes no allusion to the danger of tyranny in the Roman church. But it was this peril which Protestant observers saw as the main threat both to their own liberties and to that of Venice.

The prestige of the mixed constitution in the Renaissance owes something to post-Aristotelian theorists. Aristotle's *Politics* enumerates three varieties of good government, monarchy, aristocracy, and one based on the equality of all citizens above a certain economic level. To these correspond three corrupt forms, of which the worst, tyranny, is the corruption of the best, monarchy. Because of the danger of corruption, a tradition of political commentary probably deriving from Polybius held that the most stable form of government is one combining elements of all three 'good' forms. This view enjoys considerable popularity among Renaissance theorists; it is particularly likely that Sidney was aware of Polybius' views since he draws on the historian's account of Arcadia in the opening description of his fictional state.[37] In his lifetime Polybius's authority was invoked, and a Latin translation of the relevant part of his work published, by the Huguenot jurist François Hotman, while his ideas received their most serious challenge from Bodin, whose work Sidney had read (he alludes to Bodin's *Methodus* in the second letter to Robert, in terms which seem rather slighting; but no theory of Bodin's influence can be based on, or indeed refuted by, such a slender reference). Sixteenth-century commentators, then, place Polybius in the context of resistance to tyranny or arguments for absolute monarchy; Polybius himself more than once goes out of his way to praise the killers of tyrants.[38]

34 *Republica di Venetia Del Cardinal Contarini* (Venice, 1650), sig. B1v.
35 Gianotti, printed with Contarini, *Republica di Venetia*, sigs. H1r, I2v.
36 Contarini, *Republica di Venetia*, sigs. D12r, G11v.
37 Polybius, *Histories*, ed. and tr. W.R. Paton, 6 vols., Cambridge, Mass. and London, 1922–7 (Loeb Library), III, 272–93. See F.W. Walbank, *Polybius* (Berkeley and Los Angeles, 1973), pp. 135–7, on the ancient idea of the mixed constitution, and Elizabeth Dipple, 'Harmony and Pastoral in the Old Arcadia', *English Literary History* 35 (1968), 309–28, for Sidney's use of Polybius's account of the Arcadians.
38 *Histories*, I, 385–7; III, 284–5.

In the Aristotelian/Polybian tradition, Venetian government is praised by Contarini and others for its resemblance to a pyramid, broadly based on the equality of the *Cittadini* and rising to a point in a single supreme governor who like Aristotle's ideal Prince rules for the benefit of others, not himself. Allusions to the *Politics*, to the *Cyropaedia*, and to the pseudo-Aristotelian *Secretum Secretorum* provide a mixed classical background. As in Aristotle's *Politics*, below the level of the equal citizens there exists a class of *Artigiani* who have no political function whatever, being in the position of slaves in the ancient world.[39] But no man or group of men holds supreme power, because this is vested in the Law; individual officers are 'guardians, vicars, and ministers of the laws'. Venice under this constitution has enjoyed unparalleled felicity,[40] while disorder and tyranny (as Sidney was to write to Robert) reign in the peninsula.

The praise of Venice was frequently combined with the defence of active life. The Magnifico Stefano Maria Ugoni, for example, published four *opuscula* in 1562, one of which is a disquisition on *La dignita & eccelenza della gran citta di Venezia* and the other a *Ragionamento* on *tutti gli stati dell'umana vita* in which celibacy and contemplation are dismissed in favour of marriage and public responsibility. The same theme of the excellence of action rather than contemplation (central to the poetic of the *Apology*, as already shown, to both versions of the *Arcadia*, and constantly recurring in the letters Sidney received from Languet) is memorably expressed in a Venetian work composed in the 1570's which reveals the continuation of these patterns of thought in the political climate of the city at the time Sidney frequented it. Paolo Paruta's *Della Perfezione della Vita Civile*, published in 1579, illustrates well the antagonism between the Roman church and Venice, with its ideal of service to the state, and the relevance of Aristotelian ideas to Venetian political thought. Supposed to be a dialogue between ambassadors, some of whom are returning from the imperial court, some from the closing sessions of the Council of Trent, it eloquently defends politics as a legitimate goal for human beings against the ecclesiastical inisistence on spiritual felicity as the only true one. The Aristotelian insistence that man's ethical development can only be taken to its full extent in society leads on to a defence of human goods in general. The aristocratic values of good blood, connections, riches, and honour are declared to be the enabling factors permitting virtue to operate in the active life of the world. A eulogy of Venice follows, with a graceful reference to Contarini, developing the theory of the stability of the mixed constitution in a series of interesting comparisons with the limited monarchies of Northern

39 Contarini, *Republica di Venetia*, sigs. B8r, C6r. Cf. Aristotle, *Politics*, ed. John Warrington (London and New York, 1959), p. 74.

40 *Republica di Venetia*, sigs. B1r, G11v.

Europe.[41] These replace the contrast with the miserable condition of the other Italian states which might have been expected, and they suggest that the tradition which derived from Contarini was developing towards a demand for closer relations with countries outside Italy, though this was not to bear fruit until the next century. As Paruta succeeded Contarini in the position of official historian of Venice, the *Perfezione* may guide us to the reasons why Contarini's book might have seemed a suitable one to the young Sidney, and to how he might have read it against the contemporary Venetian background. Its grouping of Venice with the German Empire and such kingdoms as England and the elective monarchy of Poland reinforce the argument in favour of mixed constitutions as being both more just and more stable than any other kind.

Sidney's reading of Contarini and Gianotti, coinciding with the period when he was studying Aristotle on ethics and politics and frequenting Venetian society animated by the ideals expressed in Paruta's work, was part of the programme to equip him as a Protestant hero, by enabling him to compare systems and take note of the ones which particularly encouraged active, outspoken, dedicated individuals in politics. These are the modern equivalents of ancient heroes. As we shall see, *Arcadia* stresses not only the value of heroic qualities in the individual but the part played by governments in encouraging their development. In acquiring political awareness by travel and reading, it was natural for Sidney to have become familiar with the Aristotelian analysis of the different kinds of government, with special attention to the dangers of tyranny. Because of his French experiences, the examples of Italian misgovernment, and Languet's repeated warnings on the corruption of the greater part of Italy, tyranny was associated already with the Church of Rome, whose political influence he spent so much of his later life resisting. The Venetian tradition subtly reinforces this outlook.

Anti-tyranny themes had been common in the political thinking of the middle ages, as Quentin Skinner has shown.[42] Among Renaissance treatments we should include the apparently influential *Anti-Machiavel* of Innocent Gentillet. The dedication of the Latin translation of this work in 1577 to the nephew and heir of Sidney's aunt's husband, the Earl of Huntingdon, stresses the role of England as champion of oppressed Protestants against ecclesiastical tyranny and Machiavellian fraud.[43] The well-developed Huguenot theory, complete with classical examples, is commonplace among Sidney's friends and correspondents; De Mornay's

41 Paolo Paruta, *Della Perfezione della Vita Politica Libri Tre* (Venice, 1579), sigs. C3v N2r, Pp1r, Qq1r.

42 *The Foundations of Modern Political Thought*, 2 vols. (Cambridge, 1978), I, 52–5.

43 See Innocent Gentillet, *Discours Contre Machiavel*, edd A. D'Andrea and P.D. Stewart (Firenze, 1974), pp. lxi-xv.

Dela Verité de la Religion Chrétienne (1581), which Sidney planned to translate, points to the miserable end of Julius Caesar, killed by those who had fought in his company against the commonweal. Sidney himself in a love-poem refers to 'Caesar's bleeding fame' as something he does not aspire to.[44]

In Sidney's absorption of the lessons of his Italian travels and his association with the Protestant nobility of Europe we may distinguish two intellectual strands. On the one hand, the personal, subjective theme of his own career includes the great expectations entertained by his well-wishers for a young man of noble birth, high talents, virtuous character, and excellent education. His study of the laws and customs of the European states and their theoretical background was part of the formation which, it was anticipated, would bring his promise to fruition. On the other hand, the Languet correspondence suggests that this study may be seen as a survey of the available evidence about human political behaviour, rather than a course of morale-heightening indoctrination for the Protestant gentry cadres. What is stressed, for example in Machiavelli's and Guicciardini's writings, is the evidential value of history and experience, not their potential for rhetorical exploitation. Framed by the Aristotelian classification of modes of government, such a survey throws into relief the general importance of avoiding the evils of tyranny (above all), of oligarchy, and of mob rule, rather than the special role of one class, the aristocracy, as the single indispensable element in the state. On the other hand, the Polybian theory of the excellence of mixed government allowed an important role for a hereditary aristocracy, trained for their role and filled with a sense of public responsibility.

IV

Assessing the impact of these early studies and travels on the *Arcadia* is a complex task. The *Old Arcadia* is, by contrast with the revision, a work with an ethical rather than a political emphasis for most of its length. Politics are important as providing a sphere for the supreme public virtue of justice, the private one of friendship, and the subordinate one of prudence to operate in. The Arcadians' 'justice and providence' are the cause of the country's happiness in the work's opening paragraph, and in the last book numerous examples are given of their wise and virtuous laws. Duke Basilius is praised by 'the sacred titles of good, just, merciful, the father of his people' when he is thought to be dead; at the opening of the story he had been urged to let his people 'see the benefit of your justice,' and his

44 Philippe de Mornay, *A woorke concerning the trueness of the Christian Religion*, tr. Arthur Golding (1617), sig. O7r. Cf. Sidney, *Astrophel and Stella* 64.

failure to do so leads to rebellion. When the rebels attack his rural retreat, the disguised Pyrocles persuades them to desist with an oration delivered from 'the judgement seat of the duke which, according to the guise of that country, was hard before the court gate'—doubtless an emblem of his readiness to provide justice (*Old Arcadia*, pp. 4, 276, 246, 9, 113).[45]

Pyrocles' father, Euarchus, is also briefly characterised as 'a prince of such justice that he never thought himself privileged by being a prince' before disappearing from the action until Book Five. Here he is given the opportunity to display his integrity in various ways: he accepts the role of judge at the trial of Pyrocles and Musidorus; he insists that this role gives him and his successors no legal right to the throne of Arcadia; and when, having passed sentence of death, he discovers that the culprits are his own only son and nephew, he insists on there being no reprieve. It takes an apparent miracle, the revival of Basilius from a drugged sleep, to disentangle the plot and avoid a tragic outcome.

As well as this inspiring example of judicial impartiality, Euarchus offers the Arcadian people a philosophical justification for his verdict in the trial, explaining for example why persuading a daughter to elope is the equivalent of rape, and why Pyrocles and Musidorus cannot claim exemption from prosecution because of their rank.

The fourth and fifth books, compared with the earlier ones, contain much more in the way of speculation on law, justice and political systems. This may be partly an outcome of the shape of the plot, in which an erotic impasse precipitates a political crisis in the shape of the supposed death of Basilius and criminal responsibility of the other main characters. We may speculate that it was only when Sidney reached this part of his work that its political implications became fully apparent to him. Certainly there is nothing in the earlier treatment of kingship, where kings are measured on a moral yardstick but the institution of monarchy itself is hardly scrutinised, to prepare the reader for the author's comments on the condition of Arcadia:

> There was a notable example how great dissipations monarchal governments are subject unto; for now their prince and guide had left them, they had not experience to rule, and had not whom to obey. Public matters had ever been privately governed, so that they had no lively taste what was good for themselves, but everything was either vehemently desireful or extremely terrible . . . some there were that cried to have the state altered and governed no more by a prince; marry, in the alteration many would have the Lacedemonian government of a few chosen senators; others the Athenian, where

45 Quotations from the *Old Arcadia* are from the World's Classics edition, ed. Katherine Duncan-Jones, Oxford, 1985.

> the people's voice held the chief authority. But these were rather the discoursing sort of men than the active, being a matter more in imagination than practice. But they that went nearest to the present case (as in a country that knew no government without a prince) were they that strave whom they should make . . . (p. 277)

Sidney's cool account of this chaotic wrangling takes account of Aristotelian political classifications while, as in the letter to Robert Sidney, giving great weight to the political tradition of a state: the Arcadians are used to a monarch and will hardly transform their polity in response to any amount of foreign theory or example. The succeeding events make the nature of their state clearer. The nobility have some role to play; so have the people. Philanax says to Philoclea, 'I can do nothing without all the states of Arcadia' (p. 264). 'The estates of her country were ill satisfied touching her father's death,' he tells Pamela (p. 276). The nobility gather and are racked by factionalism, but when Philanax proposes calling in Euarchus as Protector and judge 'the noblemen' consent first, and 'all the popular sort followed' (p. 308). Arcadia, then, is a mixed state.

Sidney, here giving Arcadian politics a more recognisable structure than the picture we get from the gentle shepherds and villainous rebels of the earlier books, is following where his plot had been leading him throughout: back to the world of reality and political responsibility, to which the pastorals and disguises of Arcadia had never been meant to offer more than a temporary alternative. Having reached the firm ground of political actuality he may well have thought the earlier books politically naive. His European experiences, his reading of political commentators from Aristotle to Machiavelli, were in 1581 supplemented by a stint as a Member of Parliament. This may explain why the passage just quoted suggests not just exasperation at parliamentary factionalism but a real grasp of the utility of the institution. Traditional loyalties, sound laws, and a virtuously inclined people are not enough to preserve Arcadia from anarchy if the monarch proves irresponsible. The Arcadians need the habit of taking part in government; their king's neglect of their advisory, that is parliamentary, function proves almost disastrous. Euarchus's original motive for coming to Arcadia is, in fact, to admonish Basilius on the folly of withdrawing from his court 'so suddenly, without the advice or allowance of his subjects, without either good show of reasonable cause, or good provision for likely accidents' (p. 309).

V

The *New Arcadia* shows, from the beginning, a much stronger interest than the older version in the comparative efficacy of political systems. Whereas in the original version Pyrocles and Musidorus had distinguished themselves, before their arrival in Arcadia, by killing giants and dragons, rescuing ladies and the oppressed, the revised romance adds to these early exploits a more political and less chivalrous series of adventures. Having received an ideal intellectual and moral formation, the heroes set out on a Grand Tour of travel and fighting where they encounter both good and evil kinds of government and are instrumental in establishing systems of rule which reconcile differences between classes, in combating tyrannical and oligarchical misgovernment, and in resisting popular rebellion. Their experience is a continuation of their education as well as a proof of its excellence; on their travels, like Philip and Robert Sidney, they gain an overview of political systems. While none is entirely perfect, the constitution of Arcadia itself, as it weathers the shocks caused by the vagaries of its own and visiting royalty, appears in the *New Arcadia* to retain its desirable character as a mixed state; Sidney's retention of the overarching plan of the fulfilment of the oracle suggests no major upheaval in his view of the Arcadian constitution. It is worth while to examine the deployment in *Arcadia* of the account of different forms of government, in the order in which Euarchus, Pyrocles, and Musidorus experience them as well as that in which the reader learns of them.

The family history as told in the *New Arcadia* opens with an account of Euarchus as the ideal king. On coming of age after a series of minorities in the royal family, his first task is to combat the excessive power of a corrupt aristocracy, 'those great lords and little kings who in those between-times of reigning . . . had brought in . . . the worst kind of Oligarchy: that is, when men are governed indeed by a few, and yet are not taught to know who those few may be to whom they should obey' (p. 254)[46] A feature of this, as of the next corrupt form of government we encounter, is the envy of excellence, the confrontation between the heroic ideal and the deviant state: 'Men of virtue suppressed, lest their shining should discover the others' filthiness' (p. 255). When Euarchus's son and nephew, Pyrocles and Musidorus, are shipwrecked and separated at the outset of their adventures, they are washed ashore in the countries of two contrasted tyrants. Sidney here takes the opportunity to retell Cicero's tale of Damon and Pythias (*De Officiis*, III.10.45) in such a way that it turns on the incompatibility between tyranny and the virtue of friendship,

46 Quotations from the *New Arcadia* are from the Penguin edition, ed. Maurice Evans, Harmondsworth, 1977.

a point also emphatically made by Aristotle in his *Ethics* (1161a 30–b 10). In the original story, the Syracusan tyrant allowed Damon to exchange himself for Pythias, who has been condemned to death; here the tyrannical king of Phrygia permits Musidorus to give himself up to be killed in exchange for his friend. But it is Musidorus that the tyrant really wants, because he has heard prophecies of his glorious destiny and thus fears him: 'excellency grew a fault; and it was sufficient to make one guilty that he had power to be guilty' (p. 265). And while the tyrant of Syracuse was moved to remit the death sentence (and indeed to petition for inclusion in the couple's philosophical friendship) by their self-sacrificing readiness to die for each other, Musidorus is forcibly rescued from the scaffold itself by Pyrocles. At this, the Phrygians rebel with the cry of 'Liberty': 'some of the wiser (seeing that a popular licence is indeed the many-headed tyranny) prevailed with the rest to make Musidorus their chief; choosing one of them (because princes) to defend them' (pp. 269–70). Other deviant forms of government, we note, are evil because of their resemblance to tyranny. Musidorus leads the citizens against the tyrant, defeats him, and then resigns the sovereignty to 'an aged gentleman . . . of the blood royal and next to the succession . . . but with such conditions and cautions of the conditions, as might assure the people (with as much assurance as worldly matters bear) that not only that governor, of whom indeed they looked for all good, but the nature of the government, should be no way apt to decline into tyranny' (pp. 270–1).

The separation between the person of the governor and the form of the government is a signal that the travels of Pyrocles and Musidorus offer a critique of constititutions, as well as a gallery of virtues and vices; it shows that monarchy needs to be accompanied by legal safeguards for the governed. It is also noticeable that the first example of tyranny is that of a king who is not a usurper but came to the throne by legal succession—the same is true of the next specimen of this kind of misgovernment, the king of Pontus, but not of the third, who is the most memorable. This is Plexirtus, the illegitimate son of the King of Paphlagonia and the original of Shakespeare's Edmund. Sidney, we may say, states his theme of tyranny in terms which ensure that the reader will not confuse it with the mere lack of legitimacy. Plexirtus, like all examples of deviant forms of rule, is the enemy of excellence, at first of his brother 'whose just title, ennobled by courage and goodness, may one day shake the seat of a never secure tyranny' (p. 279). Later, he shows his fear of friendship by inducing a pair of devoted brothers, Tydeus and Telenor, to kill each other by trickery; he conspires with various villainous characters against Pyrocles and Musidorus, and is finally responsible for the shipwreck which once again separates them and brings them ashore in Laconia to be rescued by the Arcadian shepherds at the point where the *New Arcadia* opens.

The group of stories I have just been examining forms the first piece of Musidorus's narrative to Pamela, establishing his identity and claiming heroic value for the achievements of his and Pyrocles's recent past. It is addressed to an astute and judicious lady, herself destined to rule. The episodes in Phrygia, Pontus, and Paphlagonia are new in the revised version, and represent, I would argue, a working out in fully Aristotelian terms of the theme of deviant government. Its essential evil, tyranny, threatens the Odyssey of heroic virtue as Odysseus' monsters and enchantresses threaten his physical survival. We may notice that, just as Aristotle makes tyranny worse than oligarchy, which in turn is worse than mob rule, the crimes of Sidney's tyrants are spelt out while the indiscretions of the Phrygians rebelling against their king 'and, god knows, by the blindness of rage killing many guiltless persons, either for affinity to the tyrant or enmity to the tyrant-killers' (p. 270), are short-lived and excusable. Order is restored in the next sentence. By contrast, the evils of tyranny are insisted on throughout the *New Arcadia*, reaching their climax of psychological horror with the sufferings of the princesses in the power of Cecropia. The conducted tour of constitutional forms receives some amplification elsewhere in the revised *Arcadia*, notably in the episode of the helots of Laconia (here we are dealing with a racially oppressive society) and in the accompanying accounts of Arcadia itself.

The *New Arcadia* opens with the second shipwreck of the heroes, this time on the shores of Laconia, whose 'wasted soil' is contrasted with the 'delightful prospects' of Arcadia. The explanation of the difference is in the contrasting political conditions of the two kingdoms; Laconia is 'poor . . . by a civil war . . . within the bowels of that estate between the gentlemen and the peasants', while Arcadia is 'decked with peace and (the child of peace) good husbandry' (pp. 69–70). Apart from the body/ state imagery invoked by these brief accounts (a body with war in its bowels, a woman wearing a child like a jewel), they are accompanied by a description of Arcadia which, it has often been observed, serves as an allegory of the peaceful state in which there is harmony with variety among the classes: 'hills which garnished their proud heights with stately trees; humble valleys whose base estate seemed comforted with refreshing of silver rivers . . . each pasture stored with sheep feeding with sober security . . . here a shepherd's boy piping as though he should never be old; there a young shepherdess knitting and withal singing, and it seemed that her voice comforted her hands to work and her hands kept time to her voice's music.' The country houses are scattered through the landscape, suggesting 'an accompanable solitariness and . . . a civil wildness' (*ibid*).

The richness of this passage illustrates Sidney's assertion in the *Apology for Poetry* that the poet excels in giving the reader, like a traveller, a delightful foretaste of the journey of exploration he is about to make. The reader, like the shipwrecked Musidorus, is being introduced to a new country of Sidney's fiction—and of his moralizing and political theorizing. We absorb the various witty paradoxes of the Arcadian landscape and take in the implication that the system which provides for such happy combinations of hills and valleys, work and music, sobriety and carelessness, wilderness and civility must have much to recommend it. We expect, in fact, to hear about stable government and mutual support between classes such as are found in the mixed state. And while these expectations are met only partly by the story Sidney has to tell, they remain as a brief glimpse of the political normality to which Arcadia must at last be returned.

Before Sidney tells more of the history of Arcadia itself, however, he goes back to recount the causes of the Laconian civil war. This originated primarily from the fact that Laconia is a state founded on conquest in which the losers have 'long borne' harsh treatment by their overlords. But the 'greediness' and 'contempt' of the Lacaedemonians drove the helots to rebellion, at first with 'beastly fury' but more recently with 'soldierly discipline', against 'their king and nobility' (pp. 94–6). Laconia, then, is not, as Raitiere has pointed out, a classic mixed state;[47] rather it represents the kind of state frequently discussed by Machiavelli, where the power structure is based on colonisation. But neither is it an aristocracy or even oligarchy; it has a king, or 'kings' (pp. 96, 100, 102). It is 'king Amiclas' whose nephew Pyrocles kills and whose consequent hatred for him means that Pyrocles' expulsion from Laconia is part of the peace terms which end the civil war (p. 102). The, kings, then, are not cyphers, as in ancient Sparta, but have direct political power.

The main features of the peace articles suggest that postwar Laconia will much more nearly resemble a mixed constitution than the form of government which led to the war. The helots 'are made by public decree free men, and so capable both to give and receive voice in election of magistrates' (*ibid*). This admission to a Third Estate with a share in government is the result of Pyrocles's negotiations on behalf of the helots, his followers. It makes Laconia look more like England, more like Venice; Pyrocles's enterprise of reforming a collapsing commonwealth recalls Sidney's words to Languet when the latter was about to visit Holland, *Habebis ibi pulcherrimum campum exercendi ea in hac nova republica formanda, quae per totum vitae tempus tam sedulo didicisti.*[48] Pyrocles too has been through a rapid course of political education in the adventures which we are presently to hear narrated by him and Musidorus; here we see their fruit in a sense of the just state and in able and pragmatic negotiation and convincing rhetoric. The Odyssean voyage looks forward to the practical application of its lessons.

47 *Faire Bitts*, pp. 42–3.

48 *Correspondence of Sidney and Languet*, p. 225.

The settlement in Laconia shows a state reformed in the direction of giving each group in society a role to play in politics. It leaves the Lacaedemonians in the position of leaders and admits the helots to citizenship; their children are to be permitted to share in the 'Spartan discipline'. Kingship, we gather, remains undisturbed; we have thus a blueprint for a stable mixed constitution. Viewed in relation to the earlier political settlements implemented by the heroes in Phrygia, Pontus, and Paphlagonia, I see no reason for doubting that this too is intended as an example of high political wisdom. While Raitiere points out that, in two late asides in the revision of the *Arcadia*, we are told that the settlement was not permanent and that civil war has broken out again,[49] this does not appear to invalidate my conclusion. We may accept that this is a genuine authorial revision, since Mary Sidney knew her brother's intentions, but notice both the convenience of this detail for the rather tortuous and difficult revision of the plot which she or he, or both, had in hand, and the experience of the sixteenth century which had seen many desirable settlements in both France and Holland collapse in spite of the hopes of enlightened onlookers. The *nova republica* which Sidney hoped Languet might help to establish in Holland was not to come easily; the settlement in Phrygia too had been endowed with only 'as much assurance as worldly matters bear'.

The many states, with their laws and customs, which the heroes of *Arcadia* have visited before arriving at Arcadia itself have, then, a variety of functions. They offer the reader an image of life as a journey, a justification for the voyage of exploration which reading *Arcadia* involves, and a new introduction, a preparation for the account of the Arcadian state. Its constitution seems intended to weather the confusions of Sidney's romance (much greater in the revised version), largely, it would seem, because in the denouement 'the whole people, both of great and low estate' (p. 810) must still, in the revision, consent to the emergency drafting of Euarchus as Protector and to his judgement when they hear it, and retain their affection for the ruling house which enables Pamela to be recognised as heir: 'this assembly of people had neither meaning nor power to do any hurt to the princess, whom they all recognised as their sovereign lady' (p. 811). The 'popular sort' who are given a voice in government would appear to include the shepherds (who are not proletarians but proprietors of their sheep), but, following Aristotle and the Venetian commentators, probably not the rebellious artisans of Book II, whose trades are repeatedly stressed: the 'clowns, churls, mad multitude' (p. 379) are also 'a tailor, a butcher, a miller, a painter' (p. 380), 'ploughmen, vine-labourers, cooks' (p. 383). (Though they have got a 'young farmer' among them, he proves sensitive and rational.)

49 *Faire Bitts*, pp. 46–8; *New Arcadia*, pp. 669, 790.

The main plot of the *New Arcadia*, like that of its original, vindicates the value of the active life in public over those of privacy, leisure, and contemplation, in the tradition of Aristotle's *Ethics* and *Politics*. The greatest folly is that of Basilius in deserting his public responsibilities. Sub-plots suggest that not only are deviant political states hostile to public virtue or heroism, but sound forms predispose their citizens to heroic virtue. The heroism of the central characters is not only theirs but that of the state in which they received their education; elsewhere, while tyrants and oligarchs fear excellence, Queen Helen of Corinth elicits legendary virtues from her courtiers through her political wisdom.

Sidney's romance offers us a map of Greece as a complex of interacting states, like Europe in the sixteenth century in its variety of historical background and the varying characters and fortunes of its rulers, particularly women rulers. Those who respect the law and their obligations to their subjects (perhaps especially their nobility), who avoid tyranny, practise active virtues themselves and foster them among their subjects, may hope not only to survive but to achieve fame. The plan develops Sidney's admiration for mixed constitutions, his hostility to both rebellion and tyranny; it displays his conviction that a modern work of prose fiction could, like the *Odyssey*, the *Aeneid*, and the *Cyropaedia*, awaken a desire to know about virtue and illuminate the mind as to its nature. Thus he achieves the 'chief end of man' as stated in the *Apology*, 'the knowledge of a man's self in the ethike and politike consideration', and moves his reader towards the expression of this knowledge in action. The connection between the achievement of his late twenties and Venice, the scene of some of his early studies and enthusiasms, helps towards an understanding his great work of fiction and its sharply defined international perspective.

Prince Arthur's 'Vertuous and Gentle Discipline'

RICHARD A. McCABE

I

Despite the diversity of critical opinion that besets Spenserian scholarship, commentators have for the most part agreed in rejecting Spenser's claims for the importance of Prince Arthur to the structural design of *The Faerie Queene*.[1] At worst he is dismissed as a subsidiary figure, at best as a casualty of the work's incompletion. John Upton (1758) has remained virtually alone amongst the poem's major editors in challenging the prevailing view.[2] From the outset the critical tradition has been dominated by less enthusiastic voices. While deploring what he regarded as the poem's lack of proper 'uniformity', for example, Dryden (1693) identified Arthur as something of a Spenserian concession towards the structural demands of classical epic. However, his interpretation of the work as a *roman à clef* led him to doubt the viability of the plan, the untimely death of Sir Philip Sidney (Arthur's alleged original) rendering the eventual union with Gloriana impracticable.[3] But this is clearly to tax the poet with problems of the critic's making. More typical is the dismissive assertion of Thomas Warton (1762) that Arthur 'is only a subordinate or accessory character', an opinion supported by most modern readers.[4] According to Harry Berger (1957), for instance, 'it is perhaps not always interesting to speculate on the role of Arthur since he plays a relatively small part in the extant poem'.[5] More recent studies have concentrated upon isolated aspects of his allegorical significance to the detriment of his narrative continuity. Greater energy has been expended upon the role he might have played in the projected twelve books of 'pollliticke vertues

1 Notable exceptions are Janet Spens, *Spenser's 'Faerie Queene'* (London, 1934), p. 32; Merritt Y. Hughes, 'The Arthurs of *The Faerie Queene*', *Études Anglaises* 6 (1953), 193–213.

2 *The Faerie Queene* (London, 1758), pp. xx–xxv.

3 *Of Dramatic Poesy and Other Critical Essays*, ed. George Watson, 2 vols. (London, 1962), II, 83.

4 *Observations on the Faerie Queene of Spenser*, 2nd ed., 2 vols. (London, 1762), I, 6–8.

5 *The Allegorical Temper* (New Haven, 1957), p. 88.

. . . after that hee came to be king' than in his contribution to the six we have.[6]

Such attitudes have been immeasurably strengthened by Josephine Waters Bennett's study of *The Faerie Queene's* 'evolution'.[7] The evolutionary metaphor is revealing, since all too often its ultimate effect is to reduce the poem to a storehouse of literary 'fossils' affording evidence of Spenser's alleged failure to integrate various levels of composition into a satisfactorily unified whole. The poem is to be regarded as an organic growth rather than (as Sir Philip Sidney would have it) a rhetorical construct. It is well to remember, however, that Spenser's 'nature' is not a Darwinian force but an intellectual goddess well schooled in dialectical discrimination. By persistently attributing apparent anomalies in the romance narrative to problems in the work's 'evolution', Miss Bennett downgrades the finished product by creating the impression that the published version—the only version extant—represents a hasty and ill-conceived attempt to force an arbitrary structure upon intractable material. In the absence of any manuscript evidence, we are invited to evaluate the published poem in the light of a series of hypothetical 'early' versions, none of which can be adequately described, or accurately dated, let alone produced for comparison. Thus Arthur emerges as a 'late' addition to a poem originally conceived upon different principles, 'an afterthought' in the words of Richard Hurd (1762).[8] Yet, however many drafts there may have been, all were rejected in favour of the texts published in 1590 and 1596. We must work with what we have, and the 'Letter to Raleigh' is emphatic in assigning Prince Arthur a central role both thematic and structural. Furthermore, it is factually incorrect to represent this role as decreasing in significance as the poem proceeds.[9] Rather, with the sole exception of Book Three, where special circumstances apply, Arthur's interventions become at once more frequent and more germane to the central theme with each successive book.[10]

Since Spenser never undertakes to make his hero equally active in every legend, his relatively brief appearance in the third (extending to three

6 James Nohrnberg, *The Analogy of 'The Faerie Queene'* (Princeton, 1976), pp. 35–58; Thomas E. Vesce, 'Towards an Appreciation of Arthur's Persona in Spenser's *Faerie Queene*', *Mid-Hudson Language Studies* 4 (1981), 39–55; A. Kent Hieatt, 'The Passing of Arthur in Malory, Spenser, and Shakespeare: The Avoidance of Closure', *The Passing of Arthur: New Essays in Arthurian Tradition*, edd. Christopher Baswell and William Sharpe (New York, 1988), pp. 173–92.

7 *The Evolution of 'The Faerie Queene'* (Chicago, 1942), pp. 53–79.

8 Bennett, *ibid.*, p. 60; Richard Hurd, *Letters on Chivalry and Romance with the Third Elizabethan Dialogue*, ed. Edith J. Morley (London, 1911), p. 124.

9 Sherry L. Reames, 'Prince Arthur and Spenser's Changing Design', *'Eterne in Mutabilitie': The Unity of 'The Faerie Queene'*, ed. Kenneth John Atchity (Hamden, Connecticut, 1972), pp. 180–206, at 183–4.

10 *The Faerie Queene*, ed. A.C. Hamilton (London, 1977), pp. 483, 581.

cantos) should not call in question the poem's overall design. According to the 'Letter to Raleigh', Arthur has twelve books in which to complete his quest as the others have twelve cantos. But none is equally active in every canto. Guyon, for example, scarcely appears at all in the third canto of Book Two. The analogy seems clear. Moreover, Arthur's level of activity in Books Four and Six rivals that of the titular heroes. Whereas his intervention in Book One is essentially concerned with the rescuing of St. George, the rescuing of Guyon serves merely as the pre-lude to a series of incidents culminating in the canto-long combat with Maleger. By the time we reach the 'Legend of Courtesie', we find Arthur's adventures multiplying at a remarkable rate. Here he twice saves the life of Timias (once in the course of the action and once in flashback), escorts Serena and Timias to the dwelling of the hermit, forms an intriguing friendship with the savage man, defeats and baffles Sir Turpine and (in a separate combat) two of his mercenary agents, and vanquishes Disdain, 'sib to the great Orgoglio' of Book One. Thus Humphrey Tonkin can justly assign the Prince 'a major role' in Book Six.[11] It is generally the case that the most interesting analyses of Arthur's activity are to be found not in critiques of the overall design but in specialized studies of separate books. However, because such studies do little to relate Arthur's appearances to one another or to the progress of his own quest, they appear to support Miss Bennett's conclusion that no continuity is perceptible.[12] Yet, as in the case of Disdain, it is precisely such continuity that Spenser seems at pains to establish.

The situation is exacerbated by a common misrepresentation of Spenser's intentions as stated in the 'Letter to Raleigh'. For example, one often reads of Arthur's 'failure' to rescue the principle protagonists of Books Three to Six, although Spenser never suggested that such feats would be attempted.[13] The prevalent conception of Arthur's role is an unfortunate distortion of the plan actually announced:

> in the whole course I mention the deedes of Arthure applyable to that vertue, which I write of in that booke.

One notices that Arthur is not necessarily related to the other protagonists, as rescuer or otherwise, but to the moral concerns of the books in which they appear. In fact, in the case of Book Three, Spenser tells us that the 'succouring' involved will be performed by Britomart. The notion that Arthur fails to intervene appropriately in this and later books is born of the unfounded expectation that all books of *The Faerie Queene* should

11 *Spenser's Courteous Pastoral* (Oxford, 1972), pp. 85–6.
12 Bennett, *Evolution*, pp. 54, 58; Hughes, 'The Arthurs', p. 211.
13 Bennett, *Evolution*, pp. 55–6.

fall precisely into the pattern of the first two, the implication being that Spenser somehow or somewhere promised that they should. Yet the two books in question are themselves structurally divergent. In the first, Arthur appears midway through canto seven and leaves early in canto nine, long before George enters the allegorical 'house' of that book. In the second, he is discussed in canto three, makes no appearance in canto seven, intervenes midway through canto eight, and thereafter remains active until the close of canto eleven. During this period he enters the book's allegorical house, more than sharing the limelight with Guyon, whom he supplants completely in the eleventh canto, thereby radically altering the pattern of Book One. His defeat of Malegar is arguably as important to the furthering of temperance as the rescuing of its patron. Instead of departing from the book as previously, he here returns to the Castle of Alma to be reunited with the victorious Guyon. Comparison between two such dissimilar narratives could scarcely have been intended to raise assured expectations concerning the structure of Book Three. Book One is not a paradigm but a variant.[14]

Variation, not repetition, is Spenser's goal. As an imaginative storyteller, he must have realised that a pattern of entrances and exits repeated with clockwork regularity must ultimately prove as monotonous as clockwork and invite complacency of response. As the poem now stands, such adverse reaction is far less likely: Arthur intervenes twice in canto seven (I, IV), twice in canto eight (II, V), once in canto one (III) and once in canto five (VI) without any discernible pattern to these variations. Who could predict the structure of a seventh book?[15] Spenser has left his options open in respect of both design and incident. Allowing Arthur to rescue the chief protagonist of any legend is merely one way of having him display the appropriate virtue. Rescuing a series of lesser characters is another, as is the championing of wholly allegorical figures such as Alma and Mercilla. It remains true, of course, that whenever Arthur repeats a significant type of action in the same canto of different books the positioning enforces the coincidence and contributes to the continuity of his character. Thus he accomplishes important rescues (though not necessarily of the principle protagonist) in the eighth canto of Books One, Two, and Four, while Mirabel declines to be rescued in the same canto of Book Six. Similarly, the defeats of Malegar and Geryoneo occur in the eleventh canto of their respective books (II, V), whereas in the tenth canto of the same books Arthur assumes the relatively passive roles of reader and listener.

14 Patricia A. Parker remarks that, '*The Faerie Queene* is virtually a tour of romance forms, but of forms whose tendencies are significantly different, and the prior placing of Book I does not necessarily establish its priority' (*Inescapable Romance: Studies in the Poetics of a Mode* (Princeton, 1979), p. 74).

15 If Matthew Lownes was correct in numbering the 'Mutabilitie Cantos', Arthur could not have appeared in the sixth or seventh canto of the relevant book.

The peculiarly hybrid structure of *The Faerie Queene* demands both coincidence and divergence. Commenting upon the structure of Renaissance romance in the light of classical epic, Giraldi Cinthio points out that its subjects 'are not in the manner of Virgil's and Homer's, both of whom undertook imitating only one action of one man, whereas ours have imitated many actions not of one man only but of many, since they build the whole fabric of their work upon eight or ten persons, but they give to the work the name of that person or that action which is dominant in the whole work and on which all the others depend'. Giraldi's personal preference is for poems of multiple action on the grounds that 'diversity of actions carries with it the variety that is the spice of delight and so allows the writer a large field to use episodes, that is, pleasing digressions'.[16] He is thinking primarily of Boiardo and Ariosto, but it seems clear that what Spenser has done is to take the principle of 'eight or ten persons' more seriously by allocating each protagonist a separate book with one especially heroic character operating in all. The work could then quite legitimately take its name from the Fairy Queen who figures both as the goal of the primary quest and the motivator or supporter of most of the others.[17] In the following sections of the present study I intend to examine the continuity of Spenser's Arthurian narrative, the nature of the hero's 'magnificence', and then, by way of conclusion, the progressive refinement of his love.

II

Spenser lends continuity to Arthur's interventions in a number of ways, but most obviously by constantly reminding us of the nature of his quest, often in such a manner as to emphasise its relationship, either directly or by thematic implication, to the work in hand. This procedure is observed from the Prince's own lengthy report to Una in Book One (9.8–15) to his final departure from the poem (VI.8.30). Particularly noteworthy throughout are the unfailing persistence of the quest and the frustrating elusiveness of its goal. Having heard the account of the dream-vision, Una, herself a client of Gloriana and speaking in her allegorical role of Truth, endorses the queen's choice of lover, 'one that with his prowesse may | Defend thine honour, and thy foes confound' (I.9.16). A stanza later George goes even further in claiming that Arthur has proven himself worthy of his lady's grace to the exclusion of all rivals: 'For onely worthy you through prowes priefe | Yf *liuing* man mote worthy be, to be her liefe.' This qualification is interesting and we shall return to it later, but both

16 *On Romances*, tr. Henry L. Snuggs (Lexington, Kentucky, 1968), pp. 11, 23.

17 The principle exception is Book Four. Britomart pursues a knight who leaves her for Gloriana's service so the association is preserved.

remarks are anticipated as early as canto seven, where Una informs Arthur of her recent recourse to Gloriana's court, thereby establishing a direct association between her quest and his ambition. As we learn in canto nine, this is the first positive news Arthur has received of Gloriana in the nine months to have elapsed since his dream-vision. By espousing Una's cause he enters his lady's service directly, supplanting George for the duration of the episode. Departing 'on his way | To seeke his loue' (I.9.20), he encounters Guyon just three months later.[18] During his combat with Pyrochles he is fascinated by the portrait on Guyon's shield (II.8.43) Its appearance there leads directly to Guyon's enthusiastic description of his sovereign in the ninth canto, and that in turn leads to Arthur's renewed declaration of devotion: 'I God auow, | That sith I armes and knighthood first did plight, | My whole desire hath beene, and yet is now, | To serue that Queene' (II.9.7). Such service has again been rendered, and, as in the previous book, the point is duly noted; the 'wondrous worth' of the achievement is deemed to guarantee Arthur's eventual acceptance into the 'knights of *Maydenhed*', Gloriana's elite corps. Later in the same canto Prays-Desire, the motive-force of Arthur's life, expressly relates his chivalric endeavours to the quest for the Fairy Queen, 'glory' in Spenser's 'generall intention' (II.9.38). Presumably the fairy chronicles of canto ten, read in Arthur's presence, supply yet further evidence of Gloriana's desirability (II.10.76).

Hunting 'for glorie and renowmed praise' at the outset of Book Three, Arthur rides in pursuit of Florimell in the hope 'that Lady faire mote bee | His Faery Queene' (III.4.54). Her dwarf excites his interest even further by describing his mistress as 'a gentle lady of great sway, | And high accompt throughout all Elfin land' (III.5.4). As she is 'royally clad . . . in cloth of gold', Arthur eagerly demands her identity. The structure of stanza eight seems designed to prolong his agony, since the name is tantalizingly delayed until line seven. Despite the disappointment, however, the dwarf's concluding appeal redirects Arthur's attention to its true object:

> So may ye gaine to you full great renowne,
> Of all good Ladies through the world so wide,
> And haply in her hart find highest rowme,
> Of whom ye seeke to be most magnifide. (III.5.11)

Since magnificence is the key to Arthur's moral character he accepts, finding himself once again enlisted in the service of Gloriana through that of her subjects and clients. His avowal of undying support is entirely to be expected.

18 He has spent nine months in the search when he meets Una (I.9.15), a year when he meets Guyon (II.9.7).

This pattern continues in the following two books. Encountering Amoret and Aemylia in Book Four Arthur questions them closely as to the identity of Belphoebe—'And oft of them did earnestly inquire, | Where was her won, and how he mote her find', abandoning the interrogation only, 'when as nought according to his mind | He could outlearne' (IV.8.22). The 'Letter to Raleigh' directly links the quest for Amoret with Gloriana, and Arthur here completes it by reuniting the lady to Scudamour. Although Spenser, or the printer, seem to have omitted the requisite stanzas (displaced from the revised conclusion to Book three) towards the end of canto nine, it is clear that the union is indeed effected since Scudamour suddenly refers to 'she whom I behold' (IV.10.4), shortly after lamenting her tragic 'loss' (IV.9.38–9). Ironically, therefore, while 'resolued to pursue his *former* quest' (IV.9.17), Arthur again pursues it indirectly. The mentioning of Gloriana's name in the eighth canto of Book Five serves as the cue for his return (8.3), and his defeat of the Souldan sees him 'glorifyed' (8.51)—an important advancement—shortly before his introduction to the 'magnificke' court of Mercilla, one of the Fairy Queen's most important surrogates (9.22). The historical allegory enforces the connection: Mercilla too is Elizabeth in Spenser's 'particular' intention. Hence Arthur's eagerness to enter her service in the cause of Belge before he departs, 'and to his former iourney him addrest, | On which long way he rode, ne euer day did rest' (V.11.35).

The evidence of Book Six is crucial because any essential change in Spenser's plan must surely have emerged by such a late stage. The text affords no such indication. The 'great affaires in mynd' of which we read in the fifth canto (41) may involve no more than the disciplining of Turpine, but the conclusion to the following canto is surely emphatic: 'The morrow next the Prince did early rize, | And passed forth, to follow his first enterprize' (VI.6.44). Lest there be any doubt as to the nature of this undertaking, the lapse of a few stanzas finds Arthur, 'ryding a softly pace with portance sad, | Deuizing of his loue more, then of daunger drad' (VI.7.6). His priorities remain unaltered and his final departure from the poem follows the now familiar pattern: 'But *Arthure* with the rest, went onward still | On his first quest, in which did him betide | A great aduenture, which did him from them deuide' (VI.8.30). The phrasing here is particularly happy since it encapsulates the essential nature of the Prince's endeavours throughout the poem. It is specifically *within* his 'first quest' that his various adventures befall. In effect they form integral parts of that quest, just as all of the episodes in any given book, and not merely the concluding ones, denote essential stages in the progress of their respective knights. As he proceeds from book to book, Arthur is gaining 'glory' and, therefore, Gloriana in an allegorical sense. Ultimately her personal elusiveness proves less significant than his determined service of her subjects and surrogates, Una, Alma, Guyon, Florimell, Amoret,

Mercilla, and Serena. Having promised to appear when 'iust time' has expired, she has, in effect, appeared vicariously quite often. Instead of moving further from her, as Miss Bennett claims, Arthur is steadily approaching in the only way possible, and his love, as we shall see, is progressively refined.[19] Frustrating though the journey itself may seem, Arthur is unwittingly achieving fulfilment: 'the gentle minde by gentle deeds is knowne' (VI.3.1). Subtly the imagery points in the same direction. In Book One the precious stone, representing Gloriana, which adorns Arthur's bauldrick shines 'like *Hesperus* emongst the lesser lights' (I.7.30). In Book Three he pursues Florimell, vainly hoping she is Gloriana, 'so long that now the golden *Hesperus* | Was mounted high in top of heauen sheene' (4.51). He has mistaken the nature of his love, and the astronomical detail seems ironic. By Book Six, however, Arthur himself appears 'in siluer slomber . . . Like to the Euening starre adorn'd with deawy ray' (7.19), and the coincidence of imagery would seem to suggest a greater coincidence of moral value between the quester and his goal.

Such techniques tend to promote a unified view of Arthur's quest, a view strongly reinforced by continuity of storyline. In Book One the Prince's last discussion with George and Una centres upon his search for Gloriana, and precisely the same subject dominates his first discussion with Guyon. Similarly, the importance of the relationship between Arthur and Timias is stressed in both books and thereafter provides a thread through the complexities of the polyphonic narrative. Whereas Arthur saves Timias's life during the combat with Orgoglio and Duessa (I.8.15), the squire reciprocates during the Malegar episode (II.11.30). The pair are separated in the first canto of Book Three, and Arthur is represented as lamenting Timias's loss in canto five immediately prior to his departure from the book: 'For him he loued aboue all mankind, | Hauing him trew and faithfull euer tride, | And bold, as euer Squire that waited by knights side' (12). Spenser is supplying a narrative 'lead' and, as anticipated, Arthur is still searching for his friend in the eighth canto of Book Four (18), having failed to recognise him when they meet a canto earlier (IV.7.42–7). The allegorical significance of this we shall consider later. At present I wish to concentrate upon the tightly interlocking structure of the narrative, Since Timias's relationship with Amoret is largely responsible for his loss of identity in canto seven, the meeting of Amoret and Arthur in canto eight is far from coincidental. Moreover, the problem of Belphoebe's identity is cast in ironic perspective by the Prince's earlier discovery of her name 'engrauen' on every tree by his lovelorn squire, 'yet who was that

19 Bennett, *Evolution*, p. 29; Nohrnberg, *Analogy*, p. 675. For a typological interpretation of Gloriana's elusiveness see Jeffrey P. Fruen, '"True Glorious Type": The Place of Gloriana in *The Faerie Queene*', *Spenser Studies* 7 (New York, 1987), pp. 147–73.

Belphebe, he ne wis' (IV.8.46). But the association with Amoret has further consequences of an even more complex nature, in that it again interweaves the destinies of Arthur and Britomart, who had last met at the outset of Book Three, where he reconciled her to Guyon. Now riding in the company of Scudamour, Britomart's immediate objective is the recovery of Amoret (IV.6.35–8). If there is any sense in which Britomart may be said to have supplied Arthur's place in Book Three—which I doubt—it should also be recognised that he now supplies hers by reuniting the lovers.

We do not hear of Timias in Book Five, where his role is, to some extent, supplanted by Talus (V.8.29). However, Arthur's companionship of Artegall again involves him in the major narrative strands of Books Three to Five. As the two meet directly after Artegall's second separation from Britomart, Arthur would again appear to act in her place. Book Six resumes the Timias narrative by relating the reunion of Prince and squire in flashback, carefully emphasising the depth of the emotions involved: 'My liefe, my lifes desire, | Why haue ye me alone thus long yleft?' (VI.5.23). Their histories are further interwoven in the succeeding cantos, as they part and reunite yet once more. This pattern was clearly intended to continue in later books, for our last glimpse of Arthur sees him 'dividing' from Timias again. Book Six also expressly links Arthur's first adventures to his last by insisting upon the relationship between Disdain and Orgoglio, 'which was slaine | by *Arthure*, when as *Vnas* Knight he did maintaine' (VI.7.41) Thus the reader is led to evaluate the later combat in the light of the earlier, attempting to understand why Disdaine survives.

Further minor details of continuity are provided through Spenser's persistent attention to the armour and personal effects so elaborately described upon Arthur's intervention. The diamond shield, for example, is often in evidence, particularly in Books One and Five, where its unveiling leads to the destruction of Orgoglio (8.19) and the Souldan (8.37). In Book Six it shatters his opponent's lance (7.8). The sword Morddure (I.7.30) motivates much of the action of Book Two, since Archimago, plans to steal it as early as the third canto (18) and is shown successful in the sixth (47). Its loss obliges Arthur to oppose Pyrochles and Cymochles (appropriately) with the sword of temperance (8.40), while his own sword proves useless to his enemies (8.30). Later in the same book the positions are reversed, when Morddure proves equally ineffective against Malegar (11.41). In later books it becomes again 'his trustie sword, the seruant of his might' (VI.7.25). Similarly, the precious liquor which constitutes Arthur's gift to George (I.9.19), later reappears to heal the wounds of Amoret and Aemylia (IV.8.20). Other details of the combats may also be designed to echo former victories or problems. Adicia's transformation into a tiger (V.8.49), for instance, recalls the tiger upon which Malegar rides (II.11.20).

Perhaps the most striking features in the portrayal of Arthur are his youth and relative inexperience. His closest literary ancestor is the hero of

'Arthur of Little Britain' (republished in Lord Berners's translation in 1582), the youthful prince who pursues the Lady Florence believing her to be the fairy queen.[20] Thus Spenser frequently refers to Arthur as 'infant' or 'childe' and repeatedly has him question other characters concerning their quests or his own. On a number of occasions, but especially in Book Three, he struggles to unravel the complexities of the providential plan. Such curiosity is integral to Spenser's conception of his character, since he remains ignorant of his true identity. 'Oft and oft' he asks Merlin, 'of what loines and what lignage I did spring' (I.9.5). Other characters are in a similar position: George, Artegall, Pastorella, and Serena's savage man. In all such cases ignorance of true identity is used as a convenient metaphor for lack of self-knowledge on a number of levels. Thus George learns his personal, national, and spiritual identity at one and the same moment (I.10.61). An equivalent fate was presumably intended for Arthur, for Merlin assures him that 'time in her iust terme the truth to light should bring' (I.9.5). While one may speculate upon the nature of this moment, the extant material shows Spenser using Arthur's desire for self-knowledge as one of the major themes of his quest. However unrelated the two may at first appear, the analogy with George demonstrates the connection. Both Merlin and Gloriana insist that Arthur must abide the passage of 'iust time'.

The irony of Arthur's position in Book One is that, while professing ignorance of his identity, he wears his father's insignia on his helmet in the shape of the winged dragon which presaged his accession to the throne in Geoffrey of Monmouth's history (VIII.14–15). Since it is 'truth' that time is destined to reveal, Una is the first character to name Arthur in the poem, although the significance of this name is not disclosed. In the Castle of Alma the Prince is educated in the nature of his own humanity, especially with regard to his insatiable 'prays-desire' (II.9.36–9), but even more important are the 'Briton Chronicles', which alone can make any disclosure of identity meaningful. As Arthur himself remarks, 'how brutish is it not to understand, | How much to her we owe, that all vs gaue' (II.10.69). Spenser underscores the point by associating the encroachments of 'ambitious *Rome*' with Arthur's destined retaliation (49), and by ending the chronicle abruptly upon his father's name, 'After him *Vther*, which *Pendragon* hight, | Succeeding' (68). Arthur now possesses the name he begged from Merlin in Book One, and his warm appreciation of the chronicle does ample justice to 'the royall Ofspring of his natiue land', a land he already regards as his 'foster' parent. Until he can know Uther *as a father*, instinct must guide him in the absence of knowledge.

20 *Arthur of Little Britanie. Translated out of French by J. Bourghoher, Lord Barners*, 1582. Cf. Sarah Michie, '*The Faerie Queene* and *Arthur of Little Britain*', *Studies in Philology* 36 (1939), 105–23.

Following the theme of identity into Book Three, one begins to appreciate why Spenser engineered Arthur's meeting with Britomart at this stage: her history is as closely bound to Merlin's prophecies as his own, and the goal of her quest is none other than 'the sonne of Gorlois', Arthur's half-brother (III.3.27).[21] More important still, as events are here represented, Britomart will bear Arthur's heir in the sense that her son is destined to succeed to his throne. Spenser has altered the Galfridian account of history in order to bring his characters into a much closer relationship than would otherwise have been possible. In this way an ironic light is cast upon Arthur's desertion of Britomart in canto one, as also upon his fit of despondency in canto four. In the latter case his loss of purpose and direction contrasts sharply with the assurance of Merlin's prophecy (3.21–50), a continuation of the Briton Chronicles broken off in Book Two. Spenser has so structured Arthur's appearances that they 'frame' the prophecy without allowing him to partake of the enclosed revelation. This is appropriate, in that the obvious time gap between chronicle and prophecy exactly corresponds to the duration of Arthur's own life. Furthermore, a useful parallel is drawn between himself and Britomart, for she too lapses into despair in the same canto before deciding to continue the quest. Thus is laid the foundation for inextricably interweaving the destinies of magnificent Prince and 'Magnificke Virgin' (V.7.21).

From this point on Arthur is much concerned with the recovery of Timias, whose loss of identity, emphasised by his master's failure to recognise him, is allegorically analagous to Arthur's lack of self-knowledge. While fallen from Belphoebe's grace, Timias cannot enjoy the honour implicit in the etymology of his name. Nevertheless, under the guise of 'rude brutishnesse' Arthur detects 'that he whilome some gentle swaine had beene, | Traind vp in feats of armes and knightlinesse' (IV.7.45). Not until he is restored to the Platonic love of Belphoebe can Timias be reconciled to Arthur, whose own potential remains unfulfilled until he completes his quest for Gloriana. Just as she had promised such an outcome in 'iust time', Arthur now imitates her by leaving Timias 'till time for him should remedy prouide, | And him restore to former grace againe' (47). When their paths next cross such 'time' has elapsed and the problem of identity disappears: 'Then turning to that swaine, him well he knew | To be his Timias' (VI.5.23). Timias's reconciliation with Belphoebe may be designed to anticipate Arthur's reception by Gloriana. In any case, it associates him indirectly with another of her facets.

Throughout Books Four and Six Spenser involves Arthur in complex problems of identity such as that of Placydas and Amyas, whose bonds of

21 Geoffrey of Monmouth, *Historia regium Britanniae* VIII. 19. According to the 'Letter to Raleigh' Arthur's mother was Gorlois's wife, Igrayne (Geoffrey of Monmouth's Ygerna).

friendship are allegorically signified by their indistinguishable 'resemblaunce', a feature which amazes Arthur by demonstrating the paradoxical attainment of personal fulfilment through self-effacement in defence of Prays-Desire (IV.9.11). Similarly, he is called upon to restore Poeana to herself or to her real 'nature' (IV.9.16), and to receive the love of the savage man whose antecedents are as mysterious as his own, 'for certes he was borne of noble blood . . . As ye may know, when time shall be to tell the same' (VI.5.2). The theme is reinforced, in Arthur's absence, in the episodes of Matilda's child (VI.4.36) and Pastorella (VI.12.20), but the most important incident is undoubtedly the meeting with Artegall in Book Five.

Arthur first hears of Artegall from Guyon (II.9.6), and their blood relationship is suggested in the etymology of their names: in every sense, semantic as well as genealogical, they share the same 'root'. Artegall is ignorant of his own lineage (III.3.26) and first appears as a 'salvage' knight, apparently as alien to nobility as the wild man of Book Six (IV.4.39). Nevertheless, he is described as being 'most of might' (42), a quality, as we shall see, usually associated with 'magnificence'. The instinctive attraction which marks the encounter is all the more extraordinary for the participants' inability to explain it to themselves:

> Tho when as *Artegall* did *Arthure* vew,
> So faire a creature, and so wondrous bold,
> He much admired both his heart and hew,
> And touched with intire affection, nigh him drew. (V.8.12)

This sort of response is normally reserved for sexual attraction. In the present instance it closely recalls Artegall's earlier reaction to Britomart (IV.6.22), except that the 'intire affection' now engendered denotes a deeper sense of kinship than that of conscious recognition. Revelation of identity (whenever it occurs) will only serve to strengthen an alliance already formed through royal instinct. The problem of Arthur's identity is thus handled in a most tantalizing manner, as the hero repeatedly trembles on the verge of recognition without ever learning the truth. The proleptic introduction of 'chyld Tristram' into Book Six (2.28) was doubtless intended to herald yet another 'Arthurian' encounter at some later stage. What is demanded of Arthur himself is perseverance despite frustration. In this consists his inner 'magnificence', and according to Lodovico Castelvetro the subject of epic poetry should be both 'magnificent and royal'.[22]

22 H.B. Charlton, *Castelvetro's Theory of Poetry* (Manchester, 1913), p. 113. See also Ronald Arthur Horton, *The Unity of 'The Faerie Queene'* (Athens, Georgia, 1978), pp. 19–24.

III

Aristotle defined magnificence as liberality on a lavish scale, not solely in respect of financial outlay but also in relation to the public effect produced. The virtue is associated with nobility, honour, and wealth: 'magnificence in an achievement is excellence on a grand scale.'[23] Thus interpreted its affinities with magnanimity are obvious. Indeed, the very structure of the *Ethics* make of magnificence a stepping stone between liberality and magnanimity, and so it was frequently regarded. Renaissance Aristotelians such as Spenser's friend Lodowick Bryskett insist that magnificence and magnanimity go 'arm in arme' because the former involves expenditure 'in respect of vertue' and 'long continuance'. In effect, Bryskett argues that a magnanimous attitude towards wealth is one of the factors that distinguishes the liberal from the magnificent man.[24] Approaching the matter from the opposite direction, George Puttenham reminds us that wealth, properly used, fosters 'magnanimitie'.[25] There is much of this in Spenser's Arthur whose rich appearance symbolises an equivalent spiritual richness. He is particularly offended by those who offer their prowess for hire and twice in the poem donates the spoils of victory to others, thereby rejecting all 'meed' but honour.[26] But such outward 'magnificence' is merely symptomatic of deeper moral reserves.

Cicero's approach to magnificence, rather than Aristotle's, dominated medieval thinking. His *De Inventione* classifies the virtue as the first part or facet of fortitude: *magnificentia est rerum magnarum et excelsarum cum animi ampla quadam et splendida propositione cogitatio atque administratio* 'magnificence entails the conception and executon of great and grand enterprises in a certain spirit of sublime resolve' (II.54.163). By stressing *cogitatio* the definition subsumes important elements of Aristotle's magnanimity. The fuller, if less schematic, treatment in *De Officiis* confirms this impression by specifically relating magnificence, still a species of fortitude, to magnanimous attitudes towards wealth: *vitanda et pecuniae fugienda cupiditas; nihil enim est* tam angusti animi, tamque parvi *quam amare divitias, nihil honestius magnificentiusque quam pecuniam contemnere, si non habeas, si habeas, ad beneficentiam liberalitatemque conferre*, 'avarice is to be avoided and shunned; nothing is more narrow-minded and pusillanimous than the love of lucre, nothing more honourable and exalted than to spurn wealth if you lack it, or to employ it benevolently and liberally if you possess it' (I.20.68).

23 *Ethics*, tr. J.A.K. Thomson, rev. Hugh Tredennick, (Harmondsworth, 1976), p. 150.

24 *Literary Works*, ed. J.H.P. Pafford (Germany, 1972), pp. 223, 232.

25 *Of Poets and Poesy*, ed. G. Gregory Smith, *Elizabethan Critical Essays*, 2 vols. (Oxford, 1904), II, 44.

26 See IV. 9. 15; V. 9, 3; VI. 7. 12–15.

In the *Somnium Scipionis* Macrobius endorsed the Ciceronian view by identifying magnificence as the fourth part of fortitude, the first being magnanimity (I.8.7). As Rosemund Tuve has demonstrated, the Macrobian view was eagerly christianised in such works as Lorens d'Orleans' *Somme le Roi* (*c.*1279), which classifies magnificence as the sixth degree of fortitude ('prowesse' in the English translation), regarded not as a cardinal virtue but as one of the seven gifts of the Holy Ghost.[27] Magnificence is 'grete hiȝenesse':

> Þis vertue oure gret philosophre Ihesu Crist clepeþ perseueraunce wel lastynge, wher-bi the goode Goddes knyghtes suffreþ þe hardenesses and endureþ riȝt to þe ende in þilke hiȝe weie of parfitnesse that he haþ vndertake. Of þis vertue seiþ seynt Poule þat alle vertues rennen, but þis vertue wynneþ þe swerd'.[28]

Miss Tuve's contention is that definitions such as these established so firm a tradition of Christian magnificence as to render impossible its identification with magnanimity by Spenser and his contemporaries.[29] However, the manner in which Lorens also christianised magnanimity makes such conclusions untenable, for it emerges as a certain 'hiȝenesse' of the will whereby man undertakes 'hiȝe þinges and dredful'. Thus the magnanimous man chooses the 'weye of parfightnesse' while the magnificent man perseveres in the choice.[30] Vertues so complementary may easily be conflated. Just four years prior to the publication of the of 'Letter to Raleigh' we find the English translator of Pierre de la Primaudaye's *French Academie* (1586) asserting that the terms 'magnanimitie' and 'magnificence' are virtually synonymous, since both signify 'a doing of great and excellent things'. Magnanimity entails magnificence.[31]

Aquinas had complicated the tradition by attempting to incorporate Aristotelian detail into a fundamentally Ciceronian system. While relating magnificence to fortitude rather than to liberality, he resolved the Ciceronian definition into two separate components, one intellectual, corresponding to *cogitatio*, the other active, corresponding to *administratio*. The former is obviously related to magnanimity, as Aquinas himself acknowledges: 'just as magnanimity intends something great in every matter, it follows that magnificence does the same in every work that can be produced in external matter'. By channelling all the expenditure involved towards the service of God, he appropriated the noblest elements

27 *Allegorical Imagery* (Princeton, 1966), pp. 79–89.
28 *The Book of Vices and Virtues*, ed. W. Nelson Francis, London, 1942, (Early English Text Society 217), p. 169.1–7.
29 Tuve, *Allegorical Imagery*, p. 82.
30 *Vices and Virtues*, pp. 164–5.
31 *The French Academie*, tr. Thomas Bowes (London, 1586), p. 289.

of the Aristotelian definition in order to conclude that 'magnificence is connected with holiness, since its chief effect is directed to religion or holiness'.[32] Hence, perhaps, a new significance for Arthur's support of St George. Nevertheless, Aquinas cannot be said to have fully succeeded in reconciling his sources, and Renaissance Aristotelians, such as Francesco Piccolomini sought alternative solutions by relating liberality to charity and magnificence (liberality's highest form) to grace—a notion already implicit in Lorens's conception of fortitude as a divine gift.[33]

Within the literary tradition one finds less exactitude of definition although Cicero remains the dominant influence. For Chaucer's Parson, for example, magnanimity and magnificence are two 'speces' of fortitude, the former entailing 'greet corage', the latter 'the acomplissynge of grete goode werkes'.[34] Both are recommended as antidotes to 'accidie', the vice which seals George's fate in the combat with Orgoglio and necessitates his rescue by Arthur (I.7.4–5). For Skelton, magnificence is largely associated with the powers of majesty, Magnyfycence himself being (like Artegall) the 'man most of might'. It expands to comprehend all virtues necessary to successful government, including liberality and self-knowledge. However, the last moral virtue to which the reformed Magnyfycence is introduced is Perseveraunce, the quality Lorens recognises as central.[35] This is the essence of the Christian concept commonly regarded as uniting the powers of flesh and spirit. When, in the 'Letter to Raleigh', Spenser speaks of twelve moral virtues to be subsumed in magnificence as the perfection of the rest, he is writing in the broad chivalric tradition of such authors as Alain Chartier, whose *Breviaire des Nobles*, designed like *The Faerie Queene* to fashion gentlemen in 'vertuous and gentle discipline', is comprised of thirteen virtues. The first twelve range from *noblesce* through *amour* and *diligence* to *sobresse*, but the thirteenth, *perseverance*, encompasses them all: *O excellent, haulte vertu divine, | Qui tout parfit, acomplit et termine, | Royne puissant, Dame Perseverance.*'[36]

Thus Spenser inherited a tradition in which magnificence, in the sense of Christian perseverance, a species of fortitude, realized magnanimous ideals

32 *The Summa Theologica Part Two, Second Part, QQ. CI–CXL*, tr. the Fathers of the English Dominican Province (London, 1922), pp. 245, 297. See Richard J. DuRocher, 'Arthur's Gift, Aristotle's Magnificence, and Spenser's Allegory: A Study of *Faerie Queene* I. 9.19', *Modern Philology* 82 (1984), 185–90.

33 John Erskine Hankins, *Source and Meaning in Spenser's Allegory*, rev. ed. (Oxford, 1973), pp. 7–8.

34 *Canterbury Tales* X. 731, 735 (*The Riverside Chaucer*, 3rd ed., ed. Larry D. Benson (Oxford, 1988), pp. 312–13).

35 *Maynyfycence* 1493, 2457 ff. (*Four Morality Plays*, edited by Peter Happé (Harmondsworth, 1979), pp. 271, 306). Cf. William O. Harris, *Skelton' s 'Magnyfycence' and the Cardinal Virtue Tradition* (Chapel Hill, 1965), pp. 46–70.

36 *Poetical Works*, ed. J.C. Laidlaw (Cambridge, 1974), p. 408.

in the world of action. As seen by the other characters, even such as the depraved Archimago, Arthur is simply 'the prowest knight aliue' (II.8.1). During his first intervention in the poem he displays not merely holiness, the virtue 'applyable' to Book One, but courtesy (7.38), wisdom (7.42) loyalty (7.52), might (8.3), grace (8.19), temperance (8.34) compassion (8.39) zealous courage (8.40), patience (8.45), love (9.15), friendship (9.18), and generosity (9.19). His first showing constitutes a moral microcosm of the entire poem. In Book Two 'magnanimitie' attracts him to the fallen Guyon (8.23), and in return he finds his perseverance encouraged in the face of disappointment: 'But you, faire Sir, be not herewith dismaid, | But constant keepe the way, in which ye stand' (9.8). Only the hope of being 'magnified' in Gloriana's eyes redeems him from despondency in Book Three, where the moral value of disappointment lies in its challenge to perseverance. In Book Four Arthur's 'heroicke brest' revives the values of the Golden Age (8.30), while the essence of his adventures in Book Five is encapsulated in the line 'more in his causes truth he trusted then in might' (8.30). In Book Six, by associating himself with the hermit and baffling Turpine, he demonstrates the need for self-discipline and upholds his total commitment to the 'meed' of honour.

While functioning as an instrument of grace towards other characters, Arthur frequently needs the gift he dispenses (II.11.30), enjoying no immunity from temptation nor any special insight into the providential plan. During his long soliloquy in Book Three, he questions God's 'need' for the 'vngratious' forces of evil represented by Night, 'foule Mother of annoyance sad' (4.55). Expounding the poem's symbolism of light, he identifies 'the blessed seed, | Which darkesse shall subdew, and heauen win' as 'Dayes dearest children', concluding—in defiance of the old proverb—that 'truth' is the 'daughter' of day (59). More properly, however, as both Merlin and Gloriana suggest, she is the offspring of time, since good subsumes the effects of evil: the dream-vision occurred at night (I.9.5, 14).[37] Failure to understand this leaves Arthur so discontented that, paradoxically, the return of daylight merely deepens his sense of injustice (4.61). On the one hand his remarks constitute a commitment to the active life, as Spenser acknowledges (5.2), but on the other they reflect a spiritual trial, a moral dilemma such as Job endured. In these circumstances perseverance becomes a spiritual necessity, the quality without which none of the other virtues can succeed. When there is no external enemy to fight, 'prowesse' in the sense of physical courage is insufficient. Each quest is individually designed to test the very essence of the questor's moral character. Thus Gloriana's elusiveness becomes the touchstone of her champion's 'magnificence'.[38]

37 Fritz Saxl, 'Veritas Filia Temporis', *Philosophy and History: Essays Presented to Ernst Cassirer* (Oxford, 1936), pp. 197–222.

38 For the association between magnificence and glory see Robert Cummings, 'Spenser's "Twelve Private Morall Virtues"', *Spenser Studies* 8 (1990), pp. 35–59.

IV

The first account of Arthur's love for Gloriana falls into a conventional romance pattern, that of the inexperienced young man whose disdain for 'the idle name of loue' is justly punished by Cupid (I.9.10). The 'fresh bleeding wound' which 'rankles' in his 'riuen brest' is a component of the traditional lover's malady, as is the restlessness which accompanies it. However, the peculiarly ambivalent nature of the dream-vision, which defies the interpretation it invites, sets the experience apart. Its visionary nature seems contradicted by the physical evidence left behind, the 'pressed gras' where Gloriana lay. The terms in which her visit is described strongly suggest sexual contact ('Her daintie limbes full softly down did lay'), although Una regards the encounter as entirely honourable (9.16). Such ambiguity merely reflects the confusion in the hero's mind. Arthur is unsure 'whether dreames delude, or true it were' (14), while on a deeper level he fails to decide between the 'forced fury', which impels him 'by wayes yet never found', and the 'fatall deepe foresight', which may possibly be guiding his steps towards some predetermined goal (17).[39] Whereas George and Una emphasise Gloriana's spiritual qualities (ironically encapsulated in Arthur's allusion to her 'face diuine'), the Prince is left to wrestle with a 'passion' he can neither control nor conceal (16). Whatever he feels, it is far from the tranquillity of Platonic love.[40] In Book Two he desperately needs the sword of temperance to overcome the concupiscible and irascible passions represented by Pyrochles and Cymochles (8.40). The portrait of Gloriana on Guyon's shield impedes him during the combat (43), even though she is declared to be 'th' Idole of her makers great magnificence' (II.2.41).

The detail of the shield may be intended to remind us that in Geoffrey of Monmouth Arthur's own shield bore a likeness of the Blessed Virgin designed to keep his thoughts perpetually upon her (IX.4). The intriguing similarities between the Tudor 'cult' of the Virgin Queen and the discredited cult of the Virgin Mary could scarcely have escaped Spenser's notice.[41] In any case, Guyon's explanation of the portrait seems intended

39 See Richard A. McCabe, *The Pillars of Eternity: Time and Providence in 'The Faerie Queene'* (Dublin, 1989), pp. 154–84.

40 For Arthur's ambivalent sexual relationships see Sheila T. Cavanagh, '"Beauties Chace": Arthur and Women in *The Faerie Queene*', *The Passing of Arthur*, edd. Baswell and Sharpe, pp. 207–18. For a Lacanian reading of Arthurian desire see Elizabeth Bellamy, 'Reading Desire Backwards: Belatedness and Spenser's Arthur', *South Atlantic Quarterly* 88 (1989), 789–810.

41 Frances A. Yates, *Astraea: The Imperial Theme in the Sixteenth Century* (Harmondsworth, 1977), pp. 34–6, 78–9. 'Magnificence' is twice attributed to the Virgin Mary in Chaucer's *Canterbury Tales* (*Prioress's Prologue*, VII.474; *Second Nun's Prologue*, VIII.50) on the authority of Dante (*Paradiso*, XXXIII.20). Gawain was also Mary's knight, and bore 'in þe inore half of his

to elevate Arthur's attention in a Neo-Platonic manner from Gloriana's physical attributes to higher considerations:

> But if the beautie of her mind ye knew,
> That is her bountie, and imperiall powre,
> Thousand times fairer then her mortall hew,
> O how great wonder would your thoughts deuoure,
> And infinite desire into your spirite poure! (9.3)

Set in this context, Guyon's emphasis upon his monarch's 'chastitie' gains added force because he specifically relates it to the 'grace' and 'glory' which, in allegorical terms, constitute the goal of the quest. It is the order of *Maydenhed* he invites Arthur to join. This theme is reinforced in the House of Alma, 'a virgin bright; | That had not yet felt *Cupides* wanton rage' (9.18), on whose behalf Arthur opposes himself to the onslaughts of the five senses in canto eleven. Similarly, Antaeus, the Herculean giant upon whom Malegar is closely modelled, was allegorized from the time of Fulgentius onwards as the lust of the flesh.[42] This by no means exhausts his significance here, but it certainly forms part of it, and the combat bears all the marks of a psychomachia. The strange ineffectiveness of Arthur's sword (11.41) points in this direction, for its only previous limitation was its inability to hurt its own master (8.21). In opposing Malegar Arthur opposes his own fallen nature. Before joining combat he must first overcome impatience and impotence, 'his chiefest lets and authors of his harmes', through the assistance of grace, thereby 'riuiuing' thoughts 'of glorie and of fame' (31). By ensuring that Alma does not 'yet' fall prey to her sensual enemies, Arthur preserves the 'castle' of his own vulnerable humanity.

In Book Three the Prince rides in pursuit of Florimell hoping she may be Gloriana, 'or that his Faery Queene were such, as shee' (4.54). This qualification is important since it entails a derogation from Gloriana's true significance. As Arthur of Little Britain mistakes Florence for the Fairy Queen, so Arthur mistakes Florimell for Gloriana. By agreeing to aid the dwarf despite this disappointment, he returns from more earthly considerations, the hope of winning 'most goodly meede, the fairest Dame aliue' (1.18), to the 'eternall meede' of renown (5.11). Florimell, the perfection of physical beauty, is a far less suitable surrogate for Gloriana than Belphoebe, whose relationship with Timias (Honour)

schelde hir image depeynted' (*Sir Gawain and the Green Knight*, edd. J.R.R. Tolkien and E.V. Gordon, 2nd. ed. rev. Norman Davis (Oxford, 1967), 649, 1769). See further Davis's note on 649.

42 *Fulgentius the Mythographer*, tr. Leslie George Whitbread (Ohio, 1971), p. 69. See Philip Rollinson, 'Arthur, Malegar, and the Interpretation of *The Faerie Queene*', *Spenser Studies* 7, (1987), 103–21.

appears to reflect more accurately the nature of any future alliance between Arthur and his lady. It is Timias's decision to assail Florimell's foes rather than to seek the lady herself that leads to their encounter (1.18). Not surprisingly, he is called upon to exercise reason against passion (5. 44), the sharp distinction, drawn in canto six, between Amoret ('womanhed') and Belphoebe (virginity) serving to intensify the severely Platonic nature of the latter's makeup. In the following book the mere suspicion of Timias's affection for Amoret is sufficient to occasion his fall from grace and subsequent loss of identity (IV.7.36). If analogies may be drawn between knight and squire, it would be unfitting for Arthur to gain the 'goodly meede' of Florimell's physical beauty in Book Three, or indeed to play any large part in a book so concerned with sexual fulfilment.

The 'Legend of Friendship' provides a far more congenial habitat, and Arthur's activities there are largely concerned with the suppression of passion. His defeat of Corflambo sets his pursuit of Florimell in proper perspective, since the giant's 'infectious sight' and burning heart represent the effects and symptoms of carnal desire, 'ne was he euer vanquished afore' (8.48). The uniqueness of Arthur's victory (doubtless promoted by his earlier conquest of Malegar) marks another stage in his development. Moreover, his behaviour towards Amoret ('womanhed') is so impeccable as to recall the age of innocence when 'loyall loue had royall regiment, | And each vnto his lust did make a lawe' (8.30). Those were the Platonic days when 'beautie' was held to 'represent | The great Creatours owne resemblance bright' (8.32). Arthur himself is now depicted, not as the empassioned lover of Book One, but as one 'who goodly learned had of yore | The course of loose affection to forstall, | And Lawlesse lust to rule with reasons lore' (9.19).[43] He has consolidated the victories of Book Two, 'sith now of dayes such temperance is rare' (8.29). Amoret's private fears are, therefore, groundless. In Arthur's company, 'she was as safe as in a Sanctuary' (9.19). He cures the wounds she received in the suggestively sexual scuffle with Timias (8.20), offering the type of 'faithfull friendship', which now emerges as the highest degree in Spenser's hierarchy of love:

> For as the soule doth rule the earthly masse,
> And all the seruice of the bodie frame,
> So loue of soule doth loue of bodie passe,
> No lesse then perfect gold surmounts the meanest brasse. (9.2)

43 For Spenser's philosophy of love see Earle B. Fowler, *Spenser and the System of Courtly Love* (Louisville, 1934); *'Fowre Hymns', 'Epithalamion': A Study of Edmund Spenser's Doctrine of Love*, ed. Enid Welsford (New York, 1967), pp. 1–91.

Arthur reforms rather than destroys the castle of Corflambo because now it is his 'minde' that 'did trauell as with chylde, | Of his old loue, conceau'd in secret brest' (9.17). The subtle pun on 'conceau'd' exploits the Platonic paradox of the relationship between physical and intellectual desire. According to the *Symposium*, 'those whose procreancy is of the spirit . . . conceive and bear the things of the spirit . . . wisdom and all her sister virtues'. Ficino comments that 'the soul is as pregnant as the body, and they are both aroused to procreation by the stimuli of love. But some men, either on account of their nature or their training, are better equipped for offspring of the soul than for those of the body. Others, and certainly the majority of them, are the opposite. The former pursue heavenly love, the latter earthly'.[44] As one might expect, Scudamour's account of love and courtship assigns a special niche to those heroic spirits who, 'on chast vertue grounded their desire . . . which in their spirits kindling zealous fire, | Braue thoughts and noble deedes did euermore aspire' (10.26). The first such lover is Hercules upon whose various labours, long allegorized as spiritual trials, much of Arthur's activity in Book Five is modelled.[45]

Since Hercules was regarded as *vir scilicet omni virtute perfectus*—a man for all virtues—Spenser is at pains to establish the similarity with Arthur.[46] The Souldan, for example, is likened to the '*Thracian* Tyrant' who 'vnto his horses gaue his guests for meat' until finally destroyed by '*Alcides* great' (V.8.31). Following the suggestion in Plato's *Phaedrus*, Diomedes's horses were commonly interpreted as uncontrolled passions.[47] Throughout *The Faerie Queene* Spenser frequently uses the disposition of a knight's horse to suggest his frame of mind. Thus at the nadir of Arthur's fortunes in Book Three, his steed moves with 'lumpish pace', applying his steps to his rider's 'intent' (4.61). In the more calm reflective mood of Book Six, however, Arthur rides 'a softly pace with portance sad' (7.6). Again, Geryoneo is the son of Geryon, who 'fell | Vnder *Alcides* club', and whose 'fierce kyne' were similarly subdued (10.9–11). The triple-bodied Geryon was held to represent the eternal battle between flesh and spirit in the realms of the vegetative, sensitive, and intellectual souls. His 'kyne' were understood as *affectus corporeos et sensibiles*.[48]

44 *Plato: The Collected Dialogues*, edd. Edith Hamilton and Huntington Cairns (Princeton, 1961), p. 560; *Marsilio Ficino's Commentary on Plato's Symposium*, ed. and tr. Sears R. Jayne, Columbia, 1944, (University of Missouri Studies 19.1), p. 207.

45 Henry G. Lotspeich, *Classical Mythology in the Poetry of Edmund Spenser* (Princeton, 1932), pp. 68–9; Hughes, 'The Arthurs', pp. 205–11.

46 Coluccio Salutati, *De Laboribus Herculis*, ed. Berthold L. Ullman, 2 vols. (Zurich, 1951), I, 286.

47 *Phaedrus*, 246b-e; Salutati, *De Laboribus*, I, 286.

48 *Ibid.*, I, 328–9, 336–7.

Finally, the Malengin episode recalls aspects of Hercules's defeat of Cacus as recounted in the *Aeneid*, where Virgil specifically relates it to the story of Geryon (VIII.201–4). Cacus was assigned the sexual significance of *complexio* (coupling), and Malengin attempts to violate the Lady Samient (joining together) by stealing her 'from her self vnwarest' (9.12).[49] The relationship between love and justice is established in Book Five by Spenser's analysis of equity within the framework of Artegall's conflicting loves for Radigund and Britomart.

Arthur intervenes in the 'Legend of Ivstice' precisely at the point where Spenser opposes moral duty to the pleasures of sexual love, which 'strongly doth allure | The sense of man, and all his minde possesse' (8.1). Having previously succumbed to Radigund, as Hercules once did to Omphale (5.24), Artegall has now redeemed himself by making the famous 'choice of Hercules' in separating from Britomart in order to fulfil his quest (8.2).[50] He is now fit to meet his Herculean half-brother and proceed to the service of Mercilla, the foremost of Gloriana's surrogates. The magnificence of her state is particularly stressed (9. 22), and her court affords obvious parallels with that of Cleopolis. Belge has recourse to her much as Una and Irena have recourse to Gloriana, and the adventure is assigned after the fashion of the fairy court. In fact, all of Arthur's exploits in Book Five relate directly to Mercilla's service since Samient, his guide, is the queen's emissary. Here too, he learns to suppress even his natural compassion for womankind (Duessa), repenting of 'former fancies' in the interests of justice (9.49).[51]

The burden of Book Six is that 'vertues seat is deepe within the mynd' (pr.5), and 'great affaires in mynd' (5.41) duly preoccupy Arthur.[52] His reunion with Timias, now reconciled to Belphoebe, bespeaks a love of the qualities the squire embodies as much as of the man. Indeed, Timias is addressed in terms appropriate to Gloriana, 'my liefe, my life's desire' (5.23), in order to emphasise the association. Hence Arthur displays the correct form of *philotimia*, the virtue travestied in the person of Mammon's daughter Philotime (II.7.49). Similarly, it is Mammon's giant, Disdayne, that the Prince is called upon to fight (II.7.41). These connections with Book Two lend weight to the discomfiting in canto seven of Sir Turpine and his mercenary agents. Motivated by meed, they

49 Thomas K. Dunseath, *Spenser's Allegory of Justice in Book Five of 'The Faerie Queene'* (Princeton, 1968), pp. 198–204.

50 Erwin Panofsky, *Studies in Iconology* (London, 1939, rpt. 1972), pp. 64–5; Ronald G. Witt, *Hercules at the Crossroads: The Life, Works, and Thought of Coluccio Salutati* (Durham, N. Carolina, 1983), pp. 216–7.

51 For the historical dimension of this episode see Richard A. McCabe, 'The Masks of Duessa: Spenser, Mary Queen of Scots, and James VI', *English Literary Renaissance* 17 (1987), 224–42.

52 For the quest in Book Six see Nohrnberg, *Analogy*, pp. 655–75.

are Mammon's children. At this stage of the quest Arthur must value nothing worldly: his aim is spiritual reformation. Thus he consigns Timias and Serena to the hermit (5.41) and himself reforms Sir Enias (8.4).

The theme of love is raised more directly in the encounter with Mirabel, who has fallen victim to Scorn and Disdaine ('sib' to Orgoglio, Arthur's first opponent), having previously subjected others to the same attitudes. Arthur shows intense interest in a history which, in part, resembles his own. In his youth he too had fallen foul of Cupid:

> That idle name of loue, and louers life . . .
> I euer scornd, and ioyd to stirre vp strife,
> In middest of their mournfull Tragedy,
> Ay wont to laugh, when them I heard to cry,
> And blow the fire, which them to ashes brent. (I.9.10)

Now he 'hearkens wisely' to Mirabel's tale, 'and wondred much at *Cupids* iudgement wise' (8.25). His admission that 'the God is iust' marks the influence of Mercilla on his attitudes towards passion, 'for were no law in loue . . . His kingdome would continue but a while' (23). Only repentance and retribution may release Mirabel, and there is a hidden justice too in what Arthur describes as the 'labour'—a fittingly Herculean term—he must himself endure (I.9.15).[53]

As he proceeds from book to book, Arthur develops and deepens his character. In his youth Timon (whose name is cognate with Timias's, from τιμή, honour) had taught him to 'subdew' emotion to reason, thereby avoiding the pain of love. The immediate result was a loss of human sympathy. Punished with inevitable experience, Arthur must seek to regain a refined sense of reason, one that both acknowledges and respects the virtue of lawful desire. Thus Belphoebe demands of Timias not the suppression, but the elevation of love. The tendency is towards a Platonic emotion, a love of the 'mynd' more than the body. Union with Gloriana must ultimately prove as spiritual an affair as the 'marriage' of George and Una. Paradoxically, the more elevated the love, the more elusive the physical Gloriana. The ideal subsumes the woman. One recalls George's caution, 'yf *liuing* man mote worthy be, to be her liefe' (I.9.17), in a book which disconcertingly juxtaposes its image of the 'young Prince, when first to armes he fell', with a reference to his death (I.7.36). As in the case of Hercules, the ultimate 'glory' lies beyond the labours of the active life.[54] The apparent fragmentation of Prince Arthur's courtly

53 His hardships are travestied by those of the wanton Squire of Dames also humorously compared to '*Alcides* labours' (III.7.61).

54 In Seneca's *Hercules Oetaeus* the deified hero declares *iam virtus mihi | in astra et ipsos fecit ad superos iter* (1942–3). Spenser compares the flames of Oeta to those endured by St George in his combat with the dragon of death (I. 11. 27).

'fashioning' belies the continuity of its design, but in so doing constitutes a perfect structural expression of the poem's studied inconclusiveness. Whereas Castiglione's courtiers rejoice in their own accomplishments, the 'great affaires' that Arthur bears 'in mynd' constantly distract him from those already realized. The diverse incidents of his career are unified in his person, not in his perception, for despite his frantic activity he regards himself—paradoxically—as the instrument of greater forces, fashioned rather than self-fashioning. Such is the agitated ethos of the work that every vision prompts revision, every destination is a new point of departure.

The Meaning of Spenser's Chastity as the Fairest of Virtues

GERALD MORGAN

> Non potest esse simpliciter vera justitia aut vera castitas si desit ordinatio debita ad finem quae est per caritatem, quantumcumque aliquis se recte circa alia habeat. (Aquinas)

> O welcom pure-ey'd Faith, white-handed Hope,
> Thou hovering Angel girt with golden wings,
> And thou unblemish't form of Chastity. (Milton)

I

It is not possible to discover an author's meaning in an allegorical poem of the scope of *The Faerie Queene* merely from the inherent suggestiveness of the figure itself. What is also necessary is a knowledge of the context of its application.[1] It is for this reason that Spenser's reference of the moral basis of his allegory to 'Aristotle and the rest' (II, 486) in the Letter to Ralegh is of such vital importance.[2] I have attempted to demonstrate the coherence of the moral allegories of the Legends of Holiness and Temperance in terms of the philosophical system of Scholastic Aristotelianism in two previous articles,[3] and here I attempt to do the same in respect of the Legend of Chastity.

It may seem at first sight that the Legend of Chastity lends support to a Renaissance neo-Platonic rather than a Scholastic Aristotelian interpretation of Spenser's moral allegory. The pursuit of Florimell by Arthur and Guyon is inspired by the 'hope to win thereby | Most goodly meede, the fairest Dame alive' (III.1.18), that is, it is 'beauties chace' (III.1.19), and again the 'chace of beautie excellent' (III.4.45). Arthur and Guyon

1 On this point see P. Rollinson, *Classical Theories of Allegory and Christian Culture* (Pittsburgh and Brighton, 1981), pp. 19–22.

2 References to *The Faerie Queene* and also to the Letter to Ralegh are throughout to J.C. Smith, *Spenser's Faerie Queene*, 2 vols., Oxford, 1909.

3 'Holiness as the First of Spenser's Aristotelian Moral Virtues', *Modern Language Review* 81 (1986), 817–37 and 'The Idea of Temperance in the Second Book of *The Faerie Queene*', *Review of English Studies*, 37 (1986), 11–39. For the historical justification of a Scholastic Aristotelian reading of *The Faerie Queene* see 'Holiness as the First of Spenser's Aristotelian Moral Virtues', pp. 818–20.

are moved by 'that sweet fit, that doth true beautie love' (III.3.1). The definition of love as the desire of beauty is the language of Ficinian neo-Platonism, as we may see from his commentary on Plato's *Symposium*: *Cum amorem dicimus, pulchritudinis desiderium intelligite. Haec enim apud omnes philosophos amoris definitio est* (*In Convivium Platonis de amore commentarium* I.4).[4] The universal agreement among philosophers to which Ficino refers is not always readily apparent in their formulations. Aquinas specifies the good as the essential cause of love (*ST*, 1*a* 2*ae*, 27.1), so that it becomes necessary to explain that concealed within this formulation is the assumption of a real identity of the good and the beautiful.[5] The emphasis on love as ordered immediately to beauty is undeniably characteristic of Renaissance neo-Platonism. But Ficino's claim for the universality of the truth thus expressed may serve as a warning that the formulation of love as the desire of beauty does not imply in every text the presence of the systematic neo-Platonic philosophy of love. Attempts to read a Ficinian distinction between a heavenly and an earthly Venus, that is, between the desire of contemplating beauty and the desire of generating beauty (*In Convivium* II.7), into the allegory of the Legend of Chastity are notable for their ingenuity rather than their coherence.[6] The fact is that Spenser focuses on the moral distinction between chastity and lust that arises from the natural movement of love in the soul. The influence of his neo-Platonic inheritance is apparent in his formulation of this distinction, for he refuses the name of love to any love that is not virtuous. Thus 'love does alwayes bring forth bounteous deeds' (III.1.49), and the flame that is called love is:

4 Reference is to Ficino, *Opera*, 2nd ed., 2 vols., (Basle, 1576), II, 1322.

5 Reference to the *Summa Theologiae* is to the edition of T. Gilby and others, 61 vols (London, 1964–81). Aquinas follows Dionysius in his acceptance of the real identity of the good and the beautiful (*ST*, 1*a* 2*ae*, 27.1 *arg*. 3 and *ad* 3). The notional distinction of the good and the beautiful is expressed by Aquinas in terms of the final and formal causes of love (*ST*, 1*a* 5.4 *ad* 1).

6 R.Ellrodt, *Neoplatonism in the Poetry of Spenser* (Geneva, 1960), has demonstrated that the interpretations of Belphoebe as the heavenly Venus (M.Y. Hughes), and of Britomart as the earthly Venus (C.W. Lemmi), and also the identification of the Garden of Adonis with an exemplary realm of immaterial forms (J.W. Bennett), cannot be defended other than on the grounds of the incoherence of Spenser's allegory and the eccentricity of his neo-Platonism (esp. pp. 48–9, 74–5). Moreover, he has also shown that the doctrines of the transiency of forms and the eternity of first matter, that is, created matter (III.6.36–8) do not go beyond the medieval Platonism derived from the *Timaeus* and are 'not inconsistent either with traditional Christianity or with the prevailing Aristotelianism' (p. 72).

Not that same, which doth base affections move
In brutish minds, and filthy lust inflame,
But that sweet fit, that doth true beautie love,
And choseth vertue for his dearest Dame,
Whence spring all noble deeds and never dying fame. (III.3.1)[7]

The distinction between chastity and lust that is made here can indeed be represented symbolically by two kinds of Venus. These two Venuses, however, are not those of Ficino's *In Convivium*, but of Boccaccio's glosses to his description of the temple of Venus in the *Teseida* (VII.50–66):

> La quale Venere è doppia, perciò che l'una si può e dee intendere per ciascuno onesto e licito disiderio, sì come è disiderare d'avere moglie per avere figliuoli, e simili; a questo (. . .) La seconda Venere è quella per la quale ogni lascivia è disiderata, e che volgarmente è chiamata dea d'amore; e di questa disegna qui l'autore il tempio e l'altre cose circustanti ad esso, come nel testo appare. (p. 463)[8]

To recognize the central importance of the moral distinction between chastity and lust is not to argue for the irrelevance of metaphysical considerations in the Legend of Chastity. Indeed, it is only by resort to metaphysical considerations that we can explain both the relation of chastity to temperance and the distinction of chastity and temperance in the allegorical fiction. Chastity as a moral virtue is simply a species of temperance (*ST*, *2a 2ae*, 143), and temperance ranks beneath justice and fortitude in the hierarchy of cardinal virtues (*ST*, *1a 2ae*, 66.4). Yet Spenser announces the Legend of Chastity with the declaration that chastity is 'that fairest vertue, farre above the rest' (III.pr.1), and proceeds at once to justify these words in his fiction by displaying the decisive superiority of the Knight of Chastity to the Knight of Temperance (III.1.4–12). Indeed, not only is the superiority of Britomart to Guyon evident, but also her superiority to Red Cross when she comes to his aid at Castle Joyous (III.1.20–30). Thus Britomart disposes of five of the

7 The neo-Platonic language of this stanza obscures the consistency of Spenser's argument, for it is the same natural inclination to love in the human soul that results in good and evil loves alike. Dante's Virgil acknowledges the twofold potentiality of natural love in a more straightforward way: *'Quinci comprender puoi ch'esser convene | amor sementa in voi d'ogne virtute | e d'ogne operazion che merta pene'* (*Purgatorio*, XVII. 103–5). Reference is to G. Petrocchi, *La Commedia secondo l'antica vulgata*, 4 vols., Milan, 1966–7.

8 Reference is to the edition of the *Teseida* by Alberto Limentani (*Tutte le opere di Giovanni Boccaccio*, ed. Vittore Branca, II (Verona, 1964), pp. 229–664. The glosses have been translated by P.Boitani, *Chaucer and Boccaccio*, Oxford, 1977 (Medium Aevum Monographs, New Series 8), pp. 200–10.

assailant knights, whereas Red Cross manages to dispose of only one (III.1.29). Her superiority is awesome when it is remembered that Red Cross stands for the virtue of holiness or religion, the highest of the moral virtues (*ST*, *2a 2ae*, 81.6).[9] Such perfection of chastity among the virtues can only be explained in terms of charity, and that this is a possible meaning for chastity is evident from Milton's use of chastity in just this sense in *Comus* (215). But charity is a theological, not a moral virtue. If we are to understand the moral allegory of the Legend of Chastity, it is necessary to recognize not only the distinction between the theological and the moral virtues, but also the nature of the relationship between charity and the moral virtues.

Virtuous acts are acts that are ordered to their due standard, and this is twofold, namely God and human reason. God is the ultimate standard, to which the measure of reason must itself be referred (*ST*, *2a 2ae*, 23.6). Thus any Christian virtue is directed first towards God as the primary good, and then on secondary goods in their relation to God. This distinction is significantly made by Dante's Virgil in expounding the meaning of natural and rational love (*Purgatorio*, XVII.97–102). In accordance with this distinction there are theological virtues, infused by God and ordered to a supernatural end, namely union with God, and there are moral virtues, acquired by repeated acts and ordered to a natural end, namely conduct in accordance with right reason. It is evident that the theological virtues are superior to the moral virtues (*ST*, *2a 2ae*, 23.6). Here, then, is the reason for Guyon's swift discomfiture, for the moral virtue of temperance can be no match for the higher power infused by God. The divine infusion of theological virtue is signified in the allegory by the instrument of Britomart's victory, an 'enchaunted speare' (III.1.9), for 'the secret vertue of that weapon keene, | . . . mortall puissance mote not withstond' (III.1.10).[10] The description of chastity as 'that fairest vertue, farre above the rest' elevates it even among the theological virtues. Thus is charity

9 See my article, 'Holiness as the First of Spenser's Aristotelian Moral Virtues', p. 821.

10 It may be noted here that the doctrine of infused theological virtues necessitates the assumption of infused moral virtues proportioned to them (*ST*, 1a 2ae 63.3 *ad* 1). Aquinas explains this necessity as follows: . . . *virtutes theologicae sufficienter nos ordinant in finem supernaturalem, secundum quamdam inchoationem, quantum scilicet ad ipsum Deum immediate. Sed oportet quod per alias virtutes infusas perficiatur anima circa alias res, in ordine tamen ad Deum*' (*ST*, *1a 2ae*, 63.3 *ad* 2). The proper objects of the infused moral virtues differ from those of the acquired moral virtues. Thus the health of the body is the proper object of the acquired moral virtue of temperance and results in moderation in eating and drinking, whereas the subjection of the body to the soul is the proper object of the infused moral virtue of temperance and results in fasting (*ST*, *1a 2ae*, 63.4). In this way chaste married love and virginity can be distinguished, so that by chastity Spenser can be seen to intend the acquired and not the infused moral virtue.

elevated by St Paul (I Cor. 13: 13), and the apostle is followed by Aquinas who writes that *caritas est excellentior fide et spe, et per consequens omnibus aliis virtutibus* (*ST*, *2a 2ae*, 23.6). Chastity as charity is thus a supernatural virtue beyond the reach of reason; hence Glauce is led to observe to the impassioned Britomart that 'love can higher stye, | Then reasons reach, and oft hath wonders donne' (III.2.36). This truth is most dramatically realized in the Legend of Chastity in the passage through the 'flaming fire, ymixt with smouldry smoke' (III.11.21) that bars entrance to the castle in which Amoret is imprisoned. The flames give way before the 'utmost might' of Britomart, 'and did their force revolt' (III.11.25), but not before the 'greedy will, and envious desire' (III.11.26) of Scudamour. Britomart shows the higher power of love that is necessary for the conquest of lust. Dante too has to make his way through the flames on the seventh terrace of purgatory where the sin of lust is purged. The prompting of Virgil (or reason) is not in itself sufficient, and the inspiration of Beatrice (or love) has to be called upon (*Purgatorio*, XXVII.19–54).

Chastity is understood throughout the Legend of Chastity in terms of its order to the ultimate end, that is, God. Hence Britomart is moved to love Artegall through no chance look of a 'wandring eye', but through a glance directed by 'the streight course of heavenly destiny, | Led with eternall providence' (III.3.24). Nevertheless the central concern of Spenser's poem remains moral and not theological. It is for this very reason, indeed, that Book III is called the Legend of Chastity. This predominating moral interest becomes explicable when we consider the nature of the relationship between charity and the moral virtues. Now the form of a moral act is the end, for the principle of moral action is the will. But it is evident from the distinction of theological and moral virtue that acts have a twofold reference to an end, namely the ultimate end of infused virtue and the proximate end of acquired virtue. Thus we can view moral acts from within the limited frame of reference of human reason, and these acts, such as acts of temperance and justice, can accordingly possess a limited goodness. But the perfection of the moral act of temperance requires that it be directed also to the ultimate end, that is, God. It is so directed by charity, so that charity can be seen to be the form of temperance, as indeed it is of all the virtues:

> Manifestum est autem . . . quod per caritatem ordinantur actus omnium aliarum virtutum ad ultimum finem. Et secundum hoc ipsa dat formam actibus omnium aliarum virtutum. Et pro tanto dicitur esse forma virtutum, nam et ipsae virtutes dicuntur in ordine ad actus formatos. (*ST*, *2a 2ae*, 23.8)[11]

11 Charity is not the form of the virtues in the sense of an exemplar or substantial form, *sed magis effective, inquantum, scilicet, omnibus formam imponit* (*ST*, *2a 2ae*, 23.8 *ad* 1).

Accordingly, the act of the moral virtue of chastity can be described as an act of charity formally and an act of chastity materially.[12] The interest of Spenser in chastity *materialiter* is first of all indicated by the fact that he shows not only the superiority of chastity informed by charity to temperance considered in itself as a moral virtue, but also the essential harmony of chastity and temperance. Thus Britomart's victory over Guyon is followed at once by 'reconcilement . . . betweene them knit, | Through goodly temperance, and affection chaste' (III.1.12). In the same way the fundamental unity of chastity and holiness is established when Red Cross in his turn comes to the aid of Britomart during the commotion at Castle Joyous in the middle of the night (III.1.66). Moreover, Spenser goes to great lengths to show that Britomart's victory over Guyon is due to the power of chastity in itself and to no shortcoming in Guyon (whose own perfected temperance has just been vindicated in the destruction of the Bower of Bliss). Indeed, the poet himself, the Palmer, and Arthur are united in the desire to vindicate the name of 'good Sir *Guyon*' (III.1.5). The Palmer fears Guyon's 'toward perill and untoward blame' (III.1.9), and Arthur 'laid the blame, not to his carriage, | But to his starting steed, that swaru'd asyde, | And to the ill purveyance of his page' (III.1.11).[13] The poet expresses the universal sense of dismay that is to be felt when a knight so noble as Sir Guyon is discomfited:

> Ah gentlest knight, that ever armour bore,
> Let not thee grieve dismounted to have beene,
> And brought to ground, that never wast before;
> For not thy fault, but secret powre unseene,
> That speare enchaunted was, which layd thee on the greene.
> (III.1.7)

The title of Book III is the Legend of Chastity and not the Legend of Charity because its subject is human love and not heavenly love, albeit 'ykindled first above, | Emongst th'eternall spheres and lamping sky' (III.3.1).[14] This moral preoccupation explains the importance in the allegory of Belphoebe and Amoret, for they represent the necessary moral

12 The distinction between the formal and material dimensions of a moral act is explained by Aquinas at *ST*, *1a 2ae*, 13.1 in reference to the virtue of fortitude: *Si enim aliquis actum fortitudinis exerceat propter Dei amorem, actus quidem ille materialiter est fortitudinis, formaliter vero caritatis.*

13 A.C. Hamilton, *Edmund Spenser: The Faerie Queene* (London and New York, 1977), comments that 'while being tactful, Arthur tells the truth: Guyon is defeated because he failed to control his steed, i.e. his passions' (p. 307). This interpretation cannot be accepted. Not every element in an allegorical fiction has metaphorical status.

14 As Spenser uses chastity to include the informing power of charity, so medieval writers can use charity inclusively with reference to the moral virtue of chastity. Thus Gower ends the *Confessio Amantis* with praise of 'thilke love which that is |

distinction between virginity and chaste married love. Thus the one is 'upbrought in perfect Maydenhed' and the other is 'upbrought in goodly womanhed' (III.6.28). The notions of virginity and chaste sexual love are linked in the experience of honourable wives, and Spenser signifies the two levels of experience in his representation of Britomart. We learn of Britomart's destiny as the lover of Artegall (III.2.17–27) and as the progenitress of the race of Britons (III.3.21–50), but we know her throughout the action of the Legend of Chastity as 'this Briton Mayd' (III.2.4), 'most noble Virgin' (III. 3.21), 'the bold Virgin' (III.11.13), and 'the brave Maid' (III.12.27). But the subject of Book III is not virginity as such, for virginity belongs to the level of heroic rather than ordinary virtue:

> Hoc autem quod est conservare se immunem ab experimento venereae voluptatis habet quamdam excellentiam laudis supra hoc quod est conservare se immunem ab inordinatione venereae voluptatis. Et ideo virginitas est quaedam specialis virtus habens se ad castitatem sicut magnificentia se habet ad liberalitatem. (*ST*, *2a 2ae*, 152.3)

The fact that Chrysogone gave birth first to Belphoebe and 'bore in like cace | Faire *Amoretta* in the second place' (III.6.4) suggests the superiority of the state of virginity to the state of matrimony (*ST*, *2a 2ae*, 152.4). Belphoebe indeed 'standeth on the highest staire | Of th'honorable stage of womanhead' (III.5.54). But we are to look to Elizabeth I, the Virgin Queen herself, for such an image of heroic virtue (III.pr.5), rather than to Britomart. And indeed, it is Amoret, and not Belphoebe, who occupies our attention at the crisis of the Legend of Chastity. The reason is, as Spenser well knows, that it is 'a lesson too too hard for living clay, | From love in course of nature to refraine' (III.4.26). Spenser's chastity is thus above all an ideal of married love. The real significance of chastity informed by charity is to be found in the image of Charissa in the Legend of Holiness. Charissa is portrayed in terms of maternal fecundity, for 'her necke and breasts were ever open bare, | That ay thereof her babes might sucke their fill' (I.10.30). Such a conception of chastity is an orthodox expression of the Christian ideal of marriage, ordained 'for the procreation of children, to be brought up in the fear and nurture of the Lord' (*The Book of Common Prayer*).

It is not to be doubted, then, that the meaning of chastity in the Legend of Chastity is the moral virtue of chastity as informed by charity. At the

Withinne a mannes herte affermed, | And stant of charite confermed' (VIII. 3162–64). As E. Porter has pointed out in 'Gower's Ethical Microcosm and Political Macrocosm', (*Gower's Confessio Amantis: Responses and Reassessments*, edited by A.J. Minnis (Woodbridge, 1983), pp. 135–62, at 162), 'it would be wrong to read this praise of *caritas* as a renunciation of human love', for 'it is rather the culmination of the ethical teaching that Gower has been putting forward throughout his poem.'

same time, we may well wonder what a pagan philosopher like Aristotle has to say on the subject of charity. Here it becomes necessary to interpret the reference to 'Aristotle and the rest' in the Letter to Ralegh in terms of the christianized Aristotelianism of the medieval schoolmen, and, above all, Aquinas. It is instructive in reading Aquinas on charity (*ST*, *2a 2ae*, 34–46) to find that the Philosopher's presence there is no less pervasive than elsewhere, for charity is expounded by Aquinas in terms of Aristotle's friendship, and hence references to Books VIII and IX of the *Nicomachean Ethics* abound.

II

It now remains to explain the nature of the moral virtue of chastity as informed by charity, and our explanation may begin with a consideration of the specifically moral dimensions of the virtue. This method is justified by the fact that it is the procedure which Spenser himself adopts in the Legend of Chastity. In any case, the definition of the moral virtue of chastity is sufficiently complicated in itself, for chastity cannot be understood apart from the distinctions of natural and rational love that are assumed by Boccaccio in the glosses to the description of the temple of Venus in the *Teseida*, and explicitly formulated by Dante's Virgil in *Purgatorio*, XVII. 91–139 and XVIII. 1–75.

Natural love is the inclination of all created beings to God as the source and term of their movement, and hence a necessity of the nature of man. But natural love and rational love are not simply opposed principles, although the one is necessary and the other is free, for natural love is the source of rational love. By rational love we are to understand the exercise of choice by an intellectual being in the light of its natural inclination (*ST*, *1a 2ae*, 26.1). Thus Spenser refers to love as a 'kindly flame' (IV.pr.2) and, recognizing no freedom in respect of it, has Glauce refer to 'the tyranny of love' (III.2.40). There is no guilt in such love, for natural love is, as Virgil puts it, *sempre sanza errore* (*Purgatorio*, XVII.94). Indeed, it is manifest that resistance to such natural love is evil, so that it is fitting that Marinell who 'ever from faire Ladies love did fly' (III.4.26) should be humbled by the Knight of Chastity, who wounds him in 'his left side' (III.4.16). Thus the God of Love takes vengeance on Troilus for his 'surquidrie and foul presumpcioun' (*Troilus and Criseyde*, I.213);[15] thus 'fell proud *Marinell* upon the pretious shore' (III.4.17).[16]

15 Reference is to *The Riverside Chaucer*, 3rd ed., edd. L.D. Benson and others, Oxford, 1988.

16 Ellrodt rightly notes that it is not virginity that is condemned in Marinell, 'but insensibility to human affections for a wrong motive. Marinell does not dedicate

Natural love has to be understood in its relation to the complex nature of man, in whom are to be found both sensible and intelligible principles of loving. It is necessary, in other words, to distinguish between the sensitive or animal appetite which follows sensation and the intellectual appetite or will which follows understanding (*ST*, 1*a* 2*ae*, 6.2 and ad 1). The movements of the sensitive appetite or passions of the soul are properly subject to reason and will (*ST*, 1*a*, 81.3), and are judged good or bad in so far as they are in or out of conformity with reason and will. As judged in themselves (by neo-Platonists and Aristotelians alike) they are neither good nor bad, and are certainly not to be deplored. Hence Britomart does not scorn Malecasta in so far as she takes her to be genuinely moved by passion born of goodwill, 'for great rebuke it is, love to despise, | Or rudely sdeigne a gentle harts request' (III.1.55). Passions such as love and desire are called natural because they share in the inclination of natural appetite (*ST*, 1*a* 2*ae*, 41.3), and hence in the goodness of created being. This is presumably what Spenser has in mind when he refers to 'naturall affection faultlesse' (IV.pr.2). Likewise Glauce can find 'nothing straunge' in the 'affection' which so moves Britomart (III.2.40).[17] Indeed, the presence of passion rightly ordered to reason adds to the moral perfection of an act as expressive of the whole nature of man (*ST*, 1*a* 2*ae*, 24.3).

We turn, then, to a consideration of passion in relation to reason. What characterizes rational love is that it is free, and this freedom is expressed above all in the act of choice. Thus Red Cross would prefer death sooner than submit to the force which seeks to make him change his beloved (III.1.24), and Britomart comes to his aid, urging in the language of Chaucer's Franklin (*Canterbury Tales*, V.764–6), by that love may not 'be compeld by maisterie' (III.1.25). As a result of the freedom of choice there are two kinds of rational love, that is, two ways in which passion can be related to reason (signified by the two Venuses of Boccaccio's glosses). The first kind of rational love is a virtuous love by which passion is conformed to the rule of reason. Such is indeed the virtue of temperance (of which chastity is a species), and it consists in the perfect blending of reason and the passions of desire and pleasure of touch (hence the mixing of water and wine is an emblem of temperance). Britomart is 'the chaste damzell' (III.1.53), who demonstrates her chastity in the confrontation with Malecasta in canto 1. Thus we are

himself to a religious life, but to the acquisition of riches. Christianity has never exalted virginity apart from a religious purpose' (*Neoplatonism in the Poetry of Spenser*, p. 56, n. 55).

17 The references to Britomart's 'bleeding bowels' (III.2.39) and 'troubled bowels' (III.4.8) establish that the passion is the passion of love or desire. Thus Plato locates the inferior irrational part of the soul or appetite in the liver (*Timaeus*, 70D–72B).

assured of her chastity before we are shown the violence of her passions in canto 2. Furthermore, it is made clear that these strong passions will be chastely reciprocated by the knight who bears on his shield 'a crowned litle Ermilin' (III.2.25), which is an emblem of chastity. The end of the virtue of chastity is procreation, and its proper moral context is matrimony. Hence in canto 3 Spenser looks forward to the union of Britomart and Artegall, and 'most famous fruits of matrimoniall bowre' (III.3.3). Such reasonable love is characterized by the presence of other virtues, and especially of faithfulness. Thus Red Cross loves with an unalterable love 'the truest one on ground' (III.1.24), and Britomart will not from her 'owne love remove' (III.1.28). Spenser is already preparing us for the 'ruefull history' of Amoret, whom Busirane 'would forced have to have forlore | Her former love, and stedfast loialty' (III.6.53).

The second kind of rational love is one in which passion is at odds with reason and overwhelms the reason. This is the vice of lust, and it is characterized by servitude, for, as Boethius explains, 'the laste servage' is when the souls of men 'ben yeven to vices and han ifalle fro the possessioun of hir propre resoun' (*De consolatione philosophiae,* V.pr.2. 32–34).[18] Thus Malecasta's law of love (III.1.26–27) is a principle of servitude, enforcing infidelity. This is the evil love represented by Boccaccio in the temple of Venus, and hence it exhibits the same characteristics as Boccaccio has systematically expounded. Venus is to be found *in più secreta* | *parte del tempio* and in a place that is *oscur nel primo gire* (*Teseida*, VII.63–64). Boccaccio explains that this is because *coloro li quali adoperano male, odiano la luce* (p. 471). This is the Venus shown on the tapestry adorning the walls of the inner room of Castle Joyous (III.1.34–38). Thus she leads Adonis 'into a secret shade | . . . from bright heavens vew' (III.1.35), where 'she secretly would search each daintie lim' (III.1.36), and 'joyd his love in secret unespyde' (III.1.37). Such secrecy is the mark of Paridell's courtship of Hellenore. The evil nature of such secrecy is underlined by the use of the strongly pejorative 'privy' (the word used by Chaucer of Venus's secret abode in *The Parliament of Fowls*, 260). Thus Hellenore sent to Paridell a 'firie dart, whose hed | Empoisned was with privy lust' (III.9.28), and Paridell in return 'ever privily | In speaking, many false belgardes at her let fly' (III.9.52). The darkness of evening 'fit for lovers stealth' (III.10.12) makes possible the execution of the plan by which these lustful desires can be fulfilled, and the lovers take their leave of Malbecco's castle under the 'safe conduct' of 'Night, the patronesse of love-stealth faire' (III.10.16). The same associations are persistently developed within the House of Busirane, and especially in the tapestry in the outermost room depicting the gods who had fallen victim to Cupid (III.11.28–46). The 'goodly arras' is so tightly woven with gold

18 Reference is to Chaucer's translation.

and silk 'that the rich metall lurked privily' (III.11.28). Neptune hangs down his head, 'for privy love his brest empierced had' (III.11.41), and 'mighty *Mars*' is overcome by 'womanish teares, and . . . unwarlike smarts, | Privily moystening his horrid cheek' (III.11.44). The Masque of Cupid itself is fittingly set in the midst of darkness, when 'chearelesse Night ycovered had | Faire heaven with an universall cloud' (III.12.1).

In the *Teseida* (VII.64), Boccaccio has placed Ricchezza to keep watch at the door of the secret place in which Venus is to be found, and explains in his gloss that this is because *voluttuosa vita senza riccheza non potersi avere né lungamente seguire* (p.471). Here is an explanation of the repeated association of lust and wealth in the Legend of Chastity. Thus Malecasta is rightly called 'the *Lady of delight*' (III.1.31), for it is pleasure and not goodness that is the object of her desires, and the pursuit of such pleasure is supported by enormous wealth. 'Living wit . . . cannot display | The royall riches and exceeding cost, | Of every pillour and of every post' (III.1.32) in the great chamber of Castle Joyous, whilst the 'royaltee | And rich purveyance' of the inner room to which it leads 'might uneath be red' (III.1.33). Malecasta herself is to be found 'sitting on a sumptuous bed, | That glistred all with gold and glorious shew' (III. 1.41). By contrast Britomart despises the 'rich aray | Of pearles and pretious stones of great assay' (III.4.18) that are in her power after the defeat of Marinell.

Boccaccio's Venus holds Lascivia by the hand (*Teseida*, VII.66), and this signifies the fact that *l'opere de' voluttuosi non solamente in lussuria consistere, ma ancora in lascivia; la quale lascivia intende essere il basciare, il toccare e il cianciare e 'l motteggiare e l'altre scioccheze che intorno a ciò si fanno* (p.471). Such wantonness is represented in Castle Joyous by Malecasta's six liegemen—Gardante, Parlante, Jocante, Basciante, Bacchante, and Noctante (III.1.45). And whereas Britomart rightly does not condemn the force of passion in Malecasta, she and Red Cross are no less rightly united in disdaining 'such lascivious disport', and in loathing 'the loose demeanure of that wanton sort' (III.1.40).

III

Chastity, as Spenser represents it in the Legend of Chastity, is not limited to the virtue opposed to the bad Venus of Boccaccio's allegorical glosses. It now becomes necessary, therefore, to turn to that part of its definition which will explain its superiority to the moral virtue of temperance. This is the informing virtue of charity, which Aquinas defines as *amicitia quaedam . . . hominis ad Deum* (*ST*, 2*a* 2*ae*, 23.1). Aquinas identifies three elements as constituting such friendship, namely goodwill, mutual loving, and fellowship, and Spenser's allegory of chastity can be considered in respect of each of these elements in turn.

The definition of goodwill is developed by reference to the distinction between the love of friendship (*amor amicitiae*) and the love of desire (*amor concupiscentiae*). By the love of friendship love is directed towards the person one wishes good, and by the love of desire love is directed towards the good that one wishes for someone. In loving, therefore, one can love the object of one's love for its own sake, or for the sake of some good such as pleasure or gain that one can derive from it (*ST*, *1a 2ae*, 26.4). Thus the love of friendship is to be distinguished from the love of desire precisely because it is based on goodwill: *Dicendum quod secundum Philosophum* [*Ethics*, VIII.2], *non quilibet amor habet rationem amicitiae, sed amor qui est cum benevolentia, quando scilicet sic amamus aliquem ut ei bonum velimus* (*ST*, *2a 2ae*, 23.1). Those who love by the love of friendship are called upon to suffer for the sake of others. Consequently, such love demands great courage if it is to be exercised. Hence Britomart as the Knight of Chastity has to overcome the fears that stand in the way of the love of friendship. It is her fearlessness that is identified first by Spenser (before indeed the identification of name and sex), for the knight who unhorses Guyon comes 'fiercely forward . . . withouten dread' (III.1.5).

The fearlessness of Britomart is emphasized by the contrast with Florimell who suddenly appears 'out of the thickest brush' in full flight, her face 'through feare as white as whales bone' (III.1.15). Florimell has every reason to fear, for she is pursued by 'a griesly Foster . . . | Breathing out beastly lust her to defile' (III.1.17). But she becomes so agitated by fear that she is unable to distinguish friend from foe. Her 'needlesse dreed' (III.4.48) makes her flee from Arthur, 'affraid of him, as feend of hell' (III.4.47). By her unreasoning fears she is led away from safety into further perils and further flight (III.7.1–27, and 8.20–43). But (unlike Chaucer's Criseyde) she is not in the end undone by fear, for 'eternall thraldome was to her more liefe, | Then losse of chastitie, or chaunge of love' (III.8.42).

The need for courage if the value of chaste love is to be upheld explains why Spenser focuses so insistently upon the boldness of Britomart. Thus she continues on her quest after Arthur, Guyon, and Timias have departed in pursuit of Florimell and the forester 'with stedfast courage and stout hardiment' (III.1.19). Scudamour recognizes the 'huge heroicke magnanimity' (III.11.19) that enables her to take up the struggle on his behalf.[19] Boldness is not rashness, and Britomart does not attempt the passage through the flames without considering that 'daunger without discretion to attempt, | Inglorious and beastlike is' (III.11.23). Once entered within the

19 Magnanimity is classified by Aquinas among the parts of courage (*ST*, *2a 2ae*, 128). Dante indeed uses magnanimity as a synonym of courage in the *Convivio*, IV. 26.7: *fortezza, o vero magnanimitate, la quale vertute mostra lo loco dove è da fermarsi e da pugnare*. Reference is to *Il Convivio*, edd. G. Busnelli and G. Vandelli, 2nd ed., Florence, 1904.

House of Busirane, Britomart goes 'forward with bold steps' (III.11.50) from the first to the second room, and undaunted was her 'courage proud' as she awaits her opportunity to enter the third room (III.12.1–2). She enters the third room on the second evening, 'neither of idle shewes, nor of false charmes aghast' (III.12.29), but does not relax her vigilance until Busirane has released Amoret from these charms (III.12.37). So much attention is given to Britomart's courage because goodwill is the very foundation of charity. It is the altruistic nature of such love that accounts for the fact that the Knight of Chastity is engaged in a deadly struggle, not on behalf of her own love for Artegall (though that would be no less altruistic), but on behalf of Scudamour's love for Amoret. She could do no more, as Scudamour recognizes, if Amoret 'were thine, and thou as now am I' (III.11.19). Britomart is not in love with Scudamour, but shows the kindness towards him that proceeds from goodwill. Such kindness is noted by Aquinas as the exterior act of charity that corresponds to the interior act of goodwill (*ST*, *2a 2ae*, 31.4 *sed contra*).

But neither Spenser's Legend of Chastity nor Aquinas's definition of charity is limited to acts of goodwill. The principal act of the virtue of charity is the act of love (*ST*, *2a 2ae*, 27.1). The act of love is not the same as goodwill, but presupposes it. Here we must allow for the complexity of the rational soul of man as the principle of sensitive and intellectual appetition. Now goodwill is to be distinguished from love in respect of both; it is distinguished from the passion of love by its suddenness and lack of intensity, and from rational love by its lack of an affective union or passionate attachment of lover and loved.[20] Thus Arthur, Guyon, and Timias upon the sight of the forester pursuing Florimell 'stayd not to avise, who first should bee, | But all spurd after fast, as they mote fly, | To reskew her from shamefull villany' (III.1.18). In like manner Britomart is so moved by Scudamour's grief 'that pitty did the Virgins hart of patience rob' (III.11.8). But she is not moved by that intensity of passion that renders her unable at first to reply to Red Cross's question as to the purpose of her quest, when she 'with hart-thrilling throbs and bitter stowre, | As if she had a fever fit, did quake'

20 Cf. Aquinas, *ST*, *2a 2ae*, 27.2: *Et ideo Philosophus, in* Ethic. [IX.5], *ostendens differentiam inter benevolentiam et amorem qui est passio,* dicit quod benevolentia non habet distensionem et appetitum, *idest aliquem impetum inclinationis, sed ex solo judicio rationis homo vult bonum alicui. Similiter etiam talis amor est ex quadam consuetudine: benevolentia autem interdum oritur ex repentino, sicut accidit nobis de pugilibus qui pugnant, quorum alterum vellemus vincere. Sed amor, qui est in appetitu intellectivo, etiam differt a benevolentia. Importat enim quandam unionem secundum affectum amantis ad amatum, inquantum scilicet amans aestimat amatum quodammodo ut unum sibi, vel ad se pertinens, et sic movetur in ipsum. Sed benevolentia est simplex actus voluntatis quo volumus alicui bonum, etiam non praesupposita praedicta unione affectus ad ipsum.*

(III.2.5). The act of love that is rational is a mutual act, and it is illustrated by the passionate union of Amoret and Scudamour with which the Legend of Chastity in its original form ends (III.12.44–6).

The third element in Aquinas's definition of charity focuses on that which is shared in friendship. Thus by charity God shares his happiness with man (*ST*, 2*a* 2*ae*, 23.1). In respect of human friendship, Aristotle identifies five things that are shared, as Aquinas notes: *Praeterea, Philosophus in* Ethic. [IX.4] *ponit quinque ad amicitiam pertinentia*: *quorum primum est quod homo velit amico bonum*; *secundum est quod velit ei esse et vivere*; *tertium est quod ei convivat*; *quartum est quod eadem eligat*; *quintum est quod condoleat et congaudeat* (*ST*, 2*a* 2*ae*, 27.2 *arg.* 3). We can say in respect of the Legend of Chastity, therefore, that what is shared above all is the decisions, joys, and sorrows of married life. This aspect of Aristotle's friendship corresponds well with the Protestant emphasis in the solemnization of matrimony on 'the mutual society, help, and comfort, that the one ought to have of the other, both in prosperity and adversity' (*The Book of Common Prayer*).

There are three inward effects of charity, namely joy, peace, and mercy (preamble to *ST*, 2*a* 2*ae*, 28). The Legend of Chastity, however, is about the trials and tribulations of chaste love rather than its joyful fulfilment. Britomart rides forth on her quest 'without repose or rest' (III.4.6), that is, she remains in a state of passionate desire, seeking but not possessing the object of her love. Thus it is the effect of mercy (that is, pity for another's misfortunes) that is here chiefly to be noticed.

Aquinas draws on Aristotle's *Rhetoric* (II.8) in identifying three causes of pity (listed in ascending order in accordance with their power to move); firstly, painful and destructive evils, such as death and bodily injuries; secondly, evils due to chance, such as the deprivation of friends, and evil coming from a source where good may have been expected; and thirdly, undeserved afflictions, when *aliquis semper sectatus est bona et eveniunt ei mala* (*ST*, 2*a* 2*ae*, 30.1). Now Amoret is presented comprehensively in these terms as the object of pity. She is indeed the recipient of painful and destructive evils. Scudamour reports that Busirane 'tormenteth her most terribly, | And day and night afflicts with mortall paine' (III.11.17), but the report hardly prepares us for the horror of the injury inflicted in Amoret's breast, 'a wide wound therein (O ruefull sight) | Entrenched deepe with knife accursed keene' (III.12.20). Further, she is cut off from her friends, for Scudamour is unable to get past the flames in the porch of the House of Busirane and so come to her aid (III.11.11).[21] Indeed, evil

21 Likewise Florimell in the open sea is remote from the help of friends (III.8.27–29). Indeed the same undeserved suffering is also developed by Spenser in relation to Florimell, as is made explicit in the opening canto of the Legend of Friendship. No more piteous story was ever told than 'that of *Amorets* hart-binding chaine, | And this of *Florimels* unworthie paine' (IV.1.1).

comes to Amoret unexpectedly 'the very selfe same day that she was wedded, | Amidst the bridale feast', when she is 'ill of friends bestedded, | By way of sport, as oft in maskes is knowen', as we learn at the beginning of the Legend of Friendship (IV.1.3). But above all it is the spectacle of suffering wholly undeserved that stirs pity for Amoret. At her birth she is seen to share with her twin sister the whole store 'of bountie, and of beautie, and all vertues rare' (III.6.4), and she is entrusted by Venus to Psyche to be 'trained up in true feminitee' (III.6.51). Thus she grows up to be 'th'ensample of true love alone, | And Lodestarre of all chaste affectione' (III.6.52). Her one crime indeed is that she gives to Scudamour 'her loving hart . . . linked fast | In faithfull love' (III.6.53).[22] Aristotle explains in his *Rhetoric* (II.8) that those who are themselves most closely involved in such evils by bonds of love and kinship are moved not by pity, but by terror, for here there is a complete identification with the person enduring evils. Hence Scudamour is overwhelmed by the realization of his own impotence to aid Amoret (III.11.11) and by his sense of the injustice that allows 'goodnesse . . . no grace' and 'righteousnesse no meed' (III.11.9). The sight of Scudamour moves Britomart 'both with great ruth and terrour' (III.11.12), for the goodwill on which her chastity is based leads her to identify with Scudamour to that extent. But it is the effect of mercy that Spenser chiefly exhibits in Britomart here, and she fittingly acknowledges that 'nothing so much pitty doth implore, | As gentle Ladies helplesse misery' (III.11.18). Mercy involves not merely sorrow for another's misfortunes, but also the determination to remedy them.[23] Hence Britomart goes on to say that she will deliver Amoret from her imprisonment 'with proofe of last extremity, | . . . or with her for you dy' (III.11.18). Thus the rescue of Amoret from the House of Busirane is a poetic representation of the perfect love of charity that issues in mercy.

The first edition of Books I–III of *The Faerie Queene* in 1590 ends with joy as an effect of charity in the joyous re-union of Amoret and Scudamour, although Britomart herself, whose chaste love for Artegall remains still unfulfilled, is left 'halfe envying their blesse' (III.12.46). In prosecuting

22 A.S.P. Woodhouse, 'Nature and Grace in *The Faerie Queene*', *English Literary History* 16 (1949), 194–228, rpt. *English Literary History* in *Critical Essays on Spenser from ELH* (Baltimore and London, 1970), pp. 24–58, comments that Amoret's 'education in the Garden of Adonis, while true to nature, has yet been incomplete: it has not contained all the elements requisite for love true and chaste *at the human level.* There is some failure in integration. She cannot securely transcend the merely physical in her passion for Scudamour; hence her imprisonment by Busyrane' (p. 45). The meaning of Spenser's text at III. 6.51–53 is here misrepresented under the pressure of a false interpretation of the torments inflicted on Amoret by Busirane.

23 Such is Augustine's definition: *misericordia est alienae miseriae in nostro corde compassio, qua utique, si possumus, subvenire compellimur* (*De civitate Dei*, IX.5). It is quoted in this form by Aquinas (*ST*, 2a 2ae, 30.1).

a grander design Spenser has by 1596 reduced Amoret as well as Britomart to a state of frustrated hope, and has reserved to the Legend of Friendship the uniting of chaste lovers. Fittingly, the Legend of Friendship ends with the promised union of Florimell and Marinell (IV.12.33–35), and, no less fittingly, it is perfected in the Legend of Justice (V.3.1–3). So does the divine justice repair the undeserved misfortunes of mortals.

IV

Aquinas's systematic classification of the virtues is accompanied no less systematically by the classification of the vices opposed to them. In the same way vice is opposed to virtue in the Legend of Chastity, 'for good by paragone | Of evill, may more notably be rad' (III.9.2). The forces ranged against Britomart, therefore, are to be understood in terms of the vices opposed to charity.

As charity is founded on goodwill, so the opposed vice is rooted in simple malevolence. And such malevolence finds its outward expression in acts of cruelty. The name of Busirane, as Hamilton notes (p. 403), is derived from Busiris, a king of Egypt famous for his cruelty, and Busirane lives up to his name in the wicked torments that he inflicts on Amoret (III.11.10–11 and 16–17). As we have seen, Amoret does nothing to deserve these torments. Her faithful love of Scudamour and the joys of the wedding feast are provocation enough. Thus in *Beowulf* the monster Grendel is grievously afflicted because *he dogora gehwam dream gehyrde | hludne in healle* (88–89a), and visits upon the Danes a terrible punishment (99–169).[24] And as goodwill is maintained by courage, so such malevolent cruelty is carried out with rashness, as when Busirane 'rashly . . . did wrest' his murderous knife from Amoret and turned instead on Britomart 'his fell intent' (III.12.33). Indeed, the legends '*Be bold*' (III.11.50), '*Be bold, be bold*, and every where *Be bold*', and '*Be not too bold*' (III.11.54) over the respective doors of the three rooms in the House of Busirane are a travesty of the boldness that must accompany the love based on goodwill. The boldness of the House of Busirane is a boldness in arousing love, but not in committing oneself to love; it is the boldness of a Paridell.[25] Opposed to love as the principal act of charity is hate

24 Reference is to *Beowulf and the Fight at Finnsburg*, ed. Fr. Klaeber, 3rd ed., Boston, 1950.

25 This is the explanation of C.S. Lewis, *Spenser's Images of Life*, ed. Alastair Fowler (Cambridge, 1967), pp. 27–28. See also the excellent short article by A.K. Hieatt, 'Scudamour's Practice of "Maistrye" upon Amoret', *PMLA* 77 (1962), 509–10, which sees Scudamour's passionate love as overbold in threatening the moral integrity of Amoret. But this is a matter that belongs rather to Spenser's later development of the argument in the Legend of Friendship.

(preamble to *ST*, 2*a* 2*ae*, 34). There can be no doubt that it is Busirane's intention to destroy Amoret, and Britomart only just manages to prevent his final desperate attempt to do so (III.12.32).[26] Opposed to joy as the effect of love are sloth and envy (preamble to *ST*, 2*a* 2*ae*, 34). Sloth is represented in cantos 7 and 8 in terms of the passion of the witch's son, for he is 'a laesie loord, for nothing good to donne, | But stretched forth in idlenesse alwayes' (III.7.12), and envy in cantos 9 and 10 in terms of Malbecco's jealous love of Hellenore, for such jealousy is envy (*ST*, 1a 2*ae*, 28.4).

Love is gratuitous, but hate is a dependent principle, that is, its reality is less than the supreme reality of love. The reason is that the good to which love is ordered is identical with being, and evil is not being but a privation of being. A completely evil thing cannot by definition exist, and that which is evil presupposes a measure of goodness (*ST*, 1*a* 2*ae*, 18.1 and *ad* 1). Hence Dante defines the deadly sins in terms of their derivation from, and perversion of, the reality of love. Thus the deadly sins of pride, envy, and anger are the love of a neighbour's evil: *Che' l mal che s'ama è del prossimo* (*Purgatorio*, XVII.113). Since the good and the love of the good are the ultimate principles of reality, and since evil and hatred are derivative principles, the process whereby hatred is derived from love must consequently be set forth. And it is the purpose of Spenser's 'odious argument' (III. 9.1) to do so.

The object of love is the good, so love is evil when the good is an apparent but not a real good (*ST*, 1*a* 2*ae*, 27.1 *ad* 1). Such an evil love can be expressed in the terms of Renaissance neo-Platonism as the desire of a false and not a true beauty; hence the witch's son is no less satisfied with the false than the true Florimell as the object of his love (III.8.9–10). The seeming good is a good that is not in accord with the primary good. The separation of Busirane from the source of goodness is revealed by the fact that he is an enchanter (III.11.16), for the omnipotence and final reality of God (that is, of goodness and beauty alike) are called into question by his magic arts. The evil of necromancy constitutes a real challenge to the divine order that is taken seriously in the Legend of Chastity, as we see from the need for the reversal of his spells (III.12.34–38). When the order to the good is lacking, what remains is the order to the self, and indeed

26 T.P. Roche, Jr., *The Kindly Flame: A Study of the Third and Fourth Books of Spenser's Faerie Queene* (Princeton, New Jersey, 1964), has recognized so much of the real meaning of Busirane, but has obscured its significance by importing assumptions of Amoret's fear of physical surrender to Scudamour. He writes that Busirane 'is the great enemy to chastity; he represents a negative force of which chastity is the positive ideal. He represents the negation of chastity, and this for Spenser did not mean lust' (p. 81). Indeed, what it does mean is hate. Thus the torments of Busirane are set after the triumph of Cupid, for 'such love is hate' (III.1.50).

this is what defines the nature of the love of desire (*ST*, 1*a* 2*ae*, 27.3). Thus Paridell's interest in Hellenore is simply his own pleasure, and when he has satisfied his desire for pleasure, he abandons her; 'so had he served many one' (III.10.35). Malbecco's love for Hellenore is that of a jealously guarded possession, and is directly comparable with the fixing of his mind 'on mucky pelfe' and 'heapes of evill gotten masse' (III.9.4). Thus he finds himself in a cruel dilemma when his house is in flames and his wife is being carried off by the lover, for he was 'loth to loose his loved Dame, | And loth to leave his liefest pelfe behind' (III.10.15). In the end he opts for the money, that is 'dearest to his donghill mind' (III.10.15), for such a choice most completely defines the nature of his love. The proper word for such desire is *cupiditas* (*ST*, 1*a* 2*ae*, 30.3), and the representation of cupidity in Malbecco prepares us for the image of Cupid himself in the following canto.

The image of Cupid at the upper end of the outermost room of the House of Busirane (III.11.47–49) makes it manifest that this Cupid represents an evil and unenlightened love in which reason is subject to desire. Thus Cupid is 'blindfold' and stands in triumph over the dragon of chastity, wounded 'with a shaft . . . shot through either eye' (III.11.48). The gods, who are now subject to his power (III.11.35), transform themselves into animals to satisfy their lust, Jupiter into a ram and a bull (III.11.30), Neptune into a steer, a dolphin, and a winged horse (III.11.42), and Saturn into a centaur (III.11.43). Cupid is the 'cruell *Cupid*' (III.11.38) who holds his deadly bow in his 'cruell fist' (III.11.48), and in his cruelty does not spare his own mother (III.11.45). Such is the nature of the love of desire concerned only with the gratification of self. Thus Jupiter, transformed now into a swan, is aptly described as 'the proud Bird ruffing his fethers wyde, | And brushing his faire brest' when he invades the beautiful Leda (III.11.32). The gratification of lustful desires takes no account of the objects that have become the instruments of gratification. Thus the desires of Apollo are the death of Daphne (III.11.36), and Hyacinth and Coronis are both by his 'haplesse hand extinct' (III.11.37). The result of such desires is the 'wastefull emptinesse' of the second room (III.11.53). Such desire, making creatures its end, is indeed the death of charity (*ST*, 2*a* 2*ae*, 24.10 *ad* 2). Thus those who worship at the shrine of Cupid commit 'fowle Idolatree' (III.11.49), for in so doing they offend against the true divine source of love.

Spenser's 'odious argument' follows the course of the love of desire through cupidity and envy until it finally comes to rest in hate.[27] The

27 On the order of the passions of love, desire, fear, and sorrow, see *ST*, 1*a* 2*ae*, 25.3; on love as the cause of fear in the manner of a material disposition, see *ST*, 1*a* 2*ae*, 43.1; and on envy, that is, sorrow for a neighbour's good, as the cause of hate, see *ST*, 2*a* 2*ae*, 34.6.

odious spectacle of the torture of Amoret is fittingly represented in the final canto of the Legend of Chastity because *odium, quod huic dilectioni opponitur, non est primum in deletione virtutis, quae fit per vitia, sed ultimum* (*ST*, 2*a* 2*ae*, 34.5). It is for the same reason that Dante has reserved for the utmost depths of hell the terrible image of Ugolino della Gherardesca gnawing the skull of the Archbishop Ruggieri: *là 've 'l cervel s'aggiugne con la nuca* (*Inferno*, XXXII.129). By *si bestial segno* (XXXII.133) is represented the intense hatred (*odio*) which now consumes the whole being of Ugolino and has removed the last vestiges of his humanity. The hatred of a Busirane or of a Ugolino is the final stage of the process of corruption of the highest principle of love in the soul of man, and the truest evidence of what has been lost to human nature in the Fall. But Spenser no less than Dante denies to the unreality of evil a final triumph over the reality of good, for the Legend of Chastity comes to its first and fitting conclusion with the joyous union of Amoret and Scudamour, indistinguishable in the purity of their mutual love as 'that faire *Hermaphrodite*, | Which that rich *Romane* of white marble wrought' (III.12.46).

The Development of Romance-Epic Themes after Spenser's *Faerie Queene*

MARION WYNNE-DAVIES

In the seventeenth century romance increasingly came to incorporate the traits of national epic and political allegory. This development was initiated in Italian by Boiardo's *Orlando Innamorato* (1483, 1495), Ariosto's *Orlando Furioso* (1516, 1532), and Tasso's *Gerusalemme Liberata* (1579–81),[1] and continued in English by Sidney's *Arcadia*[2] and Spenser's *Faerie Queene*.[3] Boiardo and Ariosto combined the material of popular Italian versions of the *chansons de geste* describing Charlemagne's wars against the infidel and the adventures of his *dodici paladini*, which Pulci's *Morgante* (1482, 1489)[4] had made respectable, with the form and spirit of courtly Arthurian romances like the Prose *Lancelot*,[5] and Tasso then reinvested their frivolous treatment of Old French epic with moral and religious dignity and a classical unity of action in his *poema eroico* on the recovery of Jerusalem, which he modelled on Virgil's *Aeneid*. Sidney and Spenser, who belonged to the same literary circle and wrote at the same time, developed the romance-epic genre in opposite directions. *Arcadia* is a recreation of ancient prose romance based on Heliodorus' *Aethiopica* and Xenophon's *Cyropaedia* in a pastoral setting inspired by the *Arcadia* of Sannazaro (1502, 1504),[6] while *The Faerie Queene* is a direct imitation

1 Matteo Maria Boiardo, *Orlando Innamorato*, ed. Aldo Scaglione, 2 vols., Turin, 1951; Ludovico Ariosto, *Orlando Furioso*, edd. Marcello Turchi and Edoardo Sanguineti, 2 vols., Milan, 1974; Torquato Tasso, *Gerusalemme Liberata*, ed. Lanfranco Caretti, Turin, 1971. On the Italian epics see further C.S. Lewis, *The Allegory of Love* (Oxford, 1936), pp. 298–304; Graham Hough, *A Preface to The Faerie Queene*, (London, 1962), pp. 20–47, 59–81.

2 Sir Philip Sidney, *The Countess of Pembroke's Arcadia* (*The Old Arcadia*), ed. Jean Robertson, Oxford, 1973; *The Countess of Pembroke's Arcadia* (*The New Arcadia*), ed. Victor Skretkowicz, Oxford, 1987; *The Last Part of the Countess of Pembroke's Arcadia*, ed. Albert Feuillerat (*The Prose Works of Sir Philip Sidney*, 4 vols. (Cambridge, 1962–7), II, 1–207).

3 Edmund Spenser, *The Faerie Queene*, ed. A.C. Hamilton, London, 1980.

4 Luigi Pulci, *Morgante*, ed. Franca Ageno, Verona, 1955.

5 *Lancelot*, ed. Alexandre Micha, 9 vols., Paris, 1978–83.

6 Jacopo Sannazaro, *Arcadia* (*Opere Volgari*, ed. Alfredo Mauro (Bari, 1961), pp. 3–132).

of Ariosto's *Orlando* which brings the Arthurian component back to its British roots and adds an allegorical dimension like that of the *Queste del Saint Graal*.[7] Both were designed, however, like *Gerusalemme Liberata*, as vehicles for serious moral and political themes. This essay traces the Spenserian tradition down to the Restoration in order to show how English romance epic became identified with the monarchy, and why it was finally superseded by neo-classical epic.

I

In spite of the continued popularity of romances attested by the reprinting of Berners' translation of *Huon of Bourdeaux*, by Munday's translation of *Amadis de Gaule*,[8] and by sympathetic appraisals like those of Peacham in *The Complete Gentleman* (1622) and Cornwallys in his essay *Of the Observation and Use of Things* (1632),[9] the hostile attitude current among humanist scholars of the previous generation, epitomized in Ascham's dismissal of Malory's *Morte Darthur* as little more than 'open mans slaughter, and bold bawdrye' (1570),[10] and Harvey's rebuke to Spenser, 'If so be the Faerye Queene be fairer in your eie than the *Nine Muses*, and *Hobgoblin* runne away with the Garland from *Apollo*' (1580),[11] persisted into the new century, when Bacon was to bracket the whole genre with natural magic (1605):

> For as for that natural magic which flutters about so many books, embracing certain credulous and superstitious traditions and observations concerning sympathies and antipathies, and hidden and specific properties, with experiments for the most part frivolous, and wonderful rather for the skill with which the thing is concealed and masked rather than for the thing itself; it will not be wrong to say that it is as far differing in truth of nature from such a knowledge

7 *La Queste del Saint Graal*, ed. Albert Pauphilet, Paris, 1923. See further Rosamond Tuve, *Allegorical Imagery* (Princeton, 1966), pp. 353–6, 417–36.

8 *The Ancient Historie of Huon of Bourdeaux*, tr. Sir John Bourchier, Lord Berners, London, 1601; *The Ancient, Famovs and Honourable Historie of Amadis de Gaule*, tr. A. Munday, London, 1619.

9 Henry Peacham, *The Complete Gentleman*, ed. Virgil B. Hettzel, New York, 1962 (Folger Documents of Tudor and Stuart Civilization), p. 93; Sir William Cornwallys the Younger, *Essayes*, ed. Don Cameron Allen (Baltimore, Md., 1946), p. 51.

10 Roger Ascham, The *Scholemaster*, (Cambridge, 1904), p. 231.

11 Gabriel Harvey, 'A Gallant familiar Letter', *Spenser's Prose Works*, ed. Rudolf Gottfried, Baltimore, 1949 (*The Works of Edmund Spenser: A Variorum Edition*, edd. Edwin Greenlaw and others, 11 vols., Baltimore, 1932–57), pp. 463–77, at 432.

as we require, as the story of King Arthur of Britain, or Hugh of Bordeaux, and such like imaginary heroes, differs from Caesar's Commentaries in truth of story.[12]

The scholarly disenchantment with romance in this period is summed up by Steadman: 'The romance itself was under attack for disregarding unity of action, for basing its arguments on fables rather than on history, for violating decorum in persons and styles, and for failing to observe verisimilitude and probability.'[13] On a more popular level, there began a movement towards the burlesque treatment of romance in drama and non-dramatic literature alike, exemplified by Johnson's *Tom a Lincolne*, the anonymous *Knight of the Sea*, Beaumont and Fletcher's *Knight of the Burning Pestle*, Anton's *Moriomachia*, Shelton's translation of *Don Quixote*, Davenant's masque *Britannia Triumphans*, Whiting's *Albino and Bellona*, and Kynaston's *Leoline and Sydanis*.[14]

In view of this antagonism to romance, the poetic and imaginative force shown at the same time by romance epic may seem paradoxical. Romance epic did not, however, rely for its legitimacy on the romance tradition itself, but on a growing interest in epic, stimulated by translations of classical texts, the most important of which were Chapman's versions of Homer's *Iliad* and *Odyssey* (1616).[15] Since the ancient style of epic was unable to answer the Renaissance demand for an ethical or religious intention on its own, this demand was satisfied, as in Antiquity itself, by resorting to allegorical interpretations.[16] Yet, though the twofold nature of allegory appeared to fulfil the requirements of both form and intent, writers discovered that 'it was difficult to present the scholastic subtilties of formal ethics through heroic poetry'.[17] Romance, on the

12 Francis Bacon, *Of the Dignity and Advancement of Learning*, II. 8.3 (*The Works of Francis Bacon*, edd. J. Spedding, R.L. Ellis, and D.D.Heath (London, 1858), IV, 367).

13 John Steadman, 'The Arming of the Archetype', *Concepts of the Hero in the Middle Ages and the Renaissance*, ed. Norman T.Burns and Christopher Reagan (London, 1975), pp. 147–96, at 159.

14 Richard Johnson, *The most pleasant history of Tom a Lincolne*, 2 pts., London, 1599, 1607; *The Heroicall Adventures of the Knight of the Sea, comprised in the most famous and renowned Historie of the Illustrious (. . .) Prince Oceander*, London, 1600; Francis Beaumont and John Fletcher, *The Knight of the Burning Pestle*, London, 1613; Robert Anton, *Moriomachia*, London, 1613; Miguel de Cervantes, *The history of Don Quixote*, tr. Thomas Shelton, 2 vols., London, 1616, 1620; Sir William Davenant, *Britannia triumphans, a masque*, London, 1637; Nathaniel Whiting, *The Pleasing Historie of Albino and Bellama*, London, 1638; Sir Francis Kynaston, *Leoline and Sydanis*, London, 1642.

15 *Chapman's Homer*, ed. Allardyce Nicholl, London, 1957.

16 Steadman, 'Arming of the Archetype', pp.154–60.

17 Steadman, *ibid.*, p. 156.

other hand, with its multiplicity of actions and interlaced structure, offered the ideal vehicle for polysemous narrative, and the Renaissance had inherited from the Middle Ages a long-established and influential tradition of combining it with allegory.[18] Not surprisingly, therefore, an allegorized fusion of epic and romance, in which the latter was embued in turn with certain 'epic' qualities, such as a historical connection—often via dynastic interest—and a concern for national glory and public virtue, was readily adopted by Renaissance authors, who 'assumed that marvellous scenes symbolized and condensed complex and unseen processes, that such polyvalent figures and actions made epic and romance philosophical'.[19] Romance epic, in which the episodic, dream-like pattern of romance was combined with the national and political interests of epic, persisted well into the seventeenth century: as late as 1641, Milton, contemplating a subject for his projected epic in *The Reason of Church Government*, could couple the names of Homer and Virgil with Tasso's and consider 'what K[ing] or Knight before the conquest might be chosen in whom to lay the pattern of a Christian *Heroe*'.[20]

Spenser's *Faerie Queene* in particular, with its interweaving of narrative sequences, moral allegory, and love themes with nationalistic concerns, praise of Queen Elizabeth, and contemporary politics, had an influence upon the poetry of the seventeenth century that transcended the limits of its own genre. This commingling is perhaps embodied most perfectly in Britomart, the Knight of Chastity: her romantic quest for Artegal forms a major part of the story in Books III and IV, while at the same time she represents British monarchy, particularly Elizabeth I, and her lover Artegall (Prince Arthur's half-brother on his mother's side) represents Britain's national interests in Ireland and in France by restoring Irena and aiding Burbon (V.1, 9, 11–12). Spenser's influence was such that a sizeable group of writers attempted to perpetuate his values, methods, and themes in their own work, and several of these 'Spenserian' poets attempted to imitate him directly in various ways. In this context I shall discuss Chester's *Love's Martyr* (1601), Drayton's *Poly-Olbion* (1612, 1622), Browne's *Britannia's Pastorals* (1614, 1616), Fletcher's *Purple Island* (1633), Beaumont's *Psyche* (1648), Davenant's *Gondibert* (1651), and Chamberlayne's *Pharonnida* (1653).[21] The most thoroughgoing recrea-

18 Cf. Tuve, *Allegorical Imagery*, chapter 5.

19 Michael Murrin, *The Allegorical Epic* (Chicago, 1980), p. 25. Tasso reconciles a multiplicity of episodes with Aristotle's unity of action in his *Discourses on the Heroic Poem*, trr. Mariella Cavalchini and Irene Samuel (Oxford, 1973), pp. 75–86.

20 *Selected Prose*, ed. C.A. Patrides (Harmondsworth, 1974), pp. 49–60, at 56.

21 Robert Chester, *Loves Martyr: or, Rosalins Complaint*, ed. Alexander B. Grosart, London, 1878 (New Sakespeare Society 8.2), a page-for-page reprint

tion of Spenserian romance epic, however, is found in two unpublished works, Ralph Knevett's *Supplement to the Faery Queene* (1635) and Samuel Sheppard's *Faerie King* (1650), both of which attempt a continuation of *The Faerie Queene*.[22] Taken together, these poems show the development of romance epic in the first half of the seventeenth century and illustrate the changing attitudes towards the notions of nationhood and monarchy in the same period.

II

One of the most persistent characteristics of Renaissance epic, its nationalism, is prominent in the work of the Spenserians, who 'sought to put their country poetically on a level with Greece and Rome and Italy'.[23] The underlying motives to which Hardin drew attention in Drayton, 'the desire to place English poetry in competition with that of the ancients and moderns of other countries; to revere the past and praise the natural beauty of England; to make clear to his English readers their virtues as a people',[24] were common to them all, and for them the praise of Britain was inextricably linked to that of writers who glorified their country. Browne typified this attitude in *Britannia's Pastorals*, Song I, when he praised the British Worthies

> Whose deeds were sung by learned bards as high,
> In raptures of immortal poesy,
> As any nations, since the Grecian lads
> Were famous made by Homer's Iliads. (95–8)[25]

of the 1601 ed.; Michael Drayton, *Poly-Olbion* (*The Works of Michael Drayton*, edd. J.W. Hebel and others, 5 vols. (Oxford, 1931–41), IV; William Browne, *Britannia's Pastorals* (*The Poems of William Browne of Tavistock*, ed. G. Goodwin, 2 vols. (London, 1905), I-II, 75; Phineas Fletcher, *The Purple Island, or the isle of man* (*The Poetical Works of Giles and Phineas Fletcher*, ed. Frederick S. Boas, 2 vols. (Cambridge, 1908, 1909), II, 12–171; Joseph Beaumont, *Psyche, or Loves Mysterie* (*The Complete Poems of Dr. Joseph Beaumont*, ed. Alexander B. Grosart, 2 vols. (Edinburgh, 1880), I 11–II, 231; Sir William Davenant, *Gondibert, An Heroick Poem*, ed. D.F. Gladish, Oxford, 1971; William Chamberlayne, *Pharonnida* (*Minor Poets of the Caroline Period*, ed. George Saintsbury, 3 vols. Oxford, 1905–21) I, 4–295).

22 Ralph Knevett, *A Supplement to the Faery Queene in three Bookes. Wherein are allegorically described Affaires both military and ciuill of these times* (Cambridge, University Library, Ee. 3. 53); Samuel Sheppard, *The Faerie King* (Oxford, Bodleian Library MS Rawl. Poet 28).

23 Joan Grundy, *The Spenserian Poets*, (London, 1969), p. 70.

24 R.F. Hardin, *Michael Drayton and the Passing of Elizabethan England* (Lawrence, 1973), p. 9.

25 *Poems*, I, 191.

Later in the same song Browne narrows his praise of poets down to Spenser:

> He sung th'heroic knights of fairyland
> In lines so elegant, of such command,
> That had the Thracian play'd but half so well,
> He had not left Euridyce in hell. (991–4)[26]

Browne's national theme is coupled with a complex narrative based upon the love relationships of nymphs and shepherds, characterized by romance motifs such as the fickleness of lovers and the imprisonment of his heroine, Marina, by Limnos, who represents vice.[27]

The same combination of romance motifs and national sentiment is found in Chester's *Love's Martyr*, a curious poem which consists mainly of a dialogue between Nature and the Phoenix. It begins with Nature's complaint and journey to earth in order to encourage the Phoenix to mate and perpetuate her beauty; Nature and the Phoenix then set off on a second journey to effect a union of the latter with the Turtle, passing *en route* many notable places in Britain. Interpolated into this journey, which combines national and romance motifs, is '*The Birth, Life* and Death of honourable Arthur *King of Brittaine*'.[28] The relevance of Arthur's life has been questioned by critics. Carleton Brown, for example, asserts that 'it lacks all connexion with the allegory of the Phoenix and Turtle', an opinion in which Greenlaw and Matchett concur.[29] Its interpolation cannot be dismissed so easily, however, for digressions of such magnitude were not inserted in Renaissance poems at random. In *The Faerie Queene*, for example, the 'chronicle of Briton kings' which Arthur and Guyon read in the House of Alma (II.10) was the first installment of a legendary history of Britain which was to be continued in Merlin's prophesy to Britomart and her nurse (III.3), so that its two parts were revealed to the chief representatives of British monarchy in the poem. The Arthurian history in *Loves Martyr* fills the chronological gap between Eumnestes' book, which ended at the accession of Uther Pendragon, and Merlin's prophesy, which began with the unnamed son of Britomart and Artegall who was fated to depose Arthur's successor Constantius and thus emphasizes the thematic link between *The Faerie Queene* and

26 *Ibid.*, I, 225.

27 See further Grundy, *Spenserian Poets*, p. 145; H.E. Cory, 'The Golden Age of the Spenserian Pastoral', *PMLA* 25 (1910), pp. 241–67.

28 *Love's Martyr*, pp. 42–85 (34–77 in the 1601 ed.).

29 *Poems by Sir John Salusbury and Robert Chester*, ed. Carleton Brown, London, 1914 (Early English Text Society, Extra Series 113), p. lv; E. Greenlaw, *Studies in Spenser's Historical Allegory* (Baltimore, Maryland, 1932), pp. 37–9; W.H. Matchett, *The Phoenix and the Turtle* (The Hague, 1965), pp. 58–9.

Chester's poem, in which the Phoenix represents Elizabeth I and the Turtle Dove possibly the Earl of Essex, whom Artegall represented in the Burbon episode.[30] Here too contemporary political allegory links a historical digression to the romance as a whole, and the combination of allegory with national and monarchical themes in the rambling, quest-like structure of *Loves Martyr* shows that by the turn of the century Spenser's romance epic had already been accepted as a model to be imitated.

III

Romance epic often coupled praise of the reigning monarch with a national theme. Thus in *The Faerie Queene* Spenser glorifies Elizabeth I directly as well as allegorically, for example in the introduction to his 'chronicle of Briton kings', which associates her with the past glories of the British kings:

Who now shall giue vnto me words and sound,
  Equall vnto this haughtie enterprise?
  Or who shal lend me wings, with which from ground
  My lowly verse may loftily arise,
  And lift it selfe vnto the highest skies?
  More ample spirit, then hitherto was wount,
  Here needes me, whiles the famous auncestries
  Of my most dreaded soueraigne I recount,
By which all earthly Princes she doth farre surmount.

Ne vnder Sunne, that shines so wide and faire,
  Whence all that liues does borrow life and light,
  Liues ought, that to her linage may compaire,
  Which though from earth it be deriued right,
  Yet doth it selfe stretch forth to heauens hight,
  And all the world with wonder ouerspred;
  A labour huge, exceeding farre my might:
  How shall fraile pen, with feare disparaged,
Conceive such soueraine glory, and great bountihed?

Argument worthy of *Mæonian* quill,
  Or rather worthy of great *Phœbus* rote,
  Whereon the ruines of great *Ossa* hill,
  And triumphes of *Phlegræan Ioue* he wrote,

30 See below, p. [29]. Essex's identification with the Turtle was proposed by Grosart (*Loves Martyr*, pp. xxxiv– lxi); if so, the poem's publication might be connected with his abortive *coup d'état* in the same year.

That all the gods admird his loftie note.
But if some relish of that heauenly lay
His learned daughters would to me report,
To decke my song withall, I would assay,
Thy name, O soueraine Queene, to blazon farre away

Thy name, O soueraine Queene, thy realme and race,
From this renowmed Prince deriued arre,
Who mightily vpheld that royall mace,
Which now thou bearst, to thee descended farre
From mightie kings and conquerours in warre,
Thy fathers and great Grandfathers of old,
Whose noble deedes aboue the Northerne starre
Immortal fame for euer hath enrold;
As in that old mans booke they were in order told.

(II.1–4)[31]

Spenser was able to transmit Prince Arthur's glory directly to his supposed descendant Elizabeth Tudor. But such genealogizing became more problematic when the poet had to accommodate a non-English king, James I. Only by making Merlin prophecy the mingling of the Tudor and Stuart dynasties could Drayton link James with the Matter of Britain. In his poem *To the Majesty of King James* (1603)[32] James's birth is made to rival the fabled achievement of Brute by uniting Britain for the first time:

Two famous Kingdoms seperate thus long,
Within one Iland, and that speake one tongue
Since *Brute* first raign'd (if men of *Brute* alow)
Never before united untill now
What power, nor war could do, nor time expected,
Thy blessed birth hath happily effected. (137–42)

While this conceit was suitable for a panegyric addressed to the king, its propriety may be questioned in Songs IV and V of *Poly-Olbion*,[33] in which the Welsh, engaged in a singing competition with the Saxons for the island of Lundy, personified as 'a lustie black-brow'd Girle' (IV.17), base their claim on the legendary conquests of Arthur and the wonders of Merlin

31 Spenser here echoes Ariosto's briefer and more restrained apostrophe to Ippolito d'Este (*Orlando Furioso* III.1–4). Similar praise of the queen as embodying the virtue proper to each book, can be seen at *Fairie Queene* I. Proem 4, II. Proem 1–4, III. Proem 1–5, IV. Proem 4–5, V. Proem 11, and IV. Proem 6–7.

32 *Works*, I, 471–5.

33 *Ibid.*, IV, 69–81, 97–110.

(245–348). Sabrine (the river Severn), who judges the contest, rules nevertheless that '*Lundy* like ally'd to *Wales* and *England* is' (80), prophesying that 'th'ancient *Britan* race | Shall come againe to sit upon the soveraigne place' (80) by the union of the Tudors with the Plantagenets, and that Scotland shall then be united with England and Wales through the marriage of Margaret Tudor to its king, James IV, of the house of'Steward', which also claimed Welsh ancestry:

> This Stem to *Tudors* joyn'd (which thing all-powerfull
> Fate So happilly produc't out of that prosperous Bed,
> Whose mariages conjoynd the White-rose and the Red)
> Suppressing every Plant, shall spred itself so wide,
> As in his armes shall clip the Ile on every side.
> By whom three sever'd Realmes in one shall firmlie stand
> As Britain-founding Brute first Monarchiz'd the land.
> (62–8)

The allusion to James, which must have been obvious to seventeenth-century readers, was nevertheless made explicit by Selden, who refers to "our mighty Soveraigne" in his 'Illustrations' to the song.[34] As the climax of this long historical and poetic debate, Sabrine's tortuous dynastic solution, with its ingratiating overtones, sounds unxious and contrived. Drayton presumably intended an impression of *discordia concors*, but the debate is no more than a recital of old tales, and its solution fails even to harmonize these satisfactorily.[35]

The dichotomy between the romantic element in *Poly-Olbion* and its political and historical concerns that appears in Songs IV and V extends to every part of the work, including its title:

POLY-OLBION.
or
A Chorographicall Description of *Tracts, Riuers,*
Mountaines, Forests, and other Parts of this renowned *Isle*
of Great Britaine,
With intermixture of the most Remarquable *Stories, Antiquities, Wonders,*
Rarityes, Pleasures, and Commodities of
the same:
Digested in a Poem

This title balances the hard facts of geography, history, and political economy denoted by '*A Chorographicall* Description', '*Antiquities*', and

34 *Ibid.*, IV, 107.
35 Cf. B.C. Ewell, 'Drayton's *Poly-Olbion*: England's Body Immortalized', *Studies in Philology* 75 (1978), pp. 301–2.

'*Commodities*' against the romanctic elements represented by 'Remarquable *Stories*, '*Wonders*', '*Rarityes*', and '*Pleasures*'. His double allegiance to facts and marvels has led some critics to charge Drayton with confusion. Elton's claim that 'there is no line between legend and fact' in his poem is supported by Child: 'His real object is to preserve whatever history or legend (both are of equal importance in his eyes, and he draws no clear distinction between the two) has recorded of great deeds, and great men.'[36] Their charges imply that the poem is a haphazard conglomeration of tales and descriptions, but this tumultuous impression is surely what Drayton intended. *Poly-Olbion* is essentially a work of the imagination compacted of images culled from mythology and literature, like the catalogues of Welsh and English rivers in Song IV (119–216), which recalls the pageant of famous rivers in *The Fairie Queene* (IV.20–47), and its structure imitates the *pulcherrimae ambages* of romance, based as it is on the movements of the Muse about Britain, so that the information she gathers along the way is arranged 'chorographically' rather than logically or chronologically. The result can be seen in its many allusions to the Matter of Britain. The Muse begins her journey in Song I by travelling eastward from Land's End, so the first allusion is to the battle by the river Camel where 'British *Arthurs* blood, | By *Mordred's* murtherous hand was mingled with her flood' (183–4), and its last is the river Dart's account of the arrival of Brute (303–506). This arrangement is a striking one because of its apparent incongruity. Chronologically Brute's arrival should precede Arthur's death, and logically the first mention of Britain's greatest legendary king would be more appropriate to the Arthurian heartland of Wales than to Cornwall. Arthur's death therefore comes as a surprise that stirs the reader's interest, and the epoch-making arrival of Brute, which is narrated at some length, makes a fitting climax to the first song. As Song I suggests, the Muse's itinerary is parcelled out so as to provide strong beginnings and rhetorically effective conclusions. Song III, for example, begins with Stonehenge, 'first Wonder of the Land', transported to Salisbury Plain by Merlin's craft (41–64), and concludes with the praise of Camelot, '*Arthurs* ancient seat, | Which made the *Britaines* name through all the world so great' (395–6), and of Arthur himself, a king who would have made a greater subject than Homer's for the right poet:

> Like *Camelot*, what place, was ever yet renown'd
> Where, as at *Carlion*, oft, hee kept the *Table-round*,
> Most famous for the sports at *Pentecost* so long,

36 Oliver Elton, *Michael Drayton: A Critical Study* (London, 1905), p. 116; H.H. Child, 'Michael Drayton' (*The Cambridge History of English Literature*, edd. A.W. Ward and A.R. Waller, 15 vols. (Cambridge, 1907–27), IV, 190.

From whence all Knightlie deeds and brave atcheivement sprong.
As some soft-sliding Rill, which from a lesser head
(Yet in his going forth, by many a Fountaine fed)
Extends itself at length unto a goodlie streame:
So, almost through the world his fame flew from this Realme;
That justlie I may charge these ancient *Bards* of wrong,
So idly to neglect his glorie in their Song.
For some aboundant braine, | there had been a storie
Beyond the Blind-mans might to have inhanc't our glorie.
(397–408)

One suspects that Drayton saw his own work, which is nothing if not commendatory, as such a bid to out-Homer Homer: his comparison of Arthur's fame to a little brook swelling to a mighty river (401–4) is ideally suited to a poem full of rivers and their nymphs.

The Muse's wanderings, which determine the structure of *Poly-Olbion*, also suggest the progress of a monarch, as Grundy remarked.[37] Indeed, the tales the Muse hears from the river and wood nymphs call to mind the pageants that greeted Queen Elizabeth on these occasions, such as the Kenilworth Festivities of 1575, at which the Queen was met by a lady rising from the lake,[38] recalling in turn the past glories of the Elizabethan age, a favourite theme in *Poly-Olbion* and in Drayton's later works.[39] In *Poly-Olbion* he rejects the forward-moving linear structure of history in favour of a topographical one that imitates the sinuous patterns of romance, and the mythic associations of the Muse are reflected in the stories fitted into this framework, which do not attempt a realistic narrative of events. Instead, they emphasize the super-human powers of legendary figures like Arthur, who 'Three hundred *Saxons* slew with his owne valiant hand' (IV.271), and Brute's nephew Turnus, who is treated even more hyperbolically:

37 Grundy, *Spenserian Poets*, p. 135. Pandora, the '*Muse of Britanye*' and 'handmaide of the Fayrie Queene' in *Idea the Shepheards Garland* (*Works*, I, 47–94), VI, Arg. and line 162, who is described in VI. 90 as the sister of 'our *Phœbus*' (Sir Philip Sidney), i.e. the Countess of Pembroke (cf. Bernard H. Newdigate, *Michael Drayton and his Circle* (Oxford, 1941), p. 41), and in VI. 97 as the '*Arabian Phenix*, wonder of thy sexe', like Beta, the '*Phenix*' of III. 50 (Elizabeth), has a Britomart-like dual identity that invites speculation about the identity of the Muse in *Poly-Olbion*.

38 *Kenilworth Festivities . . . comprising Laneham's description of the pageantry,, and Gascoigne's Masques represented before Queen Elizabeth at Kenilworth Castle anno 1575*, 2 pts. (Warwick and Leamington, 1824, 1825), I, 10–11.

39 Douglas Bush, *English Literature in the Earlier Seventeenth Century*, 2nd. ed., Oxford, 1962 (*Oxford History of English Literature* VI), pp. 79–80.

Where *Turon* (of the rest) *Brutes* Sisters valiant sonne
(By whose approved deeds that day was chiefly wonne)
Sixe hundred slue out-right through his peculiar strength.
(I.459–61)

Following the example of Spenser in his catalogue of English and Irish rivers (*FQ* IV.24–44), Drayton mythologizes the geography of Britain,[40] and he carried the process a step further by introducing an Ovidian metamorphosis into the legend of Sabrina in Song VI (128–78).[41] Moylvadian, apostrophizing Sabrina's mother, tells how the implacable Queen Gwendoline cast them both into the Severn, to which Sabina gave its name:

Woe to thee Faire *Elstred*, that thou should'st thy fairer *Sabrine* see,
As she should thee behold the prey to her sterne rage
Whom kinglie Locrins death suffic'd not to assuage:
Who from the bordring Cleeves thee with thy Mother cast
Into thy cristned Flood, the whilst the Rocks aghast
Resounded with your shriekes; till in a deadlie dreame
Your corses were dissolv'd into that crystall streame,
Your curles to curled waves, which plainlie still appeare
The same in water now, that once in locks they were.
(167–76)

Drayton's version of the story, which was told by Spenser as a warning against adultery,[42] shows his romantic bias, and it also illustrates his use of Spenserian echoes to enrich his verse. The description of the weeping

40 'By turning these into deities, Spenser was doing for England (and for Ireland) what the ancient poets had already done for Greece and Italy. He was mythologizing—which is to say civilizing—his country, just as they had mythologized theirs' (C.S. Lewis, *Spenser's Images of Life*, ed. Alastair Fowler (Cambridge, 1967), pp. 127–8).

41 Glaucus describes his transformation into a sea-god in *Metamorphoses* (ed. William S. Anderson, Leipzig, 1991), XIII. 954–63. Drayton's skill in weaving his heterogeneous material into the semblance of a continuous narrative owes much to Ovid, whose ingenious transitions were compared to conjuring tricks by Quintilian: *Illa uero frigida et puerilis est in scholis adfectatio, ut ipse transitus efficiat aliquam utique sententiam et huius praestigiae plausum petat, ut Ouidius lasciuire in Metamorphosesin solet; quem tamen excusare necessitas potest, res diuersissimas in speciem unius corporis colligentem* . . . (*Institutio oratoria*, ed. M. Winterbottom, 2 vols. (Oxford, 1970), IV. 1.77). Spenser himself metamorphosized Malbecco into Gealosie in *Faerie Queene* III. 10.59–60.

42 *Ibid.*, III. 10.17–19. The story of Sabrina comes ultimately from Geoffrey of Monmouth, *Historia regum Britanniae*, II. 4–5.

Sabrina and her mother 'dropping liquid pearle' (VI.165) effectively condenses Spenser's description of Florimell:

> With that adowne out of her Christall eyne Few trickling
> teares she softly forth let fall,
> That like two Orient pearles, did purely shyne
> Vpon her snowy cheeke . . . (*FQ* III.7.9)

Sabrina's innocence and beauty recall Florimell's in her distress, and she was in turn the model for Milton's 'Sabrina fair', who also 'underwent a quick immortal change | Made goddess of the river'.[43]

IV

Drayton alone among Spenser's seventeenth-century imitators fully explored the two-fold nature of romance epic, giving equal weight to the diffuse narrative form and supernatural machinery of romance and the historical, national, and monarchical interests of epic, but the form of his work prevented him from unifying them, as Spenser did, under a single overarching theme, like Arthur's love for Gloriana, to which everything else somehow contributed. Davenant had a similar problem reconciling the poetic attractions of romance and fantasy with the weightier concerns of historical and national epic in *Gondibert*. The opening lines of Cowley's commendatory verses *To Sir Wiliam Davenant Upon His Two First Books of Gondibert* (themselves a landmark in the history of literary taste) suggest that his solution was to de-romanticize it:

> *Methinks Heroick Poesie, till now*
> *Like some fantastick Fairy land did show;*
> *Gods, Devils, Nymphs, Witches, & Giants race,*
> *And all but man in mans best work had place.*
> *Thou like some worthy Knight, with sacred Arms*
> *Dost drive the Monsters thence, and end the Charms:*
> *Instead of those dost Men and manners Plant,*
> *The things which that rich soil did chiefly want.*[44]

Yet Davenant's poem is firmly rooted in traditional romance. Its plot, like that of Sidney's *Arcadia*, is a complex interweaving of love relationships and chivalric battles which combines standard romance motifs like

43 *A Masque presented at Ludlow Castle, 1634* [*Comus*] (*The Poems of John Milton*, edd. John Cary and Alastair Fowler (London, 1968), pp. 175–229), 823–936, at 840–1.

44 *Gondibert*, ed. Gladish, pp. 270–1.

a magic stone that reveals unfaithfulness and a heroine dressed as a page (III.4.45–57) and borrowings from the classic romance epics such as 'Nature's nursery' (II.5.28), from Spenser's Garden of Adonis (*FQ* III.6.29–50), and Merlin's tomb (II.6.18), from *Orlando Furioso* (III.8, 14–15), with epic seriousness expressed in 'massive and dignified reflection' which seems too heavy for the shallow vessel that carries it.[45] In *Pharonnida*, on the other hand, 'the queen of the whole bevy' of seventeenth-century heroic poems in Saintsbury's opinion,[46] which is also modelled on *Arcadia*, Chamberlayne solved the same problem by jettisoning Sidney's moral and political concerns.

Like Davenant, Phineas Fletcher and Joseph Beaumont tried to combine romance motifs with weightier matter, in their case religious allegory. Fletcher's *Purple Island*, an allegory of the human body and the body politic of the state,[47] describes the nature of man and his fall from grace in cantos and stanzas, the traditional media of romance epic,[48] decked out with motifs such as pageants of the vices (VII.77–85 and VIII), a chivalric psychomachia (VII–XII), and a warrior princess like Bradamante or Britomart or her namesake in *Arcadia*, Sidney's Knight of the Tomb,[49] whose description echoes that of Spenser' Red Cross Knight (*FQ* I.1.1):

> With her, her sister went, a warlike Maid,
> *Parthenia*, all in steel, and gilded arms;
> In needles stead a mighty spear she swayd,
> With which in bloudy fields and fierce alarms,
> The boldest champion she down would bear,
> And like a thunderbolt wide passage tear,
> Flinging all to the earth with her enchanted spear.
>
> (X.27.2–9)

Fletcher wrote from within a long tradition of Christian allegory: his Hamartia (XII.27–31) comes from the *Hamartigenia* of Prudentius, 'the first great Christian Latin poet', who invented the genre.[50] Beaumont's *Psyche: or, Loves Mysterie* is a more intensely religious, indeed mystical poem, concerned with the soul's love for, and ultimate union with, Christ, which he hoped would show that devotional poetry could gain a hearing from men of taste:

45 Bush, *English Literature in the Earlier Seventeenth Century*, p. 356.
46 *Minor Poets*, I, xi.
47 Cf. Grundy, *Spenserian Poets*, p.188.
48 Cf. Paul Merchant, *The Epic* (London, 1971), p.49.
49 For Sidney's Parthenia see *New Arcadia*, III. 16 (ed. Skretkowicz, pp. 395–400).
50 *Aurelii Prudentii Clementis carmina*, ed. Ioannes Bergman, Vienna and Leipzig, 1926 (Corpus Scriptorum Ecclesiasticorum Latinorum 61), pp. 127–63. See further F.J.E. Raby, *A History of Christian Latin Poetry* (Oxford, 1927), pp. 44–71; J.D.

> My Desire is, That this *Book* may prompt *better Wits* to believe, that a *Divine Theam* is as capable and happy a Subject of *Poetical Ornament*, as any *Pagan* or *Humane Device* whatsoever. Which if I can obtain, and (into the Bargin,) Charm my Readers into any *true degree* of *Devotion*, I shall be bold to hope that I have partly reached my *proposed Mark*, and not continued *meerly Idle*.[51]

Perhaps to charm his readers, Beaumont also wrote in cantos and stanzas and included romance motifs such as 'The Emblematick gift of Chastitie' (III.33), a love-token consisting of a magic girdle like those of Florimell and Armida.[52] Be that as it may, both these poems are more like medieval allegory than the high Christian epic that Milton perfected in *Paradise Lost*.

V

The union of epic themes with romance techniques and structures generated anomalies in the seventeenth-century works described above, especially in that of Drayton, the most considerable poet among the Spenserians. Embodying national themes in *Poly-Olbion* must have seemed as simple to him at first as it did when he eulogized Beta (Elizabeth) in the third 'eglog' of his *Shepherd's Garland* (1593).[53] So it was to prove for Browne, and not surprisingly, as political allegory had been a stock feature of the pastoral tradition since Virgil's time and was generally accepted as one of its conventions. But the credibility of the legendary element in *Poly-Olbion* was challenged by the superior claims of historical truth, backed up by the 'illustrations' appended to each song by Selden, and the increasing emphasis placed on historical authenticity as the century went on led to the conclusion that only a rational presentation of 'Men and manners', shorn of romantic improbabilities, could satisfy the heroic ideal. Cowley's verses to Davenant echo the views expressed by Davenant himself in his *Discourse upon Gondibert* and by Hobbes in his *Answer* to it,[54] which became those of the literary establish-

Pheifer, 'Errour and Echidna in *The Faerie Queene*: A Study in Literary Tradition', *Literature and Learning in Medieval and Renaissance England*, ed. John Scattergood (Dublin, 1984), pp.127–74, at 155–8. Prudentius' allegory of original sin also inspired Milton's Sin and Death (Pheifer, *ibid.*, pp. 161–2).

51 'To the Reader' (*Complete Poems*, p. 5).

52 Florimell: *Fairie Queene* IV. 5.3; Armida: *Gerusalemme Liberata* XVI. 24–5.

53 See above, n. 37.

54 *A Discourse upon Gondibert . . . With an answer to it by Mr Hobbes*, Paris, 1650 (repr. in *Critical Essays of the Seventeenth Century*, ed. J.E. Spingarn, 3 vols. (Oxford, 1908–9), II, 1–67). Cf. Bush, *English Literature in the Earlier Seventeenth Century*, pp. 372–3.

ment. In the long run this shift towards 'realism' could only be fatal to romance epic, but in the shorter term it prompted a new emphasis on contemporary political allegory which can be seen in the two unpublished continuations of *The Faerie Queene*, Knevett's *Supplement to the Faery Queene* and Sheppard's *Faerie King*.[55] Although the *Supplement* conforms to the pattern of moral allegory established in *The Faerie Queene*, the main thrust is political, as its subtitle *Wherein are allegorically described Affaires both military and ciuill of these times* indicates, and the political allegory of *The Faerie King*, which Sheppard, a pioneer journalist in the royalist cause, composed in Newgate gaol, where he had been imprisoned in 1649 for writing seditious pamphlets, is more complex and ambiguous than Knevett's. Both poets use the romance-epic form they took over from *The Faerie Queene* to express their views on contemporary politics, especially the fortunes of the monarchy, and their poems, which were written fifteen years apart, reflect the changing attitudes towards monarchy during the Civil War period, while the tensions between their aggressive political allegory and romance-epic form gives some interesting insights into the final phase of the latter's decline.

The *Supplement* and *The Faerie King* are both monarchist poems, praising Charles I and Charles II respectively. The proem to Book VII of the *Supplement* dedicates the poem to Charles I, who 'sitt'st in Arthur's seate' (pr.2.2), that is, on the British throne, and the next stanza implicitly identifies him with Prince Arthur himself by identifying his wife Henrietta Maria with the Fairy Queen:

> Thou Gloriana ar't (oh Lady Bright)
> Whom British Arthur wonne (maugre the frowne Of adverse
> Fate) in her are blazon'd right
> Thy beauty, bounty, and thy Vertues exquisite. (pr.3.6–9)

Charles's identification with Arthur is confirmed by the description of the latter in Book VIII:

> Nor was Prince Arthur more uncomely dight,
> With purple surcote on his shoulders spred,

55 The *Supplement* was first investigated by C.B. Millican, *Spenser and the Table Round* (Cambridge, Mass., 1932), p. 201, n. 41; 'Ralph Knevett's "Supplement of The Faery Queene"', *TLS*, October 10, 1935, p. 631; 'Ralph Knevett, Author of *The Supplement* to Spenser's *Faerie Queene*,' *Review of English Studies* 14 (1938), 44–52). Millican failed to produce his promised edition, but there is one in Andrew Lavender, 'An Edition of Ralph Knevett's "Supplement of The Faery Queene" (1635)', an unpublished doctoral dissertation submitted to New York University in 1955. For *The Faerie King* see Hyder E. Rollins, 'Samuel Sheppard and his Praise of Poets', *Studies in Philology* 24 (1927), pp. 509–55.

With princely ermine lin'd; his plume was white,
A rich Caparison adorn'd his steed,
Embroiderd all with roses, white and red,
Which worke a wauy border did confine,
That those faire flowers round environed:
On his helme did a golden Lion shine,
But on his brest was figured a crosse devine. (8.30)

All the details of this description fit Charles: the 'purple surcote' and 'princely ermine' are associated with monarchs;[56] the 'roses, white and red' on the horse's caparison refer to his Tudor ancestry; the 'golden Lion' was the badge of the Scottish kings, now incorporated in the British royal arms;[57] and the 'crosse devine' is the emblem of England, previously worn by the the Red Cross Knight, who represents its patron saint (*FQ* I.1.2, 10.61). Knevett presents Arthur as a saviour-figure, as in *The Faerie Queen*, whose first task was to rescue Albanio (James I), the titular knight of Book VII, lured by Matea (μᾰτια 'folly') into a life of courtly pleasures on the Isle of Vanity, which recalls Phædria's island (*FQ* II.6):

Albanio comes to ye place,
Where Vanity doth dwell;
Prince Arthur calleth him from thence,
And doth Granvanio quell (VII.9.Arg)

The contrast between Albanio and Arthur is made visual by the description of Albanio's effete costume:

His massy coate of maile he had layd by,
And was yclad in a mandilion light,
Of sea greene Taffata, purfled with silver bright.

In stead of horrid helme he wore a bonnet,
Whereon a wanton plume did lightly waue,
And many fond love toyes were fix'd vpon it,
Like those wherewith vaine youths are wont t'embraue
Their womanish attire, when they enslaue
Their neckes to Cupids yoke, and condiscend
That passion shall triumph o're reason graue,
His bugle tipp'd with siluer at each end,
Was pendant by his side, in a greene silken bend.
(VII.9.42–3)

56 For 'purple' see T.H. Cain, *Praise in The Faerie Queene* (Lincoln, Nebraska, 1978), p.120; for 'ermine' see the portrait of Elizabeth I (1585) attributed to Sir William Segar (Roy Strong, *Tudor and Jacobean Portraits* (London, 1969), II, 202.

57 Cf. Charles Boutell, *English Heraldry*, 9th ed. rev. (London, 1907) pp. 267–80.

The next stanza opposes this array to the 'glorious armour' worn by Arthur, whose mission to is to aid Irene, not to hunt with courtiers (James's favourite pastime, represented by his hunting-horn). The prince recalls Albanio to his quest and proves his moral ascendency by defeating the monster Granvanio, as he did Orgoglio, who had previously overcome the Red Cross Knight, in *The Faerie Queene* (I.7). The superiority of *ein Heldenleben* to a life of pleasures is reaffirmed in Book VIII, where the youths on Mont Plaisant are seen training for battle (3.5).

Book VII thus establishes Charles's moral vigour indirectly through the contrast with James's indolence and effeminacy as well as directly by his identification with Arthur, and the two following books demonstrate his virtues in action. His military ambitions and Renaissance desire for honour manifest themselves in Book VIII when Arthur enters a tournament to fight for Traiecta, 'incited by the fame and brute, | Of honour great that there was to be wonne' (8.28), and again in Book IX when Arthur jousts for Queen Thalastera:

> Prince Arthur also (though desireing least,
> To winne a Mistris, or a crowne to gaine,
> But thirsteing after honour) did request
> His Ladyes license, for the entertaine
> This rare emprize, and did his sute obtaine. (11.9)

Arthur's behaviour on this occasion also hints at his counterpart's high moral character, which was rare among monarchs of any period. Charles's active foreign policy in the early part of his reign is commemorated in Book VIII. In canto 2 Arthur rescues Callimachus (Gustavus Adolphus), its titular knight (18–22), and the rest of the book allegorizes Gustavus's war against the Catholic League; his untimely death at Lützen is recalled in canto 12 (37–8). The retrenchment necessary after he dismissed parliament in 1629 left no scope for foreign ventures, but Charles' naval ambitions are allegorized in Book IX, canto 11. Prince Arthur's adventures therefore constitute a more or less continuous (though highly selective) allegory of English history from 1623, when he and Buckingham prevailed upon James to change his policy of peace at any price for a more agressive, if not a more sucessful one, to the middle years of his personal rule.[58]

Byanor, the hero of Sheppard's *Faerie King*, was identified as the exiled Prince of Wales (Charles II to his royalist supporters) when Metanoia (μετανοια, 'repentance'), recalling him and his companion Olivia to their quest, gives him a sword 'of wondrous strength and of as

58 For the historical background see Godfrey Davies, *The Early Stuarts 1603–1660*, Oxford, 1937 (*The Oxford History of England* IX), pp. 45–65, 79–84.

wondrous worth' which formerly belonged to Prince Arthur and to King Edward the Martyr (VI.1.28). He then succeeds the slain Ariodant (Charles I), whose namesake in *Orlando Furioso* had become a duke at the Scottish court, recalling Charles's Stuart ancestry,[59] as king of Ruina (England), and partners Olivia, a warrior maiden like Britomart, who thus recalls Elizabeth I and the glories of the Elizabethan age, which Charles II's return from exile was thought to promise. Byanor's identification with Charles was hinted at in his first appearance, when his blow causes the evil knight Zolamie to see stars:

> that ZOLAMIE on his horse-back doth reel the Sun, & Moone, & starres are in his sight with CHARLES HIS WAINE supported by one wheele. (III.v.28.4–6)

'CHARLES HIS WAINE', the popular name of the constellation Boötes, recalls Charlemagne as well as Charles himself, who is thus associated with the mighty emperor of Italian romance epic. The historical allegory in this poem caused its author new problems, however. Byanor is not only opposed by various forces representing the Commonwealth; his honourable love for Olivia is contrasted with Ariodant's adulterous desire for her and ill-treatment of his own queen Olympia (who also takes her name from Ariosto's poem, in which her namesake married the king of Hibernia),[60] and his success in defeating the evil enchanter Magorto (the Commonwealth) is likewise contrasted with his predecessor's ill-judged military campaigns. Effective as these contrasts are structurally and thematically, Ariodant's character and behaviour are clearly inconsistent with those of Charles I, who (unlike his sons) was a devoted husband. Admittedly, such correspondences are not always consistent in *The Faerie Queene* either. Its characters can shift their historical identities to meet the demands of the political allegory, as Artegall did when he changed from Lord Grey de Wilton, the Lord Deputy sent to pacify Ireland, whom he represented in Book V cantos 1 and 9, and in canto 11, stanzas 36–42, to the Earl of Essex, who commanded the force sent to help Henry of Navarre, in the Burbon episode (11.43–12.2), and back to Lord Grey for the rest of canto 12, and they can shed also their political significance altogether, like Artegall in cantos 2 to 8. The overriding demand of the political allegory in *The Faery King*, as in the *Supplement*, is that the heir to the throne be treated as a god-like figure of Renaissance panegyric whose reign will

59 *Orlando Furioso* V. 6–VI. 15.

60 *Ibid.*, IX. 19–X. 34, XI. 33–80. Byanor and Ariodant's rivalry for Olivia recalls that of Tristan and King Mark for Isolde, which was the mainspring of the *Roman de Tristan*.

renew the golden age, as Prince Henry was in Jonson's masque, *Oberon, the Faery Prince* (1611):[61]

> He is the matter of vertue, and plac'd high.
> His meditations, to his height, are even:
> And all their issue is a kin to heauen.
> He is a god, o're kings; yet stoupes he then
> Neerest a man, when he doth gouerne men;
> To teach them by the sweetnesse of his sway,
> And not by force. He'is such a king, as thay,
> Who'are tyrannes subiects, or ne're tasted peace,
> Would, in their wishes, forme, for their release.
> 'Tis he, that stayes the time from turning old,
> And keepes the age vp in a head of gold.
> That in his owne true circle, still doth runne;
> And holds his course, as certayne as the sunne.
> He makes it euer day, and euer spring,
> Where he doth shine, and quickens euery thing
> Like a new nature: so, that true to call
> Him, by his title, is to say, Hee's all. (341–57)

In contrast, therefore, both poems portray the old king is portrayed as lecherous and incompetent. It so happens that this characterization fitted James on both counts (in his old age at least), but Charles I was a good, even saintly man, though an unsuccessful king. Such inconsistences need not trouble Spenser's readers because his political allegory is incidental and intermittent,[62] but they do create a problem in *The Faerie King*, which is essentially a political poem like Dryden's *Absalom and Achitophel*. In fact, the primacy of the political allegory in both poems is basically incompatible with the polyphonic narrative structure they inherited from *The Faerie Queene*. Prince Arthur, whose role in the *Supplement* is limited to a series of short quests in search of earthly fame and honour, cannot adequately represent Charles I, who claimed a sovereignty as absolute as Justinian's, while Ariodant, Charles's representative in *The Faery King*, does not resemble his historical personality. The political allegory also distorts *The Faery King*'s narrative pattern. Historical verisimilitude requires Ariodant to die amidst the destruction of his troops and the ruin of his realm, as he does in Book IV, canto 6, thereby precluding a climactic confrontation between himself and Byanor, who only entered the poem effectively at Book III, canto 5, after the major part of his own

61 *Ben Jonson*, edd. C.H. Herford, Percy and Evelyn Simpson, 11 vols. (Oxford, 1925–51), VII, 341–56.

62 Cf. Hough, *Preface to The Faerie Queene*, pp. 125–30.

role had been played out, like those between the titular knights and their antitypes in the *The Faerie Queene*.

The role of the monarch was pivotal in romance epic because he served to unify the diffuse narrative structure and at the same time to exemplify the virtues of an epic hero, like Tasso's Goffredo.[63] If the fictional king can no longer able to fulfil these functions, the complex narrative and thematic structure will fall apart, as it did in the *Supplement* and *The Faerie King*, where the central figures were hobbled by the limitations of historical accuracy. So much was inevitable, given the circumstances of their composition, but their thematic basis was also undermined from within, for Knevett and Sheppard, royalists though they were, both stress industry and virtue as the qualifications for kingship rather than hereditary succession. Knevett supports this view with the somewhat dubious precedents of 'Ottoman' (Osman) and 'Tamerlane' (Timur), who rose from obscurity to found mighty dynasties:

Not alway doe the highest mountaines beare,
The tallest pines, the valleys low sometimes,
As goodly masts for vessells large doe reare:
Poore Ottoman bred in an obscure clime,
Of parentage ignoble, and infirme,
A beeing to the Turkish empire gave:
From this small root a tree sprung, so sublime,
That nations build therein, and kingdomes have,
Their nests among the branches of this Cedar brave.

Great Tamerlane who with such rage, and might,
Rush'd from the East, as if the Caspian seas,
Had broke their hilly bounds, and limits quite,
Vpon the Straites of Bosphorus to sease,
And drowne the lesser Asias provinces:
This Chieftaine was a simple Netheards sonne,
Brought up in base, and rurall offices . . . (VIII.9.2–3)

The conclusion he draws from these examples is ambiguously phrased, since it could be applied to their Turkish and Mogul descendants:

Thus Time the seedes of monarchyes doth sowe,
Which first obscur'd in base contempt may lye,
But when that Fortune doth her bright beames showe,

63 Douglas Brooks-Davies, *The Mercurian Monarch* (Manchester, 1983), pp. 1–10.

Vpon their vertue, and their industry,
They doe encrease in bounds, and glorious maiesty.
(VIII.9.5)

In the next stanza, however, he goes against the facts of history by applying it unambiguously to Callimachus, the knight that represents Gustavus Adolphus, the hereditary king of Sweden, whom he also makes rise to greatness from relative obscurity:

And though Callimachus, were fairely bred
Of princely stemme, yet were in Faery Court,
Many that did in birth farre him exceed. (VIII.9.6)[64]

Sheppard likewise distorts history by making Byanor win the right to govern Ruina without a hereditary claim (VI.4–6). It would seem that both held a view of sovereignty closer to that of Hobbes, which was based solely on power (he sanctioned the withdrawal of allegiance when the sovereign became incapable of affording protection),[65] than to the divine-right monarchy of James I and his Tudor predecessors, which was subject, in principle at least, to God. Neither theory took much notice of the rights of the subject, but the Jamesian one was a better guarantee of stability and continuity. Indeed, the idea that natural superiority gives a man the right to rule is hard to reconcile with any orderly system of government, let alone hereditary monarchy. At a practical level it is the recipe for military dictatorship, as events were to show in the 1650's.

VI

Seen in historical perspective, the problems faced by Knevett and Shepperd are symptomatic of their revolutionary century,[66] in the course of which Spenserian romance epic became more and more of an anachronism. After 1603 Elizabethan patriotism was out of date, and Drayton's efforts to forge a common British identity from King James's pedigree were, to say the least, premature, as the following decades proved, while even committed royalists like Knevett and Shepperd came to reject the quasi-theological view of monarchy held by James and his son. The

64 Knevett also rejected inherited merit and position in *Supplement* IX. 10.44–5 and in his *Funerall Elegies* (*The Shorter Poems of Ralph Knevett*, ed. A.M. Charles (Ohio, 1966), pp. 253–4).
65 Hobbes's theory of sovereignty is summarized by Bush, *English Literature in the Earlier Seventeenth Century*, pp. 252–6.
66 Cf. Davies, *Early Stuarts*, pp. xix-xxi.

fictional world of the poems, in which the monarch's role had diminished in prominence and stature, mirrored changing attitudes towards monarchy in the real one. Coupled with the rejection of divine-right monarchy was their belief in the importance of individual effort as opposed to inherited rank, which can be seen as one aspect of the independent consciousness of the individual that increased with the growth of rationalism. Rationalism, in turn, was fatal to neo-Platonism, which was the soul of romance epic. The idea that truth was a static if mysterious concept which was objectively obtainable and to which the artist as *vates* had privileged access was no longer viable. Rather, there was a sense that one must not rely upon the past but search for something fresh and move outwards in new directions beyond the confines of existing beliefs and concepts. As a result, the seventeenth century increasingly preferred a linear search for external truth to the cyclical quest for internal truth pursued by Spenser, a development that called into question the union of heroic poetry with allegory and polyphonic romance on which romance epic was based.[67] By the latter part of the century even a sympathetic critic like Rymer, in his *Preface to Rapin* (1674), regarded *The Faerie Queen* as a monstrous aberration because Spenser failed to follow Aristotle's 'rules':

> *Spencer*, I think, may be reckon'd the first of our *Heroick Poets*; he had a large spirit, a sharp judgment, and a *Genius* for *Heroic Poesie*, perhaps above any that ever writ since *Virgil*. But our misfortune is, he wanted a true *Idea*, and lost himself by following an unfaithful guide. Though besides *Homer* and *Virgil* he had read *Tasso*, yet he rather suffer'd himself to be misled by *Ariosto*; with whom blindly rambling on *marvellous* Adventures, he makes no Conscience of *Probability*. All is fanciful and chimerical, without any foundation in truth; his poem is perfect *Fairy-land*.
>
> Those who can love *Ariosto* will be ravish'd with *Spencer*, whilst men of juster thoughts lament that such great Wits have miscarried in their Travels for want of direction to set them in the right way. But the truth is, in *Spencer's* time, *Italy* it self was not well satisfied with *Tasso*; and few amongst them would then allow that he had excell'd their *divine Ariosto*. And it was the vice of those Times to affect superstitiously the *Allegory*; and nothing would then be currant without a mystical meaning. We must blame the *Italians* for debauching great *Spencer's* judgment; and they cast him on the unlucky choice of the *stanza*, which in no wise is proper for our Language.[68]

67 See further Isabel Rivers, *Classical and Christian Ideas in English Renaissance Poetry* (London, 1979), pp. 62–3.

68 Thomas Rymer, *Preface to the Translation of Rapin's Reflectins on Aristotle's Treatise of Poesie* (Spingarn, *Critical Essays*, II, 163–81, at 167–8).

Dryden, arguing from the same premisses in his *Discourse on the Originall and Progress of Satire* (1693), makes Spenser's gravest sin his lack of unity:

> For there is no uniformity in the design of Spenser: he aims at the accomplishment of no one action; he raises up a hero for every one of his adventures; and endows each of them with some particular moral virtue, which renders them all equal, without subordination, or preference. Every one is most valiant in his own legend: only we must do him that justice to observe, that magnanimity, which is the character of Prince Arthur, shines throughout the whole poem; and succours the rest, when they are in distress. The original of every knight was then living in the court of Queen Elizabeth; and he attributed to each of them that virtue, which he thought was most conspicuous in them. Had he lived to finish the poem, it had certainly been more of a piece; but could not have been more perfect, because the model was not true.[69]

Seemingly, neither Rymer nor Dryden could understand poetry written on other than neo-classical principles. Dryden did perceive the unifying role of Prince Arthur, but his remarks on *The Faerie Queene*'s structure promoted the idea that it was a *roman | clef*,[70] which was something the author of *Absalom and Achitophel* could understand. As Steadman observes, 'Neo-Aristotelian and Horatian criticism left little room for allegory; and it was the rationalistic approach to poetic imitation—the demand for probability and verisimilitude—that eventually triumphed.'[71] The romance form had been adopted to accommodate allegory to begin with, and it was abandoned when allegory ceased to be fashionable even among the religious-minded.

Thus the view of romance that Bacon took in 1605 prevailed in the end, and the 'independent truth' of seventeenth-century poetics gradually become identified with factual authenticity and/or the innate validity of a religious theme. The classical imagery beloved of Renaissance poets was condemned on both counts because the myths from which it was drawn were not literally true. Bishop Sprat condemns it on the first count in his *History of the Royal Society* (1667):

> The *Wit* of the *Fables* and *Religions* of the *Ancient World* is well-nigh consum'd : They have already serv'd the *Poets* long enough; and it is now high time to dismiss them; especially seing they have this peculiar *imperfection*, that they were only *Fictions* at

69 *Essays of John Dryden*, ed. W.P. Ker, 2 vols. (Oxford, 1900), II, 14–114, at 28.
70 Cf. Hough, *Preface to The Faerie Queene*, pp. 129–30.
71 Steadman, 'Arming of the Archetype', p. 159.

> first: whereas *Truth* is never so well express'd or amplify'd, as by those Ornaments which are *Tru* and *Real* in themselves.[72]

Cowley condemned on the second in the preface to his *Poems*, where he argues similarly that Christian truth is a better subject for poetry than pagan myths, 'the *Cold-meats* of the *Antients*, new-heated and new set forth', or romantic fictions: 'to us, who have no need of them, to us who deride their *folly* and are weried with their *impertinencies*, [mad stories of the *Gods* and *Heroes*] ought to appear no better arguments for *Verse* then those of their worthy *Successors*, the *Knights Errant*.'[73] The triumph of this view can be seen in Cowley's own *Davideis* (1656),[74] and in Milton's *Paradise Lost* (1667, 1674) and *Paradise Regain'd* (1671).[75] In *Paradise Regain'd*, a more austere poem than *Paradise Lost*, which admitted the allegory of Sin and Death (II.648–889), Milton's Christ rejects pagan philosophy and literature for the same reason as Cowley rejected pagan mythology:

> Think not but that I know these things, or think
> I know them not; not therefore am I short
> Of knowing what I ought: he who receives
> Light from above, from the fountains of light,
> No other doctrine needs, though granted true;
> But these are false, or little else but dreams,
> Conjectures, fancies, built on nothing firm. (IV.285–92)

Faced with this unholy alliance of science and religion, it is not surprising that the Spenserians yeilded so much ground to the opposition. Their discomforture goes beyond any specific criticisms of romance-epic; it is a striking instance of the wider ideological concern of their age with the nature of truth.

The Spenserians, however, while they mirror the general seventeenth-century disenchantment with romance, look back, paradoxically perhaps, to the reign of Elizabeth as a golden age of literature.[76] Browne thought Spenser a greater Orpheus, and Drayton, who speaks ironically in the preface to *Poly-Olbion* of the lack of support he experienced 'since his Majesties happy comming in',[77] makes the river Camel, lamenting the

72 Thomas Sprat, *The History of the Royal Society* (London, 1667), p. 414.
73 *English Writings*, I, 4–14, at 13.
74 *Davideis, A Sacred poem of the Troubles of David* (*The English Writings of Abraham Cowley*, ed. A.R. Waller, 2 vols. (Cambridge, 1905–6), I, 241–401).
75 *Poems of John Milton*, pp. 1077–1167.
76 Anne Barton, 'Harking Back to Elizabeth: Ben Jonson and Caroline Nostalgia', *English Literary History* 48 (1981), 706–31.
77 *Works*, IV, vi*.

passing of Arthur in Song I, contrast the meanness of the present with past glories:

> 'Even in the agedst face, where beautie once did dwell,
> And nature (in the least) but seemed to excell,
> Time cannot make such waste, but something wil appeare,
> To shewe some little tract of delicacie there.
> Or some religious worke, in building manie a day,
> That this penurious age hath suffered to decay,
> Some lim or modell, dragd out of the ruinous mass,
> The richness will declare in glorie whilst it was . . .'
>
> (194–201)[78]

The contrast with the golden age (in every sense) of Elizabeth was explicitly made by Browne, who celebrated Drayton as its last survivor in the commendatory verses prefixed to the second part of *Poly-Olbion* (1622):

> ENGLANDS brave *Genius*, raise thy head; and see,
> We have a *Muse* in this mortalitie
> Of Vertue yet survives; All met not Death,
> When wee intoomb'd our dear *Elizabeth*.
> Immortal Sidney, honoured *Colin Clout*,
> Presaging what wee feele, went timely out.
> Then why lives *Drayton*, when the *Times* refuse,
> Both *Meanes* to live, and *Matter* for a Muse?
> Onely without *Excuse* to leave us quite,
> And tell us, Durst we act, he durst to write.[79]

Drayton and his friends were interested parties, but Sheppard made the same point allegorically in the argument to Book V, canto I of his *Faerie King*, which commemorates two fictitious poets (also representing Sidney and Spenser?) and their mistress:

> PANTHEA, underneath this grasse
> with OLINDRO & AMPHIDAMAS
> (Shee high of birth, & beauteous
> They noble & magnanimous).

The most subtle (and Spenserian) expression of disillusionment with the present and nostalgia for the past, however, is Knevett's in Book IX, canto I of his *Supplement*, which relates the combat between Sir Iustine

78 William Browne, *To My Honor'd Friend Mr. Drayton* (*ibid.*, IV, 393), 1–10.

79 The 'bare, ruin'd choirs' motif recurs in Ochy's lament for the destruction of Glastonbury (*Poly-Olbion* III. 293–314).

and Sir Lereall, who contest each other's right to a shield emblazoned with a crown, a laurel wreath, and a book. Although Iustine has the support of his lady Celesia and "those Virgins nine" the Muses (IX.i.24.6), he is defeated by Lereall, who possesses Crysaker, a magic sword made by Merlin, which, however, was useless against Prince Arthur's even more powerful shield in a previos encounter. The full meaning of this episode can only be understood from the etymologies of the names and the associations of the characters and weapons involved, as Lavender has shown.[80] Iustine's name (*Iustinus*, from *iustus* 'just') signifies that his is the 'juster cause' (IX.1.21.1), and he is connected with art and/or learning through the Muses. Iustine's name also connects him with Artegal, the Knight of Justice in *The Faerie Queene*, 'whom, in a full carreere, | Hee [Lereall] did vnhorse, and layd on ground in heavy cheere' (IX.1.26.8–9) before Lereall himself was defeated by Arthur. Celesia (*caeles* 'heavenly, divine'), the name of Iustine's lady, similarly recalls Astræa, the goddess of justice, who was Artegall's governess before she returned to heaven (*FQ* V.1.5–11). Lereall's name can interpreted to mean an impudent attacker (λιρός 'bold, shameless' + ἰάλλω 'I assail', which fits the description of his confrontation with Arthur: 'swell'd up with insolence, | Hee battell 'gainst Prince Arthur durst durraine' (*Supplement*, IX.1.27.1–2). The name of Lereall's sword, Crysaker, resembles that of Artegall's sword Chrysaor 'golden sword' (χρυσός 'gold' + ἄορ 'sword'), given him by Astræa, with which

'Academia' from Cesare Ripa, *Della Novissima Iconologia* (Padua, 1625).

80 See above, n. 55. The etymologies that follow are taken, with some modifications, from Lavender's thesis.

Jove had quelled the Titans (*FQ* V.1.9–10),[81] but Crysaker may be interpreted 'coward gold' (χρυσός + ἀκήριος 'cowardly'), meaning that Lereall's weapon was slander. Lereall therefore corresponds to Spenser's Detraction, who unjustly assailed Artegall (Lord Grey) with accusations of cruelty in his treatment of Irena's enemies (*FQ* V.12.40), so he and his sword Crysaker are antitypes of Artegall and his sword Crysaor. The crown, laurel wreath, and book on the shield for which the two knights were fighting symbolize literary studies in Ripa's *Iconologia*, which portrays *Academia* as a lady wearing the crown of refined and purified thought, holding in her right hand the file of pruning and polishing, with the motto *detrahit atque polit*, and in her left a wreath of laurel, ivy, and myrtle signifying heroic, pastoral, and erotic poetry, with a great pile of books at her feet to suggest the multiplicity of knowledge the scholar must acquire.[82] Iustine's defeat at the hands of Lereall therefore signifies the overthrow of true philosophy, poetry, and learning by false and malicious attacks like those that caused the recall of Lord Grey from Ireland after the massacre at Smerwick.[83] In the context of Knevett's poem this presumably means the defeat of the spiritual and political truths embodied in *The Faerie Queene* by the forces of change, a shrewd assesment at a time when the king's friends were still firmly entrenched in the positions of civil and religious power. His pessimism was justified by events in his own day, but he underestimated the long-term vitality of the Spenserian tradition, which enjoyed a renaissance in Romantic and Victorian poetry after neoclassicism had proved itself a literary cul-de-sac, and whose combination of imaginative power and intellectual complexity has recaptured Academia in our own day, showing once again the truth of Horace's maxim

> Multa renascentur, quae iam cecidere, cadentque
> quae nunc sunt in honore . . .[84]

81 χρυσάορος adj. 'with golden sword' is an epithet of Apollo in Homer's *Iliad*, V. 509, XV. 256.

82 Cesare Ripa, *Della Novissima Iconologia* (Padua, 1625), pp. 2–6. The motto *detrahit atque polit* is an abbreviated version of the adage of Erasmus quoted in Ripa's text, *Adagiorum Chiliades Quattuor*, I.5.58 '*Limam addere*' *Lima detrahitur atque expolitur, quod redundat, quodque incultum est . . . Et elimata* [Ripa *limata*] *dicuntur expolita* (*Desiderii Erasmi Opera* (Basel, 1540), II, at 179).

83 The Italian and Spanish mercenaries beseiged by Grey in Smerwick apparently surrendered at discretion and were put to the sword. See further Edmund Spenser, *A View of the Present State of Ireland*, ed. W.L. Renwick (Oxford, 1970), pp. 106–8, with Renwick's notes on 107.27 and 34 (pp. 214–17), and H.S.V. Jones, *A Spenser Handbook* (New York, 1930), pp. 269–71.

84 *Ars poetica* (Horace, *Epistles Book II and Epistle to the Pisones* ('*Ars Poetica*'), ed. Niall Rudd (Cambridge, 1989), pp. 58–74), 47–8. These lines appear on the title-page of C.S. Lewis's *Allegory of Love* (Oxford, 1936), the book that was most influential in promoting the twentieth- century Spenserian revival.